2006
U.S.
COIN
Digest

A Guide to Average Retail Prices from the Market Experts

Edited by Joel Edler and Dave Harper

©2005 KP Books

Published by

kp books
An Imprint of F+W Publications

700 East State Street • Iola, WI 54990-0001
715-445-2214 • 888-457-2873

Our toll-free number to place an order or obtain
a free catalog is (800) 258-0929.

Library of Congress Catalog Number: 2005922621
ISBN: 0-89689-165-8

Edited by: Joel Edler and Dave Harper
Designed by: Sandra Morrison

Printed in the United States of America

Contents

Preface

Since 1952, Krause Publications has built its business and reputation by serving the needs of coin collectors. Three questions dominate every collector's thinking. The first is: "What is it?" We hope the photographs in this price guide will help you identify the coins you own. The second question is: "What's it worth? The prices contained in this volume are intended to serve as a retail guide. That means if you want to buy a specific coin in a specific grade, the price listed will be approximately what you would have to pay at the time this book was compiled. The prices listed are neither an offer to buy nor an offer to sell the coins listed. They are simply a guide assembled for your convenience by the authors. Remember that prices fluctuate. What dealers will pay to buy coins from you is a question beyond the scope of this book. The third question is: "How do I buy one (a specific coin)?" There are several thousand coin dealers across America who are ready, willing, and able to serve your needs. To find them, you can consult the phone book in your local area, but beyond that, there is a whole hobby world out there and newspapers and magazines that feature advertisements by dealers who want to fill your needs. Take a look at the Krause Web site to discover the many other fine products that the firm offers.

www.collect.com

Photo Credit:

Cover photos include a unique 1933 $20 gold piece auctioned by Sotheby's and Stack's in 2002, the reverse of a Maine state quarter, a Pine Tree shilling, the reverse of a half cent and the Walton specimen 1913 Liberty Head nickel. The 1913 nickel photo is by Donn Pearlman.

Introduction

The authors have organized this book a manner that we hope you will find both logical and useful.

Value listings

Values listed in the following price guide are average retail prices. These are the approximate prices collectors can expect to pay when purchasing coins from dealers. They are not offers to buy or sell. The pricing section should be considered a guide only; actual selling prices will vary.

The values were compiled by Krause Publications' independent staff of market analysts. They derived the values listed by monitoring auction results, business on electronic dealer trading networks, and business at major shows, and in consultation with a panel of dealers. For rare coins, when only a few specimens of a particular date and mintmark are known, a confirmed transaction may occur only once every several years. In those instances, the most recent auction result is listed.

Grading

Values are listed for coins in various states of preservation, or grades. Standards used in determining grade for U.S. coins are those set by the American Numismatic Association (www.money.org). See Chapter 4 for more on grading.

Precious metal content

Throughout this book precious metal content is indicated in troy ounces. One troy ounce equals 480 grains, or 31.103 grams. This is followed by ASW or AGW, which stand for Actual Silver (Gold) Weight.

Dates and mintmarks

The dates listed are the individual dates that appear on each coin. The letter that follows the date is the mintmark and indicates where the coin was struck: "C" – Charlotte, N.C. (1838-1861); "CC" – Carson City, Nev. (1870-1893); "D" – Dahlonega, Ga. (1838-1861), and Denver (1906-present); "O" – New Orleans (1838-1909); "P" – Philadelphia (1793-present), coins without mintmarks also were struck at Philadelphia; "S" – San Francisco (1854-present); and "W" – West Point, N.Y. (1984-present).

A slash mark in a date indicates an overdate. This means a new date was engraved on a die over an old date. For example, if the date is listed as "1899/8," an 1898 die had a 9 engraved over the last 8 in the date. Portions of the old numeral are still visible on the coin.

A slash mark in a mintmark listing indicates an overmintmark (example: "1922-P/D"). The same process as above occurred, but this time a new mintmark was engraved over an old.

See Chapter 3, "U.S. Minting Varieties and Errors," for more information on overdates and overmintmarks.

American Coin History
U.S. Mint founded in 1792

A t peak production, the U.S. Mint strikes nearly 30 billion coins a year. Who would have thought it possible at its founding? In July 1792, a site for the new U.S. Mint not yet having been secured, 1,500 silver half dismes were struck on a small screw press in the cellar of a Philadelphia building owned by sawmaker John Harper. Though some have since categorized these early emissions of the fledgling U.S. Mint as patterns, it is clear that first President George Washington – who is said to have deposited the silver from which the coins were struck – considered this small batch of half dismes to be the first official U.S. coins.

The law establishing the Mint dates to April 2, 1792. From that early legislative birth has flowed the coins that have underpinned the workings of U.S. commerce for over two centuries. It must be remembered that the Mint was born in chaos. It was a time shortly after the Revolutionary War and as hard as it was to win independence from Great Britain, setting up American government finances on a sound basis was to prove almost as daunting.

At first a cumbersome system was proposed by Robert Morris, a Revolutionary War financier and first superintendent of finance. Refinements tendered by Thomas Jefferson and Alexander Hamilton then firmly placed the nation on an easily understood decimal system of coinage. They were working with a hodgepodge system that grew up in the Colonial period. Despite a dire need for coinage in the Colonies, Great Britain considered it a royal right and granted franchises sparingly. Much of the Colonial economy, therefore, revolved around barter, with food staples, crops, and goods serving as currency. Indian wampum or bead money also was used, first in the fur trade and later as a form of money for Colonial use.

Copper pieces were produced around 1616 for Sommer Islands (now Bermuda), but coinage within the American Colonies apparently didn't begin until 1652, when John Hull struck silver threepence, sixpence and shillings under authority of the General Court of Massachusetts. This coinage continued, with design changes (willow, oak, and pine trees), through 1682. Most of the coins were dated 1652, apparently to avoid legal problems with England.

In 1658 Cecil Calvert, second Lord Baltimore, commissioned coins to be struck in England for use in Maryland. Other authorized and unauthorized coinages – including those of Mark Newby, John Holt, William Wood, and Dr. Samuel Higley –

all became part of the landscape of circulating coins. In the 1780s there were influxes of counterfeit British halfpence and various state coinages.

The Articles of Confederation had granted individual states the right to produce copper coins. Many states found this to be appealing, and merchants in the mid-1780s traded copper coins of Vermont, Connecticut, Massachusetts, New Jersey, and New York. Not all were legal issues; various entrepreneurs used this as an invitation to strike imitation state coppers and British halfpence. Mutilated and worn foreign coins also circulated in abundance. Included among these were coins of Portugal, Great Britain, and France, with the large majority of the silver arriving from Spain.

The accounting system used by the states was derived from the British system of pounds, shillings, and pence. Each state was allowed to set its own rates at which foreign gold and silver coins would trade in relation to the British pound.

In 1782 Robert Morris, newly named superintendent of finance, was appointed to head a committee to determine the values and weights of the gold and silver coins in circulation. Asked simply to draw up a table of values, Morris took the opportunity to propose the establishment of a federal mint. In his Jan. 15, 1782, report (largely prepared by his assistant, Gouverneur Morris), Morris noted that the exchange rates between the states were complicated.

He observed that a farmer in New Hampshire would be hard-pressed if asked to determine the value of a bushel of wheat in South Carolina. Morris recorded that an amount of wheat worth four shillings in his home state of New Hampshire would be worth 21 shillings and eightpence under the accounting system used in South Carolina.

Morris claimed these difficulties plagued not only farmers, but that "they are perplexing to most Men and troublesome to all." Morris further pressed for the adoption of an American coin to solve the problems of the need for small change and debased foreign coinages in circulation.

In essence, what he was advocating was a monometallic system based on silver. He said that gold and silver had fluctuated throughout history. Because these fluctuations resulted in the more valuable metal leaving the country, any nation that adopted a bimetallic coinage was doomed to have its gold or silver coins disappear from circulation.

Gouverneur Morris calculated the rate at which the Spanish dollar traded to the British pound in the various states. Leaving out South Carolina, because it threw off his calculations, Gouverneur Morris arrived at a common denominator of 1,440. Robert Morris, therefore, recommended a unit of value of 1/1,440, equivalent to a quarter grain of silver. He suggested the striking of a silver 100-unit coin, or cent; a silver 500-unit coin, or quint; a silver 1,000-unit coin, or mark; and two copper coins, one of eight units and the other of five units.

On Feb. 21, 1782, the Grand Committee of Congress approved the proposal and directed Morris to press forward and report with a plan to establish a mint. Morris had already done so. Apparently feeling confident that Congress would like his coinage ideas, Morris (as shown by his diary) began efforts at the physical establishment prior to his January 1782 report. He had already engaged Benjamin Dudley to acquire necessary equipment for the mint and hoped to have sample coins available to submit with his original report to Congress.

It wasn't until April 23, 1783, that Morris was able to send his Nova Constellatio patterns to Congress and suggest that he was ready to report on establishing a mint. Apparently nothing came of Morris' efforts. Several committees looked into the matter, but nothing was accomplished. Dudley was eventually discharged as Morris' hopes dimmed.

Thomas Jefferson was the next to offer a major plan. Jefferson liked the idea of a decimal system of coinage, but disliked Morris' basic unit of value. As chairman of the Currency Committee, Jefferson reviewed Morris' plan and formulated his own ideas.

To test public reaction, Jefferson gave his "Notes on Coinage" to *The Providence Gazette,* and *Country Journal,* which published his plan in its July 24, 1784, issue. Jefferson disagreed with Morris' suggestion for a 1/1,440 unit of value and instead proposed a decimal coinage based on the dollar, with the lowest unit of account being the mil, or 1/1,000.

"The most easy ratio of multiplication and division is that by ten," Jefferson wrote. "Every one knows the facility of Decimal Arithmetic."

Jefferson argued that although Morris' unit would have eliminated the unwanted fraction that occurred when merchants converted British farthings to dollars, this was of little significance. After all, the original idea of establishing a mint was to get rid of foreign currencies.

Morris' unit, Jefferson said, was too cumbersome for use in normal business transactions. According to Jefferson, under Morris' plan a horse valued at 80 Spanish dollars would require a notation of six figures and would be shown as 115,200 units.

Jefferson' coinage plan suggested the striking of a dollar, or unit; half dollar, or five-tenths; a double tenth, or fifth of a dollar, equivalent to a pistareen; a tenth, equivalent to a Spanish bit; and a one-fifth copper coin, relating to the British farthing. He also wanted a gold coin of $10, corresponding to the British double guinea; and a copper one-hundredth coin, relating to the British halfpence.

In reference to his coinage denominations, Jefferson said, it was important that the coins "coincide in value with some of the known coins so nearly, that the people may by quick reference in the mind, estimate their value." The Spanish dollar was the most commonly used coin in trade, so it was natural basis for the new U.S. silver dollar. In the Spanish system, the coin was called an eight reales, or piece of eight.

More than a year, however, passed without any further action on his plan or that proposed by Morris. In a letter to William Grayson, a member of the Continental Congress, Washington expressed concern for the establishment of a national coinage system, terming it "indispensably necessary." Washington also complained of the coinage in circulation: "A man must travel with a pair of scales in his pocket, or run the risk of receiving gold at one-fourth less than it counts."

On May 13, 1785, the 13-member Grand Committee, to whom Jefferson's plan had been submitted, filed its report, generally favoring Jefferson's coinage system. The committee did, however, make slight alterations, including the elimination of the gold $10 coin, the addition of a gold $5 coin, and the dropping of Jefferson's double tenth, which it replaced with a quarter dollar. The committee also added a coin equal to 1/200 of a dollar (half cent). On July 6, 1785, Congress unanimously approved the Grand Committee's plan. It failed, however, to set a standard weight for the silver dollar or to order plans drawn up for a mint.

Several proposals were offered for a contract coinage. On April 21, 1787, the board accepted a proposal by James Jarvis to strike 300 tons of copper coin at the federal standard. Jarvis, however, delivered slightly less than 9,000 pounds of his contract. The contract was voided the following year for his failure to meet scheduled delivery times, but helped to delay further action on a mint. Concerted action on a coinage system and a mint would wait until the formation of the new government.

Alexander Hamilton, named in September 1789 to head the new Treasury, offered three different methods by which the new nation could achieve economic stability, including the funding of the national debt, establishment of the Bank of North America and the founding of the U.S. Mint. On Jan. 21, 1791, Hamilton submitted to Congress a "Report on the Establishment of a Mint."

Hamilton agreed with Jefferson that the dollar seemed to be best suited to serve as the basic unit, but believed it necessary to establish a proper weight and fineness for the new coin. To do so, Hamilton had several Spanish coins assayed to determine the fine weight of the Spanish dollar. He also watched the rate at which Spanish dollars traded for fine gold (24 3/4 grains per dollar) on the world market.

From his assays and observations he determined that the Spanish dollar contained 371 grains of silver. He then multiplied 24 3/4 by 15 (the gold value of silver times his suggested bimetallic ratio) and arrived at 371 1/4 as the proper fine silver weight for the new silver dollar.

The Spanish dollar actually contained 376 grains of pure silver when new, 4 3/4 grains more than Hamilton's proposed silver dollar.

Hamilton also wanted a bimetallic ratio of 15-to-1. Hamilton said his ratio was closer to Great Britain's, which would be important for trade, and Holland's, which would be important for repaying loans from that country.

His report suggested the striking of a gold $10; gold dollar; silver dollar; silver tenth, or disme; and copper one-hundredth and half-hundredth. Hamilton felt the last of these, the half cent, was necessary because it would enable merchants to lower their prices, which would help the poor.

Congress passed the act establishing the U.S. Mint April 2, 1792. It reinstated several coin denominations left out by Hamilton and dropped his gold dollar. In gold, the act authorized at $10 coin, or "eagle"; a $5 coin, or "half eagle"; and a $2.50 coin, or "quarter eagle." In silver were to be a dollar, half dollar, quarter dollar, disme, and half disme, and in copper a cent and half cent.

Though it established a sound system of U.S. coinage, the act failed to address the problem of foreign coins in circulation. It was amended in February 1793 to cancel their legal-tender status within three years of the mint's opening.

Coinage totals at the first mint in Philadelphia were understandably low. Skilled coiners, assayers and others who could handle the mint's daily operations were in short supply in the United States. Also in want were adequate equipment and supplies of metal for coinage. Much of the former had to be built or imported. Much of the latter was also imported or salvaged from various domestic sources, including previously struck tokens and coins, and scrap metal.

Coinage began in earnest in 1793 with the striking of half cents and cents at the new mint located at Seventh Street between Market and Arch streets in Philadelphia.

Silver coinage followed in 1794, with half dimes, half dollars, and dollars. Gold coinage did not begin until 1795 with the minting of the first $5 and $10 coins. Silver dimes and quarters and gold $2.50 coins did not appear until 1796.

Under the bimetallic system of coinage by which gold and silver served as equal representations of the unit of value, much of the success and failure of the nation's coinage to enter and remain in circulation revolved around the supply and valuation of precious metals. From the Mint's beginning, slight miscalculations in the proper weight for the silver dollar and a proper bimetallic ratio led gold and silver to disappear from circulation. The U.S. silver dollar traded at par with Spanish and Mexican dollars, but because the U.S. coin was lighter, it was doomed to be exported.

A depositor at the first mint could make a profit at the mint's expense by sending the coins to the West Indies. There they could be traded at par for the heavier Spanish or Mexican eight reales, which were then shipped back to the United States for recoinage. As a result, few early silver dollars entered domestic circulation; most failed to escape the melting pots.

Gold fared no better. Calculations of the bimetallic ratio by which silver traded for gold on the world market were also askew at first and were always subject to fluctuations. Gold coins either disappeared quickly after minting or never entered circulation, languishing in bank vaults. These problems led President Jefferson to halt coinage of the gold $10 and the silver dollar in 1804.

The gold $10 reappeared in 1838 at a new, lower weight standard. The silver dollar, not coined for circulation since 1803, returned in 1836 with a limited mintage. Full-scale coinage waited until 1840.

Nor was the coinage of copper an easy matter for the first mint. Severe shortages of the metal led the mint to explore various avenues of obtaining sufficient supplies for striking cents and half cents.

Witness, for example, the half-cent issues of 1795 and 1797 struck over privately issued tokens of the New York firm of Talbot, Allum & Lee because of a shortage of copper for the federal issue. Rising copper prices and continued shortages forced the mint to lower the cent's weight from 208 grains to 168 grains in 1795.

In 1798, because of the coinage shortage, the legal-tender status of foreign coins was restored. Several more extensions were given during the 1800s, ending with the withdrawal of legal-tender status for Spanish coins in 1857.

A new law made the mint lower the standard weight of all gold coins in 1834. This reflected market conditions and in effect recognized a higher gold price when bought with silver coins. For example, $5 in silver coins bought a new, lighter $5 gold piece, meaning the buyer got less gold. This led to the melting of great numbers of the older, heavier gold coins as speculators grabbed a 4.7 percent profit.

By the 1850s discovery of gold in California made silver more expensive in terms of gold. All silver quickly disappeared from circulation. Congress reacted in 1853 by lowering the weight of the silver half dime, dime, quarter, and half dollar, hoping to keep silver in circulation. A new gold coin of $20 value, the "double eagle," was introduced to absorb a great amount of the gold from Western mines.

Not long after, silver was discovered in Nevada. By the mid-1870s the various mines that made up what was known as the Comstock Lode (named after its colorful early proprietor, Henry P. Comstock) had hit the mother lode. Large supplies of silver from the Comstock, combined with European demonetization, caused a severe drop in its value. Silver coins were made heavier as a result in 1873.

Also, it was believed that the introduction of a heavier, 420-grain silver dollar in 1873, known as the Trade dollar, would create a market for much of the Comstock silver, bolster its price, and at the same time wrest control from Great Britain of lucrative trade with the Orient. It didn't. Large numbers of Trade dollars eventually flooded back into the United States. They were demonetized in 1887.

Morgan dollars were introduced in 1878 as a panacea to the severe economic problems following the Civil War. Those who proudly carried the banner of free silver contended that by taking the rich output of the Comstock mines and turning it into silver dollars, a cheaper, more plentiful form of money would become available. This was supposed to give the economy a boost.

The Free Silver Movement reached its peak in 1896 when William Jennings Bryan attempted to gain the White House on a plank largely based on restoration of the free and unlimited coinage of the standard 412.5-grain silver dollar. He failed. Silver failed. In 1900 the United States officially adopted a gold standard.

Silver continued to be a primary coinage metal until 1964, when rising prices led the Mint to remove it from the dime and quarter. Mintage of the silver dollar had ended in 1935. The half dollar continued to be coined through 1970 with a 40 percent silver composition. It, too, was then made of copper-nickel clad metal.

Gold coinage ended in 1933 and exists today only in commemorative issues and American Eagle bullion coins with fictive face values. A clad composition of copper and nickel is now the primary coinage metal. Even the cent is no longer all copper; a copper-coated zinc composition has been used since 1982.

Precious-metal supplies were also linked to the opening of additional mints, which served the parent facility in Philadelphia. The impact of gold discoveries in the 1820s in the southern Appalachian Mountains was directly tied to the construction of branch mints in Dahlonega, Ga., and Charlotte, N.C., in 1838. These new mints struck only gold coins. New Orleans also became the site of a branch mint in the same year as Dahlonega and Charlotte. It took in some of the outflow of gold from Southern mines, but also struck silver coins.

Discovery of gold in California in the late 1840s created a gold rush, and from it sprang a great western migration. Private issues of gold coinage, often of debased quality, were prevalent, and the cost of shipping the metal eastward for coinage at Philadelphia was high. A call for an official branch mint was soon heard and heeded in 1852 with the authorization of the San Francisco Mint, which began taking deposits in 1854.

The discovery of silver in the Comstock Lode led to yet another mint. Located only a short distance via Virginia & Truckee Railroad from the fabulous Comstock Lode, the Carson City mint began receiving bullion in early 1870. It struck only silver coins during its tenure.

Denver, also located in a mineral-rich region, became the site of an assay office in 1863 when the government purchased the Clark, Gruber & Co. private mint. It became a U.S. branch mint in 1906. Now four mints exist. They are in Denver, Philadelphia, San Francisco and West Point, N.Y. The latter strikes current precious metal coinage for collectors and investors.

How Are Coins Made?
Mints are really factories

C opper, nickel, silver, and gold are pretty much the basic coin metals for the United States. When mixed with tin, copper becomes bronze, and this alloy was used in cents. Current cents have a pure zinc core. There have been patterns made of aluminum, but these never were issued for use in circulation. Platinum joined gold and silver as a precious metal used in U.S. coinage starting in 1997.

There are three basic parts of the minting process: (1) the making of the planchet, which is divided into the selection and processing of the metal and the preparation of the planchets, (2) the making of the dies, and (3) the use of the dies to strike the planchets. To help you remember these three parts, think of "P," "D," and "S" for planchet, die, and striking.

■ Making the 'blanks' ■

The piece of metal that becomes a coin is known as a "blank." This is a usually round, flat piece that has been punched or cut from a sheet or strip of coin metal.

Before a blank can become a coin it has to be processed, cleaned, softened, and given what is known as an "upset edge" – a raised ridge or rim around both sides. The blank then becomes a "planchet" and is ready to be struck into a coin by the dies. First they go through what looks like a monstrous cement mixer. A huge cylinder revolves slowly as the planchets are fed in at one end and spiral their way through. This is an annealing oven, which heats the planchets to soften them. When they come out the end, they fall into a bath where they are cleaned with a diluted acid or soap solution. As the final step, they go through the upsetting mill, the machine that puts the raised rim on the blank and turns it into a planchet, ready to be struck. In a different department the process of making the dies used to strike the coins has already begun.

■ Preparing the dies ■

For those who haven't studied metallurgy, the concept of hard metal flowing about is pretty hard to swallow, but this is actually what happens. It is basically the same process as the one used in an auto plant to turn a flat sheet of steel into a fender with multiple curves and sharp bends. The cold metal is moved about by the pressure applied.

To make the metal move into the desired design, there has to be a die. Actually, there have to be two dies, because one of the laws of physics is that for every action there has to be an equal and opposite reaction. You cannot hold a piece of metal in midair and strike one side of it. Instead you make two dies, fix one, and drive the other one against it – with a piece of metal in between to accept the design from each die.

A die is a piece of hard metal, like steel, with a design on its face that helps to form a mirror image on the struck coin. Early dies were made by hand. Engravers used hand tools, laboriously cutting each letter, each digit, and each owl or eagle or whatever design was being used into the face of the die. Notice that this is "into" the surface of the die. Each part of the die design is a hole or cavity of varying shape and depth.

This is because we want a mirror image on the coin, but we want it raised, or in "relief." To make a relief image on a coin, the image on the die has to be recessed into the face of the die, or "incuse." Of course, if we want an incuse image on the coin, such as the gold $2.50 and $5 coins of 1908-1929, the design on the die face would have to be in relief.

To fully understand this, take a coin from your pocket and a piece of aluminum foil. Press the foil down over the coin design and rub it with an eraser. When you take the foil off and look at the side that was in contact with the coin, you have a perfect copy of a die. Everywhere there is a relief design on the coin there is an incuse design on your foil "die."

■ From sketchbook to coin ■

The design process begins with an artist's sketch. This is translated into a three-dimensional relief design that is hand-carved from plaster or, in recent years, from a form of plastic.

The plaster or plastic design is then transformed into a "galvano," which is an exact copy of the design that has been plated with a thin layer of copper. This is used as a template or pattern in a reducing lathe, which cuts the design into a die blank.

This die becomes the master die, from which all of the following steps descend. The process can be reversed so that the designs will be cut in relief, forming a tool called a

A galvano of the 1976 half dollar goes on the reducing lathe.

"hub," which is simply a piece of steel with the design in relief, exactly the same as the relief design on the intended coin.

To make working dies, pieces of special steel are prepared, with one end shaped with a slight cone. The die blank is softened by heating it. Then the hub is forced into the face of the die, forming the incuse, mirror-image design in the face of the die.

The process usually has to be repeated because the die metal will harden from the pressure. The die is removed, softened, and returned to the hubbing press for a second impression from the hub. As you can imagine, it takes several hundred tons per square inch to force the hub into the die. Logically, this process is called "hubbing" a die.

The advantage of hubbing a die is that thousands of working dies can be made from a single hub, each one for all practical purposes as identical as the proverbial peas in a pod. This enables, for example, U.S. mints to strike billions of one-cent coins each year, each with the identical design.

Die making has come a long way from the early days. Philadelphia used to make all dies and then shipped them to the branch mints. Now Denver has its own die shop and creates dies of its own.

■ Striking the coin ■

Yesterday's die might strike only a few hundred coins. Today it is not unusual for a die to strike well over a million coins.

The coin press used to strike modern coins is a complicated piece of equipment that consists basically of a feed system to place the planchets in position for the stroke of the hammer die to form a coin. This process takes only a fraction of a second, so the press has to operate precisely to spew out the hundreds of coins that are struck every minute.

The end of the early hammered coinage came with the introduction of the collar, which often is called the "third" die. The collar is noth-

A binful of blanks are ready for the coin press.

ing more than a steel plate with a hole in it. This hole is the exact diameter of the intended coin and often is lined with carbide to prolong its life. It surrounds the lower, or fixed, die. Its sole purpose is to contain the coin metal to keep it from spreading too far sideways under the force of the strike.

If the intended coin has serrations, or "reeds," on the edge, then the collar has the matching design. The strike forces the coin metal against the serrations in the collar, forming the reeded edge at the same time that the two dies form the front and back, or obverse and reverse, of the coin.

Lettered-edge coins are produced usually by running the planchets through an edge-lettering die, or by using a segmented collar that is forced against the edge of the planchet during the strike by hydraulic pressure.

Several hundred tons were required to drive a hub into a die. Not as much but still significant amounts of force are needed to strike coins. A cent requires about 30 tons per square inch. A silver dollar took 150 tons. Other denominations fall between.

Modern coin presses apply pressure in a variety of ways. A ram, carrying the moving or "hammer" die, is forced against the planchet. Most commonly this is with the mechanical advantage of a "knuckle" or connected pieces to which pressure is applied from the side. When the joint straightens – like straightening your finger – the ram at the end of the piece is driven into the planchet. Once the strike is complete, at the final impact of the die pair, the coin has been produced. It is officially a coin now, and it's complete and ready to be spent.

■ Making proof coins ■

Proof coins started out as special presentation pieces. They were and still are struck on specially prepared planchets with specially prepared dies. Today the definition of a proof coin also requires that it be struck two or more times.

Currently all proof versions of circulating U.S. coins are struck at the San Francisco Mint, but some of the proof commemorative coins have been struck at the other mints. West Point currently strikes proof American Eagles of silver, gold, and platinum, and they carry a "W" mintmark.

After the proof blanks are punched from the strip, they go through the annealing oven, but on a conveyor belt rather than being tumbled in the revolving drum. After cleaning and upsetting they go into a huge vibrating machine where they are mixed with steel pellets that look like tiny footballs. The movement of the steel pellets against the planchets burnishes, or smooths, the surface so any scratches and gouges the planchets pick up during processing are smoothed over.

Proof dies get an extra polishing before the hubbing process. They are made at Philadelphia and shipped to the branch mints. When the proof dies arrive at San Francisco, they are worked on by a team of specialists who use diamond dust and other polishing agents to turn the fields of the proof dies into mirrorlike surfaces. The incuse design is sandblasted to make the surface rough, producing what is known as a "frosted" design. Because collectors like the frosted proofs, the design is periodically swabbed with acid to keep the surface rough and increase the number of frosted proofs from each die. This process has been around about a quarter century, so frosted examples of earlier proofs are considerably scarcer.

The presses that strike proof coins usually are hand-operated rather than automatic. Some of the newer presses use equipment such as vacuum suction devices to pick up the planchets, place them in the coining chamber, and then remove the struck coins. This avoids handling the pieces any more than necessary.

On a hand-operated press, the operator takes a freshly washed and dried planchet and, using tongs, places it in the collar. The ram with the die descends two or more times before the finished coin is removed from the collar and carefully stored in a box for transport to storage or the packaging line. After each strike the operator wipes the dies to make sure that lint or other particles don't stick to the dies and damage the coins as they are struck.

Proof dies are used for only a short time. Maximum die life is usually less than 10,000 coins, varying with the size of the coin and the alloy being struck.

U.S. Minting Varieties and Errors

Most are common, some are rare

■ Introduction ■

The P.D.S. cataloging system used here to list minting varieties was originally compiled by Alan Herbert in 1971. PDS stands for the three main divisions of the minting process, "planchet," "die" and "striking." Two more divisions cover collectible modifications after the strike, as well as non-collectible alterations, counterfeits and damaged coins.

This listing includes 445 classes, each a distinct part of the minting process or from a specific non-mint change in the coin. Classes from like causes are grouped together. The PDS system applies to coins of the world, but is based on U.S. coinage with added classes for certain foreign minting practices.

Price ranges are based on a U.S. coin in MS-60 grade (uncirculated.) The ranges may be applied in general to foreign coins of similar size or value although collector values are not usually as high as for U.S. coins. Prices are only a guide as the ultimate price is determined by a willing buyer and seller.

To define minting varieties, "A coin which exhibits a variation of any kind from the normal, as a result of any portion of the minting process, whether at the planchet stage, as a result of a change or modification of the die, or during the striking process. It includes those classes considered to be intentional changes, as well as those caused by normal wear and tear on the dies or other minting equipment and classes deemed to be "errors."

The three causes are represented as follows:
1. (I) = Intentional Changes
2. (W) = Wear and Tear
3. (E) = Errors
Note: A class may show more than one cause and could be listed as (IWE).

■ Rarity level ■

The rarity ratings are based on the following scale:
1 - Very Common. Ranges from every coin struck down to 1,000,000.
2 - Common. From 1,000,000 down to 100,000.
3 - Scarce. From 100,000 down to 10,000.
4 - Very Scarce. From 10,000 down to 1,000.
5 - Rare. From 1,000 down to 100.
6 - Very Rare. From 100 down to 10.
7 - Extremely Rare. From 10 down to 1.

Unknown: If there is no confirmed report of a piece fitting a particular class, it is listed as Unknown. Reports of finds by readers would be appreciated in order to update future presentations.

An Unknown does not mean that your piece automatically is very valuable. Even a Rarity 7 piece, extremely rare, even unique, may have a very low collector value because of a lack of demand or interest in that particular class.

Classes, definitions and price ranges are based on material previously offered in Alan Herbert's book, *The Official Price Guide to Minting Varieties and Errors* and in *Coin Prices* Magazine.

Pricing information has also been provided by John A. Wexler and Ken Potter, with special pricing and technical advice from Del Romines.

Also recommended is the *Cherrypicker's Guide to Rare Die Varieties* by Bill Fivaz and J.T. Stanton. Check your favorite coin shop, numismatic library or book seller for availability of the latest edition.

For help with your coin questions, to report significant new finds and for authentication of your minting varieties, include a loose first class stamp and write to Alan Herbert, 700 E. State St., Iola, WI 54990-0001. Don't include any numismatic material until you have received specific mailing instructions from me.

■ Quick check index ■

If you have a coin and are not sure where to look for the possible variety:

If your coin shows doubling, first check V-B-I.

Then try II-A, II-B, II-C, II-I (4 & 5), III-J, III-L, or IV-C.

If part of the coin is missing, check III-B, III-C, or III-D.

If there is a raised line of coin metal, check II-D, II-G.

If there is a raised area of coin metal, check II-E, II-F, or III-F.

If the coin is out of round, and too thin, check III-G.

If coin appears to be the wrong metal, check III-A, III-E, III-F-3 and III-G.

If the die appears to have been damaged, check II-E, II-G. (Damage to the coin itself usually is not a minting variety.)

If the coin shows incomplete or missing design, check II-A, II-E, III-B-3, III-B-5 or III-D.

If only part of the planchet was struck, check III-M.

If something was struck into the coin, check III-J and III-K.

If something has happened to the edge of the coin, check II-D-6, II-E-10, III-I, III-M and III-O.

If your coin shows other than the normal design, check II-A or II-C.

If a layer of the coin metal is missing, or a clad layer is missing, check III-B and III-D.

If you have an unstruck blank, or planchet, check I-G.

If your coin may be a restrike, check IV-C.

If your coin has a counterstamp, countermark, additional engraving or apparent official modifications, check IV-B and V-A-8.

Do not depend on the naked eye to examine your coins. Use a magnifying lens whenever possible, as circulation damage, wear and alterations frequently can be mistaken for legitimate minting varieties.

■ The planchet varieties ■
Division I

The first division of the PDS System includes those minting varieties that occur in the manufacture of the planchet upon which the coins will ultimately be struck and includes classes resulting from faulty metallurgy, mechanical damage, faulty processing, or equipment or human malfunction prior to the actual coin striking.

Planchet alloy mix (I-A)

This section includes those classes pertaining to mixing and processing the various metals which will be used to make a coin alloy.

I-A-1 Improper Alloy Mix (WE), Rarity Level: 3-4, Values: $5 to $10.

I-A-2 Slag Inclusion Planchet (WE), Rarity Level: 5-6, Values: $25 up.

Damaged and defective planchets (I-B)

To be a class in this section the blank, or planchet, must for some reason not meet the normal standards or must have been damaged in processing. The classes cover the areas of defects in the melting, rolling, punching and processing of the planchets up to the point where they are sent to the coin presses to be struck.

I-B-1 Defective Planchet (WE), Rarity Level: 6, Values: $25 up.

I-B-2 Mechanically Damaged Planchet (WE), Rarity Level: –, Values: No Value. (See values for the coin struck on a mechanically damaged planchet.)

I-B-3 Rolled Thin Planchet (WE), Rarity Level: 6 - (Less rare on half cents of 1795, 1797 and restrikes of 1831-52.) Values: $10 up.

I-B-4 Rolled Thick Planchet (WE), Rarity Level: 7 - (Less rare in Colonial copper coins. Notable examples occur on the restrike half cents of 1840-52.) Values: $125 up.

I-B-5 Tapered Planchet (WE), Rarity Level: 7, Values: $25 up.

I-B-6 Partially Unplated Planchet (WE), Rarity Level: 6, Values: $15 up.

I-B-7 Unplated Planchet (WE), Rarity Level: 6-7, Values: $50 up.

I-B-8 Bubbled Plating Planchet (WE), Rarity Level: 1, Values: No Value.

I-B-9 Included Gas Bubble Planchet (WE), Rarity Level: 6-7, Values: $50 up.

I-B-10 Partially Unclad Planchet (WE), Rarity Level: 6, Values: $20 up.

I-B-11 Unclad Planchet (WE), Rarity Level: 6-7, Values: $50 up.

I-B-12 Undersize Planchet (WE), Rarity Level: 7, Values: $250 up.

I-B-13 Oversize Planchet (WE), Rarity Level: 7, Values: $250 up.

I-B-14 Improperly Prepared Proof Planchet (WE), Rarity Level: 7, Values: $100 up.

I-B-15 Improperly Annealed Planchet (WE), Rarity Level: - , Values: No Value.

I-B-16 Faulty Upset Edge Planchet (WE), Rarity Level: 5-6, Values: $10 up.

I-B-17 Rolled-In Metal Planchet (WE), Rarity Level: 6-7, Values: $50 up.

I-B-18 Weld Area Planchet (WE), Rarity Level: Unknown, Values: No Value Established. (See values for the coins struck on weld area planchets.)

I-B-19 Strike Clip Planchet (WE), Rarity Level: 7, Values: $150 up.

I-B-20 Unpunched Center-Hole Planchet (WE), Rarity Level: 5-7, Values: $5 and up.

I-B-21 Incompletely Punched Center-Hole Planchet (WE), Rarity Level: 6-7, Values: $15 up.

I-B-22 Uncentered Center-Hole Planchet (WE), Rarity Level: 6-7, Values: $10 up.

I-B-23 Multiple Punched Center-Hole Planchet (WE), Rarity Level: 7, Values: $35 up.

I-B-24 Unintended Center-Hole Planchet (WE), Rarity Level: Unknown, Values: -.

I-B-25 Wrong Size or Shape Center-Hole Planchet (IWE), Rarity Level: 5-7, Values: $10 up.

Clipped planchets (I-C)

Clipped blanks, or planchets, occur when the strip of coin metal fails to move forward between successive strokes of the gang punch to clear the previously punched holes, in the same manner as a cookie cutter overlapping a previously cut hole in the dough. The size of the clip is a function of the amount of overlap of the next punch.

The overlapping round punches produce a missing arc with curve matching the outside circumference of the blanking punch. Straight clips occur when the punch overlaps the beginning or end of a strip which has had the end sheared or sawed off. Ragged clips occur in the same manner when the ends of the strip have been left as they were rolled out.

The term "clip" as used here should not be confused with the practice of clipping or shaving small pieces of metal from a bullion coin after it is in circulation.

I-C-1 Disc Clip Planchet (WE), Rarity Level: 3-5, Values: $5 up.

I-C-2 Curved Clip Planchet - (To 5%) (WE), Rarity Level: 5-6, Values: $5 up.

I-C-3 Curved Clip Planchet - (6 to 10%) (WE), Rarity Level: 6, Values: $10 up.

I-C-4 Curved Clip Planchet - (11 to 25%) (WE), Rarity Level: 5-6, Values: $15 up.

I-C-5 Curved Clip Planchet - (26 to 60%) (WE), Rarity Level: 6-7, Values: $25 up.

I-C-6 Double Curved Clip Planchet (WE), Rarity Level: 6, Values: $10 up.

I-C-7 Triple Curved Clip Planchet (WE), Rarity Level: 5-6, Values: $25 up.

I-C-8 Multiple Curved Clip Planchet (WE), Rarity Level: 6-7, Values: $35 up.

I-C-9 Overlapping Curved Clipped Planchet (WE), Rarity Level: 6-7, Values: $50 up.

I-C-10 Incompletely Punched Curved Clip Planchet (WE), Rarity Level: 6, Values: $35 up.

I-C-11 Oval Curved Clip Planchet (WE), Rarity Level: 6-7, Values: $50 up.

I-C-12 Crescent Clip Planchet - (61% or more) (WE), Rarity Level: 7, Values: $200 up.

I-C-13 Straight Clip Planchet (WE), Rarity Level: 6, Values: $30 up.

I-C-14 Incompletely Sheared Straight Clip Planchet (WE), Rarity Level: 6, Values: $50 up.

I-C-15 Ragged Clip Planchet (WE), Rarity Level: 6-7, Values: $35 up.

I-C-16 Outside Corner Clip Planchet (E), Rarity Level: -, Values: No Value.

I-C-17 Inside Corner Clip Planchet (E), Rarity Level: -, Values: No Value.

I-C-18 Irregularly Clipped Planchet (E) Rarity Level: -, Values: Value not established.

I-C-19 Incompletely Punched Scalloped or Multi-Sided Planchet (E), Rarity Level: 7, Values: $25 up.

Laminated, split, or broken planchet (I-D)

For a variety of reasons the coin metal may split into thin layers (delaminate) and either split completely off the coin, or be retained. Common causes are included gas or alloy mix problems. Lamination cracks usually enter the surface of the planchet at a very shallow angle or are at right angles to the edge. The resulting layers differ from slag in that they appear as normal metal.

Lamination cracks and missing metal of any size below a split planchet are too common in the 35 percent silver 1942-1945 nickels to be collectible or have any significant value.

I-D-1 Small Lamination Crack Planchet (W), Rarity Level: 4-5, Values: $1 up.
I-D-2 Large Lamination Crack Planchet (W), Rarity Level: 3-4, Values: $5 up.
I-D-3 Split Planchet (W), Rarity Level: 5-6, Values: $15 up.
I-D-4 Hinged Split Planchet (W), Rarity Level: 6-7, Values: $75 up.
I-D-5 Clad Planchet With a Clad Layer Missing (W), Rarity Level: 5-6, Values: $35 up.
I-D-6 Clad Planchet With Both Clad Layers Missing (W), Rarity Level: 6-7, Values: $75 up.
I-D-7 Separated Clad Layer (W), Rarity Level: 5, Values: $25 up.
I-D-8 Broken Planchet (WE), Rarity Level: 3-4, Values: $5 up.

Wrong stock planchet (I-E)

The following classes cover those cases where the wrong coin metal stock was run through the blanking press, making blanks of the correct diameter, but of the wrong thickness, alloy or metal or a combination of the wrong thickness and the wrong metal.

I-E-1 Half Cent Stock Planchet (IE), Rarity Level: Unknown, Values: No Value Established.
I-E-2 Cent Stock Planchet (IE), Rarity Level: Unknown, Values: No Value Established.
I-E-3 Two Cent Stock Planchet (E), Rarity Level: Unknown, Values: No Value Established.
I-E-4 Three Cent Silver Stock Planchet (E), Rarity Level: Unknown, Values: No Value Established.
I-E-5 Three Cent Nickel Stock Planchet (E), Rarity Level: Unknown, Values: No Value Established.
I-E-6 Half Dime Stock Planchet (E), Rarity Level: Unknown, Values: No Value Established.
I-E-7 Dime Stock Planchet (E), Rarity Level: 7, Values: $200 up.
I-E-8 Twenty Cent Stock Planchet (E), Rarity Level: Unknown, Values: No Value Established.
I-E-9 Quarter Stock Planchet (E), Rarity Level: Unknown, Values: No Value Established.
I-E-10 Half Dollar Stock Planchet (E), Rarity Level: Unknown, Values: No Value Established.
I-E-11 Dollar Stock Planchet (E), Rarity Level: 7, Values: $300 up.
I-E-12 Token or Medal Stock Planchet (E), Rarity Level: Unknown, Values: No Value Established.
I-E-13 Wrong Thickness Spoiled Planchet (IWE), Rarity Level: Unknown, Values: No Value Established.
I-E-14 Correct Thickness Spoiled Planchet (IWE), Rarity Level: Unknown, Values: No Value Established.
I-E-15 Cut Down Struck Token Planchet (IWE), Rarity Level: Unknown, Values: No Value Established.
I-E-16 Experimental or Pattern Stock Planchet (IE), Rarity Level: Unknown, Values: No Value Established.
I-E-17 Proof Stock Planchet (IE), Rarity Level: Unknown, Values: No Value Established.
I-E-18 Adjusted Specification Stock Planchet (IE), Rarity Level: 7, Values: $25 up.
I-E-19 Trial Strike Stock Planchet (IE), Rarity Level: Unknown, Values: No Value Established.
I-E-20 U.S. Punched Foreign Stock Planchet (E), Rarity Level: 7, Values: $75 up.
I-E-21 Foreign Punched Foreign Stock Planchet (E), Rarity Level: 7, Values: $75 up.
I-E-22 Non-Standard Coin Alloy Planchet (IE), Rarity Level: 7, Values: Unknown.

Extra metal on a blank, or planchet (I-F)

True extra metal is only added to the blank during the blanking operation. This occurs as metal is scraped off the sides of the blanks as they are driven down through the thimble, or lower die in the blanking press. The metal is eventually picked up by a blank passing through, welded to it by the heat of friction.

A second form of extra metal has been moved to this section, the sintered coating planchet, the metal deposited on the planchet in the form of dust during the annealing operation.

I-F-1 Extra Metal on a Type 1 Blank (W), Rarity Level: 7, Values: $50 up.
I-F-2 Extra Metal on a Type 2 Planchet (W), Rarity Level: 6-7, Values: $75 up.
I-F-3 Sintered Coating Planchet (W), Rarity Level: 7, Values: $75 up.

Normal or abnormal planchets (I-G)

This section consists of the two principal forms – the blank as it comes from the blanking press – and in the form of a planchet after it has passed through the upsetting mill. It also includes a class for purchased planchets and one for planchets produced by the mint.

I-G-1 Type I Blank (IWE), Rarity Level: 3-5, Values: $2 up.
I-G-2 Type II Planchet (IWE), Rarity Level: 3-4, Values: 50 up.
I-G-3 Purchased Planchet (I), Rarity Level: 1, Values: No Value.
I-G-4 Mint Made Planchet (I), Rarity Level: 1, Values: No Value.
I-G-5 Adjustment-Marked Planchet (I), Rarity Level: Unknown, Values: No Value.
I-G-6 Hardness Test-Marked Planchet (I), Rarity Level: -, Values: No Value Established.
Note: There are no classes between I-G-6 and I-G-23
I-G-23 Proof Planchet (IE), Rarity Level: 6-7, Values: $1 up.

Coin metal strip (I-H)

When the coin metal strip passes through the blanking press it goes directly to a chopper. This cuts the remaining web into small pieces to be sent back to the melting furnace. Pieces of the web or the chopped up web may escape into the hands of collectors.

I-H-1 Punched Coin Metal Strip (IWE), Rarity Level: 4-6, Values: $5 up, depending on size, denomination and number of holes showing.
I-H-2 Chopped Coin Metal Strip (IE), Rarity Level: 3-5, Values: $5 up.

■ The die varieties ■
Division II

Die varieties may be unique to a given die, but will repeat for the full life of the die unless a further change occurs. Anything that happens to the die will affect the appearance of the struck coin. This includes all the steps of the die making:

● Cutting a die blank from a tool steel bar.
● Making the design.
● Transferring it to a model.
● Transferring it to the master die or hub.
● The hubbing process of making the die.
● Punching in the mintmark.
● Heat treating of the die.

The completed dies are also subject to damage in numerous forms, plus wear and tear during the striking process and repair work done with abrasives. All of these factors can affect how the struck coin looks.

Engraving varieties (II-A)

In all cases in this section where a master die, or master hub is affected by the class, the class will affect all the working hubs and all working dies descending from it.

Identification as being on a master die or hub depends on it being traced to two or more of the working hubs descended from the same master tools.

II-A-1 Overdate (IE), Rarity Level: 1-7, Values: $1 up.
II-A-2 Doubled Date (IE), Rarity Level: 1-7, Values: $1 up.
II-A-3 Small Date (IE), Rarity Level: 2-5, Values: $1 up.
II-A-4 Large Date (IE), Rarity Level: 2-5, Values: $1 up.
II-A-5 Small Over Large Date (IE), Rarity Level: 4-6, Values: $15 up.
II-A-6 Large Over Small Date (IE), Rarity Level: 3-5, Values: $10 up.
II-A-7 Blundered Date (E), Rarity Level: 6-7, Values: $50 up.
II-A-8 Corrected Blundered Date (IE), Rarity Level: 3-5, Values: $5 up.
II-A-9 Wrong Font Date Digit (IE), Rarity Level: 5-6, Values: Minimal.
II-A-10 Worn, Broken or Damaged Punch (IWE), Rarity Level: 5-6, Values: $5 up.
II-A-11 Expedient Punch (IWE), Rarity Level: 5-6, Values: $10 up.
II-A-12 Blundered Digit (E), Rarity Level: 4-5, Values: $50 up.
II-A-13 Corrected Blundered Digit (IE), Rarity Level: 3-6, Values: $10 up.
II-A-14 Doubled Digit (IWE), Rarity Level: 2-6, Values: $2 up.
II-A-15 Wrong Style or Font Letter or Digit (IE), Rarity Level: 3-5, Values: Minimal.

II-A-16 One Style or Font Over Another (IE), Rarity Level: 4-6, Values: $10 up.
II-A-17 Letter Over Digit (E), Rarity Level: 6-7, Values: $25 up.
II-A-18 Digit Over Letter (E), Rarity Level: 6-7, Values: $25 up.
II-A-19 Omitted Letter or Digit (IWE), Rarity Level: 4-6, Values: $5 up.
II-A-20 Blundered Letter (E), Rarity Level: 6-7, Values: $50 up.
II-A-21 Corrected Blundered Letter (IE), Rarity Level: 1-3, Values: $10 up.
II-A-22 Doubled Letter (IWE), Rarity Level: 2-6, Values: $2 up.
II-A-23 Blundered Design Element (IE), Rarity Level: 6-7, Values: $50 up.
II-A-24 Corrected Blundered Design Element (IE), Rarity Level: 3-5, Values: $10 up.
II-A-25 Large Over Small Design Element (IE), Rarity Level: 4-6, Values: $2 up.
II-A-26 Omitted Design Element (IWE), Rarity Level: 5-7, Values: $10 up.
II-A-27 Doubled Design Element (IWE), Rarity Level: 2-6, Values: $2 up.
II-A-28 One Design Element Over Another (IE), Rarity Level: 3-6, Values: $5 up.
II-A-29 Reducing Lathe Doubling (WE), Rarity Level: 6-7, Values: $50 up.
II-A-30 Extra Design Element (IE), Rarity Level: 3-5, Values: $10 up.
II-A-31 Modified Design (IWE), Rarity Level: 1-5, Values: No Value up.
II-A-32 Normal Design (I), Rarity Level: 1, Values: No Extra Value.
II-A-33 Design Mistake (IE), Rarity Level: 2-6, Values: $1 up.
II-A-34 Defective Die Design (IWE), Rarity Level: 1, Values: No Value.
II-A-35 Pattern (I), Rarity Level: 6-7, Values: $100 up.
II-A-36 Trial Design (I), Rarity Level: 5-7, Values: $100 up.
II-A-37 Omitted Designer's Initial (IWE), Rarity Level: 3-7, Values: $1 up.
II-A-38 Layout Mark (IE), Rarity Level: 5-7, Values: Minimal.
II-A-39 Abnormal Reeding (IWE), Rarity Level: 2-5, Values: $1 up.
II-A-40 Modified Die or Hub (IWE), Rarity Level: 1-5, Values: No Value up.
II-A-41 Numbered Die (I), Rarity Level: 3-5, Values: $5 up.
II-A-42 Plugged Die (IW), Rarity Level: 5-6, Values: Minimal.
II-A-43 Cancelled Die (IE), Rarity Level: 3-6, Values: No Value up.
II-A-44 Hardness Test Marked Die (IE), Rarity Level: 7, Values: $100 up.
II-A-45 Coin Simulation (IE), Rarity Level: 6-7, Values: $100 up, but may be illegal to own.
II-A-46 Punching Mistake (IE), Rarity Level: 2-6, Values: $1 up.
II-A-47 Small Over Large Design (IE), Rarity Level: 4-6, Values: $5 up.
II-A-48 Doubled Punch (IE), Rarity Level: 5-7, Values: $5 up.
II-A-49 Mint Display Sample (I) Rarity Level: 7, Values not established.
II-A-50 Center Dot, Stud or Circle (IE) Rarity Level: 7, much more common on early cents, Values not established

Hub doubling varieties (II-B)

Rotated hub doubling   **Hub break**

This section includes eight classes of hub doubling. Each class is from a different cause, described by the title of the class. At the latest count over 2,500 doubled dies have been reported in the U.S. coinage, the most famous being examples of the 1955, 1969-S and 1972 cent dies.
II-B-I Rotated Hub Doubling (WE), Rarity Level: 3-6, Values: $1 up
II-B-II Distorted Hub Doubling (WE), Rarity Level: 3-6, Values: $1 up.
II-B-III Design Hub Doubling (IWE), Rarity Level: 3-6, Values: $1 up to five figure amounts.

II-B-IV Offset Hub Doubling (WE), Rarity Level: 4-6, Values: $15 up.
II-B-V Pivoted Hub Doubling (WE), Rarity Level: 3-6, Values: $10 up.
II-B-VI Distended Hub Doubling (WE), Rarity Level: 2-5, Values: $1 up.
II-B-VII Modified Hub Doubling (IWE), Rarity Level: 2-5, Values: $1 up.
II-B-VIII Tilted Hub Doubling (WE), Rarity Level: 4-6, Values: $5 up.

Mintmark varieties (II-C)

Double   **Triple**

Mintmarks are punched into U.S. coin dies by hand (Up to 1985 for proof coins, to 1990 for cents and nickels and 1991 for other denominations). Variations resulting from mistakes in the punching are listed in this section. Unless exceptionally mispunched, values are usually estimated at 150 percent of numismatic value. Slightly tilted or displaced mintmarks have no value.

II-C-1 Doubled Mintmark (IE), Rarity Level: 2-6, Values: 50 cents up.
II-C-2 Separated Doubled Mintmark (IE), Rarity Level: 5-6, Values: $15 up.
II-C-3 Over Mintmark (IE), Rarity Level: 3-6, Values: $2 up.
II-C-4 Tripled Mintmark (IE), Rarity Level: 3-5, Values: 50 up.
II-C-5 Quadrupled Mintmark (IE), Rarity Level: 4-6, Values: $1 up.
II-C-6 Small Mintmark (IE), Rarity Level: 2-5, Values: No Extra Value up.
II-C-7 Large Mintmark (IE), Rarity Level: 2-5, Values: No Extra Value up.
II-C-8 Large Over Small Mintmark (IE), Rarity Level: 2-5, Values: $2 up.
II-C-9 Small Over Large Mintmark (IE), Rarity Level: 3-6, Values: $5 up.
II-C-10 Broken Mintmark Punch (W), Rarity Level: 5-6, Values: $5 up.
II-C-11 Omitted Mintmark (IWE), Rarity Level: 4-7, Values: $125 up.
II-C-12 Tilted Mintmark (IE), Rarity Level: 5-7, Values: $5 up.
II-C-13 Blundered Mintmark (E), Rarity Level: 4-6, Values: $5 up.
II-C-14 Corrected Horizontal Mintmark (IE), Rarity Level: 4-6, Values: $5 up.
II-C-15 Corrected Upside Down Mintmark (IE), Rarity Level: 4-6, Values: $5 up.
II-C-16 Displaced Mintmark (IE), Rarity Level: 4-6, Values: $5 to $10.
II-C-17 Modified Mintmark (IWE), Rarity Level: 1-4, Values: No Extra Value up.
II-C-18 Normal Mintmark (I), Rarity Level: 1, Values: No Extra Value.
II-C-19 Doubled Mintmark Punch (I), Rarity Level: 6-7, Values: No Extra Value up.
II-C-20 Upside Down Mintmark (E) Rarity Level 6-7, Values: $5 up.
II-C-21 Horizontal Mintmark (E) Rarity Level 6-7, Values: $5 up.
II-C-22 Wrong Mintmark (E) Rarity Level 6-7, Values $15 up. (Example has a D mintmark in the date, but was used at Philadelphia.)

Die, collar and hub cracks (II-D)

Die cracks

Cracks in the surface of the die allow coin metal to be forced into the crack during the strike, resulting in raised irregular lines of coin metal above the normal surface of the coin. These are one of the commonest forms of die damage and wear, making them easily collectible.

Collar cracks and hub cracks are added to this section because the causes and effects are similar or closely associated.

Die cracks, collar cracks and hub cracks are the result of wear and tear on the tools, with intentional use assumed for all classes.

II-D-1 Die Crack (W), Rarity Level: 1-3, Values: 10 to $1, $25 up on a proof coin with a rarity level of 6-7.

II-D-2 Multiple Die Cracks (W), Rarity Level: 1-3, Values: 25 cents to $2.

II-D-3 Head-To-Rim Die Crack (Lincoln Cent) (W), Rarity Level: 2-6, Values: 25 to $10 for multiple die cracks.

II-D-4 Split Die (W), Rarity Level: 5-6, Values: $10 up.

II-D-5 Rim-To-Rim Die Crack (W), Rarity Level: 2-5, Values: $1 up.

II-D-6 Collar Crack (W), Rarity Level: 4-6, Values: $10 up.

II-D-7 Hub Crack (W), Rarity Level: 3-5, Values: $1-$2.

Small die break II-E-2

Clogged letter II-E-1

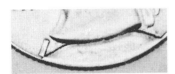

Major die break, date missing, II-E-5

Rim die break II-E-4

Die breaks (II-E)

Breaks in the surface of the die allow coin metal to squeeze into the resulting holes, causing raised irregular areas above the normal surface of the coin. Die chips and small die breaks are nearly as common as the die cracks, but major die breaks, which extend in from the edge of the coin, are quite rare on the larger coins.

If the broken piece of the die is retained, the resulting design will be above or below the level of the rest of the surface.

II-E-1 Die Chip (W), Rarity Level: 1-2, Values: 10 to $1.

II-E-2 Small Die Break (W), Rarity Level: 1-3, Values: 10 to $2.

II-E-3 Large Die Break (W), Rarity Level: 3-5, Values: $1 to $50 and up.

II-E-4 Rim Die Break (W), Rarity Level: 2-3, Values: 25 cents to $5.

II-E-5 Major Die Break (WE), Rarity Level: 3-6, Values: $5 to $100 and up.

II-E-6 Retained Broken Die (W), Rarity Level: 3-5, Values: $1 to $10 and up.

II-E-7 Retained Broken Center of the Die (W), Rarity Level: 6-7, Values: $100 up.

II-E-8 Laminated Die (W), Rarity Level: 3-5, Values: 10 cents to $5.

II-E-9 Chipped Chrome Plating (W), Rarity Level: 4-5, Values: $10 to $25 on proofs.

II-E-10 Collar Break (W), Rarity Level: 4-6, Values: $5 to $25 and up.

II-E-11 Broken Letter or Digit on an Edge Die (W), Rarity Level: 4-6, Values: Minimal.

II-E-12 "Bar" Die Break (W), Rarity Level: 3-5, Values: 25 to $20.

II-E-13 Hub Break (W), Rarity Level: 4-6, Values: 50 to $10 and up.

"BIE" varieties (II-F)

A series of small die breaks or die chips in the letters of "LIBERTY" mostly on the wheat-reverse Lincoln cent are actively collected. The name results from the resemblance to an "I" between the "B" and "E" on many of the dies, but they are found between all of the letters in different cases. Well over 1,500 dies are known and cataloged. Numerous more recent examples are known.

II-F-1 ILI Die Variety (W), Rarity Level: 4-5, Values: 25 cents to $10.

II-F-2 LII Die Variety (W), Rarity Level: 3-5, Values: 50 cents to $15.

BIE variety II-F-4

II-F-3 IIB Die Variety (W), Rarity Level: 3-5, Values: 50 cents to $15.
II-F-4 BIE Die Variety (W), Rarity Level: 3-5, Values: $1 to $20.
II-F-5 EIR Die Variety (W), Rarity Level: 3-5, Values: 50 to $15.
II-F-6 RIT Die Variety (W), Rarity Level: 4-5, Values: $2 to $25.
II-F-7 TIY Die Variety (W), Rarity Level: 4-5, Values: $5 to $30.
II-F-8 TYI Die Variety (W), Rarity Level: 4-5, Values: $2 to $25.

Worn and damaged dies, collars and hubs (II-G)

Die clashes and design transfer

Many dies are continued deliberately in service after they have been damaged, dented, clashed or show design transfer, since none of these classes actually affect anything but the appearance ofthe coin. The root cause is wear, but intent or mistakes may enter the picture.

II-G-1 Dented Die, Collar or Hub (IWE), Rarity Level: 3-5, Values: 25 to $5.
II-G-2 Damaged Die, Collar or Hub (IWE), Rarity Level: 3-5, Values: 25 to $5.
II-G-3 Worn Die, Collar or Hub (IWE), Rarity Level: 2-3, Values: No Extra Value to Minimal Value.
II-G-4 Pitted or Rusted Die, Collar or Hub (IWE), Rarity Level: 3-4, Values:No Extra Value, marker only.
II-G-5 Heavy Die Clash (IWE), Rarity Level: 4-5, Values: $1 to $10 and up.
II-G-6 Heavy Collar Clash (IWE), Rarity Level: 3-4, Values: $1 to $5 and up.
II-G-7 Heavy Design Transfer (IWE), Rarity Level: 3-4, Values: 10 cents to $1.

Die progressions (II-H)

The progression section consists of three classes. These are useful as cataloging tools for many different die varieties, but especially the die cracks and die breaks which may enlarge, lengthen or increase in number.

II-H-1 Progression (W), Rarity Level: 3-5, Values: $1 up.
II-H-2 Die Substitution (IW), Rarity Level: 2-4, Values: No Extra Value to Minimal Value.
II-H-3 Die Repeat (I), Rarity Level: 2-4, Values: No Extra Value to Minimal Value.

Die scratches, polished and abraded dies (II-I)

Die scratches II-I-1

This section consists of those classes having to do with the use of an abrasive in some form to intentionally polish proof dies, or repair the circulating die surface. Several classes which previously were referred to as "polished" now are listed as "abraded."

II-I-1 Die Scratch (IW), Rarity Level: 1-2, Values: No Extra Value to 10 cents to 25 cents, as a marker.
II-I-2 Polished (proof) Die (IW), Rarity Level: 1, Values: No Extra Value.

II-I-3 Abraded (Circulation) Die (IW), Rarity Level: 1-2, Values: No Extra Value up to $10.
II-I-4 Inside Abraded Die Doubling (IW), Rarity Level: 1-3, Values: No Extra Value to $1.
II-I-5 Outside Abraded Die Doubling (IW), Rarity Level: 1-3, Values: No Extra Value to $1.
II-I-6 Lathe Marks (IW), Rarity Level: 5-7, Values: No Extra Value, marker only.

■ Striking varieties ■
Division III

Once the dies are made and the planchets have been prepared, they are struck by a pair of dies and become a coin. In this division, we list the misstrikes resulting from human or mechanical malfunction in the striking process. These are one-of-a-kind varieties, but there may be many similar coins that fall in a given class.

Multiples and combinations of classes must be considered on a case by case basis. The first several sections match the planchet sections indicated in the title.

Struck on defective alloy mix planchets (III-A)

This section includes those classes of coins struck on planchets that were made from a defective alloy.

III-A-1 Struck on an Improper Alloy Mix Planchet (IE), Rarity Level: 2-3, Values: 10 cents to $2.
III-A-2 Struck on a Planchet With Slag Inclusions(IE), Rarity Level: 5-6, Values: $10 up.

Struck on damaged, defective or abnormal planchet (III-B)

Struck on a defective planchet III-B-1

Struck on a tapered planchet III-B-5

Coins get struck on many strange objects. The more common of course are planchets which have been damaged in some way in the production process. In most of the classes in this section intent is at least presumed, if not specifically listed as a cause.

III-B-1 Struck on a Defective Planchet (IWE), Rarity Level: 4-6, Values: $5 to $10 and up.
III-B-2 Struck on a Mechanically Damaged Planchet (IWE), Rarity Level: 5-6, Values: $10 to $20 and up.
III-B-3 Struck on a Rolled Thin Planchet (IWE), Rarity Level: 5-6, Values: $2 to $5 and up.
III-B-4 Struck on a Rolled Thick Planchet (IWE), Rarity Level: 5-6, Values: $35 to $50 and up.
III-B-5 Struck on a Tapered Planchet (WE), Rarity Level: 4-6, Values: $2 to $5 and up.
III-B-6 Struck on a Partially Unplated Planchet (WE), Rarity Level: 5, Values: $10 up.
III-B-7 Struck on an Unplated Planchet (WE), Rarity Level: 6-7, Values: $100 up.
III-B-8 Struck on a Bubbled Plating Planchet (IWE), Rarity Level: 1, Values: No Value.
III-B-9 Struck on an Included Gas Bubble Planchet (WE), Rarity Level: 5-6, Values: $5 up.
III-B-10 Struck on a Partially Unclad Planchet (WE), Rarity Level: 5-6, Values: $5 up.
III-B-11 Struck on an Unclad Planchet (WE), Rarity Level: 4-5, Values: $5 and up.
III-B-12 Struck on an Undersize Planchet (WE), Rarity Level: 4-6, Values: Minimal.
III-B-13 Struck on an Oversize Planchet (WE), Rarity Level: 6-7, Values: Minimal.
III-B-14 Struck on an Improperly Prepared Proof Planchet (IWE), Rarity Level: 3-5, Values: $5 up.
III-B-15 Struck on an Improperly Annealed Planchet (IWE), Rarity Level: 4-5, Values: $5 up.
III-B-16 Struck on a Faulty Upset Edge Planchet (IWE), Rarity Level: 4-5, Values: $1 to $2.
III-B-17 Struck on a Rolled In Metal Planchet (WE), Rarity Level: 4-6, Values: $2 up.
III-B-18 Struck on a Weld Area Planchet (WE), Rarity Level: 6, Values: $25 to $50.
III-B-19 Struck on a Strike Clip Planchet (W), Rarity Level: 6-7, Values: $25 up.
III-B-20 Struck on an Unpunched Center Hole Planchet (WE), Rarity Level: 4-6, Values: $1 and up.
III-B-21 Struck on an Incompletely Punched Center Hole Planchet (WE), Rarity Level: 6-7, Values: $5 up.

III-B-22 Struck on an Uncentered Center Hole Planchet (WE), Rarity Level: 6-7, Values: $10 up.
III-B-23 Struck on a Multiple Punched Center Hole Planchet (WE), Rarity Level: 7, Values: $25 up.
III-B-24 Struck on an Unintended Center Hole Planchet (WE), Rarity Level: 6-7, Values: $25 and up.
III-B-25 Struck on a Wrong Size or Shape Center Hole Planchet (WE), Rarity Level: 5-7, Values: $5 up.
III-B-26 Struck on Scrap Coin Metal (E), Rarity Level: 4-6, Values: $10 up.
III-B-27 Struck on Junk Non Coin Metal (E), Rarity Level: 4-6, Values: $15 up.
III-B-28 Struck on a False Planchet (E), Rarity Level: 3-5, Values: $35 up.
III-B-29 Struck on Bonded Planchets (E), Rarity Level: 6-7, Values: $50 up.

Struck on a clipped planchet (III-C)

Ragged edge clip III-C-15

Multiple clip III-C-8

Incomplete curved clip III-C-10

Coins struck on clipped blanks, or planchets, exhibit the same missing areas as they did before striking, modified by the metal flow from the strike which rounds the edges and tends to move metal into the missing areas. Values for blanks will run higher than planchets with similar clips.

III-C-1 Struck on a Disc Clip Planchet (WE), Rarity Level: 4-5, Values: $1 on regular coins, $20 and up for clad coins.
III-C-2 Struck on a Curved Clip Planchet - to 5% (WE), Rarity Level: 3-5, Values: 50 cents up.
III-C-3 Struck on a Curved Clip Planchet - (6 to 10%) (WE), Rarity Level: 4-5, Values: $1 up.
III-C-4 Struck on a Curved Clip Planchet - (11 to 25%) (WE), Rarity Level: 4-5, Values: $2 up.
III-C-5 Struck on a Curved Clip Planchet - (26 to 60%) (WE), Rarity Level: 4-6, Values: $10 up.
III-C-6 Struck on a Double Curved Clip Planchet (WE), Rarity Level: 3-4, Values: $2 up.
III-C-7 Struck on a Triple Curved Clip Planchet (WE), Rarity Level: 4-5, Values: $5 up.
III-C-8 Struck on a Multiple Curved Clip Planchet (WE), Rarity Level: 4-6, Values: $5 up.
III-C-9 Struck on an Overlapping Curved Clipped Planchet (WE), Rarity Level: 5-6, Values: $15 up.
III-C-10 Struck on an Incomplete Curved Clip Planchet (WE), Rarity Level: 4-5, Values: $10 up.
III-C-11 Struck on an Oval Clip Planchet (WE), Rarity Level: 5-6, Values: $20 up.
III-C-12 Struck on a Crescent Clip Planchet - (61% or more) (WE), Rarity Level: 6-7, Values: $100 up.
III-C-13 Struck on a Straight Clip Planchet (E), Rarity Level: 4-6, Values: $10 up.
III-C-14 Struck on an Incomplete Straight Clip Planchet (WE), Rarity Level: 5-6, Values: $20 up.
III-C-15 Struck on a Ragged Clip Planchet (E), Rarity Level: 4-6, Values: $15 up.
III-C-16 Struck on an Outside Corner Clip Planchet (E), Rarity Level: 7, Values: $100 up.
III-C-17 Struck on an Inside Corner Clip Planchet (E), Rarity Level: Unknown outside mint., Values: -.
III-C-18 Struck on an Irregularly Clipped Planchet (E), Rarity Level: 6-7, Values: $20 up.
III-C-19 Struck on an Incompletely Punched Scalloped or Multi-Sided Planchet (E), Rarity Level: 7, Values: $20 up.

Struck on a laminated, split or broken planchet (III-D)

This section has to do with the splitting, cracking or breaking of a coin parallel to the faces of the coin, or at least very nearly parallel, or breaks at right angles to the faces of the coin.

Lamination crack III-D-1

Layer peeled off III-D-2

Split planchet III-D-3

Lamination cracks and missing metal of any size below a split planchet are too common in the 35-percent silver 1942-1945 nickels to be collectible or have any significant value.

III-D-1 Struck on a Small Lamination Crack Planchet (W), Rarity Level: 3-4, Values: 10 up.

III-D-2 Struck on a Large Lamination Crack Planchet (W), Rarity Level: 3-6, Values: $1 up.

III-D-3 Struck on a Split Planchet (W), Rarity Level: 4-6, Values: $5 up.

III-D-4 Struck on a Hinged Split Planchet (W), Rarity Level: 5-6, Values: $35 up.

III-D-5 Struck on a Planchet With a Clad Layer Missing (W), Rarity Level: 4-5, Values: $15 up.

III-D-6 Struck on a Planchet With Both Clad Layers Missing (W), Rarity Level: 4-5, Values: $25 up.

III-D-7 Struck on a Separated Clad Layer or Lamination (W), Rarity Level: 6-7, Values: $75 up.

III-D-8 Struck on a Broken Planchet Before the Strike (W), Rarity Level: 3-5, Values: $10 up.

III-D-9 Broken Coin During or After the Strike (W), Rarity Level: 4-6, Values: $20 up.

III-D-10 Struck Coin Fragment Split or Broken During or After the Strike (W), Rarity Level: 3-5, Values: $5 up.

III-D-11 Reedless Coin Broken During or After the Strike (W), Rarity Level: Unknown, Values: -.

Struck on wrong stock planchets (III-E)

Quarter on dime stock
III-E-7 (lower coin edge)

These classes cover those cases where the wrong stock was run through the blanking press, making planchets of the correct diameter, but of the wrong thickness, alloy or metal or a combination of incorrect thickness and metal.

III-E-1 Struck on a Half Cent-Stock Planchet (IE), Rarity Level: Unknown, Values: No Value Established.

III-E-2 Struck on a Cent-Stock Planchet (IE), Rarity Level: Unknown, Values: No Value Established.

III-E-3 Struck on a Two-Cent-Stock Planchet (E), Rarity Level: Unknown, Values: -.

III-E-4 Struck on a Three-Cent-Silver Stock Planchet (E), Rarity Level: Unknown, Values: -.

III-E-5 Struck on a Three-Cent-Nickel Stock Planchet (E), Rarity Level: Unknown, Values: -.

III-E-6 Struck on a Half Dime-Stock Planchet (E), Rarity Level: Unknown, Values: -.

III-E-7 Struck on a Dime-Stock Planchet (E), Rarity Level: 5-6, Values: $20 up.

III-E-8 Struck on a Twenty-Cent-Stock Planchet (E), Rarity Level: Unknown, Values: -.

III-E-9 Struck on a Quarter-Stock Planchet (E), Rarity Level: 6, Values: $50 up.

III-E-10 Struck on a Half Dollar-Stock Planchet (E), Rarity Level: 6-7, Values: $100 up.

III-E-11 Struck on a Dollar-Stock Planchet (E), Rarity Level: 6-7, Values: $300 up.

III-E-12 Struck on a Token/Medal-Stock Planchet (E), Rarity Level: 7, Values: No Value Established.

III-E-13 Struck on a Wrong Thickness Spoiled Planchet (IWE), Rarity Level: 7, Values: $50 up.

III-E-14 Struck on a Correct Thickness Spoiled Planchet (IWE), Rarity Level: Unknown, Values: No Value Established.

III-E-15 Struck on a Cut Down Struck Token (IWE), Rarity Level: 6-7, Values: $50 up.

III-E-16 Struck on an Experimental or Pattern-Stock Planchet (IE), Rarity Level: 7, Values: $50 up.

III-E-17 Struck on a Proof-Stock Planchet (IE), Rarity Level: 7, Values: $100 up.

III-E-18 Struck on an Adjusted Specification-Stock Planchet (IE), Rarity Level: 3-7, Values: No Value to $5 and up.

III-E-19 Struck on a Trial Strike-Stock Planchet (IE), Rarity Level: Unknown, Values: No Value Established.

III-E-20 U.S. Coin Struck on a Foreign-Stock Planchet. (E), Rarity Level: 5, Values: $35 up.

III-E-21 Foreign Coin Struck on a Foreign-Stock Planchet (E), Rarity Level: 5-6, Values: $25 up.

III-E-22 Struck on a Non-Standard Coin Alloy (IE), Rarity Level: 4-7, Values: $20 up.

Extra metal (III-F)

Extra metal on a struck coin (III-F)

Sintered coating III-F-3

The term "extra metal" for the purpose of this section includes both extra metal added to the blank during the blanking operation and metal powder added to the planchet during the annealing operation.

III-F-1 Struck on a Type 1 Blank With Extra Metal (W), Rarity Level: Unknown, Values: -.

III-F-2 Struck on a Type 2 Planchet With Extra Metal (W), Rarity Level: 4-5, Values: $10 up.

III-F-3 Struck on a Sintered Coating Planchet (W), Rarity Level: 6-7, Values: $35 up.

Struck on normal or abnormal blanks, or planchets (III-G)

Cent on dime planchet III-G-10

Half on dime planchet III-G-10   **Half on quarter planchet III-G-11**

This section includes coins struck on either a blank, as it comes from the blanking press, or as a planchet that has passed through the upsetting mill. Added to this section are those planchets which are normal until they are struck by the wrong dies. These differ from the wrong stock planchets because the wrong stock planchets are already a variety before they are struck.

III-G-1 Struck on a Type 1 Blank (IWE), Rarity Level: 4-6, Values: $10 up.

III-G-2 Struck on a Type 2 Planchet (I), Rarity Level: 1, Values: No Extra Value.

III-G-3 Struck on a Purchased Planchet (I), Rarity Level: 1, Values: No Extra Value.

III-G-4 Struck on a Mint-Made Planchet (I), Rarity Level: 1, Values: No Extra Value.

III-G-5 Struck on an Adjustment-Marked Planchet (I), Rarity Level: 4-7, Values: Minimal, and may reduce value of coin in some cases.

III-G-6 Struck on a Hardness Test-Marked Planchet (I), Rarity Level: 6-7, Values: $10 up.

III-G-7 Wrong Planchet or Metal on a Half Cent Planchet (IE), Rarity Level: 5-7, Values: $100 up.

III-G-8 Wrong Planchet or Metal on a Cent Planchet (IE), Rarity Level: 3-6, Values: $25 up.

III-G-9 Wrong Planchet or Metal on a Nickel Planchet (E), Rarity Level: 4-6, Values: $35 up

III-G-10 Wrong Planchet or Metal on a Dime Planchet (E), Rarity Level: 4-6, Values: $50 up.

III-G-11 Wrong Planchet or Metal on a Quarter Planchet (E), Rarity Level: 4-6. Values: $100 up.

III-G-12 Wrong Planchet or Metal on a Half Dollar Planchet (E), Rarity Level: 6-7, Values: $500 up.

III-G-13 Wrong Planchet or Metal on a Dollar Planchet (E), Rarity Level: 7, Values: $500 up.

III-G-14 Wrong Planchet or Metal on a Gold Planchet (E), Rarity Level: 7, Values: $1000 up.

III-G-15 Struck on a Wrong Series Planchet (IE), Rarity Level: 6-7, Values: $1500 up.

III-G-16 U.S. Coin Struck on a Foreign Planchet (E), Rarity Level: 5-7, Values: $35 up.

III-G-17 Foreign Coin Struck on a U.S. Planchet (E), Rarity Level: 6-7, Values: $50 up.

III-G-18 Foreign Coin Struck on a Wrong Foreign Planchet (E), Rarity Level: 6-7, Values: $50 up.

III-G-19 Struck on a Medal Planchet (E), Rarity Level: 6-7, Values: $100 up.

III-G-20 Medal Struck on a Coin Planchet (IE), Rarity Level: 3-5, Values: $10 up.

III-G-21 Struck on an Official Sample Planchet (IE), Rarity Level: Unknown, Values: No Value Established.

III-G-22 Struck Intentionally on a Wrong Planchet (I), Rarity Level: 6-7, Values: Mainly struck as Presentation Pieces, full numismatic value.

III-G-23 Non-Proof Struck on a Proof Planchet (IE), Rarity Level: 6-7, Values: $500 up.

Struck on coin metal strip (III-H)

Pieces of the coin metal strip do manage at times to escape into the coin press.

III-H-1 (See I-H-1 Punched Coin Metal Strip), Rarity Level: Impossible, Values: -.

III-H-2 Struck on Chopped Coin Metal Strip (E), Rarity Level: 6-7, Values: $25 up.

Die adjustment strikes (III-I)

As the dies are set up and adjusted in the coin press, variations in the strike occur until the dies are properly set. Test strikes are normally scrapped, but on occasion reach circulation.

III-I-1 Die Adjustment Strike (IE), Rarity Level: 5-6, Values: $35 up.

III-I-2 Edge Strike (E), Rarity Level: 5-6, Values: $10 to $20 and up.

III-I-3 Weak Strike (W), Rarity Level: 1, Values: No Extra Value.

III-I-4 Strong Strike (IWE), Rarity Level: 1, Values: No value except for the premium that might be paid for a well struck coin.

III-I-5 Jam Strike (IE), Rarity Level: 7, Values: $50 up.

III-I-6 Trial Piece Strike (I), Rarity Level: 6-7, Values: $100 up.

III-I-7 Edge-Die Adjustment Strike (I), Rarity Level: 5-7, Values: $5 up.

III-I-8 Uniface Strike (I), Rarity Level 7, Values: $50 up.

Indented, brockage and counter-brockage strikes (III-J)

Indented strike III-J-1   **Counter-brockage strike III-J-11**   **Capped die strike III-J-15**

Indented and uniface strikes involve an extra unstruck planchet between one of the dies and the planchet being struck. Brockage strikes involve a struck coin between one of the dies and the planchet and a counter-brockage requires a brockage coin between one of the dies and the planchet.

A cap, or capped die strike results when a coin sticks to the die and is squeezed around it in the shape of a bottle cap.

III-J-1 Indented Strike (W), Rarity Level: 3-6, Values: $5 up.

III-J-2 Uniface Strike (W), Rarity Level: 3-5, Values: $15 up.

III-J-3 Indented Strike By a Smaller Planchet (WE), Rarity Level: 5-7, Values: $100 up.

III-J-4 Indented Second Strike (W), Rarity Level: 3-5, Values: $10 up, about the same as a regular double strike of comparable size.

III-J-5 Partial Brockage Strike (W), Rarity Level: 3-6, Values: $15 up.

III-J-6 Full Brockage Strike (W), Rarity Level: 3-6, Values: $5 up.

III-J-7 Brockage Strike of a Smaller Coin (WE), Rarity Level: 6-7, Values: $200 up.

III-J-8 Brockage Strike of a Struck Coin Fragment (WE), Rarity Level: 4-6, Values: $5 up.

III-J-9 Brockage Second Strike (WE), Rarity Level: 3-5, Values: $5 up.

III-J-10 Partial Counter-Brockage Strike (WE), Rarity Level: 3-5, Values: $10 up.

III-J-11 Full Counter-Brockage Strike (WE), Rarity Level: 5-7, Values: $100 up.

III-J-12 Counter-Brockage Second Strike (WE), Rarity Level: 4-6, Values: $10 up.
III-J-13 Full Brockage-Counter-Brockage Strike (WE), Rarity Level: 6-7, Values: $150 up.
III-J-14 Multiple Brockage or Counter-Brockage Strike (WE), Rarity Level: 5-7, Values: $100 up.
III-J-15 Capped Die Strike (WE), Rarity Level: 6-7, Values: $500 up.
III-J-16 Reversed Capped Die Strike (WE), Rarity Level: 7, Values: $1,000 up.

Struck through abnormal objects (III-K)

Struck through cloth III-K-1

Struck through a
filled die III-K-4

Struck through a
dropped filling III-K-5

This section covers most of the objects or materials which might come between the planchet and the die and be struck into the surface of the coin. Unless noted, the materials - even the soft ones - are driven into the surface of the coin.

III-K-1 Struck Through Cloth (IWE), Rarity Level: 3-6, Values: $35 up.
III-K-2 Struck Through Wire (IWE), Rarity Level: 3-6, Values: $5 up.
III-K-3 Struck Through Thread (IWE), Rarity Level: 3-6, Values: $5 up.
III-K-4 Struck Through Dirt-and-Grease-Filled Die (IWE), Rarity Level: 1-4, Values: 10 cents to 25 cents up, but no value on a worn or circulated coin.
III-K-5 Struck Through a Dropped Filling (IWE), Rarity Level: 5-6, Values: $10 up.
III-K-6 Struck Through Wrong Metal Fragments (IWE), Rarity Level: 4-6, Values: $1 up.
III-K-7 Struck Through an Unstruck Planchet Fragment (IWE), Rarity Level: 3-5, Values: $1 up.
III-K-8 Struck Through a Rim Burr (IWE), Rarity Level: 3-5, Values: $1 to $2 and up.
III-K-9 Struck Through plit-Off Reeding (IWE), Rarity Level: 5-6, Values: $25 up.
III-K-10 Struck Through a Feed Finger (IWE), Rarity Level: 5-7, Values: $25 to $50 and up.
III-K-11 Struck Through Miscellaneous Objects (IWE), Rarity Level: 4-6, Values: $1 up.
III-K-12 Struck Through Progression (IWE), Rarity Level: 4-6, Values: $1 up.

Note: Some 1987 through 1994 quarters are found without mintmarks, classed as III-K-4, a Filled Die. Values depend on market conditions. Filled dies have value ONLY on current, uncirculated grade coins.

Double strikes (III-L)

Only coins which receive two or more strikes by the die pair fall in this section and are identified by the fact that both sides of the coin are affected. Unless some object interferes, an equal area of both sides of the coin will be equally doubled.

The exception is the second strike with a loose die, which will double only one side of a coin, but is a rare form usually occurring only on proofs. A similar effect is flat field doubling from die chatter.

III-L-1 Close Centered Double Strike (WE), Rarity Level: 4-6, Values: $15 up.
III-L-2 Rotated Second Strike Over a Centered First Strike (WE), Rarity Level: 4-6, Values: $15 up.
III-L-3 Off-Center Second Strike Over a Centered First Strike (WE), Rarity Level: 4-6, Values: $15 up.
III-L-4 Off-Center Second Strike Over an Off-Center First Strike (WE), Rarity Level: 4-6, Values: $10 up.
III-L-5 Off-Center Second Strike Over a Broadstrike (WE), Rarity Level: 5-6, Values: $20 up.
III-L-6 Centered Second Strike Over an Off-Center First Strike (WE), Rarity Level: 5-6, Values: $50 up.
III-L-7 Obverse Struck Over Reverse (WE), Rarity Level: 5-6, Values: $25 up.
III-L-8 Nonoverlapping Double Strike (WE), Rarity Level: 5-6 Values: $20 up.
III-L-9 Struck Over a Different Denomination or Series (WE), Rarity Level: 6, Values: $300 and up.
III-L-10 Chain Strike (WE), Rarity Level: 6, Values: $300 up for the pair of coins that were struck together.

Off-center second strike over
centered first strike III-L-3

Non-overlapping
double strike III-L-8

Multiple strike III-L-16

Chain strike III-L-10

III-L-11 Second-Strike Doubling From a Loose Die (W), Rarity Level: 6-7, Values: $200 up.

III-L-12 Second-Strike Doubling From a Loose Screw Press Die (W), Rarity Level: 5-6, Values: $100 up.

III-L-13 Second Strike on an Edge Strike (WE), Rarity Level: 5-6, Values: $20 up.

III-L-14 Folded Planchet Strike (WE), Rarity Level: 5-7, Values: $100 up.

III-L-15 Triple Strike (WE), Rarity Level: 6-7, Values: $100 up.

III-L-16 Multiple Strike (WE), Rarity Level: 6-7, Values: $200 up.

III-L-17 U.S. Coin Struck Over a Struck Foreign Coin (WE), Rarity Level: 6-7, Values: $300 up.

III-L-18 Foreign Coin Struck over a Struck U.S. Coin (WE), Rarity Level: 6-7, Values: $400 up.

III-L-19 Foreign Coin Struck Over a Struck Foreign Coin (WE), Rarity Level: 7, Values: $500 up.

III-L-20 Double Strike on Scrap or Junk (E), Rarity Level: 6, Values: $50 up.

III-L-21 Struck on a Struck Token or Medal (E), Rarity Level: 5-6, Values: $100 up.

III-L-22 Double-Struck Edge Motto or Design (E), Rarity Level: 6-7, Values: $200 up.

III-L-23 One Edge Motto or Design Struck Over Another (E), Rarity Level: 7, Values: $300 up.

III-L-24 Flat Field Doubling (W), Rarity Level: 2-3, Values: $1 to $5.

III-L-25 Territorial Struck over Struck U.S. Coin: (I) Rarity Level: 6-7, Values: $200 up.

III-L-26 Pattern Struck over Struck U.S. Coin: (I) Rarity Level: 6-7, Values: $200 up.

III-L-27 Pattern Struck over Struck Pattern:(I) Rarity Level 6-7, Values: $200 up.

III-L-28 Pattern Struck Over Foreign Coin:(I) Rarity Level 6-7, Values - $200 up.

Collar striking varieties (III-M)

The collar is often referred to as the "Third Die," and is involved in a number of forms of misstrikes. The collar normally rises around the planchet, preventing it from squeezing sideways between the dies and at the same time forming the reeding on reeded coins.

If the collar is out of position or tilted, a partial collar strike results; if completely missing, it causes a broadstrike; if the planchet is not entirely between the dies, an off-center strike.

III-M-1 Flanged Partial Collar Strike (WE), Rarity Level: 5-6, Values: $20 up.

III-M-2 Reversed Flanged Partial Collar Strike (WE), Rarity Level: 6-7, Values: $35 up.

III-M-3 Tilted Partial Collar Strike (WE), Rarity Level: 5-6, Values: $20 up.

III-M-4 Centered Broadstrike (WE), Rarity Level: 5-6, Values: $5 up.

III-M-5 Uncentered Broadstrike (WE), Rarity Level: 5, Values: $3 up.

III-M-6 Reversed Broadstrike (WE), Rarity Level: 6, Values: $10 up.

III-M-7 Struck Off-Center 10-30% (W), Rarity Level: 3-6, Values: $3 up.

Flanged partial collar III-M-1

**Struck off center
10 to 30 percent III-M-7**

**Struck off center
31 to 70 percent III-M-8**

**Struck off center
71 percent or more
III-M-9**

III-M-8 Struck Off-Center 31-70% (W), Rarity Level: 4-6, Values: $5 up.
III-M-9 Struck Off-Center 71% or More (W), Rarity Level: 3-5, Values: $2 up.
III-M-10 Rotated Multi-sided Planchet Strike (W), Rarity Level: 5-6, Values: $10 up.
III-M-11 Wire Edge Strike (IWE), Rarity Level: 1-2, Values: No Extra Value.
III-M-12 Struck With the Collar Too High (WE), Rarity Level: 6-7, Values: $20 up.
III-M-13 Off-Center Slide Strike (W), Rarity Level:3-6 $4 up.

Misaligned and rotated (die) strike varieties (III-N)

Misaligned die III-N-1

Normal rotation   **90 degrees**   **180 degrees**

One (rarely both) of the dies may be Offset Misaligned, off to one side, or may be tilted (Vertically Misaligned). One die may either have been installed so that it is turned in relation to the other die, or may turn in the holder, or the shank may break allowing the die face to rotate in relation to the opposing die.

Vertical misaligned dies are rarely found, and like rotated dies, find only limited collector interest. Ninety and 180 degree rotations are the most popular. Rotations of 14 degrees or less have no value. The 1989-D Congress dollar is found with a nearly 180 degree rotated reverse, currently retailing for around $2,000. Only about 30 have been reported to date.

III-N-1 Offset Die Misalignment Strike (WE), Rarity Level: 3-5, Values: $2 up.
III-N-2 Vertical Die Misalignment Strike (WE), Rarity Level: 4-6, Values: $1 up.
III-N-3 Rotated Die Strike - 15 to 45 Degrees (IWE), Rarity Level: 4-6, Values: $2 up.
III-N-4 Rotated Die Strike - 46 to 135 Degrees (IWE), Rarity Level: 5-6, Values: $10 up.
III-N-5 Rotated Die Strike - 136 to 180 Degrees (IWE), Rarity Level: 5-6, Values: $25 up.

Lettered and design edge strike varieties (III-O)

Early U.S. coins and a number of foreign coins have either lettered edges, or designs on the edge of the coin. Malfunctions of the application of the motto or design to the edge fall in this section.

Overlapping edge letters III-O-1

III-O-1 Overlapping Edge Motto or Design (WE), Rarity Level: 3-4, Values: $5 to $10 and up.
III-O-2 Wrong Edge Motto or Design (WE), Rarity Level: 5-6-7, Values: $50 up.
III-O-3 Missing Edge Motto, Design or Security Edge (IWE), Rarity Level: 5-6-7, Values: $50 up.
III-O-4 Jammed Edge Die Strike (W), Rarity Level: 6, Values: $10 up.
III-O-5 Misplaced Segment of an Edge Die (E), Rarity Level: 4-7, Values: $25 up.
III-O-6 Reeded Edge Struck Over a Lettered Edge (IE), Rarity Level: 3-6, Values: No Extra Value up.

Defective strikes and mismatched dies (III-P)

The final section of the Striking Division covers coins which are not properly struck for reasons other than those in previous classes, such as coins struck with mismatched (muled) dies. The mismatched die varieties must be taken on a case by case basis, while the otherclasses presently have little collector demand or premium.

III-P-1 Defective Strike (WE), Rarity Level: 1, Values: No Extra Value.
III-P-2 Mismatched Die Strike (E), Rarity Level: 4-7, Values: $25 up.
III-P-3 Single-Strike Proof (WE), Rarity Level: 4-5, Values: Minimal.
III-P-4 Single Die-Proof Strike (IE), Rarity Level: 5-6, Values: $100 up.
III-P-5 Reversed Die Strike (I), Rarity Level: 4-5, Values: No Extra Value to Minimal.

■ Official Mint modifications ■
Division IV

Several mint produced varieties occur after the coin has been struck, resulting in the addition of the fourth division to my PDS System. Since most of these coins are either unique or are special varieties, each one must be taken on a case by case basis. All classes listed here are by definition intentional.

I have not listed values as the coins falling in these classes which are sold through regular numismatic channels, are cataloged with the regular issues or are covered in specialized catalogs in their particular area.

Matte proofs (IV-A)

**Matte proofs
IV-A-1**

Matte proofs as a section include several of the forms of proof coins which have the striking charac-teristics of a mirror proof but have been treated AFTER striking to give them a grainy, non-reflective surface.

IV-A-1 Matte Proof (I), Rarity Level: 3-5, Values: Normal Numismatic Value.
IV-A-2 Matte Proof on One Side (I), Rarity Level: 7, Values: Normal Numismatic Value.
IV-A-3 Sandblast Proof (I), Rarity Level: 4-6, Values: Normal Numismatic Value.

Additional engraving (IV-B)

Counterstamp IV-B-3

This section includes any added markings which are placed on the struck coin and struck coins which later were cut into pieces for various purposes. The warning is repeated: Anything done to a coin after the strike is extremely difficult to authenticate and is much easier to fake than a die struck coin.

IV-B-1 Counterstamp and Countermark (I), Rarity Level: 3-6, Values: Normal Numismatic Value.
IV-B-2 Perforated and Cut Coins (I), Rarity Level: 4-6, Values: Normal Numismatic Value.

Restrikes (IV-C)

Restrike with new dies IV-C-7

Restrikes cover a complicated mixture of official use of dies from a variety of sources. Whether or not some were officially sanctioned is always a problem for the collector.

IV-C-1 Restrike on the Same Denomination Planchet (I), Rarity Level: 4-6, Values: Normal Numismatic Value.
IV-C-2 Restrike on a Different Denomination or Series Planchet (I), Rarity Level: 4-6, Values: Normal Numismatic Value.
IV-C-3 Restrike on a Foreign Coin (I), Rarity Level: 6-7, Values: Normal Numismatic Value.
IV-C-4 Restrike on a Token or Medal (I), Rarity Level: 5-6, Values: Normal Numismatic Value.
IV-C-5 Restruck With the Original Dies (I), Rarity Level: 4-6, Values: Normal Numismatic Value.
IV-C-6 Restruck With Mismatched Dies (I), Rarity Level: 4-6, Values: Normal Numismatic Value.
IV-C-7 Copy Strike With New Dies (I), Rarity Level: 3-5, Values: Normal Numismatic Value.
IV-C-8 Fantasy Strike (I), Rarity Level: 4-6, Values: Normal Numismatic Value.

■ After strike modifications ■
Division V

This division includes both modifications that have value to collectors – and those that don't. I needed a couple of divisions to cover other things that happen to coins to aid in cataloging them. This avoids the false conclusion that an unlisted coin is quite rare, when the exact opposite is more likely to be the case.

Mint modification V-A-8

Collectible modifications after strike (V-A)

This section includes those classes having to do with deliberate modifications of the coin done with a specific purpose or intent which makes them of some value to collectors. Quite often these pieces were made specifically to sell to collectors, or at least to the public under the guise of being collectible.

V-A-1 Screw Thaler, Rarity Level: 5-6, Values: Normal Numismatic Value.
V-A-2 Love Token, Rarity Level: 3-6, Values: $10 up.
V-A-3 Satirical or Primitive Engraving, Rarity Level: 6-7, Values: $5 up.
V-A-4 Elongated Coin, Rarity Level: 2-7, Values: 50 cents to $1 and up.
V-A-5 Coin Jewelry, Rarity Level: 2-5, Values: $1 up.
V-A-6 Novelty Coin, Rarity Level: 1-3, Values: No Value up to $5 to $10.
V-A-7 Toning, Rarity Level: 3-6, Values: No value up, depending on coloration. Easily faked.
V-A-8 Mint Modification, Rarity Level: 4-7, Values: $5 up. Easily faked.
V-A-9 Mint Packaging Mistake, Rarity Level: 5-7, Values: Nominal $1. Very easily faked.

Alterations and damage after the strike(V-B)

Machine doubling damage V-B-1

This section includes those changes in a coin which have no collector value. In most cases their effect on the coin is to reduce or entirely eliminate any collector value - and in the case of counterfeits they are actually illegal to even own.

V-B-1 Machine Doubling Damage: NOTE: Machine doubling damage is defined as: "Damage to a coin after the strike, due to die bounce or chatter or die displacement, showing on the struck coin as scrapes on the sides of the design elements, with portions of the coin metal in the relief elements either displaced sideways or downward, depending on the direction of movement of the loose die." Machine doubling damage, or MDD, is by far the most common form of doubling found on almost any coin in the world. Rarity Level: 0, Values: Reduces the coin's value.

V-B-2 Accidental or Deliberate Damage, Rarity Level: 0, Values: Reduces the coin's value.

V-B-3 Test Cut or Mark, Rarity Level: 0, Values: Reduces value of coin to face or bullion value.

V-B-4 Alteration, Rarity Level: 0, Values: Reduces value to face or bullion value.

V-B-5 Whizzing, Rarity Level: 0, Values: Reduces value sharply and may reduce it to face or bullion value.

V-B-6 Counterfeit, Copy, Facsimile, Forgery or Fake, Rarity Level: 0, Values: No Value and may be illegal to own.

V-B-7 Planchet Deterioration. Very common on copper-plated zinc cents. Rarity level: 0, Values: No Value.

4

How to Grade
Better condition equals better value

G rading is one of the most important factors in buying and selling coins as collectibles. Unfortunately, it's also one of the most controversial. Since the early days of coin collecting in the United States, buying through the mail has been a convenient way for collectors to acquire coins. As a result, there has always been a need in numismatics for a concise way to classify the amount of wear on a coin and its condition in general.

■ A look back ■

In September 1888, Dr. George Heath, a physician in Monroe, Mich., published a four-page pamphlet titled *The American Numismatist*. Publication of subsequent issues led to the founding of the American Numismatic Association, and *The Numismatist*, as it's known today, is the association's official journal. Heath's first issues were largely devoted to selling world coins from his collection. There were no formal grades listed with the coins and their prices, but the following statement by Heath indicates that condition was a consideration for early collectors:

"The coins are in above average condition," Heath wrote, "and so confident am I that they will give satisfaction, that I agree to refund the money in any unsatisfactory sales on the return of the coins."

As coin collecting became more popular and *The Numismatist* started accepting paid advertising from others, grading became more formal. The February 1892 issue listed seven "classes" for the condition of coins (from worst to best): mutilated, poor, fair, good, fine, uncirculated, and proof. Through the years, the hobby has struggled with developing a grading system that would be accepted by all and could apply to all coins. The hobby's growth was accompanied by a desire for more grades, or classifications, to more precisely define a coin's condition. The desire for more precision, however, was at odds with the basic concept of grading: to provide a concise method for classifying a coin's condition.

For example, even the conservatively few classifications of 1892 included fudge factors.

"To give flexibility to this classification," *The Numismatist* said, "such modification of find, good and fair, as 'extremely,' 'very,' 'almost,' etc., are used to express slight variations from the general condition."

The debate over grading continued for decades in *The Numismatist*. A number of articles and letters prodded the ANA to write grading guidelines and endorse them as the association's official standards. Some submitted specific suggestions for terminology and accompanying standards for each grade. But grading remained a process of "instinct" gained through years of collecting or dealing experience.

A formal grading guide in book form finally appeared in 1958, but it was the work of two individuals rather than the ANA, *A Guide to the Grading of United States Coins* by Martin R. Brown and John W. Dunn was a break-through in the great grading debate. Now collectors had a reference that gave them specific guidelines for specific coins and could be studied and restudied at home.

The first editions of Brown and Dunn carried text only, no illustrations. For the fourth edition, in 1964, publication was assumed by Whitman Publishing Co. of Racine, Wis., and line drawings were added to illustrate the text.

The fourth edition listed six principal categories for circulated coins (from worst to best): good, very good, fine, very fine, extremely fine, and about uncirculated. But again, the desire for more precise categories were evidenced. In the book's introduction, Brown and Dunn wrote, "Dealers will sometimes advertise coins that are graded G-VG, VG-F, F-VF, VF-XF. Or the description may be ABT. G. or VG plus, etc. This means that the coin in question more than meets minimum standards for the lower grade but is not quite good enough for the higher grade."

When the fifth edition appeared, in 1969, the "New B & D Grading System" was introduced. The six principal categories for circulated coins were still intact, but variances within those categories were now designated by up to four letters: "A," "B," "C" or "D." For example, an EF-A coin was "almost about uncirculated." An EF-B was "normal extra fine" within the B & D standards. EF-C had a "normal extra fine" obverse, but the reverse was "obviously not as nice as obverse due to poor strike or excessive wear." EF-D had a "normal extra fine" reverse but a problem obverse.

But that wasn't the end. Brown and Dunn further listed 29 problem points that could appear on a coin – from No. 1 for an "edge bump" to No. 29 for "attempted re-engraving outside of the Mint." The number could be followed by the letter "O" or "R" to designate whether the problem appeared on the obverse or reverse and a Roman numeral corresponding to a clock face to designate where the problem appears on the obverse or reverse. For example, a coin described as "VG-B-9-O-X" would grade "VG-B"; the "9" designated a "single rim nick"; the "O" indicated the nick was on the obverse; and the "X" indicated it appeared at the 10 o'clock position, or upper left, of the obverse.

The author's goal was noble – to create the perfect grading system. They again, however, fell victim to the age-old grading-system problem: Precision comes at the expense of brevity. Dealer Kurt Krueger wrote in the January 1976 issues of *The Numismatist*, "Under the new B & D system, the numismatist must contend with a minimum of 43,152 different grading combinations! Accuracy is apparent, but simplicity has been lost." As a result, the "New B & D Grading System" never caught on in the marketplace.

The 1970s saw two important grading guides make their debut. The first was *Photograde* by James F. Ruddy. As the title implies, Ruddy uses photographs instead of line drawings to show how coins look in the various circulated grades. Simplicity is also a virtue of Ruddy's book. Only seven circulated grades are listed (about good, good, very good, fine, very fine, extremely fine, and about uncirculated), and the designations stop there.

In 1977 the longtime call for the ANA to issue grading standards was met with the release of *Official A.N.A. Grading Standards for United States Coins*. Like Brown and Dunn, the first edition of the ANA guide used line drawings to illustrate coins in various states of wear. But instead of using adjectival descriptions, the ANA guide adopted a numerical system for designating grades.

The numerical designations were based on a system used by Dr. William H. Sheldon in his book *Early American Cents*, first published in 1949. He used a scale of 1 to 70 to designate the grades of large cents.

"On this scale," Sheldon wrote, "1 means that the coin is identifiable and not mutilated – no more than that. A 70-coin is one in flawless Mint State, exactly as it left the dies, with perfect mint color and without a blemish or nick."

(Sheldon's scale also had its pragmatic side. At the time, a No. 2 large cent was worth about twice a No. 1 coin; a No. 4 was worth about twice a No. 2, and so on up the scale.)

With the first edition of its grading guide, the ANA adopted the 70-point scale for grading all U.S. coins. It designated 10 categories of circulated grades: AG-3, G-4, VG-8, F-12, VF-20, VF-30, EF-40, EF-45, AU-50, and AU-55. The third edition, released in 1987, replaced the line drawings with photographs, and another circulated grade was added: AU-58. A fourth edition was released in 1991.

■ Grading circulated U.S. coins ■

Dealers today generally use either the ANA guide or Photograde when grading circulated coins for their inventories. (Brown and Dunn is now out of print.) Many local coin shops sell both books. Advertisers in *Numismatic News*, *Coins* Magazine, and *Coin Prices* must indicate which standards they are using in grading their coins. If the standards are not listed, they must conform to ANA standards.

Following are some general guidelines, accompanied by photos, for grading circulated U.S. coins. Grading even circulated pieces can be subjective, particularly when attempting to draw the fine line between, for example, AU-55 and AU-58. Two longtime collectors or dealers can disagree in such a case.

But by studying some combination of the following guidelines, the ANA guide, and *Photograde*, and by looking at a lot of coins at shops and shows, collectors can gain enough grading knowledge to buy circulated coins confidently from dealers and other collectors. The more you study, the more knowledge and confidence you will gain. When you decide which series of coins you want to collect, focus on the guidelines for that particular series. Read them, reread them, and then refer back to them again and again.

AU-50

Indian cent   Lincoln cent

Buffalo nickel   Jefferson nickel

Mercury dime

Standing Liberty quarter

Washington quarter

Walking Liberty half dollar

Morgan dollar

Barber coins

AU-50 (about uncirculated): Just a slight trace of wear, result of brief exposure to circulation or light rubbing from mishandling, may be evident on elevated design areas. These imperfections may appear as scratches or dull spots, along with bag marks or edge nicks. At least half of the original mint luster generally is still evident.

XF-40

Indian cent

Lincoln cent

Buffalo nickel

Jefferson nickel

Mercury dime

Standing Liberty quarter

Washington quarter

Walking Liberty half dollar

Morgan dollar

Barber coins

XF-40 (extremely fine): The coin must show only slight evidence of wear on the highest points of the design, particularly in the hair lines of the portrait on the obverse. The same may be said for the eagle's feathers and wreath leaves on the reverse of most U.S. coins. A trace of mint luster may still show in protected areas of the coin's surface.

VF-20

Indian cent

Lincoln cent

Buffalo nickel

Jefferson nickel

Mercury dime

Standing Liberty quarter

Washington quarter

Walking Liberty half dollar

Morgan dollar

Barber coins

VF-20 (very fine): The coin will show light wear at the fine points in the design, though they may remain sharp overall. Although the details may be slightly smoothed, all lettering and major features must remain sharp.

Indian cent: All letters in "Liberty" are complete but worn. Headdress shows considerable flatness, with flat spots on the tips of the feathers.

Lincoln cent: Hair, cheek, jaw, and bow-tie details will be worn but clearly separated, and wheat stalks on the reverse will be full with no weak spots.

Buffalo nickel: High spots on hair braid and cheek will be flat but show some detail, and a full horn will remain on the buffalo.

Jefferson nickel: Well over half of the major hair detail will remain, and the pillars on Monticello will remain well defined, with the triangular roof partially visible.

Mercury dime: Hair braid will show some detail, and three-quarters of the detail will remain in the feathers. The two diagonal bands on the fasces will show completely but will be worn smooth at the middle, with the vertical lines sharp.

Standing Liberty quarter: Rounded contour of Liberty's right leg will be flattened, as will the high point of the shield.

Washington quarter: There will be considerable wear on the hair curls, with feathers on the right and left of the eagle's breast showing clearly.

Walking Liberty half dollar: All lines of the skirt will show but will be worn on the high points. Over half the feathers on the eagle will show.

Morgan dollar: Two-thirds of the hair lines from the forehead to the ear must show. Ear should be well defined. Feathers on the eagle's breast may be worn smooth.

Barber coins: All seven letters of "Liberty" on the headband must stand out sharply. Head wreath will be well outlined from top to bottom.

F-12

Indian cent

Lincoln cent

Buffalo nickel

Jefferson nickel

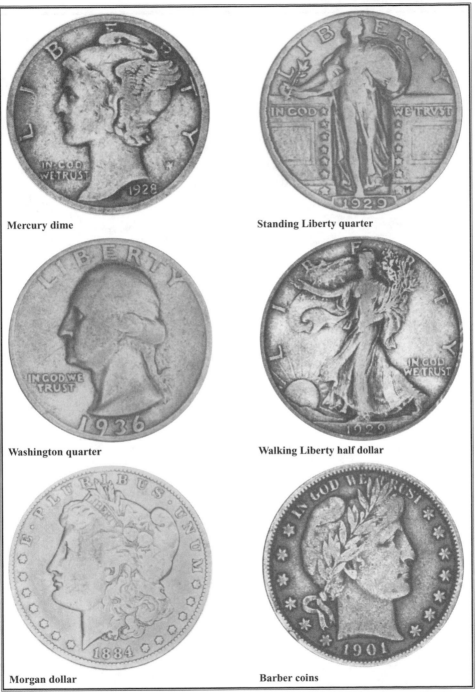

Mercury dime

Standing Liberty quarter

Washington quarter

Walking Liberty half dollar

Morgan dollar

Barber coins

F-12 (fine): Coins show evidence of moderate to considerable but generally even wear on all high points, though all elements of the design and lettering remain bold. Where the word "Liberty" appears in a headband, it must be fully visible. On 20th century coins, the rim must be fully raised and sharp.

VG-8

Indian cent

Lincoln cent

Buffalo nickel

Jefferson nickel

Mercury dime

Standing Liberty quarter

Washington quarter

Walking Liberty half dollar

Morgan dollar

Barber coins

VG-8 (very good): The coin will show considerable wear, with most detail points worn nearly smooth. Where the word "Liberty" appears in a headband, at least three letters must show. On 20th century coins, the rim will start to merge with the lettering.

G-4

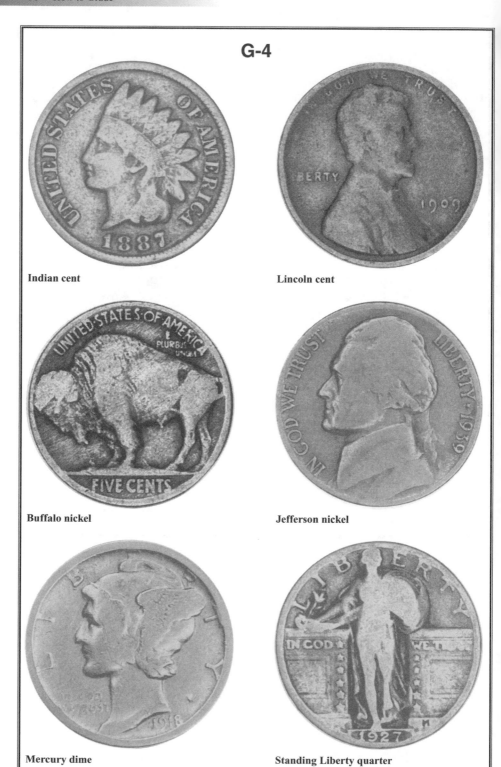

Indian cent

Lincoln cent

Buffalo nickel

Jefferson nickel

Mercury dime

Standing Liberty quarter

Washington quarter   Walking Liberty half dollar

Morgan dollar   Barber coins

G-4 (good): Only the basic design remains distinguishable in outline form, will all points of detail worn smooth. The word "Liberty" has disappeared, and the rims are almost merging with the lettering.

About good or fair: The coin will be identifiable by date and mint but otherwise badly worn, with only parts of the lettering showing. Such coins are of value only as fillers in a collection until a better example of the date and mintmark can be obtained. The only exceptions would be rare coins

■ Grading uncirculated U.S. coins ■

The subjectivity of grading and the trend toward more classifications becomes more acute when venturing into uncirculated, or mint-state, coins. A minute differ-

Collectors have a variety of grading services to choose from. This set of Arkansas half dollars that appeared in an Early American History Auctions sale used two of the services.

ence between one or two grade points can mean a difference in value of hundreds or even thousands of dollars. In addition, the standards are more difficult to articulate in writing and illustrate through drawings or photographs. Thus, the possibilities for differences of opinion on one or two grade points increase in uncirculated coins.

Back in Dr. George Heath's day and continuing through the 1960s, a coin was either uncirculated or it wasn't. Little distinction was made between uncirculated coins of varying condition, largely because there was little if any difference in value. When *Numismatic News* introduced its value guide in 1962 (the forerunner of today's Coin Market section in the *News*), it listed only one grade of uncirculated for Morgan dollars.

But as collectible coins increased in value and buyers of uncirculated coins became more picky, distinctions within uncirculated grade started to surface. In 1975 *Numismatic News* still listed only one uncirculated grade in Coin Market, but added this note: "Uncirculated and proof specimens in especially choice condition will also command proportionately higher premiums than these listed."

The first edition of the ANA guide listed two grades of uncirculated, MS-60 and MS-65, in addition to the theoretical but non-existent MS-70 (a flawless coin). MS-60 was described as "typical uncirculated" and MS-65 as "choice uncirculated." *Numismatic News* adopted both designations for Coin Market. In 1981, when the second edition of the ANA grading guide was released, MS-67 and MS-63 were added. In 1985 *Numismatic News* started listing six grades of uncirculated for Morgan dollars: MS-60, MS-63, MS-65, MS-65+, and MS-63 prooflike.

Then in 1986, a new entity appeared that has changed the nature of grading and trading uncirculated coins ever since. A group of dealers led by David Hall of Newport Beach, Calif., formed the Professional Coin Grading Service. For a fee, collectors could submit a coin through an authorized PCGS dealer and receive back a professional opinion of its grade.

The concept was not new; the ANA had operated an authentication service since 1972 and a grading service since 1979. A collector or dealer could submit a coin directly to the service and receive a certificate giving the service's opinion on authenticity and grade. The grading service was the source of near constant debate among dealers and ANA officials. Dealers charged that ANA graders were too young and inexperienced, and that their grading was inconsistent.

Grading stability was a problem throughout the coin business in the early 1980s, not just with the ANA service. Standards among uncirculated grades would tighten during a bear market and loosen during a bull market. As a result, a coin graded MS-65 in a bull market may have commanded only MS-63 during a bear market.

PCGS created several innovations in the grading business in response to these problems:

1. Coins could be submitted through PCGS-authorized dealers only.

2. Each coin would be graded by at least three members of a panel of "top graders," all prominent dealers in the business. (Since then, however, PCGS does not allow its graders to also deal in coins.)

3. After grading, the coin would be encapsulated in an inert, hard-plastic holder with a serial number and the grade indicated on the holder.

4. PCGS-member dealers pledged to make a market in PCGS-graded coins and honor the grades assigned.

5. In one of the most far-reaching moves, PCGS said it would use all 11 increments of uncirculated on the 70-point numerical scale: MS-60, MS-61, MS-62, MS-63, MS-64, MS-65, MS-66, MS-67, MS-68, MS-69, and MS-70.

Numerous other commercial grading services followed in the steps of PCGS and third-party grading is an accepted part of the hobby.

How should a collector approach the buying and grading of uncirculated coins? Collecting uncirculated coins worth thousands of dollars implies a higher level of numismatic expertise by the buyer. Those buyers without that level of expertise should cut their teeth on more inexpensive coins, just as today's experienced collectors did. Inexperienced collectors can start toward that level by studying the guidelines for mint-state coins in the ANA grading guide and looking at lots of coins at shows and shops.

Study the condition and eye appeal of a coin and compare it to other coins of the same series. Then compare prices. Do the more expensive coins look better? If so, why? Start to make your own judgments concerning relationships between condition and value. Experience remains the best teacher in the field of grading.

■ Grading U.S. proof coins ■

Because proof coins are struck by a special process using polished blanks, they receive their own grading designation. A coin does not start out being a proof and then become mint state if it becomes worn. Once a proof coin, always a proof coin.

In the ANA system, proof grades use the same numbers as circulated and uncirculated grades, and the amount of wear on the coin corresponds to those grades. But the number is preceded by the word "proof." For example, Proof-65, Proof-55, Proof-45, and so on. In addition, the ANA says a proof coin with many marks, scratches or other defects should be called an "impaired proof."

Organization is Key
Sets worth more than accumulations

T here are two major ways to organize a collection: by type, and by date and mintmark. By following either method, you will create a logically organized set that other collectors perceive as having a value greater than a random group of similar coins

Let's take collecting by type first. Look at a jar of coins, or take the change out of your pocket. You find Abraham Lincoln and the Lincoln Memorial on current cents. You find Thomas Jefferson and his home, Monticello, on the nickel. Franklin D. Roosevelt and a torch share the dime. George Washington and the eagle, or the more recent state designs, appear on the quarter. John F. Kennedy and the presidential seal are featured on the half dollar.

Each design is called a "type." If you took one of each and put the five coins in a holder, you would have a type set of the coins that are currently being produced for circulation by the U.S. Mint.

With just these five coins, you can study various metallic compositions. You can evaluate their states of preservation and assign a grade to each. You can learn about the artists who designed the coins, and you can learn of the times in which these designs were created.

As you might have guessed, many different coin types have been used in the United States over the years. You may remember seeing some of them circulating. These designs reflect the hopes and aspirations of people over time. Putting all of them together forms a wonderful numismatic mosaic of American history.

George Washington did not mandate that his image appear on the quarter. Quite the contrary. He would have been horrified. When he was president, he headed off those individuals in Congress who thought the leader of the country should have his image on its coins. Washington said it smacked of monarchy and would have nothing to do with it.

Almost a century and a half later, during the bicentennial of Washington's birth in 1932, a nation searching for its roots during troubled economic times decided that it needed his portrait on its coins as a reminder of his great accomplishments and as reassurances that this nation was the same place it had been in prosperous days.

In its broadest definition, collecting coins by type requires that you obtain an example of every design that was struck by the U.S. Mint since it was founded in 1792. That's a tall order. You would be looking for denominations like the half cent, two-cent piece, three-cent piece, and 20-cent piece, which have not been produced in over a century. You would be looking for gold coins ranging in face value from $1 to $50.

But even more important than odd-sounding denominations or high face values is the question of rarity. Some of the pieces in this two-century type set are rare and expensive. That's why type collectors often divide the challenge into more digestible units.

Type collecting can be divided into 18th, 19th, 20th and 21st century units. Starting type collectors can focus on 20th century coin designs, which are easily obtainable. The fun and satisfaction of putting the 20th or 21st century set together then creates the momentum to continue backward in time. In the process of putting a 20th century type set together, one is also learning how to grade, learning hobby jargon, and discovering how to obtain coins from dealers, the U.S. Mint, and other collectors. All of this knowledge is then refined as the collector increases the challenge to himself.

This book is designed to help. How many dollar types were struck in the 20th century? Turn to the price-guide section and check it out. We see the Morgan dollar, Peace dollar, Eisenhower dollar, and Anthony dollar. The Sacagawea dollar arrived in 2000. Hobbyists could also add the Ike dollar with the Bicentennial design of 1976 and the silver American Eagle bullion coin struck since 1986. One can also find out their approximate retail prices from the listings. The beauty of type collecting is that one can choose the most inexpensive example of each type. There is no need to select a 1903-O Morgan when the 1921 will do just as well. With the 20th century type set, hobbyists can dodge some truly big-league prices.

As a collector's hobby confidence grows, he can tailor goals to fit his desires. He can take the road less traveled if that is what suits him. Type sets can be divided by denomination. You can choose two centuries of one-cent coins. You can take just obsolete denominations or copper, silver or gold denominations.

You can even collect by size. Perhaps you would like to collect all coin types larger than 30 millimeters or all coins smaller than 20 millimeters. Many find this freedom of choice stimulating.

Type collecting has proven itself to be enduringly popular over the years. It provides a maximum amount of design variety while allowing collectors to set their own level of challenge.

The second popular method of collecting is by date and mintmark. What this means, quite simply, is that a collector picks a given type – Jefferson nickels, for example – and then goes after an example of every year, every mintmark, and every type of manufacture that was used with the Jefferson design.

Looking at this method of collecting brings up the subject of mintmarks. The "U.S. Mint" is about as specific as most non-collectors get in describing the government agency that provides everyday coins. Behind that label are the various production facilities that actually do the work.

In two centuries of U.S. coinage, there have been eight such facilities. Four are still in operation. Those eight in alphabetical order are Carson City, Nev., which used a "CC" mintmark to identify its work; Charlotte, N.C. ("C"); Dahlonega, Ga. ("D"); Denver (also uses a "D," but it opened long after the Dahlonega Mint closed, so there was never any confusion); New Orleans ("O"); Philadelphia (because it was the primary mint, it used no mintmark for much of its history, but currently uses a "P"); San Francisco ("S"); and West Point, N.Y. ("W").

A person contemplating the collecting of Jefferson nickels by date and mintmark will find that three mints produced them: San Francisco, Denver and Philadelphia. Because the first two are branch mints serving smaller populations, their output has tended over time to be smaller than that of Philadelphia. This fact, repeated in other series, has helped give mintmarks quite an allure to collectors. It provides one of the major attractions in collecting coins by date and mintmark.

The key date for Jeffersons is the 1950-D when using mintages as a guide. In that year, production was just 2.6 million pieces. Because collectors of the time were aware of the coin's low mintage, many examples were saved. As a result, prices are reasonable.

The Depression-era 1939-D comes in as the most valuable regular-issue Jefferson nickel despite a mintage of 3.5 million – almost 1 million more than the 1950-D. The reason: Fewer were saved for later generations of coin collectors.

Date and mintmark collecting teaches hobbyists to use mintage figures as a guide but to take them with a grain of salt. Rarity, after all, is determined by the number of surviving coins, not the number initially created.

The Jefferson series is a good one to collect by date and mintmark, because the mintmarks have moved around, grown in size, and expanded in number.

When the series was first introduced, the Jefferson nickel was produced at the three mints previously mentioned. In 1942, because of a diversion of certain metals to wartime use, the coin's alloy of 75 percent copper and 25 percent nickel was changed. The new alloy was 35 percent silver, 56 percent copper, and 9 percent manganese.

To denote the change, the mintmarks were moved and greatly enlarged. The pre-1942 mintmarks were small and located to the right of Monticello; the wartime mintmarks were enlarged and placed over the dome. What's more, for the first time in American history, the Philadelphia Mint used a mintmark ("P").

The war's end restored the alloy and mintmarks to their previous status. The "P" disappeared. This lasted until the 1960s, when a national coin shortage saw all mintmarks removed for three years (1965-1967) and then returned, but in a different location. Mintmarks were placed on the obverse, to the right of Jefferson's portrait near the date in 1968. In 1980 the "P" came back in a smaller form and is still used.

Another consideration arises with date and mintmark collecting: Should the hobbyist include proof coins in the set? This can be argued both ways. Suffice to say that anyone who has the desire to add proof coins to the set will have a larger one. It is not necessary nor is it discouraged.

Some of the first proof coins to carry mintmarks were Jefferson nickels. When proof coins were made in 1968 after lapsing from 1965 to 1967, production occurred at San Francisco instead of Philadelphia. The "S" mintmark was placed on the proof coins of that year, including the Jefferson nickel, to denote the change. Since that time, mintmarks used on proof examples of various denominations have included the "P," "D," "S," and "W."

For all of the mintmark history that is embodied in the Jefferson series, prices are reasonable. For a first attempt at collecting coins by date and mintmark, it provides excellent background for going on to the more expensive and difficult types. After all, if you are ever going to get used to the proper handling of a coin, it is far better to experiment on a low-cost coin than a high-value rarity.

As one progresses in date and mintmark collecting and type collecting, it is important to remember that all of the coins should be of similar states of preservation. Sets look slapdash if one coin is VG and another is MS-65 and still another is VF. Take a look at the prices of all the coins in the series before you get too far, figure out what you can afford, and then stick to that grade or range of grades.

Sure, there is a time-honored practice of filling a spot with any old example until a better one comes along. That is how we got the term "filler." But if you get a few placeholders, don't stop there. By assembling a set of uniform quality, you end up with a more aesthetically pleasing and more valuable collection.

The date and mintmark method used to be the overwhelmingly dominant form of collecting. It still has many adherents. Give it a try if you think it sounds right for you.

Before we leave the discussion of collecting U.S. coins, it should be pointed out that the two major methods of organizing a collection are simply guidelines. They are not hard-and-fast rules that must be followed without questions. Collecting should be satisfying to the hobbyist. It should never be just one more item in the daily grind. Take the elements of these aproaches that you like and ignore the rest.

It should also be pointed out that U.S. coinage history does not start with 1792 nor do all of the coins struck since that time conform precisely to the two major organizational approaches. But these two areas are good places to start.

There are coins and tokens from the American Colonial period (1607-1776) that are just as fascinating and collectible as regular U.S. Mint issues. There are federal issues struck before the Mint was actually established. See the Colonial price-guide section in this book. There are error coins covered in Chapter 3.

There are special coins called commemoratives, which have been struck by the U.S. Mint since 1892 to celebrate some aspect of American history or a contemporary event. They are not intended for circulation. There was a long interruption between 1954 and 1982, but currently numerous commemoratives are being offered for sale directly to collectors by the Mint.

Collecting commemoratives has always been considered something separate from collecting regular U.S. coinage. It is, however, organized the same way. Commemoratives can be collected by date and mintmark or by type.

Current commemoratives can be purchased from the U.S. Mint. Check the Web site at www.usmint.gov or telephone (800) USA-MINT.

Buying coins from the Mint can be considered a hobby pursuit in its own right. Some collectors let the Mint organize their holdings for them. They buy complete sets and put them away. They never buy anything from anywhere else.

Admittedly, this is a passive form of collecting, but there are individuals around the world who enjoy collecting at this level without ever really going any deeper. They like acquiring every new issue as it comes off the Mint's presses.

Once done, there is a certain knowledge that one has all the examples of the current year. Obviously, too, collectors by date and mintmark of the current types would have to buy the new coins each year, but, of course, they do not stop there.

Glossary

Adjustment marks: Marks made by use of a file to correct the weight of overweight coinage planchets prior to striking. Adjusting the weight of planchets was a common practice at the first U.S. Mint in Philadelphia and was often carried out by women hired to weigh planchets and do any necessary filing of the metal.

Altered coin: A coin that has been changed after it left the mint. Such changes are often to the date or mintmark of a common coin in an attempt to increase its value by passing to an unsuspecting buyer as a rare date or mint.

Alloy: A metal or mixture of metals added to the primary metal in the coinage composition, often as a means of facilitating hardness during striking. For example, most U.S. silver coins contain an alloy of 10 percent copper.

Anneal: To heat in order to soften. In the minting process planchets are annealed prior to striking.

Authentication: The act of determining whether a coin, medal, token or other related item is a genuine product of the issuing authority.

Bag marks: Scrapes and impairments to a coin's surface obtained after minting by contact with other coins. The term originates from the storage of coins in bags, but such marks can occur as coins leave the presses and enter hoppers. A larger coin is more susceptible to marks, which affect its grade and, therefore, its value.

Base metal: A metal with low intrinsic value.

Beading: A form of design around the edge of a coin. Beading once served a functional purpose of deterring clipping or shaving parts of the metal by those looking to make a profit and then return the debased coin to circulation.

Blank: Often used in reference to the coinage planchet or disc of metal from which the actual coin is struck. Planchets or blanks are punched out of a sheet of metal by what is known as a blanking press.

Business strike: A coin produced for circulation.

Cast copy: A copy of a coin or medal made by a casting process in which molds are used to produce the finished product. Casting imparts a different surface texture to the finished product than striking and often leaves traces of a seam where the molds came together.

Center dot: A raised dot at the center of a coin caused by use of a compass to aid the engraver in the circular positioning of die devices, such as stars, letters, and dates. Center dots are prevalent on early U.S. coinage.

Chop mark: A mark used by Oriental merchants as a means of guaranteeing the silver content of coins paid out. The merchants' chop marks, or stamped insignia, often obliterated the original design of the host coin. U.S. Trade dollars, struck from 1873 through 1878 and intended for use in trade with China, are sometimes found bearing multiple marks.

Clash marks: Marks impressed in the coinage dies when they come together without a planchet between them. Such marks will affect coins struck subsequently by causing portions of the obverse design to appear in raised form on the reverse, and vice versa.

Clipping: The practice of shaving or cutting small pieces of metal from a coin in circulation. Clipping was prevalent in Colonial times as a means of surreptitiously extracting precious metal from a coin before placing it back into circulation. The introduction of beading and a raised border helped to alleviate the problem.

Coin alignment: U.S. coins are normally struck with an alignment by which, when a coin is held by the top and bottom edge and rotated from side-to-side, the reverse will appear upside down.

Collar: A ring-shaped die between which the obverse and reverse coinage dies are held during striking. The collar contains the outward flow during striking and can be used to produce edge reeding.

Commemorative: A coin issued to honor a special event or person. United States commemorative coins have historically been produced for sale to collectors and not placed in circulation, though the 50-states quarters are circulating commemoratives.

Copy: A replica of an original issue. Copies often vary in quality and metallic composition from the original. Since passage of the Hobby Protection Act (Public Law 93-167) of Nov. 29, 1973, it has been illegal to produce or import copies of coins or other numismatic items that are not clearly and permanently marked with the word "Copy."

Counterfeit: A coin or medal or other numismatic item made fraudulently, either for entry into circulation or sale to collectors.

Denticles: The toothlike pattern found around a coin's obverse or reverse border.

Die: A cylindrical piece of metal containing an incuse image that imparts a raised image when stamped into a planchet.

Die crack: A crack that develops in a coinage die after extensive usage, or if the die is defective or is used to strike harder metals. Die cracks, which often run through border lettering, appear as raised lines on the finished coin.

Device: The principal design element.

Double eagle: Name adopted by the Act of March 3, 1849, for the gold coin valued at 20 units or $20.

Eagle: Name adopted by the Coinage Act of 1792 for a gold coin valued at 10 units or $10. Also a name used to refer to gold, silver, and platinum coins of the American Eagle bullion coinage program begun in 1986.

Edge: The cylindrical surface of a coin between the two sides. The edge can be plain, reeded, ornamented, or lettered.

Electrotype: A copy of a coin, medal, or token made by electroplating.

Exergue: The lower segment of a coin, below the main design, generally separated by a line and often containing the date, designer initials, and mintmark.

Face value: The nominal legal-tender value assigned to a given coin by the governing authority.

Fasces: A Roman symbol of authority consisting of a bound bundle of rods and an axe.

Field: The flat area of a coin's obverse or reverse, devoid of devices or inscriptions.

Galvano: A reproduction of a proposed design from an artist's original model produced in plaster or other substance and then electroplated with metal. The galvano is then used in a reducing lathe to make a die or hub.

Glory: A heraldic term for stars, rays or other devices placed as if in the sky or luminous.

Grading: The largely subjective practice of providing a numerical or adjectival ranking of the condition of a coin, token, or medal. The grade is often a major determinant of value.

Gresham's law: The name for the observation made by Sir Thomas Gresham, 16th century English financier, that when two coins with the same face value but different intrinsic values are in circulation at the same time, the one with the lesser intrinsic value will remain in circulation while the other is hoarded.

Half eagle: Name adopted by the Coinage Act of 1792 for a gold coin valued at five units or $5.

Hub: A piece of die steel showing the coinage devices in relief. The hub is used to produce a die that, in contrast, has the relief details incuse. The die is then used to produce the final coin, which looks much the same as the hub. Hubs may be reused to make new dies.

Legend: A coin' principal lettering, generally shown along its outer perimeter.

Lettered edge: Incuse or raised lettering on a coin's edge.

Matte proof: A proof coin on which the surface is granular or dull. On U.S. coins this type of surface was used on proofs of the early 20th century. The process has since been abandoned.

Magician's coin: A term sometimes used to describe a coin with two heads or two tails. Such a coin is considered impossible in normal production due to physical differences in obverse and reverse die mountings, though as of 2001 two have been certified as genuine by professional coin authenticators. The vast majority are products made outside the Mint as novelty pieces.

Medal: Made to commemorate an event or person. Medals differ from coins in that a medal is not legal tender and, in general, is not produced with the intent of circulating as money.

Medal alignment: Medals are generally struck with the coinage dies facing the same direction during striking. When held by the top and bottom edge and rotated from side-to-side, a piece struck in this manner will show both the obverse and reverse right side up.

Mintage: The total number of coins struck during a given time frame, generally one year.

Mintmark: A letter or other marking on a coin's surface to identify the mint at which the coin was struck.

Mule: The combination of two coinage dies not intended for use together.

Numismatics: The science, study or collecting of coins, tokens, medals, paper money, and related items.

Obverse: The front or "heads" side of a coin, medal, or token.

Overdate: Variety produced when one or more digits of the date are re-engraved over an old date on a die at the Mint, generally to save on dies or correct an error. Portions of the old date can still be seen under the new one.

Overmintmark: Variety created at the Mint when a different mintmark is punched over an already existing mintmark, generally done to make a coinage die already punched for one mint usable at another. Portions of the old mintmark can still be seen under the new one.

Overstrike: A coin, token or medal struck over another coin, token, or medal.

Pattern: A trial strike of a proposed coin design, issued by the Mint or authorized agent of a governing authority. Patterns can be in a variety of metals, thicknesses, and sizes.

Phrygian cap: A close-fitting, egg-shell-shaped hat placed on the head of a freed slave when Rome was in its ascendancy. Hung from a pole, it was a popular symbol of freedom during the French Revolution and in 18th century United States.

Planchet: A disc of metal or other material on which the image of the dies are impressed, resulting in a finished coin. Also sometimes called a blank.

Proof: A coin struck twice or more from specially polished dies and polished planchets. Modern proofs are prepared with a mirror finish. Early 20th century proofs were prepared with a matte surface.

Prooflike: A prooflike coin exhibits some of the characteristics of a proof despite having been struck by regular production processes. Many Morgan dollars are found with prooflike surfaces. The field will have a mirror background similar to that of a proof, and design details are frosted like some proofs.

Quarter eagle: Name adopted by the Coinage Act of 1792 for a gold coin valued at 2.5 units or $2.50.

Reeding: Serrated (toothlike) ornamentation applied to the coin's edge during striking.

Relief: The portion of a design raised above the surface of a coin, medal, or token.

Restrike: A coin, medal or token produced from original dies at a later date, often with the purpose of sale to collectors.

Reverse: The backside or "tails" side of a coin, medal or token, opposite from the principal figure of the design or obverse.

Rim: The raised area bordering the edge and surrounding the field.

Series: The complete group of coins of the same denomination and design and representing all issuing mints.

Token: A privately issued piece, generally in metal, with a represented value in trade or offer of service. Tokens are also produced for advertising purposes.

Type coin: A coin from a given series representing the basic design. A type coin is collected as an example of a particular design rather than for its date and mint-mark.

Variety: Any coin noticeably different in dies from another of the same design, date and mint. Overdate and overmintmarks are examples of varieties.

Wire edge: Created when coinage metal flows between the coinage die and collar, producing a thin flange of coin metal at the outside edge or edges of a coin.

Treasures in your set?
Discover hidden value in ultra grades

I f you like treasure hunts or believe in second chances, the dealer market is signaling it is time for both. Due to a shift in grading interpretations by commercial third-party grading services, modern commemorative coins that you bought 10 or 15 years ago from the U.S. Mint might now be worth more than you think. So get out your sets and start checking. It is even affecting Lincoln cents previously thought common.

Consider the 1986-W Statue of Liberty $5 gold piece. The proof version was sold to collectors for $170 each during the pre-issue discount period and the uncirculated version was sold for $160. They nearly tripled in price in trading on the secondary market in early 1986 before collapsing to $90, barely more than bullion value. Prices have stayed below issue price for many years. Even now, if you wanted to buy the coins on the ordinary secondary market, you probably wouldn't have to pay much more than $100 for either one. They look nice, housed as they are in the Mint's original acrylic plastic capsule. But what a difference it makes housed in a plastic slab with a new desirable grade of MS-70 or Proof-70 ultra cameo attached to it from a reputable third-party grading service. An MS-70 is retailing for $295, according to advertisements in *Numismatic News*, a popular weekly hobby newspaper. A Proof-70 UCAM is $350. With those kind of prices, it might be worth your while to pull out your coins and see if they might get the big money. The key, of course, is sending them in to third-party grading services. These services have rules you must follow and fees you must pay. In the end, your coins might not measure up to the new ultra-high grades.

What makes this new grading phenomenon so startling is that it applies to numerous commemorative issues that for many years had been considered common. Take the 1987-W Constitution $5 gold piece. This issue holds the mintage record for the gold $5 commemorative series. There are 214,225 uncirculated pieces and 651,659 proofs. In the original Mint holders they are trading for around $100, but put one in a slab with MS-70 or Proof-70 on it and the price becomes $260.

In effect, by checking over coins that you may have purchased years ago, you get a second shot at the brass ring of profit. After seeing the Statue of Liberty $5 coins soar, more than a few collectors ordered the 1987-W Constitution in hopes of a repeat performance. That didn't happen, but 16 years later, it might now be time to try again.

Throw in another factor, such as a much lower mintage, and prices go even higher. The 1997-W Franklin Delano Roosevelt $5 gold commemoratives are trading at hardly more than issue price in the $230-$250 range. But that's still more than double the ordinary Statue of Liberty and Constitution prices, reflecting the fact that mintages were lower. The uncirculated FDR $5 has a mintage of 11,805. The proof version is 29,233. Add the ultra-grade factor and the price of an MS-70 FDR $5 is $650. Do you have one in your set?

Even impatient people can get a reward. An issue as recent as the 2001-W Capitol Visitors Center $5 trades at $1,350. Its mintage is even lower than the FDR commemorative coins. The uncirculated version has a mintage of 6,761. The proof mintage is 27,652.

There is not enough space on these pages to list every single modern commemorative issue's turbocharged price in an ultra grade, but it is fair to generalize that these higher grades tend to raise the price significantly across the board. Even in the ultra grades, mintage numbers mean something. Lower mintages tend to mean higher prices.

It is also fair to say that this is a new hobby happening. When the 2003 edition of this book was assembled, nobody had ever heard of ultra-grade modern commemoratives. Condition rarity was something that was usually confined to older collector coins. Collectors, however, are nothing if not ingenious. If the concept can apply to Morgan dollars and Walking Liberty half dollars, why not the modern commemorative coins that have been struck since 1982? If the American Numismatic Association-created and sanctioned numerical grading system includes numbers up to 70, why not use them? It doesn't seem to matter that when the numerical grading system was introduced in 1977 the top numerical designation was considered to be nothing short of perfection. That accounts for the fact that for many years it was never assigned. That psychological barrier has been broken and the use of higher numbers with high price tags attached are now a fact of numismatic life.

A January 2003 auction saw a Proof-70 Deep Cameo 1963 cent sell for $39,100. The Proof-65 price is $1. With over three million 1963 proof sets to search, it is like a lottery. Will you be a prize winner?

So, what are you waiting for? If you are a loyal U.S. Mint customer with some of these issues put away, it is time to get them out and have them professionally evaluated to see if there are any ultra-grade treasures in your possession. It also pays to know that ultra grades are being applied to American Eagle gold and silver bullion coins, which have been struck since 1986, and to the 50-state quarter coins that began in 1999, and even to Roosevelt dimes. Because the hobby never stands still, it probably pays to keep an eye on every other coin series in your collection, for if it hasn't happened yet, the ultra grades will probably soon be applied to them also. For the long-suffering owner of a Statue of Liberty $5, the opportunity to more than double its value is in fact a hobby second chance.

U.S. MINT ISSUES

HALF CENT

Liberty Cap Half Cent.
Head facing left.

KM# 10   Designer: Henry Voigt. **Diameter:** 22 **Weight:** 6.7400 g. **Composition:** Copper.

Date	Mintage	G-4	VG-8	F-12	VF-20	XF-40	MS-60
1793	35,334	2,000	2,750	4,200	6,000	12,500	35,000

Liberty Cap Half Cent.
Head facing right.

KM# 14   Designer: Robert Scot (1794) and John Smith Gardner (1795). **Diameter:** 23.5 **Composition:** Copper. **Weight:** 6.74 g. (1794-95) and 5.44 g. (1795-97) **Notes:** The "lettered edge" varieties have "Two Hundred for a Dollar" inscribed around the edge. The "pole" varieties have a pole upon which the cap is hanging, resting on Liberty's shoulder. The "punctuated date" varieties have a comma after the 1 in the date. The 1797 "1 above 1" variety has a second 1 above the 1 in the date.

Date	Mintage	G-4	VG-8	F-12	VF-20	XF-40	MS-60
1794	81,600	375	650	850	1,600	3,500	18,000
1795 lettered edge, pole	25,600	425	500	850	1,500	4,250	17,500
1795 plain edge, no pole	109,000	375	475	800	1,400	3,500	16,000
1795 lettered edge, punctuated date	Inc. above	425	650	900	1,400	3,750	20,000
1795 plain edge, punctuated date	Inc. above	350	450	750	1,200	3,000	27,500
1796 pole	5,090	15,000	16,000	20,000	25,000	35,000	—
1796 no pole	1,390	27,000	32,500	47,500	90,000	—	—
1797 plain edge	119,215	400	575	950	1,900	6,000	27,500
1797 lettered edge	Inc. above	1,700	2,700	4,000	8,000	25,000	—
1797 1 above 1	Inc. above	375	475	950	1,600	3,250	20,000
1797 gripped edge	Inc. above	16,000	37,500	48,000	60,000	70,000	—

Draped Bust Half Cent.

KM# 33   Designer: Robert Scot. **Diameter:** 23.5 **Weight:** 5.4400 g. **Composition:** Copper. **Notes:** The wreath on the reverse was redesigned slightly in 1802, resulting in "reverse of 1800" and "reverse of 1802" varieties. The "stems" varieties have stems extending from the wreath above and on both sides of the fraction on the reverse. On the 1804 "crosslet 4" variety, a serif appears at the far right of the crossbar on the 4 in the date. The "spiked chin" variety appears to have a spike extending from Liberty's chin, the result of a damaged die. Varieties of the 1805 strikes are distinguished by the size of the 5 in the date. Varieties of the 1806 strikes are distinguished by the size of the 6 in the date.

Stemless   Stems

Date	Mintage	G-4	VG-8	F-12	VF-20	XF-40	MS-60
1800	211,530	50.00	75.00	100.00	200	500	2,500
1802/0 rev. 1800	14,366	15,000	22,000	30,000	—	—	—
1802/0 rev. 1802	Inc. above	800	1,200	2,750	6,500	17,000	—
1803	97,900	45.00	70.00	125	275	950	7,000
1804 plain 4, stemless wreath	1,055,312	50.00	60.00	85.00	130	250	1,400
1804 plain 4, stems	Inc. above	45.00	75.00	125	250	1,500	12,000
1804 crosslet 4, stemless	Inc. above	50.00	75.00	85.00	125	250	1,350
1804 crosslet 4, stems	Inc. above	47.00	75.00	110	175	300	1,200
1804 spiked chin	Inc. above	60.00	90.00	125	175	325	1,200
1805 small 5, stemless	814,464	50.00	75.00	90.00	135	400	3,500
1805 small 5, stems	Inc. above	675	1,200	2,400	4,500	8,000	—
1805 large 5, stems	Inc. above	49.00	65.00	85.00	125	400	3,000
1806 small 6, stems	356,000	175	325	600	1,000	2,750	—
1806 small 6, stemless	Inc. above	50.00	65.00	85.00	125	235	1,350
1806 large 6, stems	Inc. above	50.00	65.00	85.00	125	250	1,200

Date	Mintage	G-4	VG-8	F-12	VF-20	XF-40	MS-60
1807	476,000	50.00	80.00	120	175	300	1,400
1808/7	400,000	225	325	600	1,200	6,000	27,500
1808	Inc. above	50.00	65.00	90.00	135	350	5,000

Classic Head Half Cent.

KM# 41 Designer: John Reich. **Diameter:** 23.5
Weight: 5.4400 g. **Composition:** Copper. **Notes:**
Restrikes listed were produced privately in the mid-
1800s. The 1831 restrikes have two varieties with
different-size berries in the wreath on the reverse. The
1828 strikes have either 12 or 13 stars on the obverse.

Date	Mintage	G-4	VG-8	F-12	VF-20	XF-40	MS-60
1809/6	1,154,572	50.00	80.00	110	150	215	1,000
1809	Inc. above	32.00	40.00	55.00	80.00	215	800
1809 circle in 0	—	35.00	45.00	60.00	110	250	2,100
1810	215,000	45.00	60.00	120	200	600	3,250
1811	63,140	200	275	550	1,350	4,000	—
1811 restrike, reverse of 1802, uncirculated	—	—	—	—	—	—	27,500
1825	63,000	35.00	40.00	55.00	90.00	175	950
1826	234,000	35.00	40.00	60.00	90.00	150	750
1828 13 stars	606,000	30.00	37.50	52.50	60.00	75.00	300
1828 12 stars	Inc. above	40.00	60.00	80.00	125	215	850
1829	487,000	35.00	40.00	65.00	90.00	150	500
1831 original	2,200	5,000	6,000	6,500	7,000	9,750	—
1831 1st restrike, lg. berries, reverse of 1836	—	—	—	—	—	—	6,500
1831 2nd restrike, sm. berries, reverse of 1840, proof	—	—	—	—	—	—	25,000
1832	154,000	34.00	45.00	60.00	75.00	110	325
1833	120,000	34.00	45.00	60.00	75.00	110	325
1834	141,000	34.00	45.00	60.00	75.00	110	325
1835	398,000	34.00	45.00	60.00	75.00	110	325
1836 original, proof	—	—	—	—	—	—	5,000
1836 restrike, reverse of 1840, proof	—	—	—	—	—	—	18,000

Braided Hair Half Cent.

KM# 70 Designer: Christian Gobrecht. **Diameter:**
23 **Weight:** 5.4400 g. **Composition:** Copper.
Notes: 1840-1849 and 1852 strikes, both originals and
restrikes, are known in proof only; mintages are
unknown. The small-date varieties of 1849, both
originals and restrikes are known in proof only. The
Restrikes were produced clandestinely by
Philadelphia Mint personnel in the mid-1800s.

Date	Mintage	G-4	VG-8	F-12	VF-20	XF-40	MS-60	Prf-60
1840 original	—	1,000	1,200	1,500	2,000	3,000	—	5,500
1840 1st restrike	—	1,000	1,200	1,500	2,000	3,000	—	6,500
1840 2nd restrike	—	1,000	1,200	1,500	2,000	3,000	—	5,500
1841 original	—	1,000	1,200	1,500	2,000	3,000	—	5,500
1841 1st restrike	—	1,000	1,200	1,500	2,000	3,000	—	6,500
1841 2nd restrike	—	1,000	1,200	1,500	2,000	3,000	—	6,000
1842 original	—	1,000	1,200	1,500	2,000	3,000	—	6,000
1842 1st restrike	—	1,000	1,200	1,500	2,000	3,000	—	6,000
1842 2nd restrike	—	1,000	1,200	1,500	2,000	3,000	—	6,000
1843 original	—	1,000	1,200	1,500	2,000	3,000	—	6,500
1843 1st restrike	—	1,000	1,200	1,500	2,000	3,000	—	6,000
1843 2nd restrike	—	1,000	1,200	1,500	2,000	3,000	—	6,500
1844 original	—	1,000	1,200	1,500	2,000	3,000	—	6,000
1844 1st restrike	—	1,000	1,200	1,500	2,000	3,000	—	6,000
1844 2nd restrike	—	1,000	1,200	1,500	2,000	3,000	—	6,000
1845 original	—	1,000	1,200	1,500	2,000	3,000	—	6,000
1845 1st restrike	—	1,000	1,200	1,500	2,000	3,000	—	6,000
1845 2nd restrike	—	1,000	1,200	1,500	2,000	3,000	—	6,000
1846 original	—	1,000	1,200	1,500	2,000	3,000	—	6,000
1846 1st restrike	—	1,000	1,200	1,500	2,000	3,000	—	6,500
1846 2nd restrike	—	1,000	1,200	1,500	2,000	3,000	—	6,000
1847 original	—	1,000	1,200	1,500	2,000	3,000	—	6,000
1847 1st restrike	—	3,000	4,000	4,500	5,000	5,500	—	8,000
1847 2nd restrike	—	1,000	1,200	1,500	2,000	3,000	—	6,000
1848 original	—	1,000	1,200	1,500	2,000	3,000	—	6,000
1848 1st restrike	—	1,000	1,200	1,500	2,000	3,000	—	6,000
1848 2nd restrike	—	1,000	1,200	1,500	2,000	3,000	—	6,000
1849 original, small date	—	1,000	1,200	1,500	2,000	3,000	—	6,500
1849 1st restrike small date	—	1,000	1,200	1,500	2,000	3,000	—	6,000
1849 large date	39,864	40.00	45.00	75.00	100.00	150	275	—
1850	39,812	39.00	55.00	90.00	150	200	400	—

Date	Mintage	G-4	VG-8	F-12	VF-20	XF-40	MS-60	Prf-60
1851	147,672	30.00	40.00	55.00	65.00	100.00	175	—
1852 original	—	12,000	25,000	30,000	35,000	40,000	—	90,000
1852 1st restrike	—	1,000	1,200	1,500	2,000	3,000	—	5,000
1852 2nd restrike	—	1,000	1,200	1,500	2,000	3,000	—	7,000
1853	129,694	40.00	55.00	75.00	110	150	300	—
1854	55,358	40.00	55.00	75.00	110	150	300	—
1855	56,500	40.00	55.00	75.00	110	150	300	—
1856	40,430	40.00	55.00	75.00	110	150	300	—
1857	35,180	65.00	80.00	150	200	250	500	—

CENT

Flowing Hair Cent. Chain.

KM# 11 Designer: Henry Voigt. **Diameter:** 26-27
Weight: 13.4800 g. **Composition:** Copper.

Date	Mintage	G-4	VG-8	F-12	VF-20	XF-40	MS-60
1793	36,103	7,750	11,000	15,000	23,000	33,000	135,000

Flowing Hair Cent. Wreath.

KM# 12 Designer: Henry Voigt. **Diameter:** 26-28
Weight: 13.4800 g. **Composition:** Copper.

Date	Mintage	G-4	VG-8	F-12	VF-20	XF-40	MS-60
1793	63,353	1,700	2,500	4,000	8,000	12,000	30,000

Liberty Cap Cent.

KM# 13 Designer: Joseph Wright (1793-1795) and
John Smith Gardner (1795-1796). **Diameter:** 29
Composition: Copper. **Weight:** 13.48 g. (1793-95) and
10.89 g. (1795-96) **Notes:** The heavier pieces were
struck on a thicker planchet. The Liberty design on the
obverse was revised slightly in 1794, but the 1793 design
was used on some 1794 strikes. A 1795 "lettered edge"
variety has "One Hundred for a Dollar" and a leaf
inscribed on the edge.

Date	Mintage	G-4	VG-8	F-12	VF-20	XF-40	MS-60
1793 cap	11,056	5,000	6,000	9,000	20,000	26,000	—
1794	918,521	350	485	750	1,200	3,750	9,000
1794 head '93	Inc. above	1,500	2,600	4,000	7,900	12,000	—
1795	501,500	350	485	650	1,000	2,000	4,750

Liberty Cap Cent.

KM# 13a Designer: Joseph Wright (1793-1795) and
John Smith Gardner (1795-1796). **Diameter:** 29
Weight: 10.8900 g. **Composition:** Copper.

Date	Mintage	G-4	VG-8	F-12	VF-20	XF-40	MS-60
1795 lettered edge, "One Cent" high in wreath	37,000	350	550	900	1,750	3,300	11,000
1796	109,825	350	500	800	1,400	3,750	21,000

Draped Bust Cent.

KM# 22 **Designer:** Robert Scot. **Diameter:** 29 **Weight:** 10.9800 g. **Composition:** Copper. **Notes:** The "stemless" variety does not have stems extending from the wreath above and on both sides of the fraction on the reverse. The 1801 "3 errors" variety has the fraction on the reverse reading "1/000," has only one stem extending from the wreath above and on both sides of the fraction on the reverse, and "United" in "United States of America" appears as "Iinited."

 Stemless   Stems

Date	Mintage	G-4	VG-8	F-12	VF-20	XF-40	MS-60
1796	363,375	350	600	850	1,800	3,400	—
1797	897,510	130	175	250	335	1,150	3,300
1797 stemless	Inc. above	300	495	600	910	3,200	—
1798	1,841,745	90.00	130	200	350	1,300	3,100
1798/7	Inc. above	150	225	310	1,200	3,900	—
1799	42,540	3,250	4,500	7,500	16,000	35,000	—
1800	2,822,175	50.00	95.00	200	400	1,750	—
1801	1,362,837	60.00	87.00	180	325	1,000	—
1801 3 errors	Inc. above	100.00	250	700	1,500	5,500	
1802	3,435,100	50.00	75.00	150	250	775	2,250
1803	2,471,353	50.00	80.00	150	250	775	2,250
1804	96,500	1,300	2,000	2,600	3,200	7,000	—
1804 Restrike of 1860	—	325	450	500	600	900	1,100
1805	941,116	60.00	90.00	160	300	875	2,450
1806	348,000	70.00	100.00	150	375	1,100	4,700
1807	727,221	60.00	80.00	160	300	800	2,250
1807/6 large 7/6	—	60.00	80.00	160	350	1,275	
1807/6 small 7/6	—	1,900	2,900	4,200	6,000	19,000	—

Classic Head Cent.

KM# 39 **Designer:** John Reich. **Diameter:** 29 **Weight:** 10.8900 g. **Composition:** Copper.

Date	Mintage	G-4	VG-8	F-12	VF-20	XF-40	MS-60
1808	1,109,000	125	200	325	575	1,200	3,600
1809	222,867	175	300	525	1,200	2,650	6,300
1810	1,458,500	75.00	95.00	210	550	1,100	3,850
1811	218,025	110	175	400	1,000	1,500	7,000
1811/10	Inc. above	130	200	440	1,200	2,200	—
1812	1,075,500	48.00	83.00	200	525	975	2,800
1813	418,000	60.00	95.00	375	600	1,200	—
1814	357,830	45.00	80.00	200	530	975	2,800

Coronet Cent.

KM# 45 **Designer:** John Reich. **Diameter:** 28-29 **Weight:** 10.8900 g. **Composition:** Copper. **Notes:** The 1817 strikes have either 13 or 15 stars on the obverse.

Date	Mintage	G-4	VG-8	F-12	VF-20	XF-40	MS-60
1816	2,820,982	25.00	30.00	50.00	100.00	175	420
1817 13 stars	3,948,400	20.00	26.00	30.00	60.00	120	470
1817 15 stars	Inc. above	27.50	32.50	45.00	125	350	1,600
1818	3,167,000	20.00	26.00	35.00	60.00	125	270
1819	2,671,000	20.00	26.00	35.00	63.00	120	285
1820	4,407,550	20.00	26.00	35.00	65.00	120	300

Date	Mintage	G-4	VG-8	F-12	VF-20	XF-40	MS-60
1821	389,000	32.50	55.00	250	400	1,500	6,000
1822	2,072,339	25.00	30.00	50.00	100.00	195	750
1823 Included in 1824 mintage	—	90.00	150	310	690	2,750	—
1823/22 Included in 1824 mintage	—	80.00	110	300	675	2,450	—
1823 Restrike	—	700	550	675	800	900	1,300
1824	1,262,000	20.00	26.00	38.00	160	350	950
1824/22	Inc. above	28.50	36.00	100.00	400	975	3,600
1825	1,461,100	20.00	26.00	40.00	110	300	960
1826	1,517,425	20.00	26.00	40.00	84.00	175	750
1826/25	Inc. above	21.00	40.00	75.00	175	600	2,000
1827	2,357,732	20.00	26.00	40.00	75.00	160	750
1828	2,260,624	20.00	26.00	40.00	90.00	175	450
1829	1,414,500	20.00	26.00	40.00	90.00	175	425
1830	1,711,500	20.00	26.00	40.00	90.00	175	400
1831	3,359,260	20.00	26.00	40.00	80.00	175	315
1832	2,362,000	20.00	26.00	40.00	80.00	175	380
1833	2,739,000	20.00	26.00	40.00	80.00	175	300
1834	1,855,100	20.00	26.00	40.00	80.00	175	300
1835	3,878,400	20.00	26.00	40.00	80.00	200	300
1836	2,111,000	20.00	26.00	40.00	80.00	175	300
1837	5,558,300	20.00	26.00	40.00	80.00	175	300
1838	6,370,200	20.00	26.00	40.00	80.00	175	300
1839	3,128,661	20.00	26.00	40.00	80.00	175	350
1839/36	Inc. above	400	500	700	1,500	3,900	—

Braided Hair Cent.

KM# 67 Designer: Christian Gobrecht. **Diameter:** 27.5 **Weight:** 10.8900 g. **Composition:** Copper. **Notes:** 1840 and 1842 strikes are known with both small and large dates, with little difference in value. 1855 and 1856 strikes are known with both slanting and upright 5s in the date, with little difference in value. A slightly larger Liberty head and larger reverse lettering were used beginning in 1843. One 1843 variety uses the old obverse with the new reverse.

Date	Mintage	G-4	VG-8	F-12	VF-20	XF-40	MS-60
1840	2,462,700	20.00	30.00	40.00	50.00	70.00	475
1841	1,597,367	20.00	30.00	40.00	50.00	80.00	440
1842	2,383,390	20.00	30.00	40.00	50.00	70.00	425
1843	2,425,342	20.00	30.00	40.00	50.00	75.00	445
1843 obverse 1842 with reverse of 1844	Inc. above	20.00	30.00	40.00	50.00	80.00	350
1844	2,398,752	20.00	30.00	40.00	50.00	75.00	225
1844/81	Inc. above	30.00	75.00	125	175	225	600
1845	3,894,804	20.00	30.00	40.00	50.00	75.00	225
1846	4,120,800	20.00	30.00	40.00	50.00	75.00	225
1847	6,183,669	20.00	30.00	40.00	50.00	75.00	200
1848	6,415,799	20.00	30.00	40.00	50.00	75.00	200
1849	4,178,500	20.00	30.00	40.00	50.00	75.00	275
1850	4,426,844	20.00	30.00	40.00	50.00	75.00	250
1851	9,889,707	20.00	30.00	40.00	50.00	75.00	200
1851/81	Inc. above	27.00	39.00	75.00	125	290	600
1852	5,063,094	20.00	30.00	40.00	50.00	75.00	200
1853	6,641,131	20.00	30.00	40.00	50.00	75.00	200
1854	4,236,156	20.00	30.00	40.00	50.00	75.00	200
1855	1,574,829	20.00	30.00	40.00	50.00	75.00	200
1856	2,690,463	20.00	30.00	40.00	50.00	75.00	200
1857	333,456	60.00	90.00	120	150	200	400

Flying Eagle Cent.

KM# 85 Designer: James B. Longacre. **Diameter:** 19 **Weight:** 4.6700 g. **Composition:** Copper-Nickel. **Notes:** On the large-letter variety of 1858, the "A" and "M" in "America" are connected at their bases; on the small-letter variety, the two letters are separated.

 Large letters   Small letters

Date	Mintage	G-4	VG-8	F-12	VF-20	XF-40	AU-50	MS-60	MS-65	Prf-65
1856	Est. 2,500	6,250	7,250	8,000	9,900	11,000	12,800	16,500	58,000	24,500
1857	17,450,000	20.00	24.00	33.00	44.00	125	165	285	3,750	29,000
1858/7	—	65.00	90.00	175	390	750	1,500	2,500	75,000	—
1858 large letters	24,600,000	20.00	24.00	34.00	52.50	140	200	345	3,750	23,500

Date	Mintage	G-4	VG-8	F-12	VF-20	XF-40	AU-50	MS-60	MS-65	Prf-65
1858 small letters	Inc. above	20.00	24.00	33.00	44.00	125	175	290	3,800	30,000

Indian Head Cent.

KM# 87 Designer: James B. Longacre. **Diameter:** 19
Weight: 4.6700 g. **Composition:** Copper-Nickel.

Date	Mintage	G-4	VG-8	F-12	VF-20	XF-40	AU-50	MS-60	MS-65	Prf-65
1859	36,400,000	12.50	15.00	21.00	46.00	100.00	175	215	3,200	5,000

Indian Head Cent.
Shield added at top of wreath.

KM# 90 Designer: James B. Longacre. **Diameter:** 19
Weight: 4.6700 g. **Composition:** Copper-Nickel.

Date	Mintage	G-4	VG-8	F-12	VF-20	XF-40	AU-50	MS-60	MS-65	Prf-65
1860	20,566,000(1,000)	10.00	13.50	19.00	27.50	53.50	80.00	185	1,000	3,900
1861	10,100,000	20.00	30.00	41.00	52.50	90.00	160	180	1,000	7,150
1862	28,075,000	7.50	9.00	10.00	14.50	27.50	55.00	80.00	1,000	2,100
1863	49,840,000	7.50	9.00	10.00	11.00	24.00	54.00	72.50	1,000	3,200
1864	13,740,000	15.00	20.00	34.00	47.50	70.00	92.50	150	1,250	3,200

Indian Head Cent.

KM# 90a Designer: James B. Longacre. **Diameter:**
19 **Weight:** 3.1100 g. **Composition:** Bronze. **Notes:**
The 1864 "L" variety has the designer's initial in
Liberty's hair to the right of her neck.

1864 "L"

Date	Mintage	G-4	VG-8	F-12	VF-20	XF-40	AU-50	MS-60	MS-65	Prf-65
1864	39,233,714	6.00	12.00	20.00	37.50	60.00	75.00	90.00	325	4,300
1864 L	Inc. above	50.00	65.00	130	170	260	310	400	1,650	110,000
1865	35,429,286	6.00	10.00	17.50	23.00	35.00	50.00	80.00	450	1,550
1866	9,826,500	40.00	48.00	60.00	95.00	180	215	250	1,250	950
1867	9,821,000	40.00	53.00	70.00	110	175	210	265	1,250	1,050
1868	10,266,500	37.50	40.00	65.00	100.00	150	180	220	1,000	985
1869/9	6,420,000	115	155	330	440	625	685	775	1,800	—
1869	Inc. above	60.00	85.00	215	300	400	475	510	1,650	950
1870	5,275,000	45.00	70.00	200	280	375	440	515	1,600	1,075
1871	3,929,500	60.00	100.00	230	285	380	400	425	2,550	1,100
1872	4,042,000	67.50	150	375	425	575	700	775	4,100	1,100
1873	11,676,500	21.00	30.00	46.00	75.00	150	190	215	1,300	850
1874	14,187,500	15.00	20.00	35.00	55.00	95.00	125	170	700	800
1875	13,528,000	15.00	27.50	47.50	62.50	95.00	135	175	800	1,500
1876	7,944,000	27.00	35.00	62.50	125	200	265	315	1,100	925
1877	852,500	590	780	1,250	1,600	2,100	2,650	2,850	8,750	4,900
1878	5,799,850	28.00	38.00	65.00	135	225	265	315	900	490
1879	16,231,200	7.00	11.00	16.00	33.00	65.00	72.50	75.00	350	450
1880	38,964,955	4.00	6.00	8.00	11.00	25.00	37.50	60.00	350	435
1881	39,211,575	4.00	5.00	7.00	10.00	18.00	30.00	40.00	330	425
1882	38,581,100	4.00	6.00	8.00	11.00	18.00	30.00	37.50	330	425
1883	45,589,109	3.00	4.50	7.00	10.00	16.00	24.00	38.50	330	425
1884	23,261,742	4.00	6.00	8.00	14.00	27.00	38.00	65.00	500	425
1885	11,765,384	6.00	8.00	15.00	29.00	54.00	65.00	95.00	750	425
1886	17,654,290	4.00	6.00	30.00	65.00	120	175	200	1,250	460
1887	45,226,483	2.00	3.00	4.00	6.00	15.00	28.00	50.00	395	475
1888	37,494,414	2.00	2.50	4.00	7.00	20.00	28.00	42.00	950	525
1889	48,869,361	1.75	2.20	2.50	4.00	10.00	27.00	35.00	395	450
1890	57,182,854	1.50	1.80	2.50	4.00	10.00	22.00	35.00	395	500
1891	47,072,350	1.70	2.25	3.00	4.50	10.00	22.00	35.00	400	520
1892	37,649,832	2.00	2.25	3.00	5.00	16.00	20.00	34.00	395	525
1893	46,642,195	1.70	2.25	3.00	5.00	10.00	22.00	30.00	340	540
1894	16,752,132	4.00	6.00	12.00	20.00	45.00	55.00	70.00	375	525
1895	38,343,636	1.75	2.00	3.00	6.00	12.00	22.00	32.00	200	475
1896	39,057,293	1.50	2.00	2.75	5.00	10.00	21.00	33.00	230	425
1897	50,466,330	1.50	2.00	2.25	4.00	10.00	20.00	30.00	200	425
1898	49,823,079	1.50	2.00	2.25	3.00	10.00	20.00	30.00	200	425
1899	53,600,031	1.50	1.80	2.00	3.00	10.00	18.00	27.50	140	415
1900	66,833,764	1.40	1.70	2.00	4.00	12.00	20.00	25.00	175	425
1901	79,611,143	1.35	1.65	1.85	3.00	7.50	17.00	25.00	140	425
1902	87,376,722	1.35	1.65	1.85	3.00	7.00	17.00	25.00	140	425

Date	Mintage	G-4	VG-8	F-12	VF-20	XF-40	AU-50	MS-60	MS-65	Prf-65
1903	85,094,493	1.35	1.65	1.85	3.00	7.00	17.00	25.00	140	425
1904	61,328,015	1.35	1.65	1.85	3.00	7.00	17.00	25.00	140	475
1905	80,719,163	1.35	1.65	1.85	3.00	7.00	17.00	25.00	140	475
1906	96,022,255	1.35	1.65	1.85	3.00	7.00	17.00	25.00	140	395
1907	108,138,618	1.35	1.65	1.85	3.00	7.00	17.00	25.00	145	485
1908	32,327,987	1.60	2.00	2.25	3.00	7.50	18.00	26.00	145	395
1908S	1,115,000	60.00	65.00	75.00	88.00	150	185	275	650	—
1909	14,370,645	3.00	3.50	4.00	5.00	15.00	24.00	30.00	150	400
1909S	309,000	350	375	425	475	550	635	750	1,500	—

Lincoln Cent. Wheat Ears.

KM# 132   Designer: Victor D. Brenner. **Diameter:** 19
Weight: 3.1100 g. **Composition:** Bronze. **Notes:** The
1909 "VDB" varieties have the designer's initials
inscribed at the 6 o'clock position on the reverse. The
initials were removed until 1918, when they were
restored on the obverse.

Date	Mintage	G-4	VG-8	F-12	VF-20	XF-40	AU-50	MS-60	MS-65	Prf-65
1909	72,702,618	1.35	1.60	1.90	2.10	3.40	9.00	13.50	80.00	520
1909 VDB	27,995,000	4.25	4.50	4.75	5.00	5.25	5.75	9.50	100.00	6,000
1909S	1,825,000	68.50	75.00	95.00	140	195	225	285	1,300	—
1909S VDB	484,000	550	640	780	800	1,100	1,200	1,300	6,750	—
1910	146,801,218	.25	.30	.40	.50	3.75	8.00	17.50	250	700
1910S	6,045,000	7.00	9.50	11.00	13.50	28.50	60.00	65.00	800	—
1911	101,177,787	.25	.45	1.50	2.15	4.00	8.00	19.00	375	600
1911D	12,672,000	5.00	5.75	9.50	15.00	40.00	65.00	80.00	1,350	—
1911S	4,026,000	16.00	20.00	23.50	30.00	47.50	90.00	150	3,300	—
1912	68,153,060	1.25	1.50	2.20	5.50	11.00	20.00	30.00	550	950
1912D	10,411,000	6.75	7.75	9.50	22.00	50.00	85.00	150	1,900	—
1912S	4,431,000	13.50	16.75	20.00	25.00	55.00	85.00	130	4,100	—
1913	76,532,352	.65	.75	1.40	3.00	13.50	20.00	33.50	410	550
1913D	15,804,000	2.75	3.00	3.50	10.50	27.50	55.00	90.00	1,925	—
1913S	6,101,000	6.50	7.75	9.00	14.00	33.50	75.00	135	5,500	—
1914	75,238,432	.45	.70	2.00	5.25	13.50	32.50	47.50	415	600
1914D	1,193,000	125	180	260	335	575	1,250	1,600	20,000	—
1914S	4,137,000	12.00	14.00	17.00	27.00	60.00	150	275	9,800	—
1915	29,092,120	1.35	1.75	3.50	12.50	41.50	67.50	80.00	1,150	600
1915D	22,050,000	1.50	1.75	3.00	5.50	19.00	41.50	67.50	1,250	—
1915S	4,833,000	7.50	9.50	12.50	18.00	45.00	75.00	150	4,800	—
1916	131,833,677	.20	.25	.80	2.15	5.00	10.00	16.00	415	1,650
1916D	35,956,000	1.00	1.85	2.80	5.50	12.50	27.50	65.00	3,000	—
1916S	22,510,000	1.60	3.15	4.35	6.75	16.50	35.00	71.00	6,850	—
1917	196,429,785	.20	.25	.30	1.85	4.00	9.50	16.00	450	—
1917D	55,120,000	.70	1.00	2.20	4.25	14.00	30.00	60.00	3,000	—
1917S	32,620,000	.50	.80	1.25	2.15	9.50	21.50	56.00	6,850	—
1918	288,104,634	.20	.25	.30	.80	3.75	7.50	12.50	415	—
1918D	47,830,000	.80	1.30	2.20	4.00	12.50	26.00	62.50	3,550	—
1918S	34,680,000	.30	.75	1.00	2.75	8.50	30.00	57.50	6,850	—
1919	392,021,000	.20	.25	.30	.50	1.35	4.00	8.00	100.00	—
1919D	57,154,000	.80	1.00	1.25	2.75	7.00	30.00	47.50	2,500	—
1919S	139,760,000	.25	.40	1.40	2.50	4.50	16.00	41.50	4,000	—
1920	310,165,000	.20	.25	.35	.90	2.65	5.50	12.50	195	—
1920D	49,280,000	.80	1.00	1.85	2.80	12.50	31.00	62.50	2,500	—
1920S	46,220,000	.60	.65	1.50	2.15	8.50	32.50	80.00	8,000	—
1921	39,157,000	.40	.65	.80	2.15	6.75	20.00	38.00	235	—
1921S	15,274,000	1.50	1.95	2.50	4.40	25.00	67.00	100.00	5,500	—
1922D	7,160,000	10.00	12.00	14.00	17.00	27.50	47.50	75.00	1,800	—
1922 No D-T.2	Inc. above	480	645	970	1,450	2,800	4,750	7,500	180,000	—
1923	74,723,000	.35	.45	.65	.90	3.40	8.00	13.50	480	—
1923S	8,700,000	1.85	2.50	3.40	6.50	26.00	75.00	195	13,500	—
1924	75,178,000	.20	.30	.40	.60	3.00	8.00	20.00	390	—
1924D	2,520,000	15.00	18.00	22.00	35.00	85.00	150	235	8,350	—
1924S	11,696,000	1.25	1.50	2.50	400	16.00	60.00	100.00	11,000	—
1925	139,949,000	.20	.25	.30	.50	2.50	6.00	8.50	100.00	—
1925D	22,580,000	.60	1.25	1.85	4.00	10.00	23.50	50.00	4,350	—
1925S	26,380,000	.60	.80	1.50	2.15	9.50	30.00	68.50	8,400	—
1926	157,088,000	.15	.20	.25	.50	1.35	4.00	7.00	66.00	—
1926D	28,020,000	.75	1.00	1.85	2.75	10.00	27.50	65.00	4,250	—
1926S	4,550,000	4.00	5.00	7.00	9.00	18.00	56.00	110	67,500	—
1927	144,440,000	.15	.20	.25	.50	1.35	3.25	7.00	95.00	—
1927D	27,170,000	.80	1.10	1.50	2.15	4.65	20.00	55.00	1,700	—
1927S	14,276,000	1.25	1.85	2.50	4.65	11.00	32.50	62.50	6,000	—
1928	134,116,000	.15	.20	.25	.45	1.10	3.00	7.50	90.00	—
1928D	31,170,000	.80	1.00	1.50	2.15	4.65	12.50	30.00	1,100	—
1928S	17,266,000	.90	1.40	2.50	3.00	6.25	20.00	65.00	4,800	—
1929	185,262,000	.15	.20	.25	.40	.70	4.25	6.00	85.00	—
1929D	41,730,000	.40	.80	1.10	2.15	4.65	11.00	21.50	550	—

Date	Mintage	G-4	VG-8	F-12	VF-20	XF-40	AU-50	MS-60	MS-65	Prf-65
1929S	50,148,000	.50	.85	1.50	2.15	4.00	6.75	17.50	415	—
1930	157,415,000	.15	.20	.25	.40	1.10	2.25	3.75	32.50	—
1930D	40,100,000	.20	.25	.40	.55	1.95	4.00	10.50	95.00	—
1930S	24,286,000	.25	.35	.50	.65	1.10	6.50	10.00	50.00	—
1931	19,396,000	.45	.50	.80	1.85	2.50	8.00	19.00	100.00	—
1931D	4,480,000	3.75	4.40	5.00	6.25	11.00	37.50	52.00	815	—
1931S	866,000	62.50	65.00	75.00	76.00	78.50	85.00	100.00	750	—
1932	9,062,000	1.30	1.75	2.75	3.25	4.25	11.50	19.00	72.50	—
1932D	10,500,000	1.10	1.85	2.35	2.75	3.75	8.50	17.50	80.00	—
1933	14,360,000	1.10	1.65	2.35	2.75	4.00	8.50	17.50	70.00	—
1933D	6,200,000	2.50	3.15	3.75	5.00	7.75	13.50	19.00	70.00	—
1934	219,080,000	—	.15	.20	.25	.75	1.50	4.00	27.00	—
1934D	28,446,000	.15	.20	.25	.45	1.50	5.00	16.50	52.00	—
1935	245,338,000	—	.10	.15	.25	.75	1.00	2.50	13.00	—
1935D	47,000,000	—	.15	.20	.30	.95	2.50	5.50	9.50	—
1935S	38,702,000	.10	.20	.30	.40	1.00	3.00	12.00	46.00	—
1936	309,637,569	—	.10	.15	.25	.75	1.00	2.00	6.00	1,200
1936D	40,620,000	—	.10	.15	.25	.75	1.50	2.75	8.50	—
1936S	29,130,000	.10	.15	.25	.35	.85	1.75	2.75	8.50	—
1937	309,179,320	—	.10	.15	.20	.70	.90	1.75	7.00	125
1937D	50,430,000	—	.10	.15	.25	.70	1.00	2.50	9.50	—
1937S	34,500,000	—	.10	.15	.25	.60	1.25	3.00	8.50	—
1938	156,696,734	—	.10	.15	.20	.50	1.00	2.00	8.00	85.00
1938D	20,010,000	.20	.25	.35	.45	.75	1.50	3.50	12.50	—
1938S	15,180,000	.30	.40	.50	.70	1.00	2.00	2.80	8.50	—
1939	316,479,520	—	.10	.15	.20	.30	.50	1.00	5.75	78.00
1939D	15,160,000	.35	.40	.35	.60	.85	1.90	2.25	8.50	—
1939S	52,070,000	—	.15	.20	.25	.45	.90	1.35	9.50	—
1940	586,825,872	—	.15	.20	.25	.30	.45	1.00	5.75	70.00
1940D	81,390,000	—	.15	.20	.25	.35	.50	1.20	5.75	—
1940S	112,940,000	—	.15	.20	.25	.30	.75	1.25	5.85	—
1941	887,039,100	—	—	.10	.15	.25	.40	.85	5.75	65.00
1941D	128,700,000	—	—	.15	.20	.25	1.00	2.00	8.50	—
1941S	92,360,000	—	—	.15	.20	.25	1.25	2.25	11.00	—
1912	657,828,600	—	—	10	.15	.20	.25	.50	4.60	78.00
1942D	206,698,000	—	—	.10	.15	.20	.30	.50	5.75	—
1942S	85,590,000	—	—	.10	.20	.30	1.50	3.50	16.00	—

Lincoln Cent. Wheat Ears.

KM# 132a **Designer:** Victor D. Brenner. **Diameter:** 19 **Weight:** 2.7000 g. **Composition:** Zinc Coated Steel.

Date	Mintage	G-4	VG-8	F-12	VF-20	XF-40	AU-50	MS-60	MS-65	Prf-65
1943	684,628,670	—	—	.25	.30	.50	.70	.85	4.75	—
1943D	217,660,000	—	—	.25	.35	.60	.65	1.00	6.50	—
1943S	191,550,000	—	.30	.35	.40	.70	1.00	3.00	12.50	—

Lincoln Cent. Wheat Ears.

KM# A132 **Designer:** Victor D. Brenner. **Diameter:** 19 **Weight:** 3.1100 g. **Composition:** Copper-Zinc. **Notes:** KM#132 design and composition resumed.

Date	Mintage	XF-40	MS-65	Prf-65
1944	1,435,400,000	.20	2.00	—
1944D	430,578,000	.20	2.00	—
1944D/S	—	180	1,600	—
1944S	282,760,000	.20	5.50	—
1945	1,040,515,000	.20	2.00	—
1945D	226,268,000	.20	2.00	—
1945S	181,770,000	.20	5.50	—
1946	991,655,000	.20	2.00	—
1946D	315,690,000	.20	4.50	—
1946S	198,100,000	.20	4.60	—
1947	190,555,000	.20	2.25	—
1947D	194,750,000	.20	2.00	—
1947S	99,000,000	.20	5.50	—
1948	317,570,000	.20	2.00	—
1948D	172,637,000	.20	2.25	—
1948S	81,735,000	.20	5.50	—
1949	217,775,000	.20	3.50	—
1949D	153,132,000	.20	3.50	—
1949S	64,290,000	.25	6.00	—
1950	272,686,386	.20	1.75	40.00
1950D	334,950,000	.20	1.50	—
1950S	118,505,000	.20	2.50	—
1951	295,633,500	.20	2.00	40.00

Date	Mintage	XF-40	MS-65	Prf-65
1951D	625,355,000	.10	1.65	—
1951S	136,010,000	.15	3.00	—
1952	186,856,980	.15	3.00	34.00
1952D	746,130,000	.10	1.60	—
1952S	137,800,004	.15	5.00	—
1953	256,883,800	.10	1.25	28.00
1953D	700,515,000	.10	1.25	—
1953S	181,835,000	.15	1.75	—
1954	71,873,350	.15	1.25	9.00
1954D	251,552,500	.10	.50	—
1954S	96,190,000	.15	.75	—
1955	330,958,000	.10	.75	13.00
1955 doubled die	—	1,350	34,500	—

Note: The 1955 "doubled die" has distinct doubling of the date and lettering on the obverse.

Date	Mintage	XF-40	MS-65	Prf-65
1955D	563,257,500	.10	.75	—
1955S	44,610,000	.25	1.00	—
1956	421,414,384	—	.50	3.00
1956D	1,098,201,100	—	.50	—
1957	283,787,952	—	.50	2.00
1957D	1,051,342,000	—	.50	—
1958	253,400,652	—	.50	3.00
1958D	800,953,300	—	.50	—

Lincoln Cent. Lincoln Memorial.

KM# 201   Rev. Designer: Frank Gasparro. **Weight:** 3.1100 g. **Composition:** Copper-Zinc. **Notes:** The dates were modified in 1960, 1970 and 1982, resulting in large-date and small-date varieties for those years. The 1972 "doubled die" shows doubling of "In God We Trust." The 1979-S and 1981-S Type II proofs have a clearer mint mark than the Type I proofs of those years. Some 1982 cents have the predominantly copper composition; others have the predominantly zinc composition. They can be distinguished by weight.

Date	Mintage	XF-40	MS-65	Prf-65
1959	610,864,291	—	.50	1.50
1959D	1,279,760,000	—	.50	—
1960 small date	588,096,602	2.10	7.00	16.00
1960 large date	Inc. above	—	.30	1.25
1960D small date	1,580,884,000	—	.30	—
1960D large date	Inc. above	—	.30	—
1961	756,373,244	—	.30	1.00
1961D	1,753,266,700	—	.30	—
1962	609,263,019	—	.30	1.00
1962D	1,793,148,400	—	.30	—
1963	757,185,645	—	.30	1.00
1963D	1,774,020,400	—	.30	—
1964	2,652,525,762	—	.30	1.00
1964D	3,799,071,500	—	.30	—
1965	1,497,224,900	—	.30	—
1966	2,188,147,783	—	.30	—
1967	3,048,667,100	—	.50	—
1968	1,707,880,970	—	.30	—
1968D	2,886,269,600	—	.40	—
1968S	261,311,510	—	.40	1.00
1969	1,136,910,000	—	.60	—
1969D	4,002,832,200	—	.40	—
1969S	547,309,631	—	.40	1.10
1970	1,898,315,000	—	.40	—
1970D	2,891,438,900	—	.40	—
1970S	693,192,814	—	.40	1.20
1970S small date	—	—	55.00	60.00
1971	1,919,490,000	—	.35	—
1971D	2,911,045,600	—	.40	—
1971S	528,354,192	—	.25	1.20
1972	2,933,255,000	—	.25	—
1972 doubled die	—	275	715	—
1972D	2,665,071,400	—	.25	—
1972S	380,200,104	—	.25	1.15
1973	3,728,245,000	—	.25	—
1973D	3,549,576,588	—	.25	—
1973S	319,937,634	—	.25	0.80
1974	4,232,140,523	—	.25	—
1974D	4,235,098,000	—	.25	—
1974S	412,039,228	—	.25	0.75
1975	5,451,476,142	—	.25	—
1975D	4,505,245,300	—	.25	—
1975S	(2,845,450)	—	—	5.50

Date	Mintage	XF-40	MS-65	Prf-65
1976	4,674,292,426	—	.25	—
1976D	4,221,592,455	—	.25	—
1976S	(4,149,730)	—	—	5.00
1977	4,469,930,000	—	.25	—
1977D	4,149,062,300	—	.25	—
1977S	(3,251,152)	—	—	3.00
1978	5,558,605,000	—	.25	—
1978D	4,280,233,400	—	.25	—
1978S	(3,127,781)	—	—	3.50
1979	6,018,515,000	—	.25	—
1979D	4,139,357,254	—	.25	—
1979S type I, proof	(3,677,175)	—	—	4.00
1979S type II, proof	Inc. above	—	—	4.25
1980	7,414,705,000	—	.25	—
1980D	5,140,098,660	—	.25	—
1980S	(3,554,806)	—	—	2.25
1981	7,491,750,000	—	.25	—
1981S type II, proof	Inc. above	—	—	60.00
1981D	5,373,235,677	—	.25	—
1981S type I, proof	(4,063,083)	—	—	3.50
1982 large date	10,712,525,000	—	.25	—
1982 small date	—	—	.25	—
1982D large date	6,012,979,368	—	.25	—

Lincoln Cent. Lincoln Memorial.

KM# 201a **Diameter:** 19 **Weight:** 2.5000 g. **Composition:** Copper Plated Zinc.

Date	Mintage	XF-40	MS-65	Prf-65
1982 large date	—	—	.50	—
1982 small date	—	—	2.00	—
1982D large date	—	—	.30	—
1982D small date	—	—	.25	—

Lincoln Cent. Lincoln Memorial.

KM# 201b **Diameter:** 19 **Composition:** Copper Plated Zinc. **Notes:** The 1983 "doubled die reverse" shows doubling of "United States of America." The 1984 "doubled die" shows doubling of Lincoln's ear on the obverse.

Date	Mintage	XF-40	MS-65	Prf-65
1982S	(3,857,479)	—	—	3.00
1983	7,752,355,000	—	.25	—
1983 doubled die	—	—	400	—
1983D	6,467,199,428	—	.50	—
1983S	(3,279,126)	—	—	4.00
1984	8,151,079,000	—	.25	—
1984 doubled die	—	—	275	—
1984D	5,569,238,906	—	.75	—
1984S	(3,065,110)	—	—	4.50
1985	5,648,489,887	—	.25	—
1985D	5,287,399,926	—	.25	—
1985S	(3,362,821)	—	—	6.00
1986	4,491,395,493	—	1.50	—
1986D	4,442,866,698	—	1.25	—
1986S	(3,010,497)	—	—	7.50
1987	4,682,466,931	—	.25	—
1987D	4,879,389,514	—	.25	—
1987S	(4,227,728)	—	—	5.00
1988	6,092,810,000	—	.25	—
1988D	5,253,740,443	—	.25	—
1988S	(3,262,948)	—	—	12.50
1989	7,261,535,000	—	.25	—
1989D	5,345,467,111	—	.25	—
1989S	(3,220,194)	—	—	12.50
1990	6,851,765,000	—	.25	—
1990D	4,922,894,533	—	.25	—
1990S	(3,299,559)	—	—	5.75
1990 no S	—	—	—	2,750
1991	5,165,940,000	—	.25	—
1991D	4,158,442,076	—	.25	—
1991S	(2,867,787)	—	—	30.00
1992	4,648,905,000	—	.25	—
1992D	4,448,673,300	—	.25	—
1992S	(4,176,560)	—	—	5.50
1993	5,684,705,000	—	.25	—
1993D	6,426,650,571	—	.25	—
1993S	(3,394,792)	—	—	9.50
1994	6,500,850,000	—	.25	—
1994D	7,131,765,000	—	.25	—
1994S	(3,269,923)	—	—	8.50
1995	6,411,440,000	—	.25	—
1995 doubled die	—	20.00	50.00	—

Date	Mintage	XF-40	MS-65	Prf-65
1995D	7,128,560,000	—	.25	—
1995S	(2,707,481)	—	—	9.50
1996	6,612,465,000	—	.25	—
1996D	6,510,795,000	—	.25	—
1996S	(2,915,212)	—	—	6.50
1997	4,622,800,000	—	.25	—
1997D	4,576,555,000	—	.25	—
1997S	(2,796,678)	—	—	11.50
1998	5,032,155,000	—	.25	—
1998D	5,255,353,500	—	.25	—
1998S	(2,957,286)	—	—	9.50
1999	5,237,600,000	—	.25	—
1999D	6,360,065,000	—	.25	—
1999S	(3,362,462)	—	—	5.00
2000	5,503,200,000	—	.25	—
2000D	8,774,220,000	—	.25	—
2000S	(4,063,361)	—	—	4.00
2001P	4,959,600,000	—	.25	—
2001D	5,374,990,000	—	.25	—
2001S	(3,099,096)	—	—	4.00
2002P	3,260,800,000	—	.25	—
2002D	4,028,055,000	—	.25	—
2002S	(3,157,739)	—	—	4.00
2003P	—	—	.25	—
2003D	—	—	.25	—
2003S	(3,116,590)	—	—	4.00
2004S	—	—	—	—

2 CENTS

KM# 94 **Designer:** James B. Longacre. **Diameter:** 23 **Weight:** 6.2200 g. **Composition:** Copper-Tin-Zinc. **Notes:** The motto "In God We Trust" was modified in 1864, resulting in small-motto and large-motto varieties for that year.

Small motto   Large motto

Date	Mintage	G-4	VG-8	F-12	VF-20	XF-40	AU-50	MS-60	MS-65	Prf-65
1864 small motto	19,847,500	120	185	250	375	565	625	800	2,300	45,000
1864 large motto	Inc. above	14.50	15.00	18.50	25.00	34.00	65.00	70.00	500	1,400
1865	13,640,000	14.50	15.00	18.50	25.00	34.00	65.00	70.00	500	850
1866	3,177,000	14.50	17.00	20.00	28.00	34.00	65.00	70.00	630	850
1867	2,938,750	17.50	22.00	34.00	43.50	55.00	85.00	125	550	850
1868	2,803,750	17.50	22.00	34.00	43.50	57.50	95.00	135	625	850
1869	1,546,000	18.50	23.00	35.00	47.50	66.00	110	150	650	850
1870	861,250	23.50	30.00	41.50	46.00	100.00	150	235	750	850
1871	721,250	27.50	34.00	50.00	75.00	125	175	250	750	850
1872	65,000	315	360	445	625	780	860	1,100	3,300	900
1873 proof	Est. 1,100	1,175	1,300	1,400	1,475	1,525	1,600	—	—	2,500

SILVER 3 CENTS

Silver 3 Cents - Type 1.
No outlines in star.

KM# 75 **Designer:** James B. Longacre. **Diameter:** 14 **Weight:** 0.8000 g. **Composition:** 0.7500 Silver, 0.0193 oz. ASW.

Date	Mintage	G-4	VG-8	F-12	VF-20	XF-40	AU-50	MS-60	MS-65	Prf-65
1851	5,447,400	25.00	31.50	34.00	41.50	65.00	155	185	950	—
1851O	720,000	32.50	38.50	45.00	90.00	150	225	340	2,500	—
1852	18,663,500	23.50	30.00	33.50	41.50	62.50	145	160	950	—
1853	11,400,000	23.50	30.00	33.50	41.50	62.50	145	160	950	—

Silver 3 Cents - Type 2.
Three outlines in star.

KM# 80 **Designer:** James B. Longacre. **Diameter:** 14 **Weight:** 0.7500 g. **Composition:** 0.9000 Silver, 0.0218 oz. ASW.

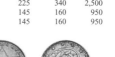

Date	Mintage	G-4	VG-8	F-12	VF-20	XF-40	AU-50	MS-60	MS-65	Prf-65
1854	671,000	25.00	31.50	34.00	47.50	100.00	225	350	3,450	33,500
1855	139,000	37.50	50.00	65.00	110	185	300	525	8,500	15,000
1856	1,458,000	26.00	34.00	39.00	57.50	100.00	190	275	4,500	15,500
1857	1,042,000	25.00	32.50	35.00	48.50	95.00	240	300	3,300	13,500
1858	1,604,000	25.00	32.50	35.00	46.00	95.00	190	240	3,300	6,400

Silver 3 Cents - Type 3.
Two outlines in star.

KM# 88 Designer: James B. Longacre. **Diameter:**
14 **Weight:** 0.7500 g. **Composition:** 0.9000 Silver,
0.0218 oz. ASW.

Date	Mintage	G-4	VG-8	F-12	VF-20	XF-40	AU-50	MS-60	MS-65	Prf-65
1859	365,000	26.00	34.00	39.00	50.00	71.00	155	170	900	2,150
1860	287,000	26.00	35.00	40.00	52.50	75.00	155	170	900	4,000
1861	498,000	25.00	32.50	35.00	45.00	66.00	150	170	900	1,800
1862	343,550	30.00	39.00	41.50	57.50	75.00	180	230	900	1,400
1863	21,460	325	355	390	420	450	585	720	2,250	1,350
1863/62 proof only; Rare	Inc. above	470	500	560	650	685	720	—	—	5,000
1864	12,470	325	355	390	420	450	585	675	1,700	1,350
1865	8,500	390	420	450	480	520	560	750	1,700	1,350
1866	22,725	325	355	390	420	440	500	650	1,900	1,325
1867	4,625	390	420	450	480	520	560	720	2,750	1,300
1868	4,100	390	420	450	480	520	560	720	5,750	1,400
1869	5,100	390	420	450	480	520	560	720	2,350	1,400
1869/68 proof only; Rare	Inc. above	—	—	—	—	—	—	—	—	—
1870	4,000	390	420	450	480	520	560	900	5,500	1,350
1871	4,360	390	420	450	480	520	560	750	1,700	1,450
1872	1,950	400	440	460	500	520	600	775	5,500	1,350
1873 proof only	600	650	685	730	800	850	975	—	—	2,000

NICKEL 3 CENTS

KM# 95 Designer: James B. Longacre. **Diameter:**
17.9 **Weight:** 1.9400 g. **Composition:** Copper-Nickel.

Date	Mintage	G-4	VG-8	F-12	VF-20	XF-40	AU-50	MS-60	MS-65	Prf-65
1865	11,382,000	14.00	15.50	16.50	23.50	32.50	55.00	100.00	675	6,500
1866	4,801,000	14.00	15.50	16.50	23.50	32.50	55.00	100.00	675	1,725
1867	3,915,000	14.00	15.50	16.50	23.50	32.50	55.00	100.00	850	1,575
1868	3,252,000	14.00	15.50	16.50	23.50	32.50	55.00	100.00	675	1,400
1869	1,604,000	14.00	16.00	17.50	25.00	34.00	60.00	115	775	1,000
1870	1,335,000	14.00	16.00	17.50	25.00	34.00	60.00	125	775	2,300
1871	604,000	14.00	16.00	19.00	26.00	35.00	62.50	135	800	1,200
1872	862,000	14.00	16.00	19.00	26.00	35.00	62.50	135	1,100	880
1873	1,173,000	14.00	16.00	19.00	26.00	35.00	62.50	135	1,400	1,050
1874	790,000	14.00	16.00	19.00	26.00	37.50	65.00	150	1,050	950
1875	228,000	15.00	17.50	20.00	27.50	41.50	75.00	170	825	1,700
1876	162,000	18.00	21.00	25.00	32.50	45.00	97.50	200	1,700	1,000
1877 proof	Est. 900	950	1,000	1,050	1,050	1,150	1,300	—	—	2,750
1878 proof	2,350	550	575	625	660	715	775	—	—	950
1879	41,200	60.00	70.00	90.00	100.00	110	150	250	850	580
1880	24,955	96.00	110	125	135	150	190	300	800	630
1881	1,080,575	15.00	15.50	18.00	25.00	34.00	55.00	100.00	715	580
1882	25,300	110	125	140	160	185	200	315	1,100	625
1883	10,609	185	200	260	285	330	375	480	4,350	580
1884	5,642	375	400	550	575	600	675	800	5,800	600
1885	4,790	435	480	640	660	700	775	850	2,300	650
1886 proof	4,290	320	330	345	385	385	415	—	—	580
1887/6 proof	7,961	350	390	415	450	450	485	—	—	750
1887	Inc. above	285	345	345	385	385	450	515	1,250	1,100
1888	41,083	47.50	57.50	62.50	70.00	90.00	135	235	725	580
1889	21,561	80.00	100.00	125	150	170	200	285	800	580

HALF DIME

Flowing Hair Half Dime.

KM# 15 Designer: Robert Scot. **Diameter:** 16.5
Weight: 1.3500 g. **Composition:** 0.8920 Silver,
0.0388 oz. ASW.

Date	Mintage	G-4	VG-8	F-12	VF-20	XF-40	MS-60
1794	86,416	1,000	1,250	1,750	2,700	4,800	13,500
1795	Inc. above	700	900	1,350	2,000	4,000	9,500

Draped Bust Half Dime. Small eagle.

KM# 23 Designer: Robert Scot. **Diameter:** 16.5
Weight: 1.3500 g. **Composition:** 0.8920 Silver,
0.0388 oz. ASW. **Notes:** Some 1796 strikes have
"Liberty" spelled as "Likerty." The 1797 strikes have
either 13, 15 or 16 stars on the obverse.

Date	Mintage	G-4	VG-8	F-12	VF-20	XF-40	MS-60
1796	10,230	1,000	1,350	2,000	3,500	6,000	13,500
1796 "Likerty"	Inc. above	1,100	1,400	2,100	3,750	6,250	14,500
1796/5	Inc. above	1,000	1,350	2,200	4,000	7,000	25,000
1797 13 stars	44,527	1,750	2,300	3,000	5,500	9,000	25,000
1797 15 stars	Inc. above	1,000	1,250	1,900	3,250	5,750	12,500
1797 16 stars	Inc. above	1,050	1,350	2,100	3,650	6,250	13,750

Draped Bust Half Dime. Heraldic eagle.

KM# 34 Designer: Robert Scot. **Diameter:** 16.5
Weight: 1.3500 g. **Composition:** 0.8920 Silver,
0.0388 oz. ASW. **Notes:** Some 1800 strikes have
"Liberty" spelled as "Libekty."

Date	Mintage	G-4	VG-8	F-12	VF-20	XF-40	MS-60
1800	24,000	575	750	1,500	2,500	4,250	9,000
1800 "Libekty"	Inc. above	600	800	1,575	2,650	4,400	9,300
1801	33,910	775	1,150	1,600	2,800	5,000	15,000
1802	13,010	17,500	25,000	40,000	65,000	85,000	185,000
1803 Large 8	37,850	750	950	1,300	2,000	4,000	9,000
1803 Small 8	Inc. above	950	1,400	1,900	3,000	5,500	11,500
1805	15,600	900	1,250	1,650	2,500	5,500	27,500

Liberty Cap Half Dime.

KM# 47 Designer: William Kneass. **Diameter:** 15.5
Weight: 1.3500 g. **Composition:** 0.8920 Silver, 0.0388
oz. ASW. **Notes:** Design modifications in 1835, 1836
and 1837 resulted in variety combinations with large and
small dates, and large and small "5C." inscriptions on the
reverse.

Date	Mintage	G-4	VG-8	F-12	VF-20	XF-40	AU-50	MS-60	MS-65
1829	1,230,000	27.50	36.00	48.00	80.00	140	250	350	2,650
1830	1,240,000	25.00	36.00	48.00	75.00	140	250	350	2,650
1831	1,242,700	25.00	36.00	48.00	75.00	140	250	350	2,600
1832	965,000	25.00	36.00	48.00	75.00	140	250	350	2,600
1833	1,370,000	25.00	36.00	48.00	75.00	140	250	350	2,650
1834	1,480,000	25.00	36.00	48.00	75.00	140	250	350	2,600
1835 lg. dt., lg. 5C.	2,760,000	25.00	36.00	48.00	75.00	140	250	350	2,600
1835 lg. dt., sm. 5C	Inc. above	25.00	36.00	48.00	75.00	140	250	350	2,600
1835 sm. dt., lg. 5C	Inc. above	25.00	36.00	48.00	75.00	140	250	350	2,600
1835 sm. dt., sm. 5C	Inc. above	25.00	36.00	48.00	75.00	140	250	350	2,600
1836 lg. 5C.	1,900,000	25.00	36.00	48.00	75.00	140	250	350	2,600
1836 sm. 5C.	Inc. above	25.00	36.00	48.00	75.00	140	250	350	2,600
1837 lg. 5C.	2,276,000	27.50	36.00	48.00	80.00	140	250	350	3,500
1837 sm. 5C.	Inc. above	33.00	40.00	55.00	100.00	200	450	950	8,750

Seated Liberty Half Dime.
No stars around rim.

KM# 60 Designer: Christian Gobrecht. **Diameter:**
15.5 **Weight:** 1.3400 g. **Composition:** 0.9000 Silver,
0.0388 oz. ASW. **Notes:** A design modification in 1837
resulted in small-date and large-date varieties for that
year.

Date	Mintage	G-4	VG-8	F-12	VF-20	XF-40	AU-50	MS-60	MS-65
1837 small date	Inc. above	30.00	42.00	62.50	115	190	485	800	3,900
1837 large date	Inc. above	34.00	46.00	70.00	125	200	375	625	3,250
1838O	70,000	80.00	125	225	400	750	1,450	2,000	25,000

Seated Liberty Half Dime.
Stars around rim. No drapery.

KM# 62.1 Designer: Christian Gobrecht. **Diameter:**
15.5 **Weight:** 1.3400 g. **Composition:** 0.9000 Silver,
0.0388 oz. ASW. **Notes:** The two varieties of 1838 are
distinguished by the size of the stars on the obverse. The
1839-O with reverse of 1838-O was struck from rusted
reverse dies. The result is a bumpy surface on this
variety's reverse.

Date	Mintage	G-4	VG-8	F-12	VF-20	XF-40	AU-50	MS-60	MS-65
1838 large stars	2,255,000	15.00	17.50	20.00	27.50	70.00	150	250	2,250
1838 small stars	Inc. above	18.00	27.50	45.00	100.00	175	315	650	3,850
1839	1,069,150	16.00	18.50	21.00	30.00	75.00	160	250	2,500
1839O	1,034,039	17.50	20.00	25.00	35.00	93.50	185	550	5,500
1839O reverse 1838O	—	375	575	750	1,200	2,250	3,500	—	—
1840	1,344,085	16.00	18.50	21.00	30.00	75.00	16.00	250	2,100
1840O	935,000	17.50	20.00	23.50	40.00	80.00	215	700	17,000

Seated Liberty Half Dime. Drapery
added to Liberty's left elbow.

KM# 62.2 Designer: Christian Gobrecht. **Diameter:**
15.5 **Weight:** 1.3400 g. **Composition:** 0.9000 Silver,
0.0388 oz. ASW. **Notes:** In 1840 drapery was added to
Liberty's left elbow. Varieties for the 1848 Philadelphia
strikes are distinguished by the size of the numerals in
the date.

Date	Mintage	G-4	VG-8	F-12	VF-20	XF-40	AU-50	MS-60	MS-65
1840	Inc. above	25.00	40.00	75.00	125	225	350	450	300
1840O	Inc. above	35.00	60.00	115	190	450	1,250	6,500	—
1841	1,150,000	15.00	17.50	21.00	28.50	56.00	115	160	1,250
1841O	815,000	17.50	20.00	25.00	43.50	110	280	650	6,500
1842	815,000	15.00	17.50	20.00	27.50	55.00	115	160	1,750
1842O	350,000	30.00	45.00	75.00	225	500	1,250	2,500	—
1843	1,165,000	15.00	17.50	20.00	27.50	55.00	110	160	1,350
1844	430,000	17.50	20.00	22.50	31.50	56.00	115	175	1,150
1844O	220,000	75.00	105	175	450	1,000	2,250	5,400	25,000
1845	1,564,000	15.00	17.50	20.00	33.50	56.00	110	160	1,150
1845/1845	Inc. above	16.00	20.00	22.50	35.00	60.00	115	160	1,200
1846	27,000	300	450	750	1,150	2,250	3,600	8,500	—
1847	1,274,000	15.00	17.50	20.00	27.50	55.00	110	160	1,150
1848 medium date	668,000	17.50	20.00	23.50	30.00	57.50	125	230	2,850
1848 large date	Inc. above	22.50	30.00	45.00	65.00	135	275	450	4,000
1848O	600,000	19.00	25.00	33.00	50.00	110	265	400	1,950
1849/8	1,309,000	28.50	35.00	47.50	62.50	125	250	625	2,600
1849/6	Inc. above	20.00	26.00	30.00	52.50	105	200	400	2,500
1849	Inc. above	16.00	18.50	27.50	50.00	65.00	125	180	1,700
1849O	140,000	29.00	40.00	95.00	225	475	975	1,950	14,000
1850	955,000	17.50	20.00	23.50	31.50	60.00	115	165	1,400
1850O	690,000	18.50	22.50	30.00	56.00	125	280	675	4,250
1851	781,000	15.00	17.50	20.00	27.50	56.00	110	160	1,500
1851O	860,000	17.50	20.00	25.00	41.50	110	220	500	4,350
1852	1,000,500	15.00	17.50	20.00	27.50	56.00	110	160	1,150
1852O	260,000	23.00	32.00	65.00	135	275	475	750	10,000
1853	135,000	32.50	43.50	67.50	125	220	385	750	3,000
1853O	160,000	225	265	375	675	1,350	2,750	500	25,000

Seated Liberty Half Dime.
Arrows at date.

KM# 76 **Designer:** Christian Gobrecht. **Weight:**
1.2400 g. **Composition:** 0.9000 Silver, 0.0362 oz. ASW.

Date	Mintage	G-4	VG-8	F-12	VF-20	XF-40	AU-50	MS-60	MS-65	Prf-65
1853	13,210,020	11.00	12.00	14.00	17.00	50.00	120	190	1,850	35,000
1853O	2,200,000	12.00	14.00	16.00	25.00	65.00	135	275	3,500	—
1854	5,740,000	10.50	12.00	14.00	17.00	45.00	110	185	1,850	16,000
1854O	1,560,000	11.00	13.00	15.00	23.00	60.00	145	250	4,250	—
1855	1,750,000	11.00	13.00	15.00	18.00	47.00	115	190	1,950	18,000
1855O	600,000	15.00	20.00	30.00	55.00	135	235	600	4,000	—

Seated Liberty Half Dime.
Arrows at date removed.

KM# A62.2 **Designer:** Christian Gobrecht. **Weight:**
1.2400 g. **Composition:** 0.9000 Silver, 0.0362 oz. ASW.
Notes: On the 1858/inverted date variety, the date was
engraved into the die upside down and then re-engraved
right side up. Another 1858 variety has the date doubled.

Date	Mintage	G-4	VG-8	F-12	VF-20	XF-40	AU-50	MS-60	MS-65	Prf-65
1856	4,880,000	13.50	16.00	17.50	23.50	50.00	115	170	1,650	15,000
1856O	1,100,000	16.00	18.50	20.00	46.00	95.00	250	550	2,000	—
1857	7,280,000	13.50	16.00	17.50	23.50	50.00	110	170	1,550	5,500
1857O	1,380,000	15.00	16.00	18.50	37.50	60.00	185	325	1,800	—
1858	3,500,000	13.50	16.00	17.50	23.50	55.00	175	300	1,700	5,500
1858 inverted date	Inc. above	30.00	43.50	62.50	90.00	185	275	675	3,000	—
1858 double date	Inc. above	45.00	60.00	90.00	175	285	425	700	—	—
1858O	1,660,000	15.00	16.00	20.00	42.50	75.00	135	265	1,600	—
1859	340,000	16.00	17.50	21.50	34.00	70.00	135	225	1,550	4,000
1859O	560,000	17.50	20.00	28.50	43.50	115	200	260	1,850	—

Seated Liberty Half Dime. "United
States of America" replaced stars.

KM# 91 **Designer:** Christian Gobrecht. **Weight:**
1.2400 g. **Composition:** 0.9000 Silver, 0.0362 oz. ASW.
Notes: In 1860 the legend "United States of America"
replaced the stars on the obverse.

Date	Mintage	G-4	VG-8	F-12	VF-20	XF-40	AU-50	MS-60	MS-65	Prf-65
1860	799,000	13.50	16.00	17.50	21.00	40.00	72.50	125	1,150	1,850
1860O	1,060,000	13.50	16.00	18.50	25.00	43.50	93.50	180	1,450	—
1861	3,361,000	13.50	16.00	17.50	21.00	40.00	72.50	125	1,175	2,500
1861/0	Inc. above	25.00	32.50	59.00	125	260	435	560	4,000	—
1862	1,492,550	20.00	25.00	33.50	43.50	55.00	93.50	160	1,150	1,650
1863	18,460	190	225	275	375	475	550	700	1,650	1,700
1863S	100,000	25.00	35.00	50.00	75.00	150	295	700	2,500	—
1864	48,470	325	425	500	600	800	1,000	1,250	2,250	1,750
1864S	90,000	50.00	65.00	100.00	150	250	450	700	3,750	—
1865	13,500	325	400	450	550	650	875	1,000	1,950	1,750
1865S	120,000	25.00	35.00	50.00	75.00	135	375	800	—	—
1866	10,725	350	450	550	650	800	1,000	1,250	2,550	1,700
1866S	120,000	25.00	35.00	50.00	75.00	135	285	450	5,000	—
1867	8,625	450	550	675	800	900	1,100	1,300	2,250	1,750
1867S	120,000	25.00	35.00	50.00	75.00	135	295	550	3,850	—
1868	89,200	55.00	70.00	110	170	250	375	570	2,400	1,750
1868S	280,000	20.00	25.00	30.00	40.00	55.00	125	300	3,250	—
1869	208,600	20.00	25.00	30.00	40.00	55.00	125	235	1,500	1,750
1869S	230,000	18.00	22.00	29.00	35.00	50.00	115	325	4,000	—
1870	536,600	18.00	22.00	29.00	35.00	50.00	125	175	1,200	1,650
1870S unique	—	—	—	—	—	—	—	—	—	—

Note: 1870S, Superior Galleries, July 1986, brilliant uncirculated, $253,000.

Date	Mintage	G-4	VG-8	F-12	VF-20	XF-40	AU-50	MS-60	MS-65	Prf-65
1871	1,873,960	14.00	16.00	17.50	21.00	37.50	75.00	125	1,250	1,650
1871S	161,000	25.00	30.00	45.00	60.00	85.00	175	250	2,450	—
1872	2,947,950	14.00	16.00	17.50	21.00	37.50	75.00	125	1,200	1,650
1872S mint mark in wreath	837,000	14.00	16.00	17.50	21.00	37.50	75.00	125	1,200	—
1872S mint mark below wreath	Inc. above	14.00	16.00	17.50	21.00	37.50	75.00	125	1,200	—
1873	712,600	14.00	16.00	17.50	21.00	37.50	75.00	125	1,300	1,750
1873S	324,000	20.00	25.00	30.00	39.00	50.00	90.00	150	1,350	—

5 CENTS

Shield Nickel. Rays between stars.

KM# 96 **Designer:** James B. Longacre. **Diameter:** 20.5 **Weight:** 5.0000 g. **Composition:** Copper-Nickel.

Date	Mintage	G-4	VG-8	F-12	VF-20	XF-40	AU-50	MS-60	MS-65	Prf-65
1866	14,742,500	27.50	38.50	50.00	70.00	155	235	250	2,700	3,400
1867	2,019,000	34.00	46.00	62.50	92.50	190	285	335	4,150	75,000

Shield Nickel. No rays between stars.

KM# 97 **Weight:** 5.0000 g. **Composition:** Copper-Nickel.

Date	Mintage	G-4	VG-8	F-12	VF-20	XF-40	AU-50	MS-60	MS-65	Prf-65
1867	28,890,500	16.00	17.50	22.00	30.00	45.00	72.50	110	950	2,750
1868	28,817,000	16.00	17.50	22.00	30.00	45.00	72.50	110	1,000	1,400
1869	16,395,000	16.00	17.50	22.00	30.00	45.00	72.50	110	775	1,025
1870	4,806,000	22.00	26.00	43.50	55.00	75.00	115	177.5	1,650	1,275
1871	561,000	60.00	72.50	100.00	135	200	240	325	2,000	1,075
1872	6,036,000	22.00	27.50	46.00	55.00	67.50	110	165	1,350	750
1873	4,550,000	22.00	27.50	43.50	52.50	65.00	100.00	160	2,400	800
1874	3,538,000	25.00	34.00	57.50	67.50	85.00	115	185	1,500	850
1875	2,097,000	30.00	41.50	68.50	90.00	115	155	200	2,000	1,750
1876	2,530,000	30.00	38.50	62.50	85.00	110	140	200	1,900	950
1877 proof	Est. 900	1,350	1,500	1,650	1,900	2,000	2,000	—	—	4,000
1878 proof	2,350	650	700	825	970	1,050	1,200	—	—	1,700
1879	29,100	375	460	575	600	650	715	850	1,800	790
1880	19,995	500	600	700	850	1,250	1,750	3,450	40,000	650
1881	72,375	235	320	430	475	570	685	775	1,650	630
1882	11,476,600	16.00	17.50	22.00	30.00	45.00	72.50	110	750	600
1883	1,456,919	17.00	22.00	28.00	37.50	50.00	75.00	115	675	570
1883/2	—	160	220	285	345	600	750	920	3,800	—

Liberty Nickel. Without "Cents" below "V".

KM# 111 **Designer:** Charles E. Barber. **Diameter:** 21.2 **Weight:** 5.0000 g. **Composition:** Copper-Nickel.

Date	Mintage	G-4	VG-8	F-12	VF-20	XF-40	AU-50	MS-60	MS-65	Prf-65
1883	5,479,519	4.75	5.50	6.50	6.25	8.00	11.50	24.00	275	1,000

Liberty Nickel. "Cents" below "V".

KM# 112 **Weight:** 5.0000 g. **Composition:** Copper Nickel.

Date	Mintage	G-4	VG-8	F-12	VF-20	XF-40	AU-50	MS-60	MS-65	Prf-65
1883	16,032,983	11.00	15.00	30.00	45.00	80.00	105	150	675	500
1884	11,273,942	17.50	27.50	38.50	52.50	80.00	125	185	2,000	575
1885	1,476,490	500	600	775	925	1,100	1,300	1,550	7,000	1,350
1886	3,330,290	195	250	375	480	630	765	850	8,250	850
1887	15,263,652	9.00	13.50	30.00	45.00	75.00	95.00	130	1,400	525
1888	10,720,483	22.50	32.50	57.50	110	160	220	275	2,000	525
1889	15,881,361	6.25	11.00	27.50	45.00	67.50	100.00	135	1,000	525
1890	16,259,272	7.00	16.00	27.50	41.50	65.00	110	160	1,950	650
1891	16,834,350	6.00	8.00	20.00	32.50	60.00	100.00	150	1,150	525
1892	11,699,642	7.00	10.00	22.00	35.00	60.00	115	150	1,500	525
1893	13,370,195	6.00	8.00	22.00	32.50	60.00	100.00	135	1,650	525

Date	Mintage	G-4	VG-8	F-12	VF-20	XF-40	AU-50	MS-60	MS-65	Prf-65
1894	5,413,132	12.00	27.00	83.50	140	200	275	330	1,500	525
1895	9,979,884	4.00	5.50	25.00	40.00	60.00	100.00	135	2,750	650
1896	8,842,920	8.00	16.00	39.00	58.50	80.00	135	190	2,400	620
1897	20,428,735	3.00	6.00	14.00	26.00	41.50	65.00	95.00	1,250	600
1898	12,532,087	2.00	4.50	10.00	21.00	36.00	70.00	140	1,250	500
1899	26,029,031	1.50	3.00	9.00	18.00	28.00	54.00	94.00	650	500
1900	27,255,995	1.50	3.00	8.00	18.00	35.00	70.00	88.00	675	500
1901	26,480,213	1.50	2.50	7.00	15.00	30.00	53.50	75.00	650	500
1902	31,480,579	1.50	2.50	5.00	15.00	27.00	53.50	77.50	650	500
1903	28,006,725	1.50	2.50	5.00	15.00	28.00	53.50	80.00	675	500
1904	21,404,984	1.50	2.50	5.00	11.00	26.00	53.50	72.50	700	725
1905	29,827,276	1.50	2.00	5.00	12.00	26.00	53.50	72.50	650	500
1906	38,613,725	1.50	2.00	5.00	12.00	26.00	53.50	70.00	1,000	500
1907	39,214,800	1.50	2.00	5.00	12.00	26.00	53.50	72.50	1,500	625
1908	22,686,177	1.50	2.00	5.00	12.00	26.00	53.50	72.50	1,250	500
1909	11,590,526	2.00	2.50	5.00	14.00	30.00	60.00	82.50	1,300	500
1910	30,169,353	1.50	2.00	5.00	11.00	23.00	48.50	65.00	750	500
1911	39,559,372	1.50	2.00	5.00	10.00	23.00	48.50	65.00	650	500
1912	26,236,714	1.50	2.00	5.00	10.00	23.00	48.50	65.00	675	575
1912D	8,474,000	2.00	3.00	9.50	32.50	65.00	150	275	2,200	—
1912S	238,000	140	170	240	480	800	1,250	1,500	6,750	—
1913 5 known	—	—	—	—	—	—	—	—	—	—

Note: 1913, Superior Sale, March 2001, Proof, $1,840,000.

Buffalo Nickel.
Buffalo standing on a mound.

KM# 133 **Designer:** James Earle Fraser. **Diameter:**
21.2 **Weight:** 5.0000 g. **Composition:** Copper-Nickel.

Date	Mintage	G-4	VG-8	F-12	VF-20	XF-40	AU-50	MS-60	MS-65	Prf-65
1913	30,993,520	7.50	9.50	10.00	11.50	18.50	23.50	32.50	150	3,500
1913D	5,337,000	12.50	15.00	19.00	25.00	35.00	50.00	62.50	315	—
1913S	2,105,000	35.00	42.00	50.00	60.00	75.00	92.50	125	700	—

Buffalo Nickel. Buffalo standing on a line.

KM# 134 **Designer:** James Earle Fraser. **Diameter:** 21.2 **Weight:** 5.0000 g. **Composition:** Copper Nickel. **Notes:** In 1913
the reverse design was modified so the ground under the buffalo was represented as a line rather than a mound. On the 1937D
3-legged variety, the buffalo's right front leg is missing, the result of a damaged die.

1918/17D

1937D 3-legged

Date	Mintage	G-4	VG-8	F-12	VF-20	XF-40	AU-50	MS-60	MS-65	Prf-65
1913	29,858,700	7.50	9.50	11.00	12.50	18.50	25.00	34.00	35.00	2,500
1913D	4,156,000	100.00	130	155	170	195	225	285	1,500	—
1913S	1,209,000	300	350	400	465	535	620	795	4,250	—
1914	20,665,738	15.00	16.50	19.00	21.50	27.50	37.50	45.00	450	2,350
1914D	3,912,000	75.00	100.00	140	185	275	340	415	1,750	—
1914S	3,470,000	23.50	33.50	43.50	62.50	90.00	135	150	2,300	—
1915	20,987,270	4.75	5.50	6.75	11.00	21.50	38.50	48.50	305	2,000
1915D	7,569,500	16.00	21.50	33.50	62.50	110	140	225	2,500	—
1915S	1,505,000	40.00	57.50	85.00	185	320	450	575	3,400	—
1916	63,498,066	3.75	5.00	5.50	6.75	12.50	19.00	41.00	350	3,850
1916/16	Inc. above	1,900	4,250	7,800	11,000	14,000	35,500	49,000	395,000	—
1916D	13,333,000	11.00	17.50	25.00	38.50	82.50	110	150	2,500	—
1916S	11,860,000	9.50	13.50	20.00	35.00	75.00	115	175	2,650	—
1917	51,424,029	3.75	5.00	6.25	8.50	13.50	31.00	55.00	540	—
1917D	9,910,800	16.00	23.00	47.50	80.00	130	255	330	4,400	—
1917S	4,193,000	23.00	35.00	70.00	110	170	285	380	5,250	—
1918	32,086,314	3.40	4.15	6.75	15.00	31.00	48.50	95.00	1,700	—
1918/17D	8,362,314	1,050	1,500	2,750	6,250	9,600	11,500	28,500	285,000	—
1918D	Inc. above	17.50	30.00	47.50	130	220	330	410	5,000	—
1918S	4,882,000	12.50	27.50	47.50	100.00	175	300	480	32,500	—
1919	60,868,000	1.35	2.10	3.25	7.00	15.00	30.00	55.00	595	—
1919D	8,006,000	12.50	23.50	55.00	115	235	335	540	8,000	—
1919S	7,521,000	8.00	20.00	47.50	110	225	360	510	19,000	—
1920	63,093,000	1.35	2.10	2.80	7.00	15.00	30.00	54.00	850	—
1920D	9,418,000	7.00	13.50	32.50	100.00	275	340	535	7,800	—

Date	Mintage	G-4	VG-8	F-12	VF-20	XF-40	AU-50	MS-60	MS-65	Prf-65
1920S	9,689,000	3.50	8.25	27.50	96.00	200	300	500	28,500	—
1921	10,663,000	3.75	6.25	8.50	25.00	53.50	70.00	115	850	—
1921S	1,557,000	65.00	110	200	545	845	1,100	1,500	8,000	—
1923	35,715,000	1.70	2.80	4.25	7.00	13.50	37.50	55.00	750	—
1923S	6,142,000	7.00	9.50	23.00	125	260	335	460	12,500	—
1924	21,620,000	1.00	1.60	4.15	9.60	19.00	41.00	70.00	950	—
1924D	5,258,000	7.50	11.00	30.00	85.00	200	285	340	5,600	—
1924S	1,437,000	16.00	32.50	96.00	470	1,100	1,700	2,250	12,000	—
1925	35,565,100	2.00	2.50	3.75	8.50	17.50	30.00	40.00	545	—
1925D	4,450,000	7.00	15.00	35.00	80.00	160	240	350	6,600	—
1925S	6,256,000	4.00	8.50	15.00	75.00	170	240	395	45,000	—
1926	44,693,000	.75	.80	2.80	5.40	11.50	20.00	30.00	185	—
1926D	5,638,000	7.50	13.50	28.50	100.00	170	285	295	5,500	—
1926S	970,000	19.00	33.50	82.50	420	920	2,800	4,500	115,000	—
1927	37,981,000	.75	.80	2.15	4.15	12.50	20.00	32.50	300	—
1927D	5,730,000	1.85	4.00	5.50	27.50	75.00	110	150	9,000	—
1927S	3,430,000	2.00	3.00	5.00	31.00	80.00	160	485	22,000	—
1928	23,411,000	.85	.90	2.20	4.15	12.50	23.00	30.00	325	—
1928D	6,436,000	1.10	2.10	3.45	15.00	40.00	45.00	50.00	1,000	—
1928S	6,936,000	1.35	1.50	2.20	11.50	27.50	100.00	215	5,500	—
1929	36,446,000	.75	.80	2.15	4.15	12.50	20.00	31.00	375	—
1929D	8,370,000	.85	1.10	3.00	6.75	32.50	42.50	55.00	2,000	—
1929S	7,754,000	.80	.85	2.25	5.00	11.50	25.00	47.50	500	—
1930	22,849,000	.75	.80	2.15	4.15	11.50	20.00	30.00	220	—
1930S	5,435,000	1.00	1.25	2.50	3.75	13.50	30.00	47.50	515	—
1931S	1,200,000	15.00	18.00	20.00	22.00	27.50	42.50	50.00	315	—
1934	20,213,003	.75	.85	2.15	4.15	10.00	19.00	47.50	440	—
1934D	7,480,000	1.35	2.50	3.40	8.50	20.00	50.00	82.50	960	—
1935	58,264,000	.75	.80	.85	1.30	1.80	8.50	19.00	115	—
1935D	12,092,000	1.35	2.20	2.50	7.50	19.50	45.00	70.00	475	—
1935S	10,300,000	.75	.80	.85	1.40	3.00	15.00	50.00	185	—
1936	119,001,420	.75	.80	.85	1.00	1.50	6.50	15.00	100.00	1,100
1936D	24,814,000	.75	.80	.85	1.00	1.50	11.00	35.00	100.00	—
1936S	14,930,000	.75	.80	.85	1.00	1.50	9.50	35.00	110	—
1937	79,485,769	.75	.80	.85	1.00	1.50	6.50	14.50	27.50	850
1937D	17,826,000	.75	.80	.85	1.10	1.50	8.00	27.50	62.50	—
1937D 3-legged	Inc. above	470	530	800	970	1,100	1,300	2,550	27,500	—
1937S	5,635,000	.90	1.00	1.20	1.50	2.25	8.00	27.50	67.50	—
1938D	7,020,000	1.50	1.75	1.90	2.00	2.80	8.00	20.00	42.50	—
1938D/D	—	2.50	4.50	6.00	8.00	10.00	17.00	20.00	60.00	—
1938D/S	Inc. above	4.50	6.75	9.00	12.50	16.00	30.00	50.00	185	—

Jefferson Nickel.

KM# 192 Designer: Felix Schlag. **Diameter:** 21.2
Weight: 5.0000 g. **Composition:** Copper-Nickel.
Notes: Some 1939 strikes have doubling of the word
"Monticello" on the reverse.

Date	Mintage	VG-8	F-12	VF-20	XF-40	MS-60	MS-65	-65FS	Prf-65
1938	19,515,365	.25	.40	.80	1.25	4.00	8.50	125	70.00
1938D	5,376,000	.90	1.00	1.25	1.75	3.50	8.00	95.00	—
1938S	4,105,000	1.75	2.00	2.50	3.00	4.75	8.50	165	—
1939 T I	—	—	—	—	—	—	—	300	70.00
1939 T II	120,627,535	—	.20	.25	.30	1.75	3.50	40.00	300
1939 doubled Monticello T II	—	30.00	50.00	80.00	140	250	750	900	—
1939D T I	—	—	—	—	—	—	—	275	—
1939D T II	3,514,000	3.00	3.50	5.00	10.00	42.00	125	250	—
1939S T I	—	—	—	—	—	—	—	250	—
1939S T II	6,630,000	.45	.60	1.50	2.75	15.00	45.00	275	—
1940	176,499,158	—	—	—	.25	1.00	3.00	35.00	65.00
1940D	43,540,000	—	.20	.30	.40	1.50	2.75	25.00	—
1940S	39,690,000	—	.20	.25	.50	2.50	6.00	45.00	—
1941	203,283,720	—	—	—	.20	.75	2.50	40.00	60.00
1941D	53,432,000	—	.20	.30	.50	2.50	6.00	25.00	—
1941S	43,445,000	—	.20	.30	.50	3.75	6.75	60.00	—
1942	49,818,600	—	—	—	.40	5.00	8.50	75.00	55.00
1942D	13,938,000	.30	.40	1.00	2.00	27.00	60.00	70.00	—

Note: Fully Struck Full Step nickels command higher prices. Bright, Fully Struck coins command even higher prices. 1938 thru 1989 - 5
Full Steps. 1990 to date - 6 Full Steps. Without bag marks or nicks on steps.

Jefferson Nickel. Mint mark above Monticello.

KM# 192a   Designer: Felix Schlag. **Diameter:** 21.2 **Composition:** Copper-Silver-Manganese, 0 oz. **Notes:** War-time composition nickels have a large mint mark above Monticello on the reverse. Composition: 0.350 Silver, .0563 oz. ASW.

1943/2P

Date	Mintage	VG-8	F-12	VF-20	XF-40	MS-60	MS-65	-65FS	Prf-65
1942P	57,900,600	.65	.85	1.00	1.75	6.00	22.50	70.00	140
1942S	32,900,000	.70	1.00	1.10	1.75	6.00	20.00	125	—
1943P	271,165,000	.50	.85	1.00	1.50	2.75	15.00	35.00	—
1943/2P	Inc. above	35.00	50.00	75.00	110	250	650	1,000	—
1943D	15,294,000	.90	1.20	1.50	1.75	4.00	13.00	30.00	—
1943S	104,060,000	.55	.70	1.00	1.50	3.00	13.00	55.00	—
1944P	119,150,000	.50	.70	1.00	1.50	4.00	22.50	100.00	—
1944D	32,309,000	.60	.80	1.00	1.75	6.50	17.50	30.00	—
1944S	21,640,000	.70	1.00	1.25	2.00	3.50	14.00	185	—
1945P	119,408,100	.50	.70	1.00	1.50	3.50	13.50	125	—
1945D	37,158,000	.55	.75	1.00	1.50	3.50	13.00	40.00	—
1945S	58,939,000	.50	.70	.80	.90	3.00	14.00	250	—

Note: Fully Struck Full Step nickels command higher prices. Bright, Fully Struck coins command even higher prices. 1938 thru 1989 - 5 Full Steps. 1990 to date - 6 Full Steps. Without bag marks or nicks on steps.

Jefferson Nickel. Pre-war design resumed.

KM# A192   Designer: Felix Schlag. **Diameter:** 21.2 **Weight:** 5.0000 g. **Composition:** Copper-Nickel. **Notes:** KM#192 design and composition resumed. The 1979-S and 1981-S Type II proofs have clearer mint marks than the Type I proofs of those years.

Date	Mintage	VG-8	F-12	VF-20	XF-40	MS-60	MS-65	-65FS	Prf-65
1946	161,116,000	—	—	.20	.25	.80	3.50	40.00	—
1946D	45,292,200	—	—	.25	.35	.95	3.50	30.00	—
1946S	13,560,000	—	—	.30	.40	.50	2.00	45.00	—
1947	95,000,000	—	—	.20	.25	.75	2.00	30.00	—
1947D	37,822,000	—	—	.20	.30	.90	2.50	30.00	—
1947S	24,720,000	—	—	.20	.25	1.00	2.25	55.00	—
1948	89,348,000	—	—	.20	.25	.50	2.50	60.00	—
1948D	44,734,000	—	—	.25	.35	1.20	4.50	30.00	—
1948S	11,300,000	—	—	.25	.50	1.20	3.50	45.00	—
1949	60,652,000	—	—	.25	.30	2.25	6.00	200	—
1949D	36,498,000	—	—	.30	.40	1.25	5.00	75.00	—
1949D/S	Inc. above	—	35.00	40.00	65.00	170	325	1,750	—
1949S	9,716,000	.25	.35	.45	.90	1.50	3.50	145	—
1950	9,847,386	.20	.30	.35	.75	1.50	4.75	150	45.00
1950D	2,630,030	9.00	9.50	10.00	11.00	16.00	27.50	45.00	—
1951	28,609,500	—	—	.40	.50	1.50	9.00	90.00	30.00
1951D	20,460,000	.25	.30	.40	.50	3.00	10.00	45.00	—
1951S	7,776,000	.30	.40	.50	1.10	1.75	5.00	150	—
1952	64,069,980	—	—	.20	.25	.85	4.50	125	26.00
1952D	30,638,000	—	—	.30	.45	2.00	7.00	65.00	—
1952S	20,572,000	—	—	.20	.25	.75	3.50	195	—
1953	46,772,800	—	—	.20	.25	.40	1.50	200	28.00
1953D	59,878,600	—	—	.20	.25	.40	1.50	100.00	—
1953S	19,210,900	—	—	.20	.25	.60	2.50	1,750	—
1954	47,917,350	—	—	—	—	.60	2.00	95.00	16.00
1954D	117,136,560	—	—	—	—	.35	2.00	175	—
1954S	29,384,000	—	—	—	.20	1.00	3.00	1,000	—
1954S/D	Inc. above	—	6.00	9.00	13.00	22.00	65.00	—	—
1955	8,266,200	.25	.35	.40	.45	.75	2.00	85.00	16.00
1955D	74,464,100	—	—	—	—	.20	1.00	150	—
1955D/S	Inc. above	—	5.00	8.50	13.00	33.00	75.00	—	—
1956	35,885,384	—	—	—	—	.30	.70	35.00	2.50
1956D	67,222,940	—	—	—	—	.25	.60	90.00	—
1957	39,655,952	—	—	—	—	.25	.60	40.00	1.50
1957D	136,828,900	—	—	—	—	.25	.60	55.00	—
1958	17,963,652	—	—	.15	.20	.30	.65	80.00	6.00
1958D	168,249,120	—	—	—	—	.25	.60	30.00	—

Note: Fully Struck Full Step nickels command higher prices. Bright, Fully Struck coins command even higher prices. 1938 thru 1989 - 5 Full Steps. 1990 to date - 6 Full Steps. Without bag marks or nicks on steps.

83

Date	Mintage	MS-65	-65FS	Prf-65
1959	28,397,291	.65	30.00	1.25
1959D	160,738,240	.55	45.00	—
1960	57,107,602	2.00	60.00	1.00
1960D	192,582,180	.55	650	—
1961	76,668,244	.55	100.00	1.00
1961D	229,342,760	.55	800	—
1962	100,602,019	1.50	75.00	1.00
1962D	280,195,720	.55	600	—
1963	178,851,645	.55	45.00	1.00
1963D	276,829,460	.55	650	—
1964	1,028,622,762	.55	55.00	1.00
1964D	1,787,297,160	.50	500	—
1965	136,131,380	.50	225	—
1966	156,208,283	.50	350	—
1967	107,325,800	.50	275	—
1968 none minted	—	—	—	—
1968D	91,227,880	.50	750	—
1968S	103,437,510	.50	300	0.75
1969 none minted	—	—	—	—
1969D	202,807,500	.50	—	—
1969S	123,099,631	.50	450	0.75
1970 none minted	—	—	—	—
1970D	515,485,380	.50	500	—
1970S	241,464,814	.50	125	0.75
1971	106,884,000	2.00	35.00	—
1971D	316,144,800	.50	25.00	—
1971S	(3,220,733)	—	—	2.00
1972	202,036,000	.50	35.00	—
1972D	351,694,600	.50	25.00	—
1972S	(3,260,996)	—	—	2.00
1973	384,396,000	.50	20.00	—
1973D	261,405,000	.50	20.00	—
1973S	(2,760,339)	—	—	1.75
1974	601,752,000	.50	75.00	—
1974D	277,373,000	.50	50.00	—
1974S	(2,612,568)	—	—	2.00
1975	181,772,000	.75	65.00	—
1975D	401,875,300	.50	60.00	—
1975S	(2,845,450)	—	—	2.25
1976	367,124,000	.75	150	—
1976D	563,964,147	.60	55.00	—
1976S	(4,149,730)	—	—	2.00
1977	585,376,000	.40	65.00	—
1977D	297,313,460	.55	35.00	—
1977S	(3,251,152)	—	—	1.75
1978	391,308,000	.40	40.00	—
1978D	313,092,780	.40	35.00	—
1978S	(3,127,781)	—	—	1.75
1979	463,188,000	.40	95.00	—
1979D	325,867,672	.40	35.00	—
1979S type I, proof	(3,677,175)	—	—	1.50
1979S type II, proof	Inc. above	—	—	1.75
1980P	593,004,000	.40	30.00	—
1980D	502,323,448	.40	25.00	—
1980S	(3,554,806)	—	—	1.50
1981P	657,504,000	.40	70.00	—
1981D	364,801,843	.40	40.00	—
1981S type I, proof	(4,063,083)	—	—	2.00
1981S type II, proof	Inc. above	—	—	2.50
1982P	292,355,000	12.50	80.00	—
1982D	373,726,544	3.50	45.00	—
1982S	(3,857,479)	—	—	3.50
1983P	561,615,000	4.00	45.00	—
1983D	536,726,276	2.50	35.00	—
1983S	(3,279,126)	—	—	4.00
1984P	746,769,000	3.00	65.00	—
1984D	517,675,146	.85	30.00	—
1984S	(3,065,110)	—	—	5.00
1985P	647,114,962	.75	60.00	—
1985D	459,747,446	.75	35.00	—
1985S	(3,362,821)	—	—	4.00
1986P	536,883,483	1.00	70.00	—
1986D	361,819,140	2.00	60.00	—
1986S	(3,010,497)	—	—	7.00
1987P	371,499,481	.75	30.00	—
1987D	410,590,604	.75	25.00	—
1987S	(4,227,728)	—	—	3.50
1988P	771,360,000	.75	30.00	—
1988D	663,771,652	.75	25.00	—

Date	Mintage	MS-65	-65FS	Prf-65
1988S	(3,262,948)	—	—	6.50
1989P	898,812,000	.75	75.00	—
1989D	570,842,474	.75	25.00	—
1989S	(3,220,194)	—	—	5.50
1990P	661,636,000	.75	25.00	—
1990D	663,938,503	.75	25.00	—
1990S	(3,299,559)	—	—	5.50
1991P	614,104,000	.75	25.00	—
1991D	436,496,678	.75	25.00	—
1991S	(2,867,787)	—	—	5.00
1992P	399,552,000	2.00	25.00	—
1992D	450,565,113	.75	25.00	—
1992S	(4,176,560)	—	—	4.00
1993P	412,076,000	.75	25.00	—
1993D	406,084,135	.75	25.00	—
1993S	(3,394,792)	—	—	4.50
1994P	722,160,000	.75	25.00	—
1994P matte	167,703	.75	—	—
1994D	715,762,110	.75	25.00	—
1994S	(3,269,923)	—	—	4.00
1995P	774,156,000	.75	25.00	—
1995D	888,112,000	.85	25.00	—
1995S	(2,707,481)	—	—	7.50
1996P	829,332,000	.75	25.00	—
1996D	817,736,000	.75	25.00	—
1996S	(2,915,212)	—	—	4.00
1997P	470,972,000	.75	25.00	—
1997P matte	25,000	200	—	—
1997D	466,640,000	2.00	25.00	—
1997S	(1,975,000)	—	—	5.00
1998P	688,272,000	.80	25.00	—
1998D	635,360,000	.80	25.00	—
1998S	(2,957,286)	—	—	4.50
1999P	1,212,000,000	.80	20.00	—
1999D	1,066,720,000	.80	20.00	—
1999S	(3,362,462)	—	—	3.50
2000P	846,240,000	.80	20.00	—
2000D	1,509,520,000	.80	20.00	—
2000S	(4,063,361)	—	—	2.00
2001P	675,704,000	.50	20.00	—
2001D	627,680,000	.50	20.00	—
2001S	(3,099,096)	—	—	2.00
2002P	539,280,000	.50	—	—
2002D	691,200,000	.50	—	—
2002S	(3,157,739)	—	—	2.00
2003P	441,840,000	.50	—	—
2003D	383,040,000	.50	—	—
2003S	3,116,590	—	—	2.00

Jefferson - Peace Reverse.
Two clasp hands, pipe and hatchet.

KM# 360   Diameter: 21.2 **Weight:** 5.0000 g.
Composition: Copper Nickel.

Date	Mintage	MS-65	-65FS	Prf-65
2004P	—	—	—	—
2004D	—	—	—	—
2004S	—	—	—	—

Jefferson - Keelboat reverse.
Lewis and Clark's Keelboat.

KM# 361   Diameter: 21.2 **Weight:** 5.0000 g.
Composition: Copper Nickel.

Date	Mintage	MS-65	-65FS	Prf-65
2004P	—	—	—	—
2004D	—	—	—	—
2004S	—	—	—	—

DIME

Draped Bust Dime. Small eagle.

KM# 24 **Designer:** Robert Scot. **Diameter:** 19
Weight: 2.7000 g. **Composition:** 0.8920 Silver,
0.0775 oz. ASW. **Notes:** 1797 strikes have either
13 or 16 stars on the obverse.

Date	Mintage	G-4	VG-8	F-12	VF-20	XF-40	MS-60
1796	22,135	1,300	1,950	2,250	3,250	5,000	12,000
1797 13 stars	25,261	1,500	2,000	2,500	3,500	6,000	12,000
1797 16 stars	Inc. above	1,500	2,000	2,500	3,500	6,000	12,000

Draped Bust Dime. Heraldic eagle.

KM# 31 **Designer:** Robert Scot. **Diameter:** 19
Weight: 2.7000 g. **Composition:** 0.8920 Silver,
0.0775 oz. ASW. **Notes:** The 1798 overdates have either
13 or 16 stars on the obverse. Varieties of the regular
1798 strikes are distinguished by the size of the 8 in the
date. The 1805 strikes have either 4 or 5 berries on the
olive branch held by the eagle.

Date	Mintage	G-4	VG-8	F-12	VF-20	XF-40	MS-60
1798	27,550	650	800	1,000	1,500	2,750	6,500
1798/97 13 stars	Inc. above	2,000	3,000	4,500	7,000	11,000	—
1798/97 16 stars	Inc. above	675	800	1,050	1,500	2,500	5,500
1798 small 8	Inc. above	900	1,150	1,700	2,400	3,600	9,500
1800	21,760	600	800	1,100	1,600	2,750	—
1801	34,640	650	850	1,300	2,500	4,500	—
1802	10,975	950	1,400	2,000	3,000	6,000	17,500
1803	33,040	550	700	950	1,500	3,600	—
1804 13 stars	8,265	1,400	1,900	2,650	5,500	13,500	—
1804 14 stars	Inc. above	1,600	2,100	3,000	6,000	15,000	—
1805 4 berries	120,780	450	650	800	1,050	2,100	5,000
1805 5 berries	Inc. above	700	1,000	1,300	1,800	2,700	5,250
1807	165,000	450	650	800	1,050	2,100	5,000

Liberty Cap Dime.

KM# 42 **Designer:** John Reich. **Diameter:** 18.8
Weight: 2.7000 g. **Composition:** 0.8920 Silver,
.0775 oz. ASW. **Notes:** Varieties of the 1814, 1821 and
1828 strikes are distinguished by the size of the
numerals in the dates. The 1820 varieties are
distinguished by the size of the 0 in the date. The 1823
overdates have either large E's or small E's in "United
States of America" on the reverse.

Date	Mintage	G-4	VG-8	F-12	VF-20	XF-40	AU-50	MS-60	MS-65
1809	51,065	150	250	450	800	1,400	3,000	4,500	22,500
1811/9	65,180	90.00	165	275	650	1,100	2,000	4,000	22,500
1814 small date	421,500	60.00	70.00	120	475	700	1,000	2,000	8,000
1814 large date	Inc. above	29.00	35.00	55.00	200	400	800	1,100	8,000
1820 large O	942,587	26.00	33.00	55.00	150	375	750	1,050	8,000
1820 small O	Inc. above	26.00	33.00	55.00	175	425	750	1,050	8,000
1821 large date	1,186,512	26.00	33.00	60.00	150	375	750	1,050	8,000
1821 small date	Inc. above	26.00	33.00	55.00	175	400	750	1,050	8,000
1822	100,000	425	600	1,100	1,700	3,000	6,000	10,000	—
1823/22 large E's	440,000	26.00	33.00	50.00	150	375	750	1,050	8,000
1823/22 small E's	Inc. above	26.00	33.00	50.00	150	375	750	1,050	8,000
1824/22 mintage undetermined	—	30.00	50.00	150	400	750	1,500	2,500	—
1825	510,000	26.00	33.00	50.00	150	450	900	1,250	8,000
1827	1,215,000	26.00	33.00	50.00	140	375	775	1,050	8,000
1828 large date	125,000	80.00	110	175	375	750	1,275	3,000	—

Liberty Cap Dime.

KM# 48 **Designer:** John Reich. **Diameter:** 18.5
Composition: Silver. **Notes:** The three varieties of 1829
strikes and two varieties of 1830 strikes are distinguished
by the size of "10C." on the reverse. On the 1833 "high
3" variety, the last 3 in the date is higher than the first 3.
The two varieties of the 1834 strikes are distinguished by
the size of the 4 in the date.

Date	Mintage	G-4	VG-8	F-12	VF-20	XF-40	AU-50	MS-60	MS-65
1828 small date	Inc. above	30.00	45.00	75.00	195	475	775	1,750	—

Date	Mintage	G-4	VG-8	F-12	VF-20	XF-40	AU-50	MS-60	MS-65
1829 very large 10C.	770,000	35.00	45.00	85.00	150	375	600	1,500	—
1829 large 10C.	—	26.00	30.00	40.00	75.00	270	400	725	8,000
1829 medium 10C.	Inc. above	26.00	30.00	40.00	70.00	270	400	725	8,000
1829 small 10C.	Inc. above	26.00	30.00	40.00	70.00	270	400	725	8,000
1829 curl base 2	—	3,200	5,000	7,500	—	—	—	—	—
1830 large 10C.	510,000	26.00	30.00	38.00	65.00	260	375	675	8,000
1830 small 10C.	Inc. above	26.00	30.00	38.00	65.00	260	375	675	8,000
1830/29	Inc. above	35.00	60.00	115	250	500	775	1,500	—
1831	771,350	26.00	30.00	38.00	65.00	260	375	675	6,000
1832	522,500	26.00	30.00	38.00	65.00	260	375	675	6,500
1833	485,000	26.00	30.00	38.00	65.00	260	375	675	6,700
1834	635,000	26.00	30.00	38.00	65.00	260	375	675	6,500
1835	1,410,000	26.00	30.00	38.00	65.00	260	375	675	6,500
1836	1,190,000	26.00	30.00	38.00	65.00	260	375	675	6,500
1837	1,042,000	26.00	30.00	38.00	65.00	260	375	675	6,600

Seated Liberty Dime.
No stars around rim.

KM# 61   Designer: Christian Gobrecht. Diameter:
17.9 Weight: 2.6700 g. Composition: 0.9000 Silver,
0.0773 oz. ASW. Notes: The two 1837 varieties are
distinguished by the size of the numerals in the date.

Date	Mintage	G-4	VG-8	F-12	VF-20	XF-40	AU-50	MS-60	MS-65
1837 small date	Inc. above	40.00	50.00	85.00	290	550	750	1,100	6,500
1837 large date	Inc. above	32.50	43.50	75.00	275	550	750	1,100	6,500
1838O	406,034	40.00	60.00	110	375	725	1,250	3,500	21,000

Seated Liberty Dime.
Stars around rim. No drapery.

No drapery
at elbow

KM# 63.1   Obv. Designer: Christian Gobrecht.
Diameter: 17.9 Weight: 2.6700 g. Composition:
0.9000 Silver, 0.0773 oz. ASW. Notes: The two 1838
varieties are distinguished by the size of the stars on the
obverse. The 1838 "partial drapery" variety has drapery
on Liberty's left elbow. The 1839-O with reverse of
1838-O variety was struck from rusted dies. This variety
has a bumpy surface on the reverse.

Date	Mintage	G-4	VG-8	F-12	VF-20	XF-40	AU-50	MS-60	MS-65
1838 small stars	1,992,500	25.00	30.00	50.00	80.00	165	350	600	—
1838 large stars	Inc. above	17.50	20.00	30.00	37.50	110	215	280	8,500
1838 partial drapery	Inc. above	30.00	45.00	65.00	125	195	325	550	—
1839	1,053,115	16.00	18.50	25.00	35.00	105	195	280	3,000
1839O	1,323,000	18.50	22.50	31.50	45.00	115	365	1,250	6,000
1839O reverse 1838O	—	145	200	350	550	950	—	—	—
1840	1,358,580	16.00	18.50	25.00	35.00	105	195	300	4,000
1840O	1,175,000	18.50	22.50	40.00	70.00	125	295	975	6,500

Seated Liberty Dime. Drapery added
to Liberty's left elbow.

Drapery
at elbow

KM# 63.2   Designer: Christian Gobrecht. Diameter:
17.9 Weight: 2.6700 g. Composition: 0.9000 Silver,
0.0773 oz. ASW.

Date	Mintage	G-4	VG-8	F-12	VF-20	XF-40	AU-50	MS-60	MS-65
1840	Inc. above	35.00	50.00	95.00	185	350	1,250	—	—
1841	1,622,500	16.00	18.50	21.50	27.50	50.00	175	260	2,700
1841O	2,007,500	18.50	22.50	28.50	42.50	75.00	250	1,500	5,000
1841O large O	Inc. above	600	900	1,200	2,500	—	—	—	—
1842	1,887,500	15.00	17.50	21.50	26.00	45.00	175	260	2,700
1842O	2,020,000	18.50	23.50	30.00	75.00	225	1,350	2,900	—
1843	1,370,000	15.00	17.50	21.50	26.00	45.00	175	260	3,000
1843/1843	—	16.00	18.50	22.50	30.00	75.00	200	295	—
1843O	150,000	35.00	65.00	125	275	800	2,250	—	—
1844	72,500	275	350	550	800	1,450	2,200	3,000	—
1845	1,755,000	16.00	18.50	21.50	27.50	45.00	120	260	2,600
1845/1845	Inc. above	17.00	20.00	35.00	55.00	100.00	175	—	—
1845O	230,000	22.00	35.00	70.00	200	550	1,350	—	—
1846	31,300	200	225	300	400	950	2,250	5,500	—
1847	245,000	19.00	25.00	40.00	75.00	150	350	950	9,000
1848	451,500	18.50	21.50	25.00	45.00	85.00	185	750	7,000
1849	839,000	17.50	19.50	23.50	33.50	60.00	140	500	4,000
1849O	300,000	21.50	30.00	45.00	120	275	750	2,200	—
1850	1,931,500	17.50	19.50	23.50	32.50	55.00	120	260	5,900
1850O	510,000	21.50	25.00	35.00	70.00	160	475	1,250	—

Date	Mintage	G-4	VG-8	F-12	VF-20	XF-40	AU-50	MS-60	MS-65
1851	1,026,500	17.50	20.00	22.50	30.00	60.00	120	325	5,000
1851O	400,000	21.50	25.00	35.00	75.00	175	500	1,850	—
1852	1,535,500	15.00	16.00	18.50	23.50	50.00	120	290	2,550
1852O	430,000	22.50	30.00	45.00	125	235	550	1,800	—
1853	95,000	70.00	100.00	130	195	300	475	800	—

Seated Liberty Dime. Arrows at date.

KM# 77 **Designer:** Christian Gobrecht. **Weight:** 2.4900 g. **Composition:** 0.9000 Silver, 0.0721 oz. ASW.

Date	Mintage	G-4	VG-8	F-12	VF-20	XF-40	AU-50	MS-60	MS-65	Prf-65
1853	12,078,010	8.00	9.00	10.00	14.00	45.00	125	330	2,500	31,500
1853O	1,100,000	11.00	14.00	20.00	45.00	145	400	900	—	—
1854	4,470,000	8.75	9.25	10.00	15.00	45.00	125	330	2,500	31,500
1854O	1,770,000	10.00	11.00	14.00	25.00	75.00	175	600	—	—
1855	2,075,000	8.75	9.25	14.00	20.00	55.00	150	350	3,800	31,500

Seated Liberty Dime. Arrows at date removed.

KM# A63.2 **Designer:** Christian Gobrecht. **Weight:** 2.4900 g. **Composition:** 0.9000 Silver, 0.0721 oz. ASW. **Notes:** The two 1856 varieties are distinguished by the size of the numerals in the date.

Date	Mintage	G-4	VG-8	F-12	VF-20	XF-40	AU-50	MS-60	MS-65	Prf-65
1856 small date	5,780,000	14.00	15.00	18.00	22.00	37.50	115	250	7,050	38,000
1856 large date	Inc. above	16.00	18.50	19.50	25.00	65.00	175	475	—	—
1856O	1,180,000	16.00	18.50	19.50	35.00	85.00	215	625	5,250	—
1856S	70,000	160	225	325	500	1,200	1,750	—	—	—
1857	5,580,000	14.00	15.50	16.50	22.50	37.50	110	260	2,600	3,400
1857O	1,540,000	14.00	16.00	18.50	25.00	65.00	200	375	2,600	—
1858	1,540,000	14.00	15.50	16.50	22.50	55.00	145	260	2,600	3,400
1858O	290,000	19.00	25.00	40.00	85.00	165	280	800	5,000	—
1858S	60,000	135	200	300	425	975	1,400	—	—	—
1859	430,000	16.00	20.00	25.00	45.00	70.00	140	350	—	3,400
1859O	480,000	16.00	20.00	25.00	45.00	80.00	225	550	—	—
1859S	60,000	150	225	325	500	1,350	3,000	—	—	—
1860S	140,000	30.00	40.00	55.00	135	300	800	—	—	—

Seated Liberty Dime. "United States of America" replaced stars.

KM# 92 **Obv. Designer:** Christian Gobrecht. **Weight:** 2.4900 g. **Composition:** 0.9000 Silver, 0.0721 oz. ASW. **Notes:** The 1873 "closed-3" and "open-3" varieties are distinguished by the amount of space between the upper left and lower left serifs of the 3 in the date.

Date	Mintage	G-4	VG-8	F-12	VF-20	XF-40	AU-50	MS-60	MS-65	Prf-65
1860	607,000	15.00	22.00	29.00	31.00	55.00	125	275	1,350	1,400
1860O	40,000	350	475	875	1,650	3,500	5,500	8,500	—	—
1861	1,884,000	12.50	15.00	17.00	20.00	35.00	72.50	135	1,250	1,400
1861S	172,500	50.00	85.00	145	275	400	900	1,400	—	—
1862	847,550	16.00	17.50	19.50	25.00	45.00	77.50	165	1,250	1,400
1862S	180,750	40.00	60.00	95.00	175	350	775	1,000	—	—
1863	14,460	350	450	600	700	875	1,100	1,300	—	1,400
1863S	157,500	34.00	44.00	75.00	125	275	550	1,200	—	—
1864	11,470	350	450	575	650	775	1,000	1,200	—	1,400
1864S	230,000	28.00	35.00	60.00	95.00	225	425	1,200	—	—
1865	10,500	400	500	650	750	900	1,100	1,250	—	1,400
1865S	175,000	35.00	45.00	75.00	125	300	850	—	—	—
1866	8,725	450	550	700	800	975	1,200	1,800	—	1,750
1866S	135,000	40.00	50.00	85.00	145	325	675	1,900	—	—
1867	6,625	550	700	950	1,100	1,450	1,600	1,800	—	1,750
1867S	140,000	40.00	50.00	85.00	145	295	625	1,200	—	—
1868	464,000	18.00	22.00	29.00	39.00	80.00	175	300	—	1,400
1868S	260,000	25.00	35.00	50.00	85.00	165	300	600	—	—
1869	256,600	25.00	35.00	45.00	75.00	135	250	600	—	1,400
1869S	450,000	20.00	25.00	35.00	45.00	75.00	175	400	—	—
1870	471,000	18.00	22.00	30.00	40.00	50.00	80.00	150	—	1,400
1870S	50,000	275	350	450	550	675	950	2,000	—	—
1871	907,710	16.00	20.00	25.00	33.00	55.00	160	300	—	1,400
1871CC	20,100	1,400	1,850	2,950	4,000	7,500	10,500	—	—	—

Date	Mintage	G-4	VG-8	F-12	VF-20	XF-40	AU-50	MS-60	MS-65	Prf-65
1871S	320,000	35.00	55.00	75.00	130	195	350	900	—	—
1872	2,396,450	12.00	15.00	17.00	20.00	31.00	95.00	175	—	1,400
1872CC	35,480	425	650	975	1,950	5,500	—	—	—	—
1872S	190,000	40.00	60.00	80.00	150	235	450	1,100	—	—
1873 closed 3	1,568,600	12.50	15.00	18.00	22.00	50.00	100.00	200	—	1,400
1873 open 3	Inc. above	22.00	30.00	40.00	60.00	110	225	650	—	—
1873CC	12,400	—	—	—	—	—	—	—	—	—

Note: 1873-CC, Heritage Sale, April 1999, MS-64, $632,500.

Seated Liberty Dime. Arrows at date.

KM# 105 Designer: Christian Gobrecht. **Weight:**
2.5000 g. **Composition:** 0.9000 Silver, 0.0724 oz. ASW.

Date	Mintage	G-4	VG-8	F-12	VF-20	XF-40	AU-50	MS-60	MS-65	Prf-65
1873	2,378,500	15.00	18.50	25.00	55.00	150	350	500	4,500	4,500
1873CC	18,791	1,400	1,850	2,950	4,000	8,500	—	—	—	—
1873S	455,000	20.00	30.00	40.00	70.00	190	400	1,500	—	—
1874	2,940,700	13.50	17.50	22.50	50.00	150	315	500	4,500	4,500
1874CC	10,817	3,500	5,500	8,000	12,500	25,000	—	—	—	—
1874S	240,000	60.00	75.00	100.00	160	250	450	1,500	—	—

Seated Liberty Dime.
Arrows at date removed.

KM# A92 Designer: Christian Gobrecht. **Weight:**
2.5000 g. **Composition:** 0.9000 Silver, 0.0724 oz. ASW.
Notes: On the 1876-CC doubled-obverse variety,
doubling appears in the words "of America" in the
legend.

Date	Mintage	G-4	VG-8	F-12	VF-20	XF-40	AU-50	MS-60	MS-65	Prf-65
1875	10,350,700	12.50	15.00	17.00	20.00	27.50	72.50	125	2,250	4,600
1875CC mint mark in wreath	4,645,000	15.00	16.00	18.50	26.00	42.50	90.00	190	2,700	—
1875CC mint mark under wreath	Inc. above	15.00	16.00	22.50	37.50	65.00	165	235	3,000	—
1875S mint mark in wreath	9,070,000	20.00	25.00	30.00	43.00	65.00	125	225	3,100	—
1875S mint mark under wreath	Inc. above	12.50	15.50	17.50	20.00	27.50	72.50	125	1,100	—
1876	11,461,150	12.00	15.00	17.00	20.00	24.00	72.50	125	1,100	1,200
1876CC	8,270,000	15.00	16.00	18.50	26.00	42.50	82.50	180	—	—
1876CC doubled obverse	Inc. above	16.00	20.00	30.00	80.00	135	300	500	—	—
1876S	10,420,000	12.50	15.00	17.00	20.00	35.00	72.50	125	1,750	—
1877	7,310,510	12.00	15.00	17.00	20.00	27.50	72.50	125	1,100	1,200
1877CC	7,700,000	15.00	16.00	18.50	26.00	42.50	82.50	180	1,100	—
1877S	2,340,000	14.00	18.00	20.00	30.00	50.00	105	225	—	—
1878	1,678,800	12.50	15.00	17.00	20.00	36.00	72.50	125	1,500	1,200
1878CC	200,000	60.00	75.00	125	190	300	475	775	3,900	—
1879	15,100	225	250	300	350	425	525	675	1,750	1,500
1880	37,335	185	215	250	300	350	400	500	1,750	1,500
1881	24,975	200	225	275	325	400	500	650	2,500	1,600
1882	3,911,100	12.50	15.00	17.00	20.00	27.50	72.50	125	1,100	1,200
1883	7,675,712	12.50	15.00	17.00	20.00	27.50	72.50	125	1,100	1,200
1884	3,366,380	12.50	15.00	17.00	20.00	27.50	72.50	125	1,100	1,200
1884S	564,969	30.00	35.00	45.00	55.00	125	280	650	—	—
1885	2,533,427	12.50	15.00	17.00	20.00	27.50	72.50	125	1,100	1,200
1885S	43,690	375	525	725	1,450	2,200	3,600	5,000	—	—
1886	6,377,570	12.50	15.00	17.00	20.00	27.50	72.50	125	1,100	1,200
1886S	206,524	50.00	70.00	80.00	125	175	280	600	—	—
1887	11,283,939	12.50	15.00	17.00	20.00	27.50	72.50	125	1,100	1,200
1887S	4,454,450	12.50	15.00	17.00	20.00	38.00	80.00	125	1,100	—
1888	5,496,487	12.50	15.00	17.00	20.00	27.50	72.50	125	1,100	1,200
1888S	1,720,000	12.50	15.00	17.00	25.00	40.00	95.00	200	—	—
1889	7,380,711	12.50	15.00	17.00	20.00	27.50	72.50	125	1,100	1,200
1889S	972,678	14.00	18.00	25.00	45.00	70.00	150	475	4,500	—
1890	9,911,541	12.50	15.00	17.00	20.00	27.50	72.50	125	1,100	1,200
1890S	1,423,076	14.00	15.00	22.50	50.00	85.00	155	400	4,900	—
1891	15,310,600	12.50	15.00	17.00	20.00	27.50	72.50	125	1,100	1,200
1891O	4,540,000	12.50	15.00	17.00	20.00	27.50	72.50	175	1,750	—
1891O /horizontal O	Inc. above	65.00	95.00	125	175	225	400	—	—	—
1891S	3,196,116	13.50	15.00	17.50	20.00	30.00	75.00	225	1,650	—
1891S/S	Inc. above	25.00	30.00	40.00	85.00	135	250	—	—	—

Barber Dime.

KM# 113 Designer: Charles E. Barber. **Diameter:** 17.9 **Weight:** 2.5000 g. **Composition:** 0.9000 Silver, 0.0724 oz. ASW.

Date	Mintage	G-4	VG-8	F-12	VF-20	XF-40	AU-50	MS-60	MS-65	Prf-65
1892	12,121,245	4.25	5.75	16.00	23.50	27.50	70.00	110	750	1,450
1892O	3,841,700	8.50	13.00	30.00	47.50	57.50	82.50	152.5	1,275	—
1892S	990,710	60.00	105	185	200	260	295	400	4,000	—
1893	3,340,792	7.50	12.50	20.00	27.50	40.00	74.00	100.00	1,000	1,450
1893O	1,760,000	28.50	45.00	115	150	190	225	300	3,250	—
1893S	2,491,401	11.00	20.00	30.00	41.50	67.50	125	285	4,350	—
1894	1,330,972	20.00	38.50	110	135	160	375	275	1,200	1,450
1894O	720,000	62.50	95.00	200	260	370	650	1,550	14,500	—
1894S	24	—	—	—	—	—	—	—	—	—
Note: 1894S, Eliasberg Sale, May 1996, Prf-64, $451,000.										
1895	690,880	80.00	135	345	470	535	600	720	2,800	2,000
1895O	440,000	360	500	795	1,100	2,200	3,300	6,000	17,500	—
1895S	1,120,000	41.50	55.00	125	165	225	285	485	7,800	—
1896	2,000,762	10.00	22.00	55.00	75.00	95.00	115	160	1,500	1,450
1896O	610,000	75.00	150	275	345	445	700	1,000	8,400	—
1896S	575,056	82.50	150	275	315	385	515	770	4,600	—
1897	10,869,264	2.00	3.45	7.50	13.50	30.00	73.50	125	700	1,450
1897O	666,000	66.00	110	275	355	445	600	975	4,700	—
1897S	1,342,844	22.00	35.00	96.00	115	155	230	450	4,250	—
1898	16,320,735	2.00	2.75	6.75	11.00	25.00	72.50	110	720	1,450
1898O	2,130,000	11.00	25.00	80.00	115	175	230	450	4,150	—
1898S	1,702,507	6.75	13.50	28.50	41.50	67.50	150	370	3,850	—
1899	19,580,846	2.50	2.80	7.50	11.00	25.00	70.00	100.00	700	1,450
1899O	2,650,000	8.25	17.00	70.00	100.00	135	225	415	4,850	—
1899S	1,867,493	7.00	13.50	22.00	30.00	47.50	100.00	300	5,000	—
1900	17,600,912	2.80	4.00	7.00	11.00	23.50	780	100.00	825	1,450
1900O	2,010,000	17.50	35.00	110	150	215	355	595	6,000	—
1900S	5,168,270	4.25	5.50	11.50	16.00	27.50	75.00	155	1,900	—
1901	18,860,478	2.50	2.75	6.50	9.50	25.00	62.50	110	850	1,450
1901O	5,620,000	3.45	4.00	13.50	25.00	60.00	150	450	4,500	—
1901S	593,022	80.00	140	345	400	470	650	1,000	5,500	—
1902	21,380,777	3.00	3.45	5.50	8.00	22.00	62.50	100.00	700	1,450
1902O	4,500,000	3.45	5.00	13.50	27.50	55.00	130	125	4,650	—
1902S	2,070,000	7.00	19.50	55.00	75.00	115	195	385	4,000	—
1903	19,500,755	2.50	2.80	3.75	8.00	23.50	62.50	110	1,150	1,450
1903O	8,180,000	3.50	4.75	12.50	20.00	41.50	100.00	250	5,100	—
1903S	613,300	75.00	115	340	475	800	845	1,150	3,750	—
1904	14,601,027	2.75	3.00	6.25	9.50	25.00	62.50	110	1,950	1,450
1904S	800,000	40.00	65.00	150	225	320	480	750	4,500	—
1905	14,552,350	2.80	3.45	5.60	8.00	23.50	62.50	100.00	700	1,450
1905O	3,400,000	3.75	8.00	34.00	55.00	78.00	140	285	1,900	—
1905S	6,855,199	2.75	3.45	8.50	16.00	38.50	96.00	220	800	—
1906	19,958,406	1.75	2.20	3.75	6.75	22.00	62.50	100.00	700	1,450
1906D	4,060,000	2.75	3.45	6.25	15.00	35.00	80.00	175	1,600	—
1906O	2,610,000	4.80	12.50	47.50	68.50	96.00	135	200	1,300	—
1906S	3,136,640	2.50	4.65	11.50	20.00	43.50	110	240	1,300	—
1907	22,220,575	1.75	2.15	3.35	6.00	20.00	60.00	110	700	1,450
1907D	4,080,000	2.80	4.00	8.50	17.00	45.00	110	275	4,600	—
1907O	5,058,000	3.45	6.75	31.50	47.50	62.50	110	210	1,350	—
1907S	3,178,470	2.75	4.65	13.50	25.00	65.00	140	400	2,500	—
1908	10,600,545	2.15	2.50	3.40	6.75	22.00	62.50	110	700	1,450
1908D	7,490,000	2.15	2.50	4.65	9.50	30.00	62.50	130	1,000	—
1908O	1,789,000	4.65	11.00	42.50	57.50	90.00	140	300	1,700	—
1908S	3,220,000	2.80	4.45	11.00	20.00	41.50	175	325	2,750	—
1909	10,240,650	2.15	2.50	3.40	6.75	22.00	62.50	110	700	1,700
1909D	954,000	6.75	16.00	60.00	90.00	130	225	500	3,000	—
1909O	2,287,000	3.00	6.00	9.50	20.00	38.50	90.00	190	2,000	—
1909S	1,000,000	7.00	19.00	85.00	125	190	315	535	3,200	—
1910	11,520,551	1.85	2.15	3.40	8.50	22.00	62.50	100.00	700	1,450
1910D	3,490,000	2.50	4.00	8.50	18.50	43.50	110	175	1,550	—
1910S	1,240,000	5.00	10.00	48.50	71.00	100.00	200	435	2,600	—
1911	18,870,543	1.75	2.10	3.40	6.75	22.00	62.50	110	700	1,700
1911D	11,209,000	1.75	2.10	3.40	6.75	25.00	62.50	110	750	—
1911S	3,520,000	2.50	3.45	8.00	17.50	38.50	100.00	200	1,300	—
1912	19,350,700	1.75	2.10	3.40	6.75	22.00	62.50	110	700	1,700
1912D	11,760,000	1.75	2.10	3.75	6.75	22.00	62.50	110	700	—
1912S	3,420,000	2.20	2.75	5.60	12.50	32.50	92.50	160	850	—
1913	19,760,622	1.75	2.10	3.00	6.50	22.00	62.50	110	700	1,450
1913S	510,000	15.00	27.50	90.00	140	225	300	500	1,450	—
1914	17,360,655	1.75	2.10	3.00	6.50	22.00	62.50	110	700	1,700
1914D	11,908,000	1.75	2.10	3.40	6.50	22.00	62.50	110	700	—

Date	Mintage	G-4	VG-8	F-12	VF-20	XF-40	AU-50	MS-60	MS-65	Prf-65
1914S	2,100,000	3.00	4.00	8.00	17.50	38.50	80.00	150	1,350	—
1915	5,620,450	2.10	2.50	3.00	6.50	22.00	62.50	110	700	2,000
1915S	960,000	5.00	9.50	31.50	45.00	65.00	135	250	1,600	—
1916	18,490,000	1.75	2.15	3.40	8.00	22.00	62.50	110	700	—
1916S	5,820,000	1.75	2.15	4.00	8.00	23.50	65.00	110	850	—

Mercury Dime.

KM# 140   Designer: Adolph A. Weinman. **Diameter:** 17.9 **Weight:** 2.5000 g. **Composition:** 0.9000 Silver, 0.0724 oz. ASW. **Notes:** All specimens listed as -65FSB are for fully struck MS-65 coins with fully split and rounded horizontal bands on the fasces.

Mint mark   1942/41

Date	Mintage	G-4	VG-8	F-12	VF-20	XF-40	AU-50	MS-60	MS-63	MS-65	-65FSB
1916	22,180,080	3.50	4.50	6.00	6.25	9.00	21.50	30.00	40.00	90.00	120
1916D	264,000	775	1,100	2,100	3,450	5,250	7,750	9,350	12,500	22,500	44,500
1916S	10,450,000	3.90	4.20	7.75	8.50	18.00	24.00	35.00	55.00	155	600
1917	55,230,000	1.85	2.00	2.50	5.00	7.50	12.50	30.00	60.00	155	400
1917D	9,402,000	4.00	5.00	10.00	21.50	42.00	92.50	120	300	1,100	6,000
1917S	27,330,000	1.80	2.00	3.50	5.75	10.00	26.50	62.00	170	470	1,150
1918	26,680,000	2.50	2.75	5.50	10.00	25.00	42.00	70.00	95.00	420	1,150
1918D	22,674,800	2.65	3.00	4.50	10.00	21.50	44.00	105	210	600	33,500
1918S	19,300,000	2.40	2.75	3.50	8.50	16.00	37.00	90.00	230	660	6,600
1919	35,740,000	1.90	2.00	3.00	5.00	10.00	22.50	37.00	100.00	320	700
1919D	9,939,000	3.35	6.00	11.00	21.50	35.00	72.00	175	420	1,400	38,500
1919S	8,850,000	2.75	3.00	8.00	15.00	31.00	72.00	175	450	1,000	13,000
1920	59,030,000	1.35	1.45	2.00	3.50	6.50	13.50	27.50	70.00	235	515
1920D	19,171,000	2.40	2.75	4.00	7.00	18.00	44.00	105	310	750	4,000
1920S	13,820,000	2.40	2.75	4.00	7.50	15.00	40.00	110	300	1,300	8,000
1921	1,230,000	41.50	68.50	110	275	565	885	1,000	1,500	3,200	4,400
1921D	1,080,000	60.00	110	170	360	640	1,100	1,150	1,650	3,200	5,600
1923	50,130,000	1.20	1.60	2.00	3.50	6.00	14.00	27.50	40.00	110	295
1923S	6,440,000	2.40	2.75	7.00	12.50	65.00	100.00	160	370	1,150	6,900
1924	24,010,000	1.35	1.60	2.50	4.25	12.00	26.50	42.00	88.00	175	520
1924D	6,810,000	2.75	4.00	6.00	14.00	44.00	100.00	160	300	950	1,400
1924S	7,120,000	2.75	3.50	4.00	8.75	44.00	95.00	170	450	1,100	14,000
1925	25,610,000	1.15	1.45	2.00	3.75	7.50	16.00	27.00	78.00	195	1,000
1925D	5,117,000	4.00	4.25	11.50	38.00	110	190	350	700	1,750	3,500
1925S	5,850,000	2.40	2.75	7.00	12.50	65.00	100.00	175	460	1,400	4,400
1926	32,160,000	1.10	1.45	1.70	2.75	4.25	12.00	25.00	60.00	240	525
1926D	6,828,000	2.75	4.00	4.50	8.50	24.00	43.00	125	260	550	2,650
1926S	1,520,000	8.00	11.00	25.00	55.00	225	420	900	1,475	3,000	6,500
1927	28,080,000	1.10	1.45	1.75	3.50	4.50	11.00	26.00	48.00	125	400
1927D	4,812,000	2.75	5.00	7.25	18.50	65.00	92.50	175	360	1,200	8,500
1927S	4,770,000	2.10	3.50	4.75	8.00	23.00	48.00	280	550	1,400	7,700
1928	19,480,000	1.10	1.45	1.75	3.50	4.00	16.00	27.50	48.00	110	300
1928D	4,161,000	3.00	3.25	8.00	18.50	44.00	85.00	170	310	875	2,500
1928S	7,400,000	1.80	2.10	2.75	5.50	16.00	37.00	125	260	425	1,900
1929	25,970,000	1.35	1.60	1.95	2.75	4.00	9.50	20.00	30.00	60.00	265
1929D	5,034,000	1.80	3.00	3.50	6.25	14.50	20.00	25.00	28.00	70.00	225
1929S	4,730,000	1.35	1.60	2.00	4.00	7.00	20.00	32.50	42.00	120	525
1930	6,770,000	1.35	1.50	2.00	3.50	7.00	13.00	26.00	48.00	115	525
1930S	1,843,000	2.50	3.50	4.80	6.25	15.00	45.00	75.00	115	200	565
1931	3,150,000	2.10	2.50	2.75	4.25	8.75	21.00	35.00	62.50	135	725
1931D	1,260,000	8.00	10.00	14.00	17.00	32.50	56.00	85.00	100.00	225	350
1931S	1,800,000	3.00	3.50	5.00	8.00	13.50	41.50	85.00	90.00	225	2,100
1934	24,080,000	1.00	1.45	1.75	3.00	5.00	10.00	21.50	26.50	40.00	150
1934D	6,772,000	1.60	2.10	2.75	4.00	8.00	18.50	50.00	57.50	72.00	360
1935	58,830,000	.80	1.00	1.50	2.15	4.25	7.50	8.00	13.00	30.00	70.00
1935D	10,477,000	1.25	1.75	2.50	3.75	7.50	18.00	34.00	42.00	72.00	600
1935S	15,840,000	1.00	1.50	1.75	3.00	5.50	14.00	24.00	25.00	31.50	500
1936	87,504,130	.80	1.00	1.50	2.25	3.50	6.50	8.00	13.00	25.00	90.00
1936D	16,132,000	1.00	1.25	1.50	3.00	6.50	14.00	26.00	31.50	42.00	295
1936S	9,210,000	1.00	1.25	1.50	2.50	3.00	8.00	20.00	26.00	31.50	85.00
1937	56,865,756	.80	1.00	1.50	2.00	3.25	6.00	8.00	12.00	23.00	42.00
1937D	14,146,000	1.00	1.25	1.50	3.00	5.50	9.50	21.00	26.00	43.00	100.00
1937S	9,740,000	1.00	1.25	1.50	3.00	5.50	7.50	24.00	26.00	34.00	195
1938	22,198,728	.80	1.00	1.50	2.25	3.50	5.00	13.00	22.00	27.50	80.00
1938D	5,537,000	1.50	1.75	2.00	3.50	6.00	9.50	16.00	24.00	28.00	65.00
1938S	8,090,000	1.35	1.55	1.75	2.35	3.75	9.00	20.00	27.50	35.00	135
1939	67,749,321	.80	1.00	1.50	2.00	3.25	5.00	8.50	13.50	25.00	170
1939D	24,394,000	1.00	1.25	1.50	2.00	3.50	6.00	7.50	12.00	26.00	45.00
1939S	10,540,000	1.25	1.50	2.00	2.50	4.25	8.50	21.00	28.00	35.00	750

Date	Mintage	G-4	VG-8	F-12	VF-20	XF-40	AU-50	MS-60	MS-63	MS-65	-65FSB
1940	65,361,827	.60	.70	.90	1.10	2.50	4.00	6.00	10.00	26.00	57.50
1940D	21,198,000	.60	.70	.90	1.10	1.50	5.00	8.00	14.00	30.00	55.00
1940S	21,560,000	.60	.70	.90	1.10	1.50	4.50	8.50	12.50	30.00	95.00
1941	175,106,557	.60	.70	.90	1.10	1.50	3.00	5.00	8.00	30.00	42.00
1941D	45,634,000	.60	.70	.90	1.10	1.50	4.00	8.00	14.00	23.00	40.00
1941S	43,090,000	.60	.70	.90	1.10	1.50	4.50	7.00	9.50	30.00	50.00
1942	205,432,329	.60	.70	.90	1.10	1.50	2.00	5.50	9.00	24.00	52.50
1942/41	Inc. above	550	580	625	715	835	1,250	1,900	4,000	12,500	38,500
1942D	60,740,000	.60	.70	.90	1.10	1.50	4.00	8.00	12.75	27.50	40.00
1942/41D	Inc. above	500	560	625	750	850	1,150	2,250	3,550	5,600	19,500
1942S	49,300,000	.60	.70	.90	1.10	1.50	4.50	9.50	16.00	24.00	140
1943	191,710,000	.60	.70	.90	1.10	1.50	2.00	5.50	9.00	30.00	50.00
1943D	71,949,000	.60	.70	.90	1.10	1.50	3.00	7.50	10.00	27.50	40.00
1943S	60,400,000	.60	.70	.90	1.10	1.50	4.50	8.25	12.50	25.00	66.00
1944	231,410,000	.60	.70	.90	1.10	1.50	2.00	5.50	9.00	23.00	80.00
1944D	62,224,000	.60	.70	.90	1.10	1.50	3.00	6.50	11.00	23.00	40.00
1944S	49,490,000	.60	.70	.90	1.10	1.50	4.00	6.50	10.00	30.00	50.00
1945	159,130,000	.60	.70	.90	1.10	1.50	2.00	5.50	9.00	23.00	8,000
1945D	40,245,000	.60	.70	.90	1.10	1.50	2.00	6.00	9.00	24.00	40.00
1945S	41,920,000	.60	.70	.90	1.10	1.50	4.00	6.50	9.50	24.00	135
1945S micro S	Inc. above	1.00	1.25	1.50	3.00	4.25	7.00	26.00	29.00	85.00	650

Roosevelt Dime.

KM# 195 **Designer:** John R. Sinnock. **Diameter:** 17.9 **Weight:** 2.5000 g. **Composition:** 0.9000 Silver, 0.0724 oz. ASW.

   Mint mark 1946-69

Date	Mintage	G-4	VG-8	F-12	VF-20	XF-40	AU-50	MS-60	MS-65	Prf-65
1946	225,250,000				.50	.65	.95	3.10	9.00	—
1946D	61,043,500	—	—	—	.50	.65	1.10	3.50	8.00	—
1946S	27,900,000	—	—	—	.50	.65	.90	4.00	11.00	—
1947	121,520,000	—	—	—	.50	.65	.95	5.00	12.00	—
1947D	46,835,000	—	—	—	.50	.95	1.50	7.00	15.00	—
1947S	34,840,000	—	—	—	.50	.95	1.25	4.50	16.00	—
1948	74,950,000	—	—	—	.50	.95	1.50	3.00	14.00	—
1948D	52,841,000	—	—	—	.50	1.20	2.00	3.00	10.00	—
1948S	35,520,000	—	—	—	.50	.95	1.10	2.75	11.00	—
1949	30,940,000	—	—	—	1.00	1.50	4.00	23.50	42.00	—
1949D	26,034,000	—	—	.60	.80	1.25	2.00	9.50	22.00	—
1949S	13,510,000	—	1.00	1.25	1.50	2.75	6.00	33.50	60.00	—
1950	50,181,500	—	—	—	.50	.95	1.35	7.00	13.50	50.00
1950D	46,803,000	—	—	—	.50	.65	1.60	3.65	8.00	—
1950S	20,440,000	—	.85	1.00	1.10	1.25	6.00	34.50	50.00	—
1951	102,937,602	—	—	—	.50	.85	1.00	1.75	5.00	65.00
1951D	56,529,000	—	—	—	.50	.65	.95	1.75	5.00	—
1951S	31,630,000	—	—	—	.75	1.05	3.25	9.75	24.00	—
1952	99,122,073	—	—	—	.50	.90	1.10	1.35	5.00	30.00
1952D	122,100,000	—	—	—	.50	.65	.95	1.35	5.00	—
1952S	44,419,500	—	—	—	.75	1.05	1.50	4.25	11.00	—
1953	53,618,920	—	—	—	.50	.65	1.00	2.15	5.00	30.00
1953D	136,433,000	—	—	—	.50	.65	.95	2.15	5.00	—
1953S	39,180,000	—	—	—	.50	.65	.75	1.00	4.00	—
1954	114,243,503	—	—	—	.50	.65	.75	1.00	4.00	12.00
1954D	106,397,000	—	—	—	.50	.65	.75	1.00	3.25	—
1954S	22,860,000	—	—	—	.50	.65	.80	1.00	3.15	—
1955	12,828,381	—	—	—	.70	.80	.85	1.00	5.00	12.00
1955D	13,959,000	—	—	—	.50	.55	.60	1.00	4.00	—
1955S	18,510,000	—	—	—	.50	.60	.65	1.00	5.00	—
1956	109,309,384	—	—	—	.50	.50	.60	1.00	3.00	3.50
1956D	108,015,100	—	—	—	.50	.50	.60	1.00	3.25	—
1957	161,407,952	—	—	—	.50	.50	.60	1.00	3.00	2.75
1957D	113,354,330	—	—	—	.50	.50	.60	1.00	4.00	—
1958	32,785,652	—	—	—	.50	.50	.60	1.00	4.00	3.50
1958D	136,564,600	—	—	—	.50	.50	.60	1.00	4.00	—
1959	86,929,291	—	—	—	.50	.50	.60	1.00	3.00	2.50
1959D	164,919,790	—	—	—	.50	.50	.60	1.00	3.25	—
1960	72,081,602	—	—	—	.50	.50	.60	1.00	3.00	2.50
1960D	200,160,400	—	—	—	.50	.50	.60	1.00	3.00	—
1961	96,758,244	—	—	—	.50	.50	.60	1.00	3.00	2.00
1961D	209,146,550	—	—	—	.50	.50	.60	1.00	3.00	—
1962	75,668,019	—	—	—	.50	.50	.60	1.00	3.00	2.00
1962D	334,948,380	—	—	—	.50	.50	.60	1.00	3.00	—
1963	126,725,645	—	—	—	.50	.50	.60	1.00	3.00	2.00

Date	Mintage	G-4	VG-8	F-12	VF-20	XF-40	AU-50	MS-60	MS-65	Prf-65
1963D	421,476,530	—	—	—	.50	.50	.60	1.00	3.00	—
1964	933,310,762	—	—	—	.50	.50	.60	1.00	3.00	2.00
1964D	1,357,517,180	—	—	—	.50	.50	.60	1.00	3.00	—

Roosevelt Dime.

KM# 195a   Designer: John R. Sinnock. **Diameter:** 17.9 **Weight:** 2.2700 g. **Composition:** Copper-Nickel Clad Copper. **Notes:** The 1979-S and 1981-S Type II proofs have clearer mint marks than the Type I proofs of those years. On the 1982 no-mint-mark variety, the mint mark was inadvertently left off.

1982 No mint mark

Mint mark 1968 - present

Date	Mintage	MS-65	Prf-65	Date	Mintage	MS-65	Prf-65
1965	1,652,140,570	1.00	—	1986P	682,649,693	1.70	—
1966	1,382,734,540	.80	—	1986D	473,326,970	1.60	—
1967	2,244,007,320	.80	—	1986S	(3,010,497)	—	2.75
1968	424,470,000	.70	—	1987P	762,709,481	.75	—
1968D	480,748,280	.80	—	1987D	653,203,402	.75	—
1968S	(3,041,506)	—	1.00	1987S	(4,227,728)	—	1.25
1969	145,790,000	2.00	—	1988P	1,030,550,000	.80	—
1969D	563,323,870	1.00	—	1988D	962,385,488	.80	—
1969S	(2,934,631)	—	0.80	1988S	(3,262,948)	—	3.00
1970	345,570,000	.70	—	1989P	1,298,400,000	1.00	—
1970D	754,942,100	.70	—	1989D	896,535,597	.50	—
1970S	(2,632,810)	—	0.65	1989S	(3,220,194)	—	4.00
1971	162,690,000	1.00	—	1990P	1,034,340,000	1.00	—
1971D	377,914,240	.80	—	1990D	839,995,824	.80	—
1971S	(3,220,733)	—	0.65	1990S	(3,299,559)	—	2.75
1972	431,540,000	.70	—	1991P	927,220,000	.80	—
1972D	330,290,000	.70	—	1991D	601,241,114	1.00	—
1972S	(3,260,996)	—	1.00	1991S	(2,867,787)	—	3.25
1973	315,670,000	.70	—	1992P	593,500,000	.75	—
1973D	455,032,426	.75	—	1992D	616,273,932	.80	—
1973S	(2,760,339)	—	1.00	1992S	(2,858,981)	—	4.00
1974	470,248,000	.70	—	1993P	766,180,000	.80	—
1974D	571,083,000	.70	—	1993D	750,110,166	.80	—
1974S	(2,612,568)	—	1.25	1993S	(2,633,439)	—	7.00
1975	585,673,900	.70	—	1994P	1,189,000,000	.80	—
1975D	313,705,300	.75	—	1994D	1,303,268,110	.80	—
1975S	(2,845,450)	—	1.50	1994S	(2,484,594)	—	5.00
1976	568,760,000	1.20	—	1995P	1,125,500,000	.80	—
1976D	695,222,774	.80	—	1995D	1,274,890,000	1.20	—
1976S	(4,149,730)	—	1.50	1995S	(2,010,384)	—	20.00
1977	796,930,000	.70	—	1996P	1,421,163,000	1.00	—
1977D	376,607,228	.70	—	1996D	1,400,300,000	1.00	—
1977S	(3,251,152)	—	1.75	1996W	1,457,949	15.00	—
1978	663,980,000	.70	—	1996S	(2,085,191)	—	3.50
1978D	282,847,540	.70	—	1997P	991,640,000	1.00	—
1978S	(3,127,781)	—	1.50	1997D	979,810,000	.75	—
1979	315,440,000	.70	—	1997S	(1,975,000)	—	9.00
1979D	390,921,184	.70	—	1998P	1,163,000,000	.80	—
1979 type I	—	—	1.00	1998D	1,172,250,000	.80	—
1979S type I	(3,677,175)	—	1.00	1998S	(2,078,494)	—	2.50
1979S type II	Inc. above	—	1.25	1999P	2,164,000,000	.80	—
1980P	735,170,000	.70	—	1999D	1,397,750,000	.80	—
1980D	719,354,321	.70	—	1999S	(2,557,897)	—	3.00
1980S	(3,554,806)	—	1.00	2000P	1,842,500,000	.80	—
1981P	676,650,000	.70	—	2000D	1,818,700,000	.75	—
1981D	712,284,143	.70	—	2000S	(3,097,440)	—	2.00
1981S type I	—	—	1.00	2001P	1,369,590,000	.80	—
1981S type II	—	—	4.00	2001D	1,412,800,000	.75	—
1982P	519,475,000	7.00	—	2001S	(2,249,496)	—	3.00
1982 no mint mark		225	—	2002P	1,187,500,000	.75	—
1982D	542,713,584	3.00	—	2002D	1,379,500,000	.75	—
1982S	(3,857,479)	—	2.00	2002S	(2,268,913)	—	2.00
1983P	647,025,000	8.00	—	2003P	1,085,500,000	.75	—
1983D	730,129,224	2.00	—	2003D	986,500,000	.75	—
1983S	(3,279,126)	—	1.25	2003S	(2,076,165)	—	2.00
1984P	856,669,000	1.00	—	2004S	—	—	—
1984D	704,803,976	1.20	—				
1984S	(3,065,110)	—	2.00				
1985P	705,200,962	.80	—				
1985D	587,979,970	.80	—				
1985S	(3,362,821)	—	1.00				

Roosevelt Dime.

KM# A195 **Composition:** Silver.

Date	Mintage	Prf-65	Date	Mintage	Prf-65
1992S	(1,317,579)	5.00	1998S	(878,792)	8.00
1993S	(761,353)	9.00	1999S	(804,565)	6.50
1994S	(785,329)	8.50	2000S	(965,921)	4.00
1995S	(838,953)	25.00	2001S	(849,600)	5.00
1996S	(830,021)	8.00	2002S	(888,826)	5.00
1997S	(821,678)	26.00	2003S	1,090,425	3.50

20 CENTS

KM# 109 **Designer:** William Barber. **Diameter:** 22
Weight: 5.0000 g. **Composition:** 0.9000 Silver,
0.1447 oz. ASW.

Date	Mintage	G-4	VG-8	F-12	VF-20	XF-40	AU-50	MS-60	MS-65	Prf-65
1875	39,700	110	125	175	215	280	440	650	5,500	9,500
1875S	1,155,000	85.00	92.50	105	135	175	295	470	5,000	—
1875CC	133,290	160	185	250	315	400	580	850	10,000	—
1876	15,900	150	175	260	315	385	525	650	5,200	9,500
1876CC	10,000	—	—	—	—	—	—	—	—	—

Note: 1876CC, Eliasberg Sale, April 1997, MS-65, $148,500. Heritage 1999 ANA, MS-63, $86,500.

Date	Mintage	G-4	VG-8	F-12	VF-20	XF-40	AU-50	MS-60	MS-65	Prf-65
1877 proof	510	1,600	1,800	2,250	2,600	280	3,150	—	—	10,500
1878 proof	600	1,350	1,525	1,850	2,000	2,300	2,600	—	—	9,700

QUARTER

Draped Bust Quarter. Small eagle.

KM# 25 **Designer:** Robert Scot. **Diameter:** 27.5
Weight: 6.7400 g. **Composition:** 0.8920 Silver,
0.1935 oz. ASW.

Date	Mintage	G-4	VG-8	F-12	VF-20	XF-40	AU-50	MS-60	MS-65
1796	6,146	6,250	9,250	15,000	21,500	30,000	34,000	50,000	125,000

Draped Bust Quarter. Heraldic eagle.

KM# 36 **Designer:** Robert Scot. **Diameter:** 27.5
Weight: 6.7400 g. **Composition:** 0.8920 Silver,
.1935 oz. ASW.

Date	Mintage	G-4	VG-8	F-12	VF-20	XF-40	AU-50	MS-60	MS-65
1804	6,738	2,000	2,400	3,500	5,000	11,000	20,000	43,000	110,000
1805	121,394	200	275	500	950	1,600	3,500	5,000	62,000
1806	206,124	200	275	500	900	1,450	3,300	4,650	46,500
1806/5	Inc. above	225	375	650	1,400	2,500	4,000	6,250	62,500
1807	220,643	200	275	500	925	1,700	3,400	4,650	48,500

Liberty Cap Quarter.
"E Pluribus Unum" above eagle.

KM# 44 Designer: John Reich. **Diameter:** 27
Weight: 6.7400 g. **Composition:** 0.8920 Silver,
0.1935 oz. ASW. **Notes:** Varieties of the 1819 strikes are
distinguished by the size of the 9 in the date. Varieties of
the 1820 strikes are distinguished by the size of the 0 in
the date. One 1822 variety and one 1828 variety have
"25" engraved over "50" in the denomination. The 1827
restrikes were produced privately using dies sold as
scrap by the U.S. Mint.

Date	Mintage	G-4	VG-8	F-12	VF-20	XF-40	AU-50	MS-60	MS-65
1815	89,235	55.00	70.00	175	475	1,000	1,650	2,750	25,000
1818	361,174	50.00	65.00	150	450	900	1,500	2,500	16,000
1818/15	Inc. above	55.00	70.00	200	575	1,100	1,750	2,800	20,000
1819 small 9	144,000	55.00	65.00	150	425	875	1,500	2,500	22,000
1819 large 9	Inc. above	55.00	65.00	150	425	875	1,500	2,500	22,000
1820 small O	127,444	60.00	75.00	150	425	875	1,500	2,500	28,000
1820 large O	Inc. above	50.00	65.00	150	425	875	1,500	2,500	25,000
1821	216,851	50.00	60.00	150	450	675	1,250	1,850	16,500
1822	64,080	65.00	90.00	200	550	1,200	2,000	3,750	—
1822 25/50C.	Inc. above	1,500	3,000	4,250	7,000	12,500	19,000	—	—
1823/22	17,800	10,000	14,000	20,000	30,000	40,000	55,000	—	—

Note: 1823/22, Superior, Aug. 1990, Proof, $62,500.

Date	Mintage	G-4	VG-8	F-12	VF-20	XF-40	AU-50	MS-60	MS-65
1824/2 mintage unrecorded	—	80.00	130	350	850	1,900	3,500	6,250	—
1825/22	168,000	70.00	100.00	200	500	1,100	1,900	2,800	22,500
1825/23	Inc. above	50.00	65.00	140	425	875	1,500	2,500	16,500
1825/24	Inc. above	50.00	65.00	140	425	875	1,500	2,500	16,500
1827 original	4,000	—	—	—	—	—	—	—	—

Note: Eliasberg, April 1997, VF-20, $39,600.

Date	Mintage	G-4	VG-8	F-12	VF-20	XF-40	AU-50	MS-60	MS-65
1827 restrike	Inc. above	—	—	—	—	—	—	—	—

Note: 1827 restrike, Eliasberg, April 1997, Prf-65, $77,000.

Date	Mintage	G-4	VG-8	F-12	VF-20	XF-40	AU-50	MS-60	MS-65
1828	102,000	50.00	65.00	140	375	775	1,600	2,850	19,500
1828 25/50C.	Inc. above	150	325	550	1,050	1,850	4,000	8,500	—

Liberty Cap Quarter. "E Pluribus Unum" removed from above eagle.

KM# 55 Designer: William Kneass. **Diameter:** 24.3
Composition: 0.8920 Silver. **Notes:** Varieties of the
1831 strikes are distinguished by the size of the lettering
on the reverse.

Date	Mintage	G-4	VG-8	F-12	VF-20	XF-40	AU-50	MS-60	MS-65
1831 small letter	398,000	55.00	65.00	75.00	120	350	850	1,000	13,500
1831 large letter	Inc. above	55.00	65.00	75.00	120	350	850	1,000	18,500
1832	320,000	55.00	65.00	75.00	120	350	850	1,000	16,000
1833	156,000	55.00	65.00	75.00	120	350	850	1,000	13,500
1834	286,000	55.00	65.00	75.00	120	350	850	1,000	13,500
1835	1,952,000	55.00	65.00	75.00	120	350	850	1,000	13,500
1836	472,000	55.00	65.00	75.00	120	350	850	1,000	14,500
1837	252,400	55.00	65.00	75.00	120	350	850	1,000	13,500
1838	832,000	55.00	65.00	75.00	120	350	850	1,000	14,750

Seated Liberty Quarter. No drapery.

KM# 64.1 Designer: Christian Gobrecht. **Diameter:**
24.3 **Weight:** 6.6800 g. **Composition:** 0.9000 Silver,
0.1934 oz. ASW.

Date	Mintage	G-4	VG-8	F-12	VF-20	XF-40	AU-50	MS-60	MS-65
1838	Inc. above	26.00	30.00	46.00	85.00	350	550	1,250	30,000
1839	491,146	25.00	29.00	44.00	75.00	350	550	1,250	34,000
1840O	425,200	28.50	35.00	60.00	400	375	575	1,350	38,500

Seated Liberty Quarter. Drapery added to Liberty's left elbow.

KM# 64.2 Designer: Christian Gobrecht. **Diameter:** 24.3 **Weight:** 6.6800 g. **Composition:** 0.9000 Silver, 0.1934 oz. ASW. **Notes:** Two varieties for 1842 and 1842-O are distinguished by the size of the numerals in the date. 1852 obverse dies were used to strike the 1853 no-arrows variety, with the 2 being recut to form a 3.

Date	Mintage	G-4	VG-8	F-12	VF-20	XF-40	AU-50	MS-60	MS-65
1840	188,127	30.00	55.00	80.00	125	225	350	950	12,000
1840O	Inc. above	29.00	39.00	70.00	115	250	450	1,000	—
1841	120,000	75.00	90.00	120	185	300	385	750	11,000
1841O	452,000	21.50	27.50	50.00	85.00	165	350	700	10,000
1842 small date	88,000	—	—	—	—	—	—	—	—
Note: 1842 small date, Eliasberg, April 1997, Prf-63, $66,000.									
1842 large date	Inc. above	85.00	120	170	275	350	800	1,250	—
1842O small date	769,000	425	650	1,100	1,850	4,000	—	—	—
1842O large date	Inc. above	22.50	27.50	37.50	50.00	125	300	900	4,000
1843	645,600	20.00	25.00	31.50	40.00	70.00	150	400	6,750
1843O	968,000	25.00	31.50	47.50	100.00	250	750	2,000	11,000
1844	421,200	20.00	25.00	31.50	41.50	70.00	160	450	5,500
1844O	740,000	25.00	28.50	40.00	75.00	140	280	1,000	6,000
1845	922,000	20.00	25.00	31.50	40.00	70.00	150	465	5,000
1846	510,000	20.00	25.00	36.50	50.00	75.00	160	475	6,000
1847	734,000	20.00	25.00	31.50	40.00	70.00	150	450	5,000
1847O	368,000	27.50	40.00	60.00	120	275	700	1,900	—
1848	146,000	40.00	55.00	100.00	185	225	375	1,000	10,000
1849	340,000	20.00	25.00	36.00	65.00	125	275	750	9,000
1849O mintage unrecorded	—	425	600	1,000	1,700	2,900	5,750	—	—
1850	190,800	35.00	45.00	75.00	110	150	275	800	—
1850O	412,000	20.00	30.00	50.00	100.00	150	450	1,300	—
1851	160,000	60.00	75.00	125	225	285	400	850	8,500
1851O	88,000	150	265	375	575	1,000	2,250	4,000	—
1852	177,060	50.00	60.00	100.00	185	225	350	500	4,800
1852O	96,000	175	250	350	595	1,200	3,500	8,000	—
1853 recut date	44,200	350	500	700	900	1,200	1,600	2,600	9,000

Seated Liberty Quarter. Arrows at date. Rays around eagle.

KM# 78 Designer: Christian Gobrecht. **Diameter:** 24.3 **Weight:** 6.2200 g. **Composition:** 0.9000 Silver, 0.1800 oz. ASW.

Date	Mintage	G-4	VG-8	F-12	VF-20	XF-40	AU-50	MS-60	MS-65	Prf-65
1853	15,210,020	15.00	20.00	27.50	45.00	150	275	950	19,000	90,000
1853/4	Inc. above	40.00	65.00	100.00	200	275	750	1,750	—	—
1853O	1,332,000	18.00	35.00	50.00	100.00	275	1,100	2,750	—	—

Seated Liberty Quarter. Rays around eagle removed.

KM# 81 Designer: Christian Gobrecht. **Diameter:** 24.3 **Weight:** 6.6800 g. **Composition:** 0.9000 Silver, .1934 oz. ASW. **Notes:** The 1854-O "huge O" variety has an oversized mint mark.

Date	Mintage	G-4	VG-8	F-12	VF-20	XF-40	AU-50	MS-60	MS-65	Prf-65
1854	12,380,000	15.00	20.00	27.50	35.00	75.00	225	440	7,500	17,500
1854O	1,484,000	17.00	24.00	35.00	60.00	125	300	1,750	—	—
1854O huge O	Inc. above	—	—	—	—	—	—	—	—	—
1855	2,857,000	15.00	20.00	27.50	35.00	75.00	225	440	8,500	18,500
1855O	176,000	50.00	75.00	110	240	475	950	2,750	—	—
1855S	396,400	40.00	60.00	80.00	225	500	1,250	2,000	—	—

Seated Liberty Quarter.
Arrows at date removed.

KM# A64.2 **Designer:** Christian Gobrecht.
Diameter: 24.3 **Weight:** 6.2200 g. **Composition:**
0.9000 Silver, 0.1800 oz. ASW.

Date	Mintage	G-4	VG-8	F-12	VF-20	XF-40	AU-50	MS-60	MS-65	Prf-65
1856	7,264,000	15.00	20.00	27.50	35.00	60.00	145	290	4,250	15,000
1856O	968,000	20.00	30.00	40.00	60.00	110	250	1,000	8,500	—
1856S	286,000	45.00	65.00	110	250	450	900	2,200	—	—
1856S/S	Inc. above	70.00	100.00	185	375	875	1,250	—	—	—
1857	9,644,000	15.00	20.00	27.50	35.00	60.00	145	290	4,000	9,500
1857O	1,180,000	15.00	20.00	29.00	40.00	80.00	275	975	—	—
1857S	82,000	100.00	145	250	400	600	950	2,750	—	—
1858	7,368,000	15.00	20.00	27.50	35.00	60.00	160	300	4,000	6,500
1858O	520,000	25.00	30.00	45.00	70.00	135	360	1,350	—	—
1858S	121,000	60.00	100.00	175	275	650	1,250	—	—	—
1859	1,344,000	17.00	24.00	30.00	40.00	75.00	175	375	6,000	7,000
1859O	260,000	25.00	30.00	50.00	80.00	150	400	1,000	15,000	—
1859S	80,000	100.00	135	225	450	1,350	2,500	—	—	—
1860	805,400	18.00	22.00	28.00	33.00	60.00	160	500	—	5,250
1860O	388,000	20.00	30.00	40.00	55.00	100.00	275	1,200	—	—
1860S	56,000	175	325	575	900	3,500	6,000	—	—	—
1861	4,854,600	16.00	19.00	27.00	32.00	55.00	150	290	4,200	5,500
1861S	96,000	80.00	125	235	400	1,250	2,750	—	—	—
1862	932,550	18.00	22.00	33.00	40.00	65.00	165	300	4,350	5,350
1862S	67,000	80.00	125	200	300	700	1,600	2,750	—	—
1863	192,060	30.00	45.00	60.00	120	185	300	650	4,350	5,500
1864	94,070	75.00	100.00	135	200	300	400	650	5,000	5,500
1864S	20,000	375	575	875	1,250	2,350	3,750	7,000	—	—
1865	59,300	75.00	100.00	150	200	290	375	875	9,500	5,500
1865S	41,000	100.00	135	200	350	650	1,250	2,350	11,500	—
1866 unique	—	—	—	—	—	—	—	—	—	—

Seated Liberty Quarter.
"In God We Trust" above eagle.

KM# 98 **Designer:** Christian Gobrecht. **Diameter:**
24.3 **Weight:** 6.2200 g. **Composition:** 0.9000 Silver,
0.1800 oz. ASW. **Notes:** The 1873 closed-3 and open-3
varieties are distinguished by the amount of space
between the upper left and lower left serifs in the 3.

Date	Mintage	G-4	VG-8	F-12	VF-20	XF-40	AU-50	MS-60	MS-65	Prf-65
1866	17,525	450	575	700	950	1,200	1,500	2,250	7,500	3,000
1866S	28,000	250	325	550	900	1,450	2,000	3,000	—	—
1867	20,625	225	300	450	625	800	975	1,200	—	2,450
1867S	48,000	275	350	600	900	1,350	1,700	—	—	—
1868	30,000	185	250	325	400	500	650	900	7,000	3,450
1868S	96,000	80.00	100.00	185	300	625	1,350	2,000	—	—
1869	16,600	325	425	550	675	775	950	1,275	—	2,500
1869S	76,000	90.00	115	225	375	700	1,400	2,400	16,000	—
1870	87,400	55.00	80.00	125	200	285	375	850	6,000	2,750
1870CC	8,340	3,800	5,500	8,000	12,000	16,000	25,000	35,000	—	—
1871	119,160	40.00	65.00	75.00	150	195	350	650	6,000	2,500
1871CC	10,890	2,250	3,800	5,500	9,500	14,500	25,000	40,000	—	—
1871S	30,900	300	450	550	800	1,100	1,850	3,000	10,000	—
1872	182,950	30.00	40.00	80.00	110	155	300	600	6,500	2,500
1872CC	22,850	650	850	1,500	2,950	5,900	7,500	14,000	—	—
1872S	83,000	900	1,250	1,650	2,100	3,500	4,500	7,500	—	—
1873 closed 3	212,600	150	225	325	525	600	1,000	2,000	—	2,600
1873 open 3	Inc. above	30.00	42.50	80.00	120	175	250	450	5,000	—
1873CC 6 known	4,000	—	75,000	—	—	—	—	—	—	—

Note: 1873CC, Heritage, April 1999, MS-62, $106,375.

Seated Liberty Quarter.
Arrows at date.

KM# 106 Designer: Christian Gobrecht. **Diameter:**
24.3 **Weight:** 6.2500 g. **Composition:** 0.9000 Silver,
0.1808 oz. ASW.

Date	Mintage	G-4	VG-8	F-12	VF-20	XF-40	AU-50	MS-60	MS-65	Prf-65
1873	1,271,700	16.00	23.00	30.00	60.00	200	400	775	4,250	8,000
1873CC	12,462	2,250	3,500	5,250	8,500	14,500	18,000	35,000	—	—
1873S	156,000	25.00	40.00	85.00	140	275	550	1,200	8,000	—
1874	471,900	20.00	26.00	40.00	70.00	220	420	850	4,000	6,750
1874S	392,000	23.00	30.00	50.00	110	240	425	900	4,500	—

Seated Liberty Quarter.
Arrows at date removed.

KM# A98 Designer: Christian Gobrecht. **Diameter:**
24.3 **Weight:** 6.2500 g. **Composition:** 0.9000 Silver,
0.1808 oz. ASW. **Notes:** The 1876-CC fine-reeding
variety has a more finely reeded edge.

Date	Mintage	G-4	VG-8	F-12	VF-20	XF-40	AU-50	MS-60	MS-65	Prf-65
1875	4,293,500	14.00	17.00	25.00	30.00	50.00	135	225	1,600	2,300
1875CC	140,000	60.00	90.00	175	300	550	850	1,600	15,000	—
1875S	680,000	25.00	36.00	67.00	110	175	275	575	3,200	—
1876	17,817,150	14.00	17.00	25.00	30.00	50.00	135	225	1,600	2,250
1876CC	4,944,000	17.00	20.00	30.00	40.00	70.00	150	325	3,600	—
1876CC fine reeding	Inc. above	18.00	28.00	33.00	42.00	72.00	150	325	3,600	—
1876S	8,596,000	16.00	19.00	25.00	30.00	50.00	135	225	2,000	—
1877	10,911,710	14.00	17.00	25.00	30.00	50.00	135	225	1,600	2,250
1877CC	4,192,000	18.00	28.00	33.00	42.00	72.00	150	325	2,000	—
1877S	8,996,000	14.00	17.00	25.00	30.00	50.00	135	225	1,600	—
1877S /horizontal S	Inc. above	32.00	48.00	75.00	125	225	375	650	—	—
1878	2,260,800	16.00	18.00	28.00	34.00	55.00	145	250	2,750	2,300
1878CC	996,000	19.00	29.00	45.00	85.00	110	150	450	3,500	—
1878S	140,000	150	185	285	350	600	850	1,450	—	—
1879	14,700	190	235	285	325	400	485	575	1,700	2,250
1880	14,955	190	235	285	325	400	485	575	1,600	2,250
1881	12,975	200	250	300	350	425	500	600	1,650	2,200
1882	16,300	200	250	300	350	425	500	600	1,850	2,200
1883	15,439	210	265	315	365	435	525	625	2,450	2,200
1884	8,875	325	400	485	585	675	750	850	1,900	2,200
1885	14,530	210	265	315	365	435	525	625	2,600	2,200
1886	5,886	500	600	700	800	900	1,000	1,250	2,600	2,400
1887	10,710	300	350	400	485	585	625	750	2,350	2,200
1888	10,833	250	300	350	400	475	550	650	2,000	2,350
1888S	1,216,000	15.00	20.00	27.50	30.00	60.00	160	245	2,450	—
1889	12,711	225	285	325	385	450	500	625	1,750	2,350
1890	80,590	65.00	85.00	100.00	125	200	300	425	—	2,350
1891	3,920,600	15.00	20.00	27.50	30.00	60.00	160	245	1,750	2,350
1891O	68,000	150	225	325	550	950	1,250	3,000	14,500	—
1891S	2,216,000	16.00	22.00	29.00	65.00	52.50	185	275	2,400	—

Barber Quarter.

KM# 114 Designer: Charles E. Barber. **Diameter:**
24.3 **Weight:** 6.2500 g. **Composition:** 0.9000 Silver,
0.1809 oz. ASW.

Date	Mintage	G-4	VG-8	F-12	VF-20	XF-40	AU-50	MS-60	MS-65	Prf-65
1892	8,237,245	5.25	6.75	22.50	43.50	75.00	120	220	1,300	2,000
1892O	2,640,000	11.00	17.50	37.50	52.50	96.00	140	300	1,650	—
1892S	964,079	25.00	47.50	80.00	110	160	300	480	4,850	—
1893	5,484,838	5.00	7.00	26.00	38.50	71.00	120	210	1,750	2,000
1893O	3,396,000	6.75	11.00	27.50	50.00	90.00	160	275	1,900	—
1893S	1,454,535	15.00	30.00	60.00	105	135	300	480	8,400	—
1894	3,432,972	5.50	7.50	32.50	47.50	93.50	150	250	1,550	2,000
1894O	2,852,000	8.00	13.50	41.50	65.00	110	225	340	3,000	—
1894S	2,648,821	7.50	11.00	38.00	62.50	100.00	205	315	3,000	—

Date	Mintage	G-4	VG-8	F-12	VF-20	XF-40	AU-50	MS-60	MS-65	Prf-65
1895	4,440,880	5.50	8.00	30.00	41.50	78.50	135	230	1,900	2,000
1895O	2,816,000	10.00	15.00	41.50	67.50	115	225	400	2,750	—
1895S	1,764,681	13.50	22.00	52.50	85.00	125	250	400	4,000	—
1896	3,874,762	5.00	6.50	25.00	41.50	78.50	135	235	1,600	2,000
1896O	1,484,000	15.00	30.00	100.00	250	415	750	850	7,750	—
1896S	188,039	650	1,000	1,650	2,500	4,000	5,250	7,500	45,000	—
1897	8,140,731	5.00	6.25	21.50	33.50	71.50	120	220	1,300	2,000
1897O	1,414,800	13.50	32.50	100.00	220	375	625	800	3,750	—
1897S	542,229	85.00	110	250	300	430	700	1,000	7,000	—
1898	11,100,735	5.00	6.25	22.50	33.50	71.50	120	220	1,300	2,000
1898O	1,868,000	11.00	22.00	65.00	125	285	415	625	10,000	—
1898S	1,020,592	8.00	16.00	42.50	60.00	96.00	210	400	7,200	—
1899	12,624,846	5.00	6.25	22.50	33.50	71.50	120	215	1,300	2,000
1899O	2,644,000	9.50	16.00	32.50	55.00	110	275	400	3,350	—
1899S	708,000	15.00	27.50	70.00	85.00	135	275	440	3,700	—
1900	10,016,912	6.00	8.00	21.50	35.00	71.50	135	215	1,300	2,000
1900O	3,416,000	11.00	23.00	62.50	100.00	135	345	585	3,800	—
1900S	1,858,585	7.50	15.00	38.00	55.00	80.00	135	385	5,400	—
1901	8,892,813	8.00	11.00	22.50	38.00	80.00	125	215	2,250	2,200
1901O	1,612,000	38.50	55.00	130	250	440	685	900	6,000	—
1901S	72,664	5,500	10,000	13,500	16,000	19,500	22,000	26,000	55,000	—
1902	12,197,744	6.00	8.00	19.50	33.50	66.00	115	215	1,300	2,100
1902O	4,748,000	8.00	16.00	45.00	80.00	135	220	450	4,800	—
1902S	1,524,612	12.50	19.00	47.50	75.00	130	235	530	3,600	—
1903	9,670,064	5.75	8.00	19.00	33.50	66.00	115	215	2,600	2,000
1903O	3,500,000	7.00	11.00	38.00	60.00	105	250	450	5,800	—
1903S	1,036,000	14.00	23.00	45.00	75.00	125	275	450	2,900	—
1904	9,588,813	5.75	8.00	19.00	33.50	66.00	115	215	1,475	2,000
1904O	2,456,000	8.50	17.50	55.00	90.00	210	400	840	3,250	—
1905	4,968,250	7.50	9.50	27.50	33.50	72.50	125	215	1,650	2,000
1905O	1,230,000	15.00	30.00	80.00	150	230	375	515	6,600	—
1905S	1,884,000	8.50	15.00	40.00	62.50	105	225	350	3,650	—
1906	3,656,435	5.75	8.00	19.00	33.50	70.00	115	215	1,300	2,000
1906D	3,280,000	6.25	8.00	25.00	42.50	71.50	155	220	2,200	—
1906O	2,056,000	6.25	8.50	38.00	57.50	96.00	200	300	1,400	—
1907	7,192,575	5.25	8.00	17.50	33.50	66.00	115	215	1,300	2,000
1907D	2,484,000	6.00	9.00	29.00	52.50	80.00	180	250	2,750	—
1907O	4,560,000	5.25	8.00	17.50	38.50	70.00	135	220	2,600	—
1907S	1,360,000	8.50	15.00	42.50	62.50	125	265	480	3,500	—
1908	4,232,545	5.00	6.25	18.50	33.50	70.00	115	215	1,300	2,200
1908D	5,788,000	5.00	6.25	17.50	32.50	70.00	120	250	1,750	—
1908O	6,244,000	5.00	8.50	17.50	33.50	75.00	125	215	1,300	—
1908S	784,000	16.00	35.00	80.00	140	295	480	775	5,100	—
1909	9,268,650	5.00	6.25	17.50	33.50	66.00	115	215	1,300	2,000
1909D	5,114,000	6.25	7.50	20.50	38.50	75.00	162.5	215	2,350	—
1909O	712,000	16.00	38.50	90.00	185	330	520	825	9,000	—
1909S	1,348,000	7.00	9.50	33.50	47.50	80.00	200	300	2,400	—
1910	2,244,551	7.00	8.50	28.50	46.00	78.50	140	215	1,300	2,000
1910D	1,500,000	7.00	9.00	42.50	65.00	110	260	375	2,250	—
1911	3,720,543	5.25	8.00	17.50	33.50	72.50	125	215	1,300	2,000
1911D	933,600	7.50	19.00	95.00	215	310	500	700	6,250	—
1911S	988,000	6.25	12.00	51.50	75.00	150	300	400	1,500	—
1912	4,400,700	5.75	8.00	17.50	33.50	70.00	115	215	1,300	2,000
1912S	708,000	8.00	14.00	42.50	75.00	115	230	390	2,750	—
1913	484,613	12.50	21.50	71.50	160	415	535	960	4,250	2,200
1913D	1,450,800	7.50	12.00	34.00	55.00	85.00	185	275	1,400	—
1913S	40,000	950	1,600	3,500	5,250	6,000	6,500	7,300	16,000	—
1914	6,244,610	5.00	6.25	17.50	30.00	57.50	115	215	1,300	2,200
1914D	3,046,000	5.00	6.25	17.50	30.00	57.50	115	215	1,300	—
1914S	264,000	62.50	90.00	185	300	500	700	930	3,550	—
1915	3,480,450	5.00	6.25	17.50	30.00	66.00	115	215	1,300	2,200
1915D	3,694,000	5.00	6.25	17.50	30.00	66.00	115	215	1,300	—
1915S	704,000	8.00	11.00	32.50	52.50	96.00	220	255	1,300	—
1916	1,788,000	5.00	9.50	17.50	27.50	57.50	115	215	1,300	—
1916D	6,540,800	5.00	6.25	17.50	30.00	57.50	115	215	1,300	—

Standing Liberty Quarter. Right breast exposed; Type 1.

KM# 141   Designer: Hermon A. MacNeil. **Diameter:** 24.3 **Weight:** 6.2500 g. **Composition:** 0.9000 Silver, 0.1809 oz. ASW.

Date	Mintage	G-4	VG-8	F-12	VF-20	XF-40	AU-50	MS-60	MS-65	-65FH
1916	52,000	3,500	6,000	8,500	9,500	11,500	13,500	15,000	27,500	35,000
1917	8,792,000	22.00	38.00	50.00	65.00	95.00	185	250	1,200	1,500
1917D	1,509,200	28.00	39.00	55.00	70.00	115	195	275	950	2,500
1917S	1,952,000	30.00	39.00	60.00	80.00	160	220	400	1,600	3,500

Standing Liberty Quarter. Right breast covered; Type 2.
Three stars below eagle.

KM# 145   Designer: Hermon A. MacNeil. **Diameter:** 24.3 **Weight:** 6.2500 g. **Composition:** 0.9000 Silver, 0.1809 oz. ASW.

Mint mark

Date	Mintage	G-4	VG-8	F-12	VF-20	XF-40	AU-50	MS-60	MS-65	-65FH
1917	13,880,000	25.00	25.00	30.00	35.00	48.00	85.00	150	650	1,200
1917D	6,224,400	39.00	50.00	80.00	90.00	100.00	160	225	1,400	3,500
1917S	5,522,000	35.00	44.00	60.00	71.50	85.00	125	180	1,150	4,100
1918	14,240,000	18.50	30.00	30.00	38.00	48.00	90.00	140	625	1,800
1918D	7,380,000	28.00	36.00	57.00	65.00	90.00	150	220	1,450	5,500
1918S	11,072,000	18.00	24.00	35.00	44.00	60.00	120	225	1,500	14,500
1918/17S	Inc. above	1,500	2,150	3,750	4,200	7,000	11,500	1,500	110,000	300,000
1919	11,324,000	35.00	55.00	62.50	65.00	75.00	110	175	625	1,800
1919D	1,944,000	85.00	145	185	275	440	575	1,000	2,900	27,500
1919S	1,836,000	85.00	200	250	325	520	725	1,100	4,500	30,000
1920	27,860,000	16.00	21.00	30.00	35.00	45.00	75.00	120	540	1,950
1920D	3,586,400	55.00	60.00	88.00	120	160	200	300	2,600	6,750
1920S	6,380,000	20.00	29.00	35.00	45.00	66.00	125	250	2,400	27,500
1921	1,916,000	180	240	325	400	480	650	800	1,850	4,750
1923	9,716,000	15.00	21.00	35.00	40.00	50.00	80.00	125	1,000	4,500
1923S	1,360,000	260	390	550	660	900	1,050	1,500	2,200	4,600
1924	10,920,000	16.00	20.00	25.00	30.00	36.00	75.00	120	525	1,800
1924D	3,112,000	55.00	75.00	100.00	140	180	215	280	650	4,600
1924S	2,860,000	28.00	33.00	41.50	55.00	105	240	375	2,000	5,750
1925	12,280,000	3.00	4.00	7.00	15.00	35.00	72.50	125	525	1,200
1926	11,316,000	3.00	4.00	7.00	15.00	35.00	75.00	125	525	2,000
1926D	1,716,000	7.00	9.00	16.00	30.00	65.00	100.00	140	525	26,000
1926S	2,700,000	3.00	4.00	12.00	30.00	110	275	345	2,200	28,000
1927	11,912,000	3.00	4.00	6.00	15.00	40.00	80.00	125	525	1,200
1927D	976,400	12.50	17.50	23.00	60.00	130	175	220	700	3,100
1927S	396,000	25.00	30.00	90.00	300	1,250	3,000	4,000	16,000	175,000
1928	6,336,000	3.00	4.00	5.00	15.00	35.00	75.00	105	525	2,500
1928D	1,627,600	4.00	6.00	8.00	18.00	40.00	100.00	150	525	6,250
1928S	2,644,000	4.00	5.00	6.00	15.00	32.00	72.00	150	525	1,050
1929	11,140,000	3.00	4.00	6.00	11.50	36.00	75.00	130	525	1,250
1929D	1,358,000	4.00	5.00	8.00	14.00	34.00	72.00	150	525	6,750
1929S	1,764,000	3.00	4.00	5.00	15.00	35.00	75.00	150	525	900
1930	5,632,000	3.00	4.00	4.50	12.50	35.00	75.00	125	525	900
1930S	1,556,000	4.00	5.00	6.00	16.00	39.00	80.00	130	650	1,000

Washington Quarter.

KM# 164 **Designer:** John Flanagan. **Diameter:** 24.3 **Weight:** 6.2500 g. **Composition:** 0.9000 Silver, 0.1809 oz. ASW.

Mint mark 1932-64

Date	Mintage	G-4	VG-8	F-12	VF-20	XF-40	AU-50	MS-60	MS-65	Prf-65
1932	5,404,000	4.00	5.50	6.00	7.25	9.50	15.00	24.00	415	—
1932D	436,800	140	150	165	170	275	550	1,000	26,500	—
1932S	408,000	140	150	160	165	190	235	500	7,800	—
1934	31,912,052	2.00	2.50	3.00	3.50	5.00	9.00	25.00	90.00	—
1934D	3,527,200	3.75	5.50	6.50	10.00	15.00	80.00	220	1,500	—
1935	32,484,000	1.75	2.00	2.25	2.50	4.00	8.00	20.00	110	—
1935D	5,780,000	2.25	3.00	5.00	10.00	20.00	115	220	975	—
1935S	5,660,000	2.00	2.50	4.50	6.00	13.00	32.00	85.00	330	—
1936	41,303,837	1.75	1.85	2.00	2.50	4.00	8.50	20.00	95.00	1,050
1936D	5,374,000	3.75	4.40	5.65	20.00	47.50	260	600	1,850	—
1936S	3,828,000	2.25	2.50	3.50	5.00	12.00	45.00	100.00	425	—
1937	19,701,542	2.00	2.25	3.00	3.50	4.50	16.00	22.00	90.00	380
1937D	7,189,600	2.00	2.50	3.25	5.00	12.50	28.00	60.00	140	—
1937S	1,652,000	4.00	4.50	6.00	13.50	27.50	85.00	120	345	—
1938	9,480,045	3.75	4.50	5.00	6.00	14.00	41.50	85.00	250	225
1938S	2,832,000	4.50	5.00	5.50	7.00	19.00	52.50	95.00	235	—
1939	33,548,795	1.65	1.75	2.10	2.50	3.25	7.00	20.00	60.00	150
1939D	7,092,000	2.00	2.25	3.00	4.50	8.50	16.00	37.50	100.00	—
1939S	2,628,000	3.50	3.75	4.00	6.75	16.00	45.00	100.00	325	—
1940	35,715,246	1.65	1.75	2.00	2.50	3.25	6.00	25.00	65.00	150
1940D	2,797,600	2.50	3.00	6.00	10.00	23.50	55.00	115	325	—
1940S	8,244,000	2.25	2.50	5.00	6.00	8.00	14.00	20.00	53.00	—
1941	79,047,287	—	—	1.65	2.00	2.50	3.50	12.50	45.00	110
1941D	16,714,800	—	—	2.25	3.00	4.50	12.50	35.00	95.00	—
1941S	16,080,000	—	—	2.00	2.50	3.50	10.00	30.00	80.00	—
1942	102,117,123	—	—	1.65	2.00	3.00	3.50	7.00	40.00	110
1942D	17,487,200	—	—	1.75	2.50	3.75	8.00	15.00	45.00	—
1942S	19,384,000	—	—	2.00	3.00	5.00	20.00	75.00	225	—
1943	99,700,000	—	—	1.50	2.00	2.25	3.00	5.00	45.00	—
1943D	16,095,600	—	—	2.00	3.50	6.00	12.50	27.50	70.00	—
1943S	21,700,000	—	—	3.00	5.00	7.50	15.00	30.00	70.00	—
1944	104,956,000	—	—	1.50	2.00	2.25	3.00	5.00	42.00	—
1944D	14,600,800	—	—	1.75	2.50	3.75	8.50	15.00	45.00	—
1944S	12,560,000	—	—	2.00	2.75	4.00	9.00	15.00	40.00	—
1945	74,372,000	—	—	1.50	1.75	2.00	2.50	5.00	42.00	—
1945D	12,341,600	—	—	2.00	3.50	6.50	11.00	17.50	44.00	—
1945S	17,004,001	—	—	1.75	2.50	3.50	6.00	10.00	42.00	—
1946	53,436,000	—	—	1.50	1.75	2.00	2.50	5.00	42.00	—
1946D	9,072,800	—	—	1.50	2.00	2.50	4.00	8.00	45.00	—
1946S	4,204,000	—	—	2.50	2.75	3.00	3.50	8.00	43.00	—
1947	22,556,000	—	—	1.65	2.10	2.75	4.00	10.00	45.00	—
1947D	15,338,400	—	—	1.65	2.25	3.00	4.00	10.00	45.00	—
1947S	5,532,000	—	—	2.25	2.50	2.75	4.00	10.00	45.00	—
1948	35,196,000	—	—	1.65	2.00	2.25	3.00	4.00	43.00	—
1948D	16,766,800	—	—	1.75	2.10	2.75	5.50	10.00	55.00	—
1948S	15,960,000	—	—	1.75	2.10	2.50	4.00	11.00	70.00	—
1949	9,312,000	—	—	2.00	3.00	6.50	14.00	35.00	75.00	—
1949D	10,068,400	—	—	2.25	2.50	5.00	7.00	25.00	52.50	—
1950	24,971,512	—	—	1.50	1.75	2.25	3.00	5.50	30.00	55.00
1950D	21,075,600	—	—	1.65	2.00	2.50	3.00	5.00	32.00	—
1950D/S	Inc. above	30.00	33.00	40.00	60.00	140	215	275	2,250	—
1950S	10,284,004	—	—	2.25	2.50	3.25	4.50	9.00	40.00	—
1950S/D	Inc. above	32.00	36.00	44.00	70.00	180	315	400	850	—
1951	43,505,602	—	—	1.50	1.75	2.25	3.50	6.00	32.00	40.00
1951D	35,354,800	—	—	1.50	2.00	2.50	3.50	7.00	38.00	—
1951S	9,048,000	—	—	3.00	4.50	6.00	9.00	24.00	52.00	—
1952	38,862,073	—	—	1.50	1.75	2.75	3.50	5.50	35.00	37.00
1952D	49,795,200	—	—	1.50	1.65	2.75	3.25	5.00	32.00	—
1952S	13,707,800	—	—	2.50	4.00	6.00	9.00	21.00	42.00	—
1953	18,664,920	—	—	1.50	1.65	1.75	3.00	5.50	30.00	25.00
1953D	56,112,400	—	—	1.50	1.65	1.75	2.75	4.25	29.00	—
1953S	14,016,000	—	—	1.50	1.75	2.10	2.75	5.00	30.00	—
1954	54,645,503	—	—	—	1.50	1.75	2.75	5.00	30.00	13.00
1954D	42,305,500	—	—	—	1.50	1.75	2.75	4.75	30.00	—
1954S	11,834,722	—	—	—	1.50	1.75	2.75	4.00	25.00	—
1955	18,558,381	—	—	—	1.65	1.75	2.75	3.50	25.00	14.00

Date	Mintage	G-4	VG-8	F-12	VF-20	XF-40	AU-50	MS-60	MS-65	Prf-65
1955D	3,182,400	—	—	2.00	2.25	2.50	2.75	3.25	45.00	—
1956	44,813,384	—	—	—	1.65	2.00	2.75	4.00	22.00	4.00
1956D	32,334,500	—	—	—	1.75	2.00	2.50	3.00	26.00	—
1957	47,779,952	—	—	—	1.65	1.75	2.25	3.50	23.00	4.00
1957D	77,924,160	—	—	—	1.65	1.75	2.00	2.25	26.00	—
1958	7,235,652	—	—	—	2.00	2.25	2.50	2.75	20.00	6.00
1958D	78,124,900	—	—	—	1.65	1.75	2.00	2.50	20.00	—
1959	25,533,291	—	—	—	1.65	1.75	2.00	2.75	20.00	4.25
1959D	62,054,232	—	—	—	1.65	1.75	2.00	2.75	25.00	—
1960	30,855,602	—	—	—	1.65	1.75	2.00	2.50	17.00	3.75
1960D	63,000,324	—	—	—	1.65	1.75	2.00	2.50	17.00	—
1961	40,064,244	—	—	—	1.65	1.75	2.00	2.75	19.00	3.50
1961D	83,656,928	—	—	—	1.65	1.75	2.00	2.50	16.00	—
1962	39,374,019	—	—	—	1.65	1.75	2.00	2.50	18.00	3.50
1962D	127,554,756	—	—	—	1.65	1.75	2.00	2.50	16.00	—
1963	77,391,645	—	—	—	1.50	1.60	2.00	2.50	15.00	3.50
1963D	135,288,184	—	—	—	1.50	1.60	2.00	2.50	15.00	—
1964	564,341,347	—	—	—	1.50	1.60	2.00	2.50	15.00	3.50
1964D	704,135,528	—	—	—	1.50	1.60	2.00	2.50	15.00	—

Washington Quarter.

KM# 164a **Designer:** John Flanagan. **Diameter:** 24.3 **Weight:** 5.6700 g. **Composition:** Copper-Nickel Clad Copper.

Date	Mintage	MS-65	Prf-65	Date	Mintage	MS-65	Prf-65
1965	1,819,717,540	8.00	—	1971D	258,634,428	2.50	—
1966	821,101,500	4.50	—	1971S	(3,220,733)	—	3.00
1967	1,524,031,848	6.50	—	1972	215,048,000	4.00	—
1968	220,731,500	7.50	—	1972D	311,067,732	5.50	—
1968D	101,534,000	5.00	—	1972S	(3,260,996)	—	3.00
1968S	(3,041,506)	—	3.50	1973	346,924,000	7.00	—
1969	176,212,000	7.50	—	1973D	232,977,400	9.00	—
1969D	114,372,000	6.50	—	1973S	(2,760,339)	—	3.00
1969S	(2,934,631)	—	3.50	1974	801,456,000	6.50	—
1970	136,420,000	6.50	—	1974D	353,160,300	10.00	—
1970D	417,341,364	6.00	—	1974S	(2,612,568)	—	3.00
1970S	(2,632,810)	—	3.00	1975 none minted	—	—	—
1971	109,284,000	6.00	—	1975D none minted	—	—	—
				1975S none minted	—	—	—

Washington Quarter. Bicentennial design, drummer boy.

KM# 204 **Rev. Designer:** Jack L. Ahr. **Diameter:** 24.3 **Weight:** 5.6700 g. **Composition:** Copper-Nickel Clad Copper.

Mint mark
1968 - present

Date	Mintage	G-4	VG-8	F-12	VF-20	XF-40	MS-60	MS-65	Prf-65
1976	809,784,016	—	—	—	—	—	.60	3.50	—
1976D	860,118,839	—	—	—	—	—	.60	4.00	—
1976S	(4,149,730)	—	—	—	—	—	—	—	3.00

Washington Quarter. Bicentennial design, drummer boy.

KM# 204a **Rev. Designer:** Jack L. Ahr. **Diameter:** 24.3 **Weight:** 5.7500 g. **Composition:** Silver Clad, 0.074 oz.

Date	Mintage	G-4	VG-8	F-12	VF-20	XF-40	MS-60	MS-65	Prf-65
1976S	4,908,319(3,998,621)	—	—	—	—	—	1.25	3.00	3.00

Washington Quarter. Regular design resumed.

KM# A164a **Diameter:** 24.3 **Weight:** 5.6700 g. **Composition:** Copper-Nickel Clad Copper. **Notes:** KM#164 design and composition resumed. The 1979-S and 1981 Type II proofs have clearer mint marks than the Type I proofs for those years.

Date	Mintage	MS-65	Prf-65	Date	Mintage	MS-65	Prf-65
1977	468,556,000	6.50	—	1979S T-II	—	—	3.00
1977D	256,524,978	4.00	—	1980P	635,832,000	5.00	—
1977S	(3,251,152)	—	1.50	1980D	518,327,487	4.75	—
1978	521,452,000	6.00	—	1980S	(3,554,806)	—	2.00
1978D	287,373,152	8.00	—	1981P	601,716,000	6.00	—
1978S	(3,127,781)	—	3.00	1981D	575,722,833	4.00	—
1979	515,708,000	6.00	—	1981S T-I	—	—	1.75
1979D	489,789,780	4.00	—	1981S T-II	—	—	5.00
1979S T-I	—	—	2.00	1982P	500,931,000	18.50	—

Date	Mintage	MS-65	Prf-65
1982D	480,042,788	10.00	—
1982S	(3,857,479)	—	2.75
1983P	673,535,000	45.00	—
1983D	617,806,446	30.00	—
1983S	(3,279,126)	—	2.75
1984P	676,545,000	10.00	—
1984D	546,483,064	7.00	—
1984S	(3,065,110)	—	2.75
1985P	775,818,962	10.00	—
1985D	519,962,888	6.00	—
1985S	(3,362,821)	5.00	1.75
1986P	551,199,333	7.00	—
1986D	504,298,660	10.00	—
1986S	(3,010,497)	—	3.00
1987P	582,499,481	7.00	—
1987D	655,594,696	5.00	—
1987S	(4,227,728)	—	1.75
1988P	562,052,000	9.00	—
1988D	596,810,688	8.00	—
1988S	(3,262,948)	—	2.25
1989P	512,868,000	9.00	—
1989D	896,535,597	3.00	—
1989S	(3,220,194)	—	2.25
1990P	613,792,000	9.00	—
1990D	927,638,181	3.00	—
1990S	(3,299,559)	—	6.00
1991P	570,968,000	8.00	—
1991D	630,966,693	7.00	—
1991S	(2,867,787)	—	2.50
1992P	384,764,000	12.00	—
1992D	389,777,107	15.00	—

Date	Mintage	MS-65	Prf-65
1992S	(2,858,981)	—	3.00
1993P	639,276,000	6.00	—
1993D	645,476,128	7.50	—
1993S	(2,633,439)	—	4.50
1994P	825,600,000	12.00	—
1994D	880,034,110	7.00	—
1994S	(2,484,594)	—	4.00
1995P	1,004,336,000	10.00	—
1995D	1,103,216,000	9.00	—
1995S	(2,010,384)	—	16.50
1996P	925,040,000	5.00	—
1996S	—	—	4.00
1996D	906,868,000	5.00	—
1997P	595,740,000	4.00	—
1997D	599,680,000	4.00	—
1997S	(1,975,000)	—	9.50
1998P	896,268,000	4.00	—
1998D	821,000,000	4.00	—
1998S	—	—	11.00

Washington Quarter.

KM# A164b   **Composition:** Silver.

Date	Mintage	Prf-65
1992S	(1,317,579)	3.50
1993S	(761,353)	6.50
1994S	(785,329)	12.50
1995S	(838,953)	18.00
1996S	—	11.50
1997S	—	19.00
1998S	—	10.00

50 State Quarters

Connecticut

KM# 297   **Composition:** Copper-Nickel Clad Copper.

Date	Mintage	MS-63	MS-65	Prf-65
1999P	688,744,000	.75	1.00	—
1999D	657,480,000	.75	1.00	—
1999S	(3,713,359)	—	—	10.00

KM# 297a   **Composition:** 0.9000 Silver.

Date	Mintage	MS-63	MS-65	Prf-65
1999S	(804,565)	—	—	40.00

Delaware

KM# 293   **Diameter:** 24.3 **Weight:** 5.6700 g.
Composition: Copper-Nickel Clad Copper.

Date	Mintage	MS-63	MS-65	Prf-65
1999P	373,400,000	1.25	1.50	—
1999D	401,424,000	1.25	1.50	—
1999S	(3,713,359)	—	—	10.00

KM# 293a   **Composition:** 0.9000 Silver.

Date	Mintage	MS-63	MS-65	Prf-65
1999S	(804,565)	—	—	40.00

Georgia

KM# 296a   **Composition:** 0.9000 Silver.

Date	Mintage	MS-63	MS-65	Prf-65
1999S	(804,565)	—	—	40.00

KM# 296   **Composition:** Copper-Nickel Clad Copper.

Date	Mintage	MS-63	MS-65	Prf-65
1999P	451,188,000	.75	1.00	—
1999D	488,744,000	.75	1.00	—
1999S	(3,713,359)	—	—	10.00

New Jersey

KM# 295 **Composition:** Copper-Nickel Clad Copper.

Date	Mintage	MS-63	MS-65	Prf-65
1999P	363,200,000	1.00	1.50	—
1999D	299,028,000	1.00	1.75	—
1999S	(3,713,359)	—	—	10.00

KM# 295a **Composition:** 0.9000 Silver.

Date	Mintage	MS-63	MS-65	Prf-65
1999S	(804,565)	—	—	40.00

Pennsylvania

KM# 294 **Diameter:** 24.3 **Weight:** 5.6700 g.
Composition: Copper-Nickel Clad Copper.

Date	Mintage	MS-63	MS-65	Prf-65
1999P	349,000,000	1.50	2.00	—
1999D	358,332,000	1.25	1.50	—
1999S	(3,713,359)	—	—	10.00

KM# 294a **Composition:** 0.9000 Silver.

Date	Mintage	MS-63	MS-65	Prf-65
1999S	(804,565)	—	—	40.00

Maryland

KM# 306 **Composition:** Copper-Nickel Clad Copper.

Date	Mintage	MS-63	MS-65	Prf-65
2000P	678,200,000	.75	1.00	—
2000D	556,526,000	.75	1.00	—
2000S	(4,078,747)	—	—	5.00

KM# 306a **Composition:** 0.9000 Silver.

Date	Mintage	MS-63	MS-65	Prf-65
2000S	(965,921)	—	—	7.50

Massachusetts

KM# 305 **Composition:** Copper-Nickel Clad Copper.

Date	Mintage	MS-63	MS-65	Prf-65
2000P	629,800,000	.75	1.00	—
2000D	535,184,000	.75	1.00	—
2000S	(4,078,747)	—	—	5.00

KM# 305a **Composition:** 0.9000 Silver.

Date	Mintage	MS-63	MS-65	Prf-65
2000S	(965,921)	—	—	7.50

New Hampshire

KM# 308a **Composition:** 0.9000 Silver.

Date	Mintage	MS-63	MS-65	Prf-65
2000S	(965,921)	—	—	7.50

KM# 308 **Composition:** Copper-Nickel Clad Copper.

Date	Mintage	MS-63	MS-65	Prf-65
2000P	673,040,000	.75	1.00	—
2000D	495,976,000	.75	1.00	—
2000S	(4,078,747)	—	—	5.00

South Carolina

Date	Mintage	MS-63	MS-65	Prf-65
2000D	566,208,000	.75	1.00	—
2000S	(4,078,747)	—	—	5.00

KM# 307a **Composition:** 0.9000 Silver.

Date	Mintage	MS-63	MS-65	Prf-65
2000S	(965,921)	—	—	7.50

KM# 307 **Composition:** Copper-Nickel Clad Copper.

Date	Mintage	MS-63	MS-65	Prf-65
2000P	742,756,000	.75	1.00	—

Virginia

KM# 309   **Composition:** Copper-Nickel Clad Copper.

Date	Mintage	MS-63	MS-65	Prf-65
2000P	943,000,000	.75	1.00	—
2000D	651,616,000	.75	1.00	—
2000S	(4,078,747)	—	—	5.00

KM# 309a   **Composition:** 0.9000 Silver.

Date	Mintage	MS-63	MS-65	Prf-65
2000S	(965,921)	—	—	7.50

Kentucky

KM# 322   **Composition:** Copper-Nickel Clad Copper.

Date	Mintage	MS-63	MS-65	Prf-65
2001P	353,000,000	.75	1.00	—
2001D	370,564,000	.75	1.00	—
2001S	(3,009,800)	—	—	6.50

KM# 322a   **Composition:** 0.9000 Silver.

Date	Mintage	MS-63	MS-65	Prf-65
2001S	(849,500)	—	—	22.50

New York

KM# 318   **Composition:** Copper-Nickel Clad Copper.

Date	Mintage	MS-63	MS-65	Prf-65
2001P	655,400,000	.75	1.00	—
2001D	619,640,000	.75	1.00	—
2001S	(3,009,800)	—	—	6.50

KM# 318a   **Composition:** 0.9000 Silver.

Date	Mintage	MS-63	MS-65	Prf-65
2001S	(849,600)	—	—	22.50

North Carolina

KM# 319   **Composition:** Copper-Nickel Clad Copper.

Date	Mintage	MS-63	MS-65	Prf-65
2001P	627,600,000	.75	1.00	—
2001D	427,876,000	.75	1.00	—
2001S	(3,009,800)	—	—	6.50

KM# 319a   **Composition:** 0.9000 Silver.

Date	Mintage	MS-63	MS-65	Prf-65
2001S	(849,600)	—	—	22.50

Rhode Island

KM# 320   **Composition:** Copper-Nickel Clad Copper.

Date	Mintage	MS-63	MS-65	Prf-65
2001P	423,000,000	.75	1.00	—
2001D	447,100,000	.75	1.00	—
2001S	(3,009,800)	—	—	6.50

KM# 320a   **Composition:** 0.9000 Silver.

Date	Mintage	MS-63	MS-65	Prf-65
2001S	(849,600)	—	—	22.50

Vermont

Date	Mintage	MS-63	MS-65	Prf-65
2001P	423,400,000	.75	1.00	—
2001D	459,404,000	.75	1.00	—
2001S	(3,009,800)	—	—	6.50

KM# 321a   **Composition:** 0.9000 Silver.

Date	Mintage	MS-63	MS-65	Prf-65
2001S	(849,600)	—	—	22.50

KM# 321   **Composition:** Copper-Nickel Clad Copper.

Indiana

KM# 334 **Composition:** Copper-Nickel Clad Copper.

Date	Mintage	MS-63	MS-65	Prf-65
2002P	362,600,000	.75	1.00	—
2002D	327,200,000	.75	1.00	—
2002S	(3,084,185)	—	—	6.00

KM# 334a **Composition:** 0.9000 Silver.

Date	Mintage	MS-63	MS-65	Prf-65
2002S	(892,229)	—	—	18.00

Louisiana

KM# 333 **Composition:** Copper-Nickel Clad Copper.

Date	Mintage	MS-63	MS-65	Prf-65
2002P	362,000,000	.75	1.00	—
2002D	402,204,000	.75	1.00	—
2002S	(3,084,185)	—	—	6.00

KM# 333a **Composition:** 0.9000 Silver.

Date	Mintage	MS-63	MS-65	Prf-65
2002S	(892,229)	—	—	18.00

Mississippi

KM# 335 **Composition:** Copper-Nickel Clad Copper.

Date	Mintage	MS-63	MS-65	Prf-65
2002P	290,000,000	.75	1.00	—
2002D	289,600,000	.75	1.00	—
2002S	(3,084,185)	—	—	6.00

KM# 335a **Composition:** 0.9000 Silver.

Date	Mintage	MS-63	MS-65	Prf-65
2002S	(892,229)	—	—	18.00

Ohio

KM# 332a **Composition:** 0.9000 Silver.

Date	Mintage	MS-63	MS-65	Prf-65
2002S	(892,229)	—	—	18.00

KM# 332 **Composition:** Copper-Nickel Clad Copper.

Date	Mintage	MS-63	MS-65	Prf-65
2002P	217,200,000	.75	1.00	—
2002D	414,832,000	.75	1.00	—
2002S	(3,084,185)	—	—	6.00

Tennessee

KM# 331a **Composition:** 0.9000 Silver.

Date	Mintage	MS-63	MS-65	Prf-65
2002S	(892,229)	—	—	18.00

KM# 331 **Composition:** Copper-Nickel Clad Copper.

Date	Mintage	MS-63	MS-65	Prf-65
2002P	361,600,000	1.25	2.00	—
2002D	286,468,000	.85	1.25	—
2002S	(3,084,185)	—	—	6.00

Alabama

Date	Mintage	MS-63	MS-65	Prf-65
2003D	232,400,000	.75	1.00	—
2003S	(3,270,603)	—	—	5.00

KM# 344a **Composition:** 0.9000 Silver.

Date	Mintage	MS-63	MS-65	Prf-65
2003S	—	—	—	9.00

KM# 344 **Composition:** Copper-Nickel Clad Copper.

Date	Mintage	MS-63	MS-65	Prf-65
2003P	225,000,000	.75	1.00	—

Arkansas

KM# 347 **Composition:** Copper-Nickel Clad Copper.

Date	Mintage	MS-63	MS-65	Prf-65
2003P	228,000,000	.75	1.00	—
2003D	229,800,000	.75	1.00	—
2003S	(3,270,603)	—	—	5.00

KM# 347a **Composition:** 0.9000 Silver.

Date	Mintage	MS-63	MS-65	Prf-65
2003S	—	—	—	9.00

Illinois

KM# 343 **Composition:** Copper-Nickel Clad Copper.

Date	Mintage	MS-63	MS-65	Prf-65
2003P	225,800,000	.75	1.00	—
2003D	237,400,000	.75	1.00	—
2003S	(3,270,603)	—	—	5.00

KM# 343a **Composition:** 0.9000 Silver.

Date	Mintage	MS-63	MS-65	Prf-65
2003S	—	—	—	9.00

Maine

KM# 345a **Composition:** 0.9000 Silver.

Date	Mintage	MS-63	MS-65	Prf-65
2003S	—	—	—	9.00

KM# 345 **Composition:** Copper-Nickel Clad Copper.

Date	Mintage	MS-63	MS-65	Prf-65
2003P	217,400,000	.75	1.00	—
2003D	213,400,000	.75	1.00	—
2003S	(3,270,603)	—	—	5.00

Missouri

KM# 346 **Composition:** Copper-Nickel Clad Copper.

Date	Mintage	MS-63	MS-65	Prf-65
2003P	225,000,000	.75	1.00	—
2003D	228,200,000	.75	1.00	—
2003S	(3,270,603)	—	—	5.00

KM# 346a **Composition:** 0.9000 Silver.

Date	Mintage	MS-63	MS-65	Prf-65
2003S	—	—	—	9.00

Florida

KM# 356 **Composition:** Copper-Nickel Clad Copper.

Date	Mintage	MS-63	MS-65	Prf-65
2004D	241,600,000	.75	1.00	—
2004S	—	—	—	—
2004P	240,200,000	.75	1.00	—

KM# 356a **Composition:** 0.9000 Silver.

Date	Mintage	MS-63	MS-65	Prf-65
2004S	—	—	—	—

Iowa

KM# 358 **Composition:** Copper-Nickel Clad Copper.

Date	Mintage	MS-63	MS-65	Prf-65
2004P	—	—	—	—
2004D	—	—	—	—
2004S	—	—	—	—

KM# 358a **Composition:** 0.9000 Silver.

Date	Mintage	MS-63	MS-65	Prf-65
2004S	—	—	—	—

Michigan

KM# 355a **Composition:** 0.9000 Silver.

Date	Mintage	MS-63	MS-65	Prf-65
2004S	—	—	—	—

Michigan continued

KM# 355 **Composition:** Copper-Nickel Clad Copper.

Date	Mintage	MS-63	MS-65	Prf-65
2004P	233,800,000	.75	1.00	—
2004D	225,800,000	.75	1.00	—
2004S	—	—	—	—

Texas

KM# 357 **Composition:** Copper-Nickel Clad Copper.

Date	Mintage	MS-63	MS-65	Prf-65
2004D	—	—	—	—
2004S	—	—	—	—
2004P	—	—	—	—

KM# 357a **Composition:** 0.9000 Silver.

Date	Mintage	MS-63	MS-65	Prf-65
2004S	—	—	—	—

Wisconsin

KM# 359 **Composition:** Copper-Nickel Clad Copper.

Date	Mintage	MS-63	MS-65	Prf-65
2004P	—	—	—	—
2004D	—	—	—	—
2004S	—	—	—	—

KM# 359a **Composition:** 0.9000 Silver.

Date	Mintage	MS-63	MS-65	Prf-65
2004S	—	—	—	—

HALF DOLLAR

Flowing Hair Half Dollar.

KM# 16   Designer: Robert Scot. **Diameter:** 32.5 **Weight:** 13.4800 g. **Composition:** 0.8920 Silver, 0.3869 oz. ASW. **Notes:** The 1795 "recut date" variety had the date cut into the dies twice, so both sets of numbers are visible on the coin. The 1795 "3 leaves" variety has three leaves under each of the eagle's wings on the reverse.

Date	Mintage	G-4	VG-8	F-12	VF-20	XF-40	MS-60
1794	23,464	2,400	4,000	6,000	13,000	20,000	90,000
1795	299,680	650	900	1,700	3,500	7,500	22,000
1795 recut date	Inc. above	700	950	1,750	3,750	7,750	25,000
1795 3 leaves	Inc. above	1,050	1,800	3,000	6,000	12,500	—

Draped Bust Half Dollar. Small eagle.

KM# 26   Designer: Robert Scot. **Diameter:** 32.5 **Weight:** 13.4800 g. **Composition:** 0.8920 Silver, 0.3869 oz. ASW. **Notes:** The 1796 strikes have either 15 or 16 stars on the obverse.

Date	Mintage	G-4	VG-8	F-12	VF-20	XF-40	MS-60
1796 15 stars	3,918	29,000	35,000	40,000	55,000	80,000	175,000
1796 16 stars	Inc. above	30,000	36,000	42,000	60,000	85,000	200,000
1797	Inc. above	29,000	35,000	40,000	55,000	80,000	175,000

Draped Bust Half Dollar. Heraldic eagle.

KM# 35   Designer: Robert Scot. **Diameter:** 32.5 **Weight:** 13.4800 g. **Composition:** 0.8920 Silver, 0.3869 oz. ASW. **Notes:** The two varieties of the 1803 strikes are distinguished by the size of the 3 in the date. The several varieties of the 1806 strikes are distinguished by the style of 6 in the date, size of the stars on the obverse, and whether the stem of the olive branch held by the reverse eagle extends through the claw.

Date	Mintage	G-4	VG-8	F-12	VF-20	XF-40	MS-60
1801	30,289	225	300	700	1,500	5,000	35,000
1802	29,890	225	300	700	1,500	4,500	40,000
1803 small 3	188,234	150	170	300	600	1,500	8,500
1803 large 3	Inc. above	125	150	250	500	1,000	9,000
1805	211,722	125	150	250	550	1,050	9,000
1805/4	Inc. above	190	300	500	1,000	2,500	26,000
1806 round-top 6, large stars	839,576	125	150	190	450	1,100	6,000
1806 round-top 6, small stars	Inc. above	125	140	180	450	1,100	6,250
1806 knobbed 6, stem not through claw	—	—	35,000	40,000	50,000	65,000	—
1806 pointed-top 6, stem not through claw	Inc. above	115	130	250	340	1,000	5,750
1806 pointed-top 6, stem through claw	Inc. above	120	150	250	340	1,000	5,750
1806/5	Inc. above	125	160	275	500	1,400	8,000
1806 /inverted 6	Inc. above	200	350	600	1,200	2,100	15,000
1807	301,076	120	150	250	340	1,000	5,750

108

Bust Half Dollar. "50 C." below eagle.

KM# 37   Designer: John Reich. **Diameter:** 32.5
Weight: 13.4800 g. **Composition:** 0.8920 Silver,
0.3869 oz. ASW. **Notes:** There are three varieties of the
1807 strikes. Two are distinguished by the size of the
stars on the obverse. The third was struck from a reverse
die that had a 5 cut over a 2 in the "50C" denomination.
Two varieties of the 1811 are distinguished by the size of
the 8 in the date. A third has a period between the 8 and
second 1 in the date. One variety of the 1817 has a period
between the 1 and 7 in the date. Two varieties of the
1819/18 overdate are distinguished by the size of the 9 in
the date. Two varieties of the 1820 are distinguished by
the size of the date. On the 1823 varieties, the "broken 3"
appears to be almost separated in the middle of the 3 in
the date; the "patched 3" has the error repaired; the "ugly
3" has portions of its detail missing. The 1827 "curled-2"
and "square-2" varieties are distinguished by the
numeral's base -- either curled or square. Among the
1828 varieties, "knobbed 2" and "no knob" refers to
whether the upper left serif of the digit is rounded. The
1830 varieties are distinguished by the size of the 0 in the
date. The four 1834 varieties are distinguished by the
sizes of the stars, date and letters in the inscriptions. The
1836 "50/00" variety was struck from a reverse die that
had "50" recut over "00" in the denomination.

Date	Mintage	G-4	VG-8	F-12	VF-20	XF-40	AU-50	MS-60	MS-65
1807 small stars	750,500	65.00	105	200	475	800	3,500	5,900	35,000
1807 large stars	Inc. above	60.00	100.00	180	475	800	3,500	5,500	—
1807 50/20 C.	Inc. above	55.00	92.50	140	250	500	2,100	4,000	30,000
1807 bearded goddess	—	300	500	900	1,500	2,750	7,500	—	—
1808	1,368,600	50.00	57.50	65.00	100.00	260	600	1,800	15,000
1808/7	Inc. above	52.50	62.50	92.50	160	330	900	1,850	17,500
1809	1,405,810	50.00	57.50	65.00	100.00	210	525	1,600	15,000
1810	1,276,276	52.50	57.50	66.00	100.00	175	475	1,550	13,000
1811 small 8	1,203,644	52.50	60.00	65.00	100.00	140	375	800	7,500
1811 large 8	Inc. above	50.00	57.50	62.50	95.00	150	500	1,000	8,500
1811 dated 18.11	Inc. above	55.00	60.00	80.00	150	300	800	2,100	12,000
1812	1,628,059	52.50	60.00	65.00	100.00	150	340	775	7,500
1812/1 small 8	Inc. above	53.50	61.00	90.00	160	250	700	2,000	12,000
1812/1 large 8	Inc. above	1,350	1,900	3,500	4,850	7,500	15,500	—	—
1813	1,241,903	52.50	60.00	65.00	100.00	165	500	1,250	11,000
1813 50/UNI reverse	1,241,903	55.00	62.50	92.50	135	300	900	1,900	12,000
1814	1,039,075	52.50	60.00	66.00	100.00	165	500	1,350	9,800
1814/3	Inc. above	62.50	75.00	110	150	275	850	2,000	16,500
1815/2	47,150	840	11,500	1,550	1,900	3,000	4,750	11,000	60,000
1817	1,215,567	52.50	60.00	66.00	90.00	160	385	900	10,000
1817/3	Inc. above	80.00	125	175	385	800	1,800	3,750	43,500
1817/4	—	50,000	60,000	115,000	145,000	190,000	240,000	—	—
1817 dated 181.7	Inc. above	54.00	62.50	70.00	100.00	175	650	1,500	12,500
1818	1,960,322	52.50	60.00	66.00	85.00	135	375	900	8,500
1818/7	Inc. above	60.00	72.50	85.00	105	160	700	1,500	11,000
1819	2,208,000	52.50	60.00	66.00	85.00	125	375	900	9,000
1819/8 small 9	Inc. above	57.50	62.50	75.00	100.00	200	550	1,300	1,150
1819/8 large 9	Inc. above	57.50	62.50	75.00	100.00	200	550	1,300	11,500
1820 small date	751,122	53.50	61.00	75.00	145	260	650	1,500	12,500
1820 large date	Inc. above	53.50	61.00	75.00	125	250	660	1,350	12,000
1820/19	Inc. above	62.50	75.00	85.00	150	300	900	2,000	15,000
1821	1,305,797	52.50	60.00	66.00	80.00	140	525	1,200	9,750
1822	1,559,573	52.50	60.00	66.00	85.00	125	300	750	7,700
1822/1	Inc. above	60.00	68.50	92.50	150	250	800	1,750	11,000
1823	1,694,200	47.50	52.50	57.50	66.00	110	300	825	7,500
1823 broken 3	Inc. above	55.00	66.00	92.50	140	360	900	1,750	12,000
1823 patched 3	Inc. above	52.50	62.50	85.00	115	180	400	1,300	13,500
1823 ugly 3	Inc. above	53.50	67.50	88.00	135	235	900	1,700	14,000
1824	3,504,954	47.50	52.50	66.00	75.00	110	260	650	7,500
1824/21	Inc. above	52.50	60.00	66.00	85.00	150	400	1,000	8,000
1824 1824/various dates	Inc. above	52.50	60.00	70.00	125	200	750	1,750	12,000
1825	2,943,166	47.50	52.50	66.00	75.00	110	260	550	7,000
1826	4,004,180	47.50	52.50	66.00	75.00	110	260	550	7,000
1827 curled 2	5,493,400	47.50	52.50	66.00	100.00	130	345	900	8,500
1827 square 2	Inc. above	47.50	52.50	60.00	75.00	110	260	650	7,500
1827/6	Inc. above	57.50	68.50	80.00	100.00	150	375	975	9,000
1828 curled-base 2, no knob	3,075,200	47.50	52.50	66.00	75.00	110	260	650	7,000
1828 curled-base 2, knobbed 2	Inc. above	47.50	52.50	66.00	85.00	120	270	700	7,250
1828 small 8s, square-base 2, large letters	Inc. above	47.50	52.50	66.00	75.00	110	260	550	6,250
1828 small 8s, square-base 2, small letters	Inc. above	52.50	70.00	95.00	135	220	720	1,200	9,500
1828 large 8s, square-base 2	Inc. above	48.50	52.50	66.00	75.00	110	260	750	9,000
1829	3,712,156	45.00	50.00	53.50	60.00	100.00	250	600	9,000

Date	Mintage	G-4	VG-8	F-12	VF-20	XF-40	AU-50	MS-60	MS-65
1829/7	Inc. above	47.50	57.50	67.50	85.00	165	330	925	11,750
1830 small letter rev.	4,764,800	45.00	50.00	53.50	60.00	100.00	250	500	7,000
1830 large letter rev.	Inc. above	1,250	1,850	2,250	3,300	4,500	7,500	—	—
1831	5,873,660	45.00	50.00	53.50	60.00	100.00	250	500	7,000
1832 small letters	4,797,000	45.00	50.00	53.50	60.00	100.00	250	575	7,000
1832 large letters	Inc. above	45.00	50.00	64.00	90.00	155	315	700	7,500
1833	5,206,000	45.00	50.00	53.50	60.00	100.00	250	575	7,000
1834 small date, large stars, small letters	6,412,004	45.00	50.00	53.50	60.00	100.00	250	575	7,000
1834 small date, small stars, small letters	Inc. above	45.00	50.00	53.50	60.00	100.00	250	575	7,000
1834 large date, small letters	Inc. above	45.00	50.00	53.50	60.00	100.00	250	575	7,000
1834 large date, large letters	Inc. above	45.00	50.00	53.50	60.00	100.00	250	575	7,000
1835	5,352,006	45.00	50.00	53.50	60.00	100.00	275	600	9,000
1836	6,545,000	45.00	50.00	53.50	60.00	100.00	250	500	7,000
1836 50/00	Inc. above	55.00	80.00	100.00	185	300	800	1,750	10,000

Bust Half Dollar.
"50 Cents" below eagle.

KM# 58 Designer: Christian Gobrecht. **Diameter:** 30 **Weight:** 13.3600 g. **Composition:** 0.9000 Silver, 0.3867 oz. ASW.

Date	Mintage	G-4	VG-8	F-12	VF-20	XF-40	AU-50	MS-60	MS-65
1836	1,200	700	1,000	1,200	1,500	2,250	3,200	6,000	40,000
1837	3,629,820	50.00	60.00	75.00	110	165	325	750	12,500

Bust Half Dollar.
"Half Dol." below eagle.

KM# 65 Designer: Christian Gobrecht. **Diameter:** 30 **Weight:** 13.3600 g. **Composition:** 0.9000 Silver, 0.3867 oz. ASW.

Date	Mintage	G-4	VG-8	F-12	VF-20	XF-40	AU-50	MS-60	MS-65
1838	3,546,000	50.00	60.00	75.00	110	165	475	825	17,000
1838O proof only	Est. 20	85,000	105,000	115,000	125,000	150,000	180,000	—	—
1839	1,392,976	56.00	66.00	82.50	115	185	375	990	30,000
1839O	178,976	135	215	300	400	675	1,200	2,500	45,000

Seated Liberty Half Dollar.

KM# 68 Designer: Christian Gobrecht. **Diameter:** 30.6 **Weight:** 13.3600 g. **Composition:** 0.9000 Silver, .3867 oz. ASW. **Notes:** The 1839 varieties are distinguished by whether there's drapery extending from Liberty's left elbow. One variety of the 1840 strikes has smaller lettering; another used the old reverse of 1838. Varieties of 1842 and 1846 are distinguished by the size of the numerals in the date.

Date	Mintage	G-4	VG-8	F-12	VF-20	XF-40	AU-50	MS-60	MS-65
1839 no drapery from elbow	Inc. above	38.00	65.00	110	315	725	1,650	4,500	150,000
1839 drapery	Inc. above	20.00	30.00	50.00	75.00	145	265	450	—
1840 small letters	1,435,008	23.00	32.00	47.50	67.00	110	350	575	8,250
1840 reverse 1838	Inc. above	125	175	250	325	575	1,100	2,900	12,000
1840O	855,100	23.00	28.00	45.00	80.00	125	275	430	—
1841	310,000	39.00	49.00	80.00	130	200	300	1,100	5,700
1841O	401,000	19.00	28.00	44.00	75.00	125	250	550	5,900
1842 small date	2,012,764	35.00	42.00	60.00	110	185	325	1,300	12,000
1842 large date	Inc. above	18.00	28.00	43.00	52.00	100.00	175	1,250	12,000
1842O small date	957,000	650	850	1,400	2,250	4,000	—	—	—
1842O large date	Inc. above	22.00	29.00	48.00	115	225	750	1,750	—
1843	3,844,000	17.00	28.00	43.00	52.00	100.00	180	350	4,500
1843O	2,268,000	17.00	28.00	43.00	60.00	115	250	550	—

Date	Mintage	G-4	VG-8	F-12	VF-20	XF-40	AU-50	MS-60	MS-65
1844	1,766,000	17.00	28.00	43.00	52.00	100.00	210	350	4,500
1844O	2,005,000	18.00	28.00	43.00	52.00	100.00	225	525	—
1844/1844O	Inc. above	500	775	1,000	1,375	2,300	4,900	—	—
1845	589,000	30.00	40.00	60.00	110	200	375	900	—
1845O	2,094,000	18.00	28.00	43.00	52.00	125	240	550	—
1845O no drapery	Inc. above	25.00	35.00	65.00	115	185	375	750	—
1846 medium date	2,210,000	18.00	28.00	43.00	52.00	100.00	200	500	9,000
1846 tall date	Inc. above	22.00	30.00	60.00	85.00	145	250	650	12,000
1846 /horizontal 6	Inc. above	175	235	300	400	575	1,000	2,500	—
1846O medium date	2,304,000	18.00	28.00	43.00	52.00	100.00	225	550	12,000
1846O tall date	Inc. above	135	245	325	575	950	2,000	3,600	—
1847/1846	1,156,000	2,000	2,750	3,200	4,250	6,500	—	—	—
1847	Inc. above	25.00	35.00	55.00	70.00	115	250	480	9,000
1847O	2,584,000	18.00	28.00	43.00	52.00	95.00	250	640	7,000
1848	580,000	40.00	60.00	85.00	170	265	475	1,000	9,000
1848O	3,180,000	18.00	28.00	43.00	52.00	110	285	750	9,000
1849	1,252,000	26.00	40.00	55.00	90.00	150	365	1,250	9,000
1849O	2,310,000	17.00	28.00	43.00	60.00	110	250	650	9,000
1850	227,000	275		325	400	500	675	1,000	1,500	—
1850O	2,456,000	20.00	28.00	45.00	80.00	135	275	650	9,000
1851	200,750	425	500	700	900	1,000	1,250	1,950	—
1851O	402,000	37.00	45.00	75.00	105	175	300	675	9,000
1852	77,130	400	500	650	850	1,000	1,200	1,650	—
1852O	144,000	100.00	125	200	350	525	1,050	1,850	—
1853O mintage unrecorded	—	—	—	—	—	—	—	—	—

Note: 1853O, Eliasberg Sale, 1997, VG-8, $154,000.

Seated Liberty Half Dollar.
Arrows at date. Rays around eagle.
KM# 79   Designer: Christian Gobrecht.   **Weight:**
12.4400 g. **Composition:** 0.9000 Silver, 0.3600 oz. ASW.

Date	Mintage	G-4	VG-8	F-12	VF-20	XF-40	AU-50	MS-60	MS-65	Prf-65
1853	3,532,708	17.00	27.00	40.00	90.00	250	505	1,700	21,500	—
1853O	1,328,000	21.00	32.00	50.00	125	290	700	2,100	21,500	—

Seated Liberty Half Dollar.
Rays around eagle removed.
KM# 82   Designer: Christian Gobrecht.   **Weight:**
12.4400 g. **Composition:** 0.9000 Silver, 0.3600 oz. ASW.

Date	Mintage	G-4	VG-8	F-12	VF-20	XF-40	AU-50	MS-60	MS-65	Prf-65
1854	2,982,000	17.00	28.00	43.00	55.00	100.00	270	675	8,000	—
1854O	5,240,000	17.00	28.00	43.00	55.00	100.00	270	600	8,000	—
1855	759,500	23.00	33.00	45.00	75.00	150	325	1,200	8,000	22,500
1855/4	Inc. above	35.00	60.00	80.00	125	225	400	1,500	—	—
1855O	3,688,000	17.00	28.00	43.00	55.00	100.00	270	650	8,000	—
1855S	129,950	250	350	600	1,300	2,400	6,000	—	—	—

Seated Liberty Half Dollar.
Arrows at date removed.
KM# A68   Designer: Christian Gobrecht.   **Weight:**
12.4400 g. **Composition:** 0.9000 Silver, 0.3600 oz. ASW.

Date	Mintage	G-4	VG-8	F-12	VF-20	XF-40	AU-50	MS-60	MS-65	Prf-65
1856	938,000	19.00	31.00	43.00	55.00	90.00	195	425	6,500	12,500
1856O	2,658,000	17.00	28.00	43.00	52.00	90.00	190	385	12,500	—
1856S	211,000	85.00	120	160	260	475	1,250	3,500	19,000	—
1857	1,988,000	17.00	28.00	43.00	52.00	90.00	190	385	5,150	12,500
1857O	818,000	21.00	31.00	43.00	65.00	125	275	885	12,500	—
1857S	158,000	100.00	120	145	285	575	975	3,500	19,000	—
1858	4,226,000	17.00	28.00	43.00	52.00	90.00	190	385	6,500	12,500
1858O	7,294,000	17.00	28.00	43.00	52.00	90.00	190	385	12,500	—
1858S	476,000	25.00	35.00	50.00	95.00	185	400	950	12,500	—
1859	748,000	17.00	28.00	43.00	60.00	110	200	650	6,600	5,500
1859O	2,834,000	17.00	28.00	43.00	50.00	90.00	190	450	6,500	—
1859S	566,000	25.00	38.00	55.00	85.00	215	375	750	12,500	—
1860	303,700	25.00	35.00	47.50	80.00	110	350	1,000	6,500	5,500
1860O	1,290,000	17.00	28.00	43.00	52.00	90.00	190	450	5,150	—
1860S	472,000	20.00	30.00	50.00	75.00	130	245	850	12,500	—
1861	2,888,400	17.00	28.00	43.00	52.00	90.00	190	440	5,150	5,500
1861O	2,532,633	18.00	29.00	50.00	65.00	100.00	190	450	5,150	—
1861S	939,500	18.00	29.00	43.00	60.00	110	195	975	9,500	—
1862	253,550	28.00	40.00	55.00	95.00	175	285	750	5,150	5,500
1862S	1,352,000	18.00	29.00	43.00	65.00	110	195	460	9,000	—
1863	503,660	20.00	32.00	43.00	75.00	130	250	750	5,150	5,500
1863S	916,000	18.00	29.00	43.00	60.00	100.00	195	460	9,000	—
1864	379,570	29.00	35.00	60.00	95.00	175	250	750	5,150	5,500
1864S	658,000	18.00	28.00	45.00	60.00	115	215	675	9,000	—
1865	511,900	28.00	37.00	55.00	85.00	135	275	750	5,150	5,500
1865S	675,000	18.00	29.00	43.00	60.00	100.00	235	500	9,000	—
1866 proof, unique	—	—	—	—	—	—	—	—	—	—
1866S	60,000	90.00	135	215	375	795	1,500	5,000	—	—

Seated Liberty Half Dollar.
"In God We Trust" above eagle.

KM# 99   Designer: Christian Gobrecht. **Weight:**
12.4400 g. **Composition:** 0.9000 Silver, 0.3600 oz. ASW.
Notes: In 1866 the motto "In God We Trust" was added to
the reverse. The "closed-3" and "open-3" varieties are
distinguished by the amount of space between the upper
and lower left serifs of the 3.

Date	Mintage	G-4	VG-8	F-12	VF-20	XF-40	AU-50	MS-60	MS-65	Prf-65
1866	745,625	18.00	27.00	45.00	70.00	110	225	350	4,800	3,750
1866S	994,000	19.00	29.00	45.00	60.00	100.00	275	650	5,000	—
1867	449,925	25.00	35.00	55.00	90.00	145	250	350	4,800	3,750
1867S	1,196,000	19.00	29.00	40.00	60.00	100.00	250	350	7,000	—
1868	418,200	35.00	49.00	80.00	135	225	300	525	7,100	3,750
1868S	1,160,000	19.00	29.00	41.00	60.00	110	250	350	7,000	—
1869	795,900	19.00	29.00	41.00	60.00	110	190	385	4,600	3,750
1869S	656,000	20.00	29.00	41.00	60.00	120	265	600	7,000	—
1870	634,900	21.00	31.00	42.00	70.00	125	250	475	7,000	3,750
1870CC	54,617	800	1,200	1,750	2,900	10,000	—	—	—	—
1870S	1,004,000	19.00	31.00	45.00	70.00	125	275	575	7,000	—
1871	1,204,560	18.00	29.00	41.00	60.00	110	165	350	7,000	3,750
1871CC	153,950	200	325	600	1,200	1,950	10,000	15,000	—	—
1871S	2,178,000	18.00	29.00	41.00	55.00	110	215	400	7,000	—
1872	881,550	18.00	29.00	40.00	55.00	110	195	430	2,850	3,750
1872CC	272,000	70.00	100.00	200	325	1,500	4,000	8,000	50,000	—
1872S	580,000	28.00	33.00	60.00	110	185	375	975	7,000	—
1873 closed 3	801,800	23.00	30.00	50.00	90.00	135	250	500	4,500	3,750
1873 open 3	Inc. above	2,200	2,700	4,100	5,500	7,500	—	—	—	—
1873CC	122,500	170	225	325	800	1,500	2,500	4,100	9,000	3,750
1873S no arrows	5,000	—	—	—	—	—	—	—	—	—

Note: 1873S no arrows, no specimens known to survive.

Seated Liberty Half Dollar.
Arrows at date.

KM# 107   Designer: Christian Gobrecht. **Weight:**
12.5000 g. **Composition:** 0.9000 Silver, 0.3618 oz. ASW.

Date	Mintage	G-4	VG-8	F-12	VF-20	XF-40	AU-50	MS-60	MS-65	Prf-65
1873	1,815,700	18.00	27.00	40.00	85.00	210	400	850	17,500	9,000
1873CC	214,560	115	220	335	725	1,700	2,400	5,700	42,000	—
1873S	233,000	42.50	62.50	100.00	200	375	675	2,200	40,000	—
1874	2,360,300	18.00	27.00	40.00	85.00	210	400	850	12,750	9,000
1874CC	59,000	400	550	950	1,500	2,500	4,500	8,000	—	—
1874S	394,000	30.00	40.00	70.00	160	315	600	1,600	—	—

Seated Liberty Half Dollar.
Arrows at date removed.

KM# A99 Designer: Christian Gobrecht. **Weight:**
12.5000 g. **Composition:** 0.9000 Silver, 0.3618 oz. ASW.

Date	Mintage	G-4	VG-8	F-12	VF-20	XF-40	AU-50	MS-60	MS-65	Prf-65
1875	6,027,500	17.00	25.00	39.00	47.00	70.00	160	425	3,500	3,200
1875CC	1,008,000	20.00	34.00	53.00	95.00	185	300	540	5,450	—
1875S	3,200,000	17.00	26.00	40.00	47.00	80.00	165	340	2,700	—
1876	8,419,150	17.00	25.00	39.00	45.00	70.00	160	340	5,300	3,200
1876CC	1,956,000	18.00	30.00	48.00	85.00	175	275	560	4,200	—
1876S	4,528,000	17.00	25.00	39.00	45.00	70.00	160	340	2,700	—
1877	8,304,510	17.00	25.00	39.00	45.00	70.00	160	340	2,700	3,750
1877CC	1,420,000	18.00	33.00	43.00	75.00	145	275	630	3,250	—
1877S	5,356,000	17.00	25.00	39.00	45.00	70.00	160	340	2,700	—
1878	1,378,400	20.00	28.00	36.00	55.00	115	170	425	3,650	3,200
1878CC	62,000	375	525	875	1,250	2,750	5,000	7,000	42,500	—
1878S	12,000	15,000	17,500	22,000	27,500	33,000	40,000	52,500	125,000	—
1879	5,900	295	325	375	425	525	600	825	2,900	3,250
1880	9,755	275	310	365	415	500	575	800	2,900	3,250
1881	10,975	275	300	350	400	485	550	800	2,900	3,250
1882	5,500	350	400	425	500	585	650	850	3,600	3,250
1883	9,039	275	310	365	415	500	575	800	2,900	3,250
1884	5,275	375	425	450	550	600	675	825	2,900	3,250
1885	6,130	350	400	425	500	585	650	800	2,900	3,250
1886	5,886	375	425	475	575	625	700	850	4,800	3,250
1887	5,710	450	500	575	650	750	800	900	2,900	3,250
1888	12,833	280	310	365	400	485	550	800	2,900	3,250
1889	12,711	275	300	350	400	485	550	800	2,900	3,250
1890	12,590	285	310	365	415	500	550	800	3,250	3,250
1891	200,600	50.00	60.00	80.00	115	165	290	500	3,250	3,250

Barber Half Dollar.

KM# 116 Designer: Charles E. Barber. **Diameter:**
30.6 **Weight:** 12.5000 g. **Composition:** 0.9000 Silver,
0.3618 oz. ASW.

Mint mark

Date	Mintage	G-4	VG-8	F-12	VF-20	XF-40	AU-50	MS-60	MS-65	Prf-65
1892	935,245	27.50	38.50	65.00	125	190	295	475	3,000	3,300
1892O	390,000	285	375	480	535	570	635	850	4,750	—
1892O micro O	—	2,000	3,750	4,500	7,000	10,000	17,500	—	55,000	—
1892S	1,029,028	235	330	400	480	580	625	925	5,500	—
1893	1,826,792	19.00	27.50	75.00	135	205	325	535	5,500	3,300
1893O	1,389,000	35.00	62.50	110	205	360	435	650	10,500	—
1893S	740,000	140	195	285	440	515	580	1,200	27,500	—
1894	1,148,972	27.50	45.00	100.00	160	275	380	500	3,375	3,300
1894O	2,138,000	22.00	31.00	90.00	155	260	345	525	7,250	—
1894S	4,048,690	15.00	22.00	65.00	110	220	350	500	12,250	—
1895	1,835,218	16.00	22.00	67.50	130	200	325	595	3,500	3,300
1895O	1,766,000	20.00	34.00	110	165	200	385	595	7,850	—
1895S	1,108,086	30.00	50.00	115	220	285	385	575	9,000	—
1896	950,762	20.00	25.00	85.00	140	250	340	565	6,000	3,400
1896O	924,000	38.50	52.50	170	255	440	715	1,500	15,500	—
1896S	1,140,948	85.00	130	190	335	480	675	1,400	11,750	—
1897	2,480,731	12.50	15.00	46.00	96.00	155	325	485	4,300	3,300

Date	Mintage	G-4	VG-8	F-12	VF-20	XF-40	AU-50	MS-60	MS-65	Prf-65
1897O	632,000	125	225	450	800	1,000	1,250	1,700	10,000	—
1897S	933,900	150	205	345	520	825	1,050	1,500	8,500	—
1898	2,956,735	12.50	15.00	38.50	88.50	160	325	485	3,850	3,300
1898O	874,000	32.50	75.00	220	335	480	600	1,150	12,000	—
1898S	2,358,550	22.00	44.00	75.00	135	250	395	970	10,500	—
1899	5,538,846	13.50	15.00	38.50	92.50	155	310	485	4,800	3,900
1899O	1,724,000	23.00	34.00	75.00	150	275	395	650	8,500	—
1899S	1,686,411	22.00	32.50	72.50	130	220	360	660	7,000	—
1900	4,762,912	13.50	15.50	37.50	85.00	155	310	485	4,300	3,300
1900O	2,744,000	16.00	20.00	56.00	135	275	375	850	16,500	—
1900S	2,560,322	14.00	18.00	47.50	100.00	205	320	650	12,500	—
1901	4,268,813	12.50	15.00	35.00	90.00	160	300	485	4,500	3,500
1901O	1,124,000	15.00	25.00	67.50	165	310	475	1,350	17,000	—
1901S	847,044	27.50	47.50	150	320	580	960	1,850	21,250	—
1902	4,922,777	12.50	13.50	32.50	105	210	295	485	4,250	3,700
1902O	2,526,000	13.00	16.00	52.50	105	210	360	725	8,500	—
1902S	1,460,670	15.00	19.00	62.50	130	235	415	750	9,350	—
1903	2,278,755	12.50	15.00	46.00	100.00	205	340	500	11,000	3,825
1903O	2,100,000	12.50	16.00	55.00	110	215	345	680	10,000	—
1903S	1,920,772	13.50	16.00	53.50	110	235	380	610	5,750	—
1904	2,992,670	12.00	13.50	34.00	80.00	155	310	1,300	6,600	4,100
1904O	1,117,600	17.50	28.50	78.50	205	385	580	1,100	13,300	—
1904S	553,038	30.00	60.00	225	500	890	1,500	6,250	37,500	—
1905	662,727	19.00	26.00	82.50	155	250	345	575	8,500	3,900
1905O	505,000	24.00	41.00	115	225	310	440	760	5,250	—
1905S	2,494,000	12.50	15.00	48.50	110	225	360	565	10,000	—
1906	2,638,675	12.00	13.50	31.00	85.00	160	300	485	3,100	3,300
1906D	4,028,000	12.00	13.50	34.00	85.00	155	300	485	4,750	—
1906O	2,446,000	12.00	13.50	44.00	96.00	165	325	625	6,700	—
1906S	1,740,154	12.50	16.00	55.00	110	220	310	610	6,250	—
1907	2,598,575	12.00	13.50	30.00	80.00	155	300	485	3,000	4,000
1907D	3,856,000	12.00	13.50	30.00	75.00	155	300	485	3,400	—
1907O	3,946,000	12.00	13.50	31.00	85.00	155	325	595	3,700	—
1907S	1,250,000	16.00	22.00	80.00	160	325	650	1,275	13,500	—
1908	1,354,545	12.00	13.50	30.00	80.00	155	295	485	3,000	4,000
1908D	3,280,000	12.00	13.50	30.00	80.00	155	295	485	3,000	—
1908O	5,360,000	12.00	13.50	30.00	90.00	155	325	550	3,000	—
1908S	1,644,828	16.50	22.50	68.50	135	255	385	595	6,850	—
1909	2,368,650	12.50	16.00	31.00	80.00	160	295	485	3,000	4,000
1909O	925,400	13.50	20.00	60.00	125	300	525	775	5,250	—
1909S	1,764,000	12.00	13.50	35.00	96.00	190	350	595	5,000	—
1910	418,551	13.00	25.00	80.00	155	300	420	625	4,000	4,250
1910S	1,948,000	12.50	16.00	34.00	100.00	185	350	650	6,850	—
1911	1,406,543	12.00	13.50	30.00	80.00	155	300	485	3,000	3,300
1911D	695,080	12.50	15.00	41.00	85.00	200	295	575	3,350	—
1911S	1,272,000	12.50	16.00	41.00	92.50	165	330	580	6,000	—
1912	1,550,700	12.00	13.50	30.00	80.00	155	300	485	4,200	4,000
1912D	2,300,800	12.00	13.50	30.00	80.00	155	325	485	3,000	—
1912S	1,370,000	12.50	15.00	37.50	92.50	165	340	550	6,000	—
1913	188,627	45.00	62.50	190	355	535	825	1,100	4,850	3,800
1913D	534,000	13.00	15.00	46.00	96.00	200	300	500	5,500	—
1913S	604,000	14.00	20.00	50.00	120	220	365	625	5,250	—
1914	124,610	100.00	110	290	540	750	1,000	1,350	7,500	4,300
1914S	992,000	15.00	19.00	41.00	92.50	185	315	580	5,000	—
1915	138,450	62.50	80.00	225	375	550	850	1,200	6,500	4,250
1915D	1,170,400	12.00	13.50	30.00	77.50	155	295	485	3,000	—
1915S	1,604,000	14.00	18.50	38.50	85.00	155	295	485	3,050	—

Walking Liberty Half Dollar.

KM# 142   Designer: Adolph A. Weinman. **Diameter:** 30.6 **Weight:** 12.5000 g. **Composition:** 0.9000 Silver, 0.3618 oz. ASW. **Notes:** The mint mark appears on the obverse below the word "Trust" on 1916 and some 1917 issues. Starting with some 1917 issues and continuing through the remainder of the series, the mint mark was changed to the reverse, at about the 8 o'clock position near the rim.

Obverse mint mark   Reverse mint mark

Date	Mintage	G-4	VG-8	F-12	VF-20	XF-40	AU-50	MS-60	MS-65	Prf-65
1916	608,000	40.00	46.00	90.00	160	220	275	350	1,800	—
1916D	1,014,400	35.00	41.00	75.00	125	200	265	375	2,250	—

Date	Mintage	G-4	VG-8	F-12	VF-20	XF-40	AU-50	MS-60	MS-65	Prf-65
1916S	508,000	110	115	260	445	600	750	1,100	6,250	—
1917D obv.	765,400	20.00	30.00	75.00	150	220	330	625	8,000	—
1917S obv.	952,000	25.00	41.50	115	350	700	1,200	2,250	19,000	—
1917	12,292,000	4.00	5.25	8.75	20.00	40.00	75.00	135	1,000	—
1917D rev.	1,940,000	10.00	16.50	45.00	135	275	575	925	18,500	—
1917S rev.	5,554,000	4.50	8.00	16.50	33.00	54.00	160	340	13,000	—
1918	6,634,000	4.50	6.50	16.00	60.00	150	275	580	3,800	—
1918D	3,853,040	8.00	12.50	33.50	85.00	220	500	1,100	25,000	—
1918S	10,282,000	4.50	5.75	15.00	32.00	62.50	200	525	18,000	—
1919	962,000	19.00	30.00	75.00	260	515	900	1,300	7,500	—
1919D	1,165,000	14.50	32.50	90.00	300	725	1,550	6,000	130,000	—
1919S	1,552,000	16.50	27.50	70.00	290	800	1,800	3,300	19,000	—
1920	6,372,000	4.50	5.50	16.00	38.50	75.00	150	350	5,250	—
1920D	1,551,000	10.00	16.00	65.00	235	435	950	1,500	12,000	—
1920S	4,624,000	5.00	7.50	20.00	67.50	235	500	850	12,500	—
1921	246,000	155	200	300	750	1,525	2,750	4,325	17,750	—
1921D	208,000	250	305	450	890	2,150	3,250	4,800	23,500	—
1921S	548,000	43.50	62.50	190	700	4,800	8,600	13,500	85,000	—
1923S	2,178,000	8.50	11.50	25.00	100.00	275	700	1,400	15,000	—
1927S	2,392,000	6.25	6.75	13.50	45.00	150	385	1,000	10,000	—
1928S	1,940,000	6.25	6.75	15.00	65.00	180	470	1,000	10,500	—
1929D	1,001,200	8.00	12.00	16.00	45.00	110	210	415	3,500	—
1929S	1,902,000	5.75	7.25	12.50	28.50	110	230	415	3,550	—
1933S	1,786,000	7.50	12.00	14.00	20.00	55.00	250	600	4,600	—
1934	6,964,000	3.25	3.50	3.75	4.00	9.50	26.00	85.00	475	—
1934D	2,361,400	5.00	5.50	6.00	9.50	29.00	90.00	155	1,250	—
1934S	3,652,000	3.75	4.00	4.25	5.50	27.00	105	395	5,200	—
1935	9,162,000	3.25	3.50	3.75	4.50	6.75	22.50	45.00	485	—
1935D	3,003,800	3.75	4.00	5.50	10.00	31.50	67.50	140	2,500	—
1935S	3,854,000	3.25	3.50	3.75	8.00	28.50	100.00	295	2,700	—
1936	12,617,901	3.25	3.50	3.75	4.00	6.00	22.00	38.50	220	6,600
1936D	4,252,400	3.25	3.50	4.00	6.75	20.00	55.00	80.00	530	—
1936S	3,884,000	3.25	3.50	4.00	6.50	21.50	62.50	135	800	—
1937	9,527,728	3.25	3.50	3.75	4.00	8.00	22.50	40.00	265	1,700
1937D	1,676,000	6.00	7.00	8.00	13.50	33.50	110	225	600	—
1937S	2,090,000	3.50	4.00	4.75	7.75	25.00	62.50	165	600	—
1938	4,118,152	4.25	5.50	5.50	6.00	9.50	41.50	70.00	420	1,275
1938D	491,600	65.00	70.00	77.50	92.50	125	260	525	1,425	—
1939	6,820,808	3.25	3.50	3.75	4.00	5.50	22.50	42.50	160	1,150
1939D	4,267,800	3.25	3.50	3.75	4.00	7.25	23.50	43.50	200	—
1939S	2,552,000	5.00	6.00	7.00	10.00	23.00	75.00	150	330	—
1940	9,167,279	3.25	3.50	3.75	4.00	4.75	11.00	30.00	150	1,000
1940S	4,550,000	3.30	3.60	3.85	4.00	10.00	22.00	52.50	435	—
1941	24,207,412	3.25	3.50	3.75	4.00	4.50	11.00	32.00	160	850
1941D	11,248,400	3.25	3.50	3.75	4.00	6.50	18.00	38.50	280	—
1941S	8,098,000	3.25	3.50	3.75	4.00	5.50	27.50	75.00	1,500	—
1942	47,839,120	3.25	3.50	3.75	4.00	4.50	11.00	32.00	150	850
1942D	10,973,800	3.25	3.50	3.75	4.00	6.50	19.00	38.50	380	—
1942S	12,708,000	3.25	3.50	3.75	4.00	5.50	17.50	38.50	850	—
1943	53,190,000	3.25	3.50	3.75	4.00	4.50	11.00	33.50	150	—
1943D	11,346,000	3.25	3.50	3.75	4.00	7.50	25.00	43.50	350	—
1943S	13,450,000	3.25	3.50	3.75	4.00	5.50	18.50	43.50	560	—
1944	28,206,000	3.25	3.50	3.75	4.00	4.50	11.00	33.00	175	—
1944D	9,769,000	3.25	3.50	3.75	4.00	6.50	20.00	36.00	195	—
1944S	8,904,000	3.25	3.50	3.75	4.00	5.50	16.00	38.50	775	—
1945	31,502,000	3.25	3.50	3.75	4.00	4.50	11.00	32.00	160	—
1945D	9,966,800	3.25	3.50	3.75	4.00	6.50	19.00	34.00	160	—
1945S	10,156,000	3.25	3.50	3.75	4.00	5.50	17.50	35.00	235	—
1946	12,118,000	3.25	3.50	3.75	4.00	5.00	11.00	32.00	235	—
1946D	2,151,000	4.00	5.50	6.50	9.00	25.00	38.50	50.00	125	—
1946S	3,724,000	3.25	3.50	3.75	4.00	7.50	19.00	43.50	175	—
1947	4,094,000	3.25	4.00	4.75	5.50	9.00	22.00	50.00	250	—
1947D	3,900,600	3.25	4.00	4.75	6.25	11.00	31.50	50.00	165	—

Franklin Half Dollar.

KM# 199   Designer: John R. Sinnock. **Diameter:** 30.6 **Weight:** 12.5000 g. **Composition:** 0.9000 Silver, 0.3618 oz. ASW.

Mint mark

Date	Mintage	G-4	VG-8	F-12	VF-20	XF-40	AU-50	MS-60	MS-65	-65FBL	-65CAM
1948	3,006,814	—	4.00	4.50	5.00	6.50	10.00	15.00	80.00	200	—
1948D	4,028,600	—	3.50	3.75	4.50	5.50	11.00	15.00	130	200	—
1949	5,614,000	—	3.75	4.00	4.50	6.00	12.00	38.50	145	300	—
1949D	4,120,600	—	3.50	3.75	4.25	8.00	25.00	43.50	850	1,750	—
1949S	3,744,000	—	3.75	4.25	7.00	11.00	30.00	62.50	155	650	—
1950	7,793,509	—	—	3.25	3.75	6.00	10.00	26.00	110	250	3,700
1950D	8,031,600	—	—	3.50	4.00	7.50	11.50	22.00	425	1,150	—
1951	16,859,602	—	—	3.00	3.50	4.50	5.50	11.00	75.00	235	2,200
1951D	9,475,200	—	—	3.75	4.75	7.50	17.50	26.00	170	525	—
1951S	13,696,000	—	—	3.50	3.75	4.00	15.00	23.50	125	775	—
1952	21,274,073	—	—	2.75	3.25	3.75	4.50	8.50	80.00	200	1,100
1952D	25,395,600	—	—	2.75	3.25	3.75	5.50	7.75	135	450	—
1952S	5,526,000	—	4.00	4.50	5.50	10.00	28.50	46.00	75.00	1,250	—
1953	2,796,920	—	4.00	4.50	5.00	6.00	15.00	23.50	165	850	475
1953D	20,900,400	—	—	2.75	3.50	4.00	5.25	8.00	160	400	—
1953S	4,148,000	—	3.50	4.00	4.75	6.00	15.00	25.00	65.00	16,000	—
1954	13,421,503	—	—	2.50	3.50	4.00	5.00	7.00	80.00	250	250
1954D	25,445,580	—	—	2.50	3.25	3.50	4.25	7.00	110	200	—
1954S	4,993,400	—	3.50	4.00	4.75	6.00	8.50	13.50	105	425	—
1955	2,876,381	15.00	16.00	17.00	18.00	19.00	22.00	25.00	55.00	185	195
1955 Bugs Bunny	—	16.00	17.00	18.00	19.00	20.00	24.00	27.00	100.00	750	—
1956	4,701,384	6.50	7.00	7.50	8.00	8.50	9.00	14.00	45.00	95.00	75.00
1957	6,361,952	—	4.00	4.25	4.50	4.75	5.60	7.00	42.00	95.00	135
1957D	19,966,850	—	—	—	2.75	3.25	4.40	6.25	42.00	65.00	—
1958	4,917,652	—	4.00	4.25	4.50	4.75	5.00	6.25	42.00	100.00	250
1958D	23,962,412	—	—	—	2.50	3.25	4.40	6.25	42.00	75.00	—
1959	7,349,291	—	4.00	4.25	4.50	4.75	5.00	6.25	105	250	475
1959D	13,053,750	—	—	—	2.50	2.75	4.40	6.25	135	190	—
1960	7,715,602	—	—	4.00	4.25	4.50	4.75	5.95	135	350	75.00
1960D	18,215,812	—	—	—	2.50	2.75	4.40	5.95	475	1,250	—
1961	11,318,244	—	—	—	2.50	2.75	4.40	5.95	145	1,750	75.00
1961D	20,276,442	—	—	—	2.50	2.75	4.40	5.95	200	875	—
1962	12,932,019	—	—	—	2.50	2.75	4.40	5.95	160	1,850	50.00
1962D	35,473,281	—	—	—	2.50	2.75	4.40	5.95	225	775	—
1963	25,239,645	—	—	—	2.50	2.75	4.40	5.95	55.00	775	50.00
1963D	67,069,292	—	—	—	2.50	2.75	4.40	5.95	70.00	125	—

Kennedy Half Dollar.

KM# 202   Obv. Designer: Gilroy Roberts. **Rev.
Designer:** Frank Gasparro. **Diameter:** 30.6 **Weight:**
12.5000 g. **Composition:** 0.9000 Silver, 0.3618 oz. ASW.

Mint mark 1964

Date	Mintage	G-4	VG-8	F-12	VF-20	XF-40	MS-60	MS-65	Prf-65
1964	277,254,766	—	—	—	—	—	3.00	9.00	10.00
1964D	156,205,446	—	—	—	—	—	3.50	12.00	—

Kennedy Half Dollar.

KM# 202a   Obv. Designer: Gilroy Roberts. **Rev.
Designer:** Frank Gasparro. **Diameter:** 30.6 **Weight:**
11.5000 g. **Composition:** 0.4000 Silver, 0.1480 oz. ASW.

Mint mark 1968 - present

Date	Mintage	G-4	VG-8	F-12	VF-20	XF-40	MS-60	MS-65	Prf-65
1965	65,879,366	—	—	—	—	—	1.25	9.50	—
1965 SMS	2,360,000	—	—	—	—	—	—	9.50	—
1966	108,984,932	—	—	—	—	—	1.40	11.00	—
1966 SMS	2,261,583	—	—	—	—	—	—	11.00	—
1967	295,046,978	—	—	—	—	—	1.50	9.50	—
1967 SMS	18,633,440	—	—	—	—	—	—	9.50	—
1968D	246,951,930	—	—	—	—	—	1.25	9.00	—
1968S	3,041,506	—	—	—	—	—	—	—	5.00
1969D	129,881,800	—	—	—	—	—	1.25	7.50	—
1969S	2,934,631	—	—	—	—	—	—	—	5.00
1970D	2,150,000	—	—	—	—	—	10.00	32.00	—
1970S	2,632,810	—	—	—	—	—	—	—	10.00

Kennedy Half Dollar.

KM# 202b **Obv. Designer:** Gilroy Roberts. **Rev. Designer:** Frank Gasparro. **Diameter:** 30.6 **Weight:** 11.3400 g. **Composition:** Copper-Nickel Clad Copper.

Date	Mintage	G-4	VG-8	F-12	VF-20	XF-40	MS-60	MS-65	Prf-65
1971	155,640,000	—	—	—	—	—	1.50	12.00	—
1971D	302,097,424	—	—	—	—	—	1.00	5.00	—
1971S	3,244,183	—	—	—	—	—	—	—	3.00
1972	153,180,000	—	—	—	—	—	1.00	9.00	—
1972D	141,890,000	—	—	—	—	—	1.00	6.00	—
1972S	3,267,667	—	—	—	—	—	—	—	2.50
1973	64,964,000	—	—	—	—	—	1.00	6.00	—
1973D	83,171,400	—	—	—	—	—	—	5.50	—
1973S	(2,769,624)	—	—	—	—	—	—	—	2.50
1974	201,596,000	—	—	—	—	—	1.00	5.00	—
1974D	79,066,300	—	—	—	—	—	1.00	6.00	—
1974S	(2,617,350)	—	—	—	—	—	—	—	3.00
1975		—	—	—	—	—	—	—	—
1975D none minted		—	—	—	—	—	—	—	—
1975S none minted		—	—	—	—	—	—	—	—

Kennedy Half Dollar. Bicentennial design, Independence Hall.

KM# 205 **Rev. Designer:** Seth Huntington.
Composition: Copper-Nickel Clad Copper.

Date	Mintage	G-4	VG-8	F-12	VF-20	XF-40	MS-60	MS-65	Prf-65
1976	234,308,000	—	—	—	—	—	1.00	10.00	—
1976D	287,565,248	—	—	—	—	—	1.00	7.00	—
1976S	(7,059,099)	—	—	—	—	—	—	—	2.00

Kennedy Half Dollar. Bicentennial design, Independence Hall.

KM# 205a **Rev. Designer:** Seth Huntington. **Weight:** 11.5000 g. **Composition:** 0.4000 Silver, 0.1480 oz. ASW.

Date	Mintage	G-4	VG-8	F-12	VF-20	XF-40	MS-60	MS-65	Prf-65
1976S	4,908,319(3,998,621)	—	—	—	—	—	—	13.00	5.00

Kennedy Half Dollar. Regular design resumed.

KM# A202b **Diameter:** 30.6 **Weight:** 11.3400 g. **Composition:** Copper-Nickel Clad Copper. **Notes:** KM#202b design and composition resumed. The 1979-S and 1981-S Type II proofs have clearer mint marks than the Type I proofs of those years.

Date	Mintage	MS-65	Prf-65	Date	Mintage	MS-65	Prf-65
1977	43,598,000	6.50	—	1986D	15,336,145	12.00	—
1977D	31,449,106	6.00	—	1986S	(2,411,180)	—	7.50
1977S	(3,251,152)	—	2.00	1987P	2,890,758	12.00	—
1978	14,350,000	6.50	—	1987D	2,890,758	10.00	—
1978D	13,765,799	6.50	—	1987S	(4,407,728)	—	3.50
1978S	(3,127,788)	—	2.00	1988P	13,626,000	10.00	—
1979	68,312,000	5.50	—	1988D	12,000,096	10.00	—
1979D	15,815,422	6.00	—	1988S	(3,262,948)	—	7.00
1979S type I, proof	(3,677,175)	—	2.00	1989P	24,542,000	10.00	—
1979S type II, proof	Inc. above	—	18.00	1989D	23,000,216	8.00	—
1980P	44,134,000	5.00	—	1989S	(3,220,194)	—	7.00
1980D	33,456,449	4.50	—	1990P	22,780,000	15.00	—
1980S	(3,547,030)	—	2.00	1990D	20,096,242	15.00	—
1981P	29,544,000	6.00	—	1990S	(3,299,559)	—	5.00
1981D	27,839,533	5.50	—	1991P	14,874,000	10.00	—
1981S type I, proof	(4,063,083)	—	2.00	1991D	15,054,678	12.00	—
1981S type II, proof	Inc. above	—	14.50	1991S	(2,867,787)	—	11.50
1982P	10,819,000	5.00	—	1992P	17,628,000	7.00	—
1982D	13,140,102	7.00	—	1992D	17,000,106	8.00	—
1982S	(38,957,479)	—	3.50	1992S	(2,858,981)	—	10.00
1983P	34,139,000	10.00	—	1993P	15,510,000	8.00	—
1983D	32,472,244	10.00	—	1993D	15,000,006	12.00	—
1983S	(3,279,126)	—	3.00	1993S	(2,633,439)	—	14.00
1984P	26,029,000	6.50	—	1994P	23,718,000	6.00	—
1984D	26,262,158	7.00	—	1994D	23,828,110	6.00	—
1984S	(3,065,110)	—	4.00	1994S	(2,484,594)	—	8.00
1985P	18,706,962	10.00	—	1995P	26,496,000	6.00	—
1985D	19,814,034	12.00	—	1995D	26,288,000	6.00	—
1985S	(3,962,138)	—	4.50	1995S	(2,010,384)	—	47.50
1986P	13,107,633	16.00	—	1996P	24,442,000	6.00	—

Date	Mintage	MS-65	Prf-65
1996D	24,744,000	6.00	—
1996S	2,085,191	—	10.00
1997P	20,882,000	7.00	—
1997D	19,876,000	6.00	—
1997S	(1,975,000)	—	25.00
1998P	15,646,000	9.00	—
1998D	15,064,000	8.00	—
1998S	(2,078,494)	—	14.00
1998S matte	62,350	—	400
1999P	8,900,000	6.00	—
1999D	10,682,000	6.00	—
1999S	(2,557,897)	—	10.00
2000P	22,600,000	6.00	—
2000D	19,466,000	6.00	—
2000S	(3,082,944)	—	4.50
2001P	21,200,000	6.00	—
2001D	19,504,000	6.00	—
2001S	(2,235,000)	—	10.00
2002P	3,100,000	15.00	—
2002D	2,500,000	10.00	—
2002S	(2,268,913)	—	7.00

Date	Mintage	MS-65	Prf-65
2003P	2,500,000	10.00	—
2003D	2,500,000	10.00	—
2003S	2,076,165	—	7.00
2004S	—	—	—

Kennedy Half Dollar.
KM# B202b **Composition:** Silver.

Date	Mintage	Prf-65
1992S	(1,317,579)	15.00
1993S	(761,353)	25.00
1994S	(785,329)	35.00
1995S	(838,953)	100.00
1996S	(830,021)	50.00
1997S	(821,678)	100.00
1998S	(878,792)	30.00
1999S	(804,565)	15.00
2000S	(965,921)	12.50
2001S	(849,600)	12.50
2002S	(888,816)	—
2003S	1,040,425	—

DOLLAR

Flowing Hair Dollar.
KM# 17 **Designer:** Robert Scot. **Diameter:** 39-40 **Weight:** 26.9600 g. **Composition:** 0.8920 Silver, 0.7737 oz. ASW. **Notes:** The two 1795 varieties have either two or three leaves under each of the eagle's wings on the reverse.

Date	Mintage	F-12	VF-20	XF-40	AU-50	MS-60	MS-63
1794	1,758	45,000	80,000	140,000	250,000	—	—
1795 2 leaves	203,033	3,250	5,750	10,000	17,000	38,000	58,000
1795 3 leaves	Inc. above	3,000	5,500	9,500	15,000	34,000	55,000

Draped Bust Dollar. Small eagle.

KM# 18 **Designer:** Robert Scot. **Diameter:** 39-40 **Weight:** 26.9600 g. **Composition:** 0.8920 Silver, 0.7737 oz. ASW. **Notes:** The 1796 varieties are distinguished by the size of the numerals in the date and letters in "United States of America." The 1797 varieties are distinguished by the number of stars to the left and right of the word "Liberty" and by the size of the letters in "United States of America." The 1798 varieties have either 13 or 15 stars on the obverse.

Date	Mintage	F-12	VF-20	XF-40	AU-50	MS-60	MS-63
1795	Inc. above	2,000	3,300	5,900	7,800	24,500	57,500
1796 small date, small letters	72,920	2,000	3,300	5,900	7,800	24,500	—
1796 small date, large letters	Inc. above	2,050	11,350	6,000	8,000	25,500	—

Date	Mintage	F-12	VF-20	XF-40	AU-50	MS-60	MS-63
1796 large date, small letters	Inc. above	1,975	3,250	5,850	7,750	27,000	65,000
1797 9 stars left, 7 stars right, small letters	7,776	3,000	4,800	9,000	16,500	42,500	70,000
1797 9 stars left, 7 stars right, large letters	Inc. above	2,050	3,350	6,000	7,750	28,500	60,000
1797 10 stars left, 6 stars right	Inc. above	1,975	3,250	5,850	7,750	24,500	60,000
1798 13 stars	327,536	1,875	3,350	6,250	9,500	28,500	—
1798 15 stars	Inc. above	2,350	3,800	8,000	12,500	33,500	—

Draped Bust Dollar. Heraldic eagle.

KM# 32   Designer: Robert Scot. **Diameter:** 39-40 **Weight:** 26.9600 g. **Composition:** 0.8920 Silver, 0.7737 oz. ASW. **Notes:** The 1798 "knob 9" variety has a serif on the lower left of the 9 in the date. The 1798 varieties are distinguished by the number of arrows held by the eagle on the reverse and the number of berries on the olive branch. On the 1798 "high-8" variety, the 8 in the date is higher than the other numerals. The 1799 varieties are distinguished by the number and positioning of the stars on the obverse and by the size of the berries in the olive branch on the reverse. On the 1700 "irregular date" variety, the first 9 in the date is smaller than the other numerals. Some varieties of the 1800 strikes had letters in the legend cut twice into the dies; as the dies became worn, the letters were touched up. On the 1800 "very wide date, low 8" variety, the spacing between the numerals in the date are wider than other varieties and the 8 is lower than the other numerals. The 1800 "small berries" variety refers to the size of the berries in the olive branch on the reverse. The 1800 "12 arrows" and "10 arrows" varieties refer to the number of arrows held by the eagle. The 1800 "Americai" variety appears to have the faint outline of an "I" after "America" in the reverse legend. The "close" and "wide" varieties of 1802 refer to the amount of space between the numerals in the date. The 1800 large-3 and small-3 varieties are distinguished by the size of the 3 in the date.

Date	Mintage	F-12	VF-20	XF-40	AU-50	MS-60	MS-63
1798 knob 9	Inc. above	1,125	1,775	2,850	4,200	16,750	34,500
1798 10 arrows	Inc. above	1,125	1,775	2,850	4,200	16,750	34,500
1798 4 berries	Inc. above	1,125	1,775	2,850	4,200	16,750	34,500
1798 5 berries, 12 arrows	Inc. above	1,125	1,775	2,850	4,200	16,750	34,500
1798 high 8	Inc. above	1,125	1,775	2,850	7,200	16,750	34,500
1798 13 arrows	Inc. above	1,125	1,775	2,850	4,200	16,750	34,500
1799/98 13-star reverse	423,515	1,350	2,050	3,300	6,000	18,500	36,000
1799/98 15-star reverse	Inc. above	1,225	1,825	3,000	6,200	19,500	36,000
1799 irregular date, 13-star reverse	Inc. above	1,200	1,850	2,900	4,650	18,500	38,500
1799 irregular date, 15-star reverse	Inc. above	1,175	1,825	2,850	4,600	16,500	36,000
1799 perfect date, 7- and 6-star obverse, no berries	Inc. above	1,100	1,750	2,750	4,800	13,500	33,500
1799 perfect date, 7- and 6-star obverse, small berries	Inc. above	1,100	1,350	2,750	4,200	13,500	33,500
1799 perfect date, 7- and 6-star obverse, medium large berries	Inc. above	1,125	1,350	2,750	4,200	13,500	33,500
1799 perfect date, 7- and 6-star obverse, extra large berries	Inc. above	1,125	1,350	2,750	4,200	13,500	33,500
1799 8 stars left, 5 stars right on obverse	Inc. above	1,200	1,850	2,900	4,650	19,000	42,500
1800 "R" in "Liberty" double cut	220,920	1,175	1,825	2,850	4,600	16,500	36,000
1800 first "T" in "States" double cut	Inc. above	1,175	1,825	2,850	4,600	16,500	36,000
1800 both letters double cut	Inc. above	1,175	1,825	2,850	4,600	16,500	36,000
1800 "T" in "United" double cut	Inc. above	1,175	1,825	2,850	4,600	16,500	36,000
1800 very wide date, low 8	Inc. above	1,175	1,825	2,850	4,600	16,500	36,000
1800 small berries	Inc. above	1,200	1,850	2,900	4,650	17,000	—
1800 dot date	Inc. above	1,350	2,050	3,300	6,000	16,500	39,500
1800 12 arrows	Inc. above	1,175	1,825	2,850	4,600	16,500	36,000
1800 10 arrows	Inc. above	1,175	1,825	2,850	4,600	16,500	36,000
1800 "Americai"	Inc. above	1,350	2,050	3,300	6,000	16,500	39,500
1801	54,454	1,300	2,100	3,000	4,600	20,000	40,000
1801 proof restrike	—	—	—	—	—	—	—
1802/1 close	Inc. above	1,350	2,050	3,300	6,000	15,500	—
1802/1 wide	Inc. above	1,350	2,050	3,300	6,000	15,500	—
1802 close, perfect date	Inc. above	1,200	1,850	2,900	4,650	15,500	—
1802 wide, perfect date	Inc. above	1,175	1,825	2,850	4,600	16,500	—
1802 proof restrike, mintage unrecorded							
1803 large 3	85,634	1,225	1,925	3,000	5,400	15,500	37,500
1803 small 3	Inc. above	1,350	2,050	3,300	6,000	16,500	38,500
1803 proof restrike, mintage unrecorded							
1804 15 known	—	—	—	—	— 1,000,000	—	—

Note: 1804, Childs Sale, Aug. 1999, Prf-68, $4,140,000.

Gobrecht Dollar. "C. Gobrecht F." below base. Eagle flying left amid stars.

KM# 59.1   Obv. Designer: Christian Gobrecht. **Diameter:** 38.1 **Weight:** 26.7300 g. **Composition:** 0.9000 Silver, 0.7736 oz. ASW.

Date	Mintage	VF-20	XF-40	AU-50	Prf-60
1836	1,000	3,750	4,750	—	12,500

"C. Gobrecht F." below base. Eagle flying in plain field.

KM# 59.2   Obv. Designer: Christian Gobrecht.. **Diameter:** 38.1 **Weight:** 26.7300 g. **Composition:** 0.9000 Silver, 0.7736 oz. ASW.

Date	Mintage	VF-20	XF-40	AU-50	Prf-60
1836 Restrike	—	—	—	—	—

"C. Gobrecht F." on base.

KM# 59a.1   Diameter: 38.1 **Weight:** 26.7300 g. **Composition:** 0.9000 Silver, 0.7736 oz. ASW.

Date	Mintage	VF-20	XF-40	AU-50	Prf-60
1836	600	—	—	—	—

"C. Gobrecht F." on base. Eagle flying left amid stars.

KM# 59a.2   Diameter: 38.1 **Weight:** 26.7300 g. **Composition:** 0.9000 Silver, 0.7736 oz. ASW.

Date	Mintage	VF-20	XF-40	AU-50	Prf-60
1836 Restrike	—	—	—	—	—

Designer's name omitted. Eagle in plain field.

KM# 59a.3   Diameter: 38.1 **Weight:** 26.7300 g. **Composition:** 0.9000 Silver, 0.7736 oz. ASW.

Date	Mintage	VF-20	XF-40	AU-50	Prf-60
1839	300	—	—	—	—

Seated Liberty Dollar. No motto above eagle.

KM# 71   Designer: Christian Gobrecht. **Diameter:** 38.1 **Weight:** 26.7300 g. **Composition:** 0.9000 Silver, 0.7736 oz. ASW.

Date	Mintage	G-4	VG-8	F-12	VF-20	XF-40	AU-50	MS-60	MS-63	MS-65	Prf-65
1840	61,005	160	180	225	300	525	750	1,750	12,500	—	—
1841	173,000	145	165	210	250	360	625	1,500	4,200	42,500	—
1842	184,618	145	165	210	250	350	600	1,100	3,750	24,000	—
1843	165,100	145	165	210	250	350	625	1,400	4,350	24,000	—
1844	20,000	180	245	300	385	500	850	3,000	7,000	44,500	—
1845	24,500	200	260	285	350	550	800	4,850	17,000	—	—
1846	110,600	145	165	225	275	385	625	1,450	4,650	30,000	—
1846O	59,000	150	250	300	475	1,250	3,000	12,000	24,500	—	—
1847	140,750	145	165	210	250	350	600	950	3,500	26,500	—
1848	15,000	250	300	425	550	750	1,500	3,000	7,500	40,000	—

Date	Mintage	G-4	VG-8	F-12	VF-20	XF-40	AU-50	MS-60	MS-63	MS-65	Prf-65
1849	62,600	165	190	250	325	400	700	1,650	4,600	32,500	—
1850	7,500	500	675	800	900	1,000	2,000	4,500	13,000	47,500	—
1850O	40,000	250	300	375	650	1,275	2,850	6,250	15,500	55,000	—
1851	1,300	4,000	5,000	8,000	9,500	13,500	21,500	27,500	35,000	60,000	—
1852	1,100	3,800	4,800	7,500	8,500	11,500	21,500	26,500	33,500	55,000	—
1853	46,110	185	235	285	375	600	850	2,350	6,500	26,500	—
1854	33,140	1,000	1,200	1,600	2,350	3,650	4,850	7,000	9,800	24,500	—
1855	26,000	900	1,150	1,400	1,900	2,950	3,800	6,500	15,000	—	—
1856	63,500	400	500	600	750	975	1,650	3,450	6,500	—	—
1857	94,000	375	475	550	750	950	1,300	2,750	4,200	27,500	—
1858 proof	Est. 800	2,250	2,650	3,350	4,200	5,500	6,250	9,000	12,000	—	—

Note: Proof Only restruck in later years.

Date	Mintage	G-4	VG-8	F-12	VF-20	XF-40	AU-50	MS-60	MS-63	MS-65	Prf-65
1859	256,500	180	220	300	450	600	850	1,800	5,000	15,000	13,500
1859O	360,000	145	175	220	275	375	600	950	2,600	32,000	—
1859S	20,000	235	300	400	600	1,350	3,000	8,000	25,500	60,000	—
1860	218,930	165	200	275	350	475	600	1,100	2,600	26,000	13,500
1860O	515,000	145	165	210	250	350	550	900	2,500	15,000	—
1861	78,500	440	500	650	800	1,000	1,500	2,800	4,600	22,500	13,500
1862	12,090	450	525	675	850	1,100	1,600	2,750	5,000	34,500	13,500
1863	27,660	375	425	500	650	1,200	2,350	3,800	11,250	1,400	13,500
1864	31,170	240	265	315	425	600	1,200	2,300	4,600	20,000	13,500
1865	47,000	225	245	290	400	560	1,150	2,150	4,450	32,500	13,500
1866 2 known without motto	—										

Seated Liberty Dollar. "In God We Trust" above eagle.

KM# 100 **Designer:** Christian Gobrecht. **Diameter:** 38.1 **Weight:** 26.7300 g. **Composition:** 0.9000 Silver, 0.7736 oz. ASW. **Notes:** In 1866 the motto "In God We Trust" was added to the reverse above the eagle.

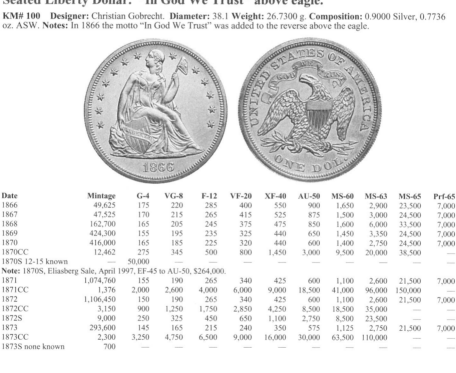

Date	Mintage	G-4	VG-8	F-12	VF-20	XF-40	AU-50	MS-60	MS-63	MS-65	Prf-65
1866	49,625	175	220	285	400	550	900	1,650	2,900	23,500	7,000
1867	47,525	170	215	265	415	525	875	1,500	3,000	24,500	7,000
1868	162,700	165	205	245	375	475	850	1,600	6,000	33,500	7,000
1869	424,300	155	195	235	325	440	650	1,450	3,350	24,500	7,000
1870	416,000	165	185	225	320	440	600	1,400	2,750	24,500	7,000
1870CC	12,462	275	345	500	800	1,450	3,000	9,500	20,000	38,500	—
1870S 12-15 known	—	50,000	—	—	—	—	—	—	—	—	—

Note: 1870S, Eliasberg Sale, April 1997, EF-45 to AU-50, $264,000.

Date	Mintage	G-4	VG-8	F-12	VF-20	XF-40	AU-50	MS-60	MS-63	MS-65	Prf-65
1871	1,074,760	155	190	265	340	425	600	1,100	2,600	21,500	7,000
1871CC	1,376	2,000	2,600	4,000	6,000	9,000	18,500	41,000	96,000	150,000	—
1872	1,106,450	150	190	265	340	425	600	1,100	2,600	21,500	7,000
1872CC	3,150	900	1,250	1,750	2,850	4,250	8,500	18,500	35,000	—	—
1872S	9,000	250	325	450	650	1,100	2,750	8,500	23,500	—	—
1873	293,600	145	165	215	240	350	575	1,125	2,750	21,500	7,000
1873CC	2,300	3,250	4,750	6,500	9,000	16,000	30,000	63,500	110,000	—	—
1873S none known	700	—	—	—	—	—	—	—	—	—	—

Trade Dollar.

KM# 108 **Designer:** William Barber. **Diameter:** 38.1 **Weight:** 27.2200 g. **Composition:** 0.9000 Silver, 0.7878 oz. ASW.

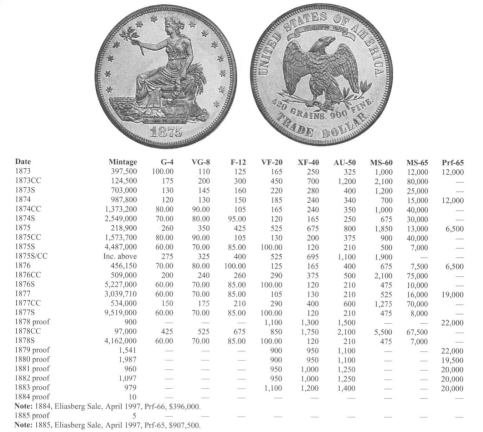

Date	Mintage	G-4	VG-8	F-12	VF-20	XF-40	AU-50	MS-60	MS-65	Prf-65
1873	397,500	100.00	110	125	165	250	325	1,000	12,000	12,000
1873CC	124,500	175	200	300	450	700	1,200	2,100	80,000	—
1873S	703,000	130	145	160	220	280	400	1,200	25,000	—
1874	987,800	120	130	150	185	240	340	700	15,000	12,000
1874CC	1,373,200	80.00	90.00	105	165	240	350	1,000	40,000	—
1874S	2,549,000	70.00	80.00	95.00	120	165	250	675	30,000	—
1875	218,900	260	350	425	525	675	800	1,850	13,000	6,500
1875CC	1,573,700	80.00	90.00	105	130	200	375	900	40,000	—
1875S	4,487,000	60.00	70.00	85.00	100.00	120	210	500	7,000	—
1875S/CC	Inc. above	275	325	400	525	695	1,100	1,900	—	—
1876	456,150	70.00	80.00	100.00	125	165	400	675	7,500	6,500
1876CC	509,000	200	240	260	290	375	500	2,100	75,000	—
1876S	5,227,000	60.00	70.00	85.00	100.00	120	210	475	10,000	—
1877	3,039,710	60.00	70.00	85.00	105	130	210	525	16,000	19,000
1877CC	534,000	150	175	210	290	400	600	1,275	70,000	—
1877S	9,519,000	60.00	70.00	85.00	100.00	120	210	475	8,000	—
1878 proof	900	—	—	—	1,100	1,300	1,500	—	—	22,000
1878CC	97,000	425	525	675	850	1,750	2,100	5,500	67,500	—
1878S	4,162,000	60.00	70.00	85.00	100.00	120	210	475	7,000	—
1879 proof	1,541	—	—	—	900	950	1,100	—	—	22,000
1880 proof	1,987	—	—	—	900	950	1,100	—	—	19,500
1881 proof	960	—	—	—	950	1,000	1,250	—	—	20,000
1882 proof	1,097	—	—	—	950	1,000	1,250	—	—	20,000
1883 proof	979	—	—	—	1,100	1,200	1,400	—	—	20,000
1884 proof	10	—	—	—	—	—	—	—	—	—
Note: 1884, Eliasberg Sale, April 1997, Prf-66, $396,000.
1885 proof	5	—	—	—	—	—	—	—	—	—
Note: 1885, Eliasberg Sale, April 1997, Prf-65, $907,500.

Morgan Dollar.

KM# 110 **Designer:** George T. Morgan. **Diameter:** 38.1 **Weight:** 26.7300 g. **Composition:** 0.9000 Silver, 0.7736 oz. ASW. **Notes:** "65DMPL" values are for coins grading MS-65 deep-mirror prooflike. The 1878 "8 tail feathers" and "7 tail feathers" varieties are distinguished by the number of feathers in the eagle's tail. On the "reverse of 1878" varieties, the top of the top feather in the arrows held by the eagle is straight across and the eagle's breast is concave. On the "reverse of 1879 varieties," the top feather in the arrows held by the eagle is slanted and the eagle's breast is convex. The 1890-CC "tail-bar variety has a bar extending from the arrow feathers to the wreath on the reverse, the result of a die gouge.

8 tail feathers

7 tail feathers

7/8 tail feathers

Date	Mintage	VG-8	F-12	VF-20	XF-40	AU-50	MS-60	MS-63	MS-64	MS-65	65DMPL	Prf-65
1878 8 tail feathers	750,000	24.00	25.00	27.50	32.50	50.00	125	160	435	1,400	6,300	7,500

U.S. MINT ISSUES

Date	Mintage	VG-8	F-12	VF-20	XF-40	AU-50	MS-60	MS-63	MS-64	MS-65	65DMPL	Prf-65
1878 7 tail feathers, reverse of 1878	Inc. above	16.00	17.50	20.00	22.00	40.00	56.00	95.00	390	1,500	6,300	—
1878 7 tail feathers, reverse of 1879	Inc. above	16.00	17.50	19.50	22.00	40.00	67.50	140	640	3,000	8,800	9,000
1878 7 over 8 tail feathers	9,759,550	19.00	20.00	21.50	28.00	50.00	125	350	550	3,350	14,500	—
1878CC	2,212,000	96.00	98.00	105	100.00	110	220	410	640	2,000	3,450	—
1878S	9,744,000	15.50	17.50	19.50	21.50	33.00	46.00	70.00	105	285	2,250	—
1879	14,807,100	13.50	13.00	15.00	16.50	20.00	30.00	60.00	135	1,250	6,950	6,000
1879CC	756,000	105	110	160	580	1,250	2,700	6,250	9,300	25,000	65,000	—
1879O	2,887,000	13.50	13.00	15.00	17.00	20.50	72.50	180	480	3,300	16,500	—
1879S reverse of 1878	9,110,000	14.00	17.00	25.00	30.00	50.00	90.00	360	1,450	8,300	22,000	—
1879S reverse of 1879	9,110,000	14.00	13.00	16.00	17.00	21.00	40.00	42.50	63.50	165	450	—
1880	12,601,335	14.00	13.50	15.00	17.00	20.00	30.00	55.00	115	800	3,450	5,900
1880CC reverse of 1878	591,000	100.00	125	150	185	250	495	640	1,100	3,000	11,000	—
1880CC reverse of 1879	591,000	115	150	165	225	300	495	515	800	1,450	3,650	—
1880O	5,305,000	13.50	14.50	15.00	16.75	20.50	60.00	385	2,000	24,000	70,000	—
1880S	8,900,000	14.00	14.50	15.00	17.00	21.00	33.00	46.00	63.50	165	450	—
1881	9,163,975	14.00	14.50	15.00	17.00	20.00	30.00	55.00	150	850	13,750	6,250
1881CC	296,000	315	330	345	370	430	500	560	625	850	1,450	—
1881O	5,708,000	13.50	14.50	15.00	16.50	20.00	30.00	48.00	160	1,650	15,000	—
1881S	12,760,000	13.50	14.50	15.00	16.50	20.00	30.00	46.00	63.50	165	450	—
1882	11,101,100	13.50	14.50	15.00	16.50	20.00	30.00	46.00	63.50	450	4,100	5,900
1882CC	1,133,000	90.00	92.50	95.00	96.00	100.00	215	220	270	500	725	—
1882O	6,090,000	13.00	14.50	15.00	16.75	20.00	32.50	46.00	75.00	800	4,200	—
1882S	9,250,000	13.50	14.50	15.00	16.50	25.00	33.00	46.00	63.50	165	1,100	—
1883	12,291,039	13.50	14.50	15.00	16.50	20.00	30.00	46.00	63.50	170	760	5,900
1883CC	1,204,000	95.00	97.50	105	115	120	220	240	280	500	830	—
1883O	8,725,000	13.50	14.50	15.00	16.50	20.00	30.00	46.00	65.00	165	575	—
1883S	6,250,000	13.50	16.00	17.00	33.00	165	500	2,750	5,500	22,000	94,500	—
1884	14,070,875	13.50	14.00	15.00	16.50	20.00	30.00	46.00	63.50	300	2,200	5,900
1884CC	1,136,000	100.00	110	120	130	160	220	240	280	500	600	—
1884O	9,730,000	13.50	14.50	15.00	16.50	20.00	30.00	46.00	63.50	165	670	—
1884S	3,200,000	14.00	15.00	17.50	41.50	280	6,000	31,500	110,000	200,000	220,000	—
1885	17,787,767	13.50	14.50	14.50	16.50	20.00	30.00	46.00	60.00	165	570	5,900
1885CC	228,000	375	390	440	465	500	600	640	800	1,800	1,450	—
1885O	9,185,000	13.50	14.50	14.50	16.50	20.00	30.00	46.00	63.50	165	490	—
1885S	1,497,000	17.50	21.50	27.50	57.50	125	200	250	650	2,000	16,500	—
1886	19,963,886	13.50	14.50	14.50	16.50	20.00	30.00	46.00	62.00	165	575	5,900
1886O	10,710,000	13.50	14.50	14.50	18.00	80.00	505	4,400	10,000	215,000	283,500	—
1886S	750,000	30.00	34.50	55.00	65.00	125	285	470	695	3,250	16,500	—
1887	20,290,710	14.00	15.00	15.00	17.50	20.00	30.00	46.00	63.50	165	530	5,900
1887O	11,550,000	13.50	15.00	14.75	17.00	22.00	54.00	105	425	4,100	8,500	—
1887S	1,771,000	14.50	15.50	17.50	20.00	39.00	100.00	285	700	4,000	27,000	—
1888	19,183,833	13.50	14.50	14.50	16.50	20.00	30.00	46.00	63.50	215	2,350	6,000
1888O	12,150,000	13.50	15.00	16.00	17.00	20.00	30.00	46.00	64.50	460	1,600	—
1888S	657,000	45.00	90.00	110	130	150	240	440	850	3,500	10,500	—
1889	21,726,811	13.50	14.50	14.50	16.50	20.00	29.00	46.00	62.00	310	2,950	5,900
1889CC	350,000	625	900	1,700	3,500	6,500	22,000	34,000	5,150	315,000	285,000	—
1889O	11,875,000	13.50	14.50	15.00	17.50	30.00	140	465	900	5,550	14,500	—
1889S	700,000	33.50	46.00	57.50	68.50	100.00	200	440	575	1,950	7,550	—
1890	16,802,590	13.50	14.50	15.00	16.50	20.00	30.00	50.00	115	2,300	12,500	5,900
1890CC	2,309,041	90.00	92.50	15.00	160	210	350	850	2,300	6,300	9,750	—
1890CC tail bar	Inc. above	135	145	180	500	900	1,600	4,000	8,500	—	9,800	—
1890O	10,701,000	13.50	14.50	15.00	18.00	24.00	56.00	110	340	1,750	7,500	—
1890S	8,230,373	13.50	14.50	15.00	16.50	20.00	56.00	110	300	1,050	8,200	—
1891	8,694,206	13.50	14.50	15.00	16.50	21.50	51.00	135	575	7,500	25,000	5,900
1891CC	1,618,000	90.00	92.50	95.00	160	210	345	850	1,350	5,000	20,000	—
1891O	7,954,529	13.50	14.50	15.00	18.00	34.00	135	350	750	9,000	21,500	—
1891S	5,296,000	13.50	14.50	15.00	19.50	24.00	60.00	125	275	1,300	7,250	—
1892	1,037,245	17.00	19.00	21.00	30.00	72.50	150	400	1,000	4,000	15,750	5,900
1892CC	1,352,000	125	135	225	440	575	945	2,600	3,700	11,000	27,000	—
1892O	2,744,000	14.50	19.00	19.50	30.00	60.00	160	325	700	5,250	27,000	—
1892S	1,200,000	20.00	22.00	55.00	200	1,750	35,000	57,500	96,000	170,000	170,000	—
1893	378,792	140	165	195	220	285	635	1,300	2,500	7,750	38,000	5,900
1893CC	677,000	195	265	550	1,700	2,300	3,500	7,800	13,500	54,500	85,000	—
1893O	300,000	180	240	350	600	1,000	1,500	6,750	20,000	220,000	201,500	—
1893S	100,000	2,800	4,200	6,150	9,600	24,000	80,000	107,500	250,000	415,000	380,000	—
1894	110,972	1,125	1,175	1,500	2,250	3,000	4,500	6,250	9,250	37,500	44,000	6,500
1894O	1,723,000	43.50	50.00	62.50	115	315	550	3,750	8,500	50,000	56,500	—
1894S	1,260,000	34.00	52.00	70.00	130	525	625	1,150	1,850	5,750	19,000	—
1895 proof only	12,880	21,000	27,500	29,000	33,500	37,000	—	—	—	—	—	67,500
1895O	450,000	330	440	580	900	1,650	14,000	55,000	100,000	225,000	—	—
1895S	400,000	200	275	340	515	1,700	3,500	5,600	8,000	21,000	40,500	—

Date	Mintage	VG-8	F-12	VF-20	XF-40	AU-50	MS-60	MS-63	MS-64	MS-65	65DMPL	Prf-65
1896	9,967,762	12.50	16.00	16.25	16.50	20.00	29.00	46.00	67.50	230	975	5,900
1896O	4,900,000	13.00	16.00	16.50	18.00	190	1,000	7,350	46,000	185,000	170,000	—
1896S	5,000,000	17.50	27.00	47.50	185	750	1,400	3,250	4,400	16,000	25,000	—
1897	2,822,731	13.00	16.00	16.25	17.00	20.00	30.00	46.00	63.50	260	2,900	5,900
1897O	4,004,000	13.50	16.00	16.50	24.00	110	675	5,500	15,500	50,000	56,500	—
1897S	5,825,000	13.50	16.00	16.50	17.50	24.00	56.00	115	170	700	1,700	—
1898	5,884,735	16.00	16.50	17.00	18.00	20.00	30.00	46.00	63.50	265	1,075	5,900
1898O	4,440,000	17.00	21.00	22.00	23.00	25.00	30.00	46.00	63.50	165	510	—
1898S	4,102,000	20.00	23.00	27.50	37.50	95.00	260	465	890	2,500	11,250	—
1899	330,846	35.00	51.50	62.50	78.50	100.00	160	285	445	900	2,250	6,000
1899O	12,290,000	15.00	16.00	16.50	19.00	21.00	30.00	45.00	63.50	165	825	—
1899S	2,562,000	15.00	18.75	25.00	41.50	100.00	330	480	800	2,200	8,600	—
1900	8,880,938	13.00	15.00	16.00	18.00	20.00	30.00	46.00	63.50	210	11,000	5,900
1900O	12,590,000	13.00	25.00	16.00	20.00	24.00	32.00	46.00	63.50	165	3,000	—
1900O/CC	Inc. above	21.50	23.00	34.00	66.00	135	230	675	1,250	2,750	19,000	—
1900S	3,540,000	16.00	17.00	19.50	36.00	83.00	275	400	500	1,575	9,450	—
1901	6,962,813	19.00	23.00	30.00	72.50	350	2,000	15,500	55,000	215,000	220,000	6,500
1901O	13,320,000	13.00	14.50	16.00	19.00	20.00	32.00	46.00	67.50	230	3,800	—
1901S	2,284,000	15.00	20.00	29.00	45.00	220	400	695	960	4,000	12,500	—
1902	7,994,777	16.50	17.50	18.00	19.00	23.00	42.50	105	140	525	15,750	5,900
1902O	8,636,000	13.00	17.50	18.00	20.00	21.00	30.00	46.00	63.50	165	3,600	—
1902S	1,530,000	41.50	55.00	100.00	135	285	415	600	1,000	3,350	15,000	—
1903	4,652,755	43.50	47.50	50.00	57.50	62.50	67.50	78.50	100.00	300	9,150	5,900
1903O	4,450,000	240	260	285	315	340	415	450	470	720	4,650	—
1903S	1,241,000	43.50	55.00	115	285	1,800	4,150	6,500	7,500	8,500	40,000	—
1904	2,788,650	19.50	20.00	20.50	21.50	33.00	80.00	265	680	4,500	38,000	5,900
1904O	3,720,000	19.50	20.00	20.50	21.00	24.00	33.00	46.00	72.50	165	550	—
1904S	2,304,000	27.50	34.00	66.00	220	550	1,150	3,400	4,300	8,000	19,000	—
1921	44,690,000	11.00	11.25	11.50	11.75	13.50	19.50	32.50	50.00	130	8,800	—
1921D	20,345,000	11.00	11.25	11.50	11.75	14.00	40.00	66.00	135	315	15,000	—
1921S	21,695,000	11.00	11.25	11.50	12.00	15.00	40.00	68.50	175	1,450	22,000	—

Peace Dollar.

KM# 150   **Designer:** Anthony DeFrancisci. **Diameter:** 38.1 **Weight:** 26.7300 g. **Composition:** 0.9000 Silver, 0.7736 oz. ASW. **Notes:** Commonly called Peace dollars.

Mint mark

Date	Mintage	G-4	VG-8	F-12	VF-20	XF-40	AU-50	MS-60	MS-63	MS-64	MS-65
1921	1,006,473	60.00	85.00	92.50	100.00	110	155	220	385	825	2,500
1922	51,737,000	8.00	8.50	9.25	9.50	9.75	10.00	16.00	33.50	52.50	160
1922D	15,063,000	8.00	8.50	9.25	10.00	11.00	12.00	24.00	48.00	85.00	365
1922S	17,475,000	8.00	8.50	9.25	10.25	12.00	13.00	23.00	67.50	230	2,250
1923	30,800,000	8.00	8.50	9.25	9.50	9.75	10.00	16.00	33.50	52.50	160
1923D	6,811,000	8.00	8.50	10.00	10.50	11.00	18.00	53.00	120	260	1,000
1923S	19,020,000	8.00	8.50	10.00	10.50	11.00	13.00	28.00	67.50	200	5,750
1924	11,811,000	8.00	8.50	9.50	10.00	10.50	11.00	16.00	33.50	52.50	160
1924S	1,728,000	11.00	16.00	27.50	31.00	35.00	55.00	195	550	1,100	9,000
1925	10,198,000	8.00	8.50	9.25	9.50	9.75	12.50	16.00	33.50	52.50	160
1925S	1,610,000	9.00	13.50	17.50	20.00	23.50	38.50	75.00	160	550	20,000
1926	1,939,000	9.00	13.00	14.50	15.00	15.50	16.50	34.00	70.00	105	360
1926D	2,348,700	8.00	12.50	14.50	14.75	17.50	27.00	60.00	135	270	600
1926S	6,980,000	8.00	11.00	13.50	14.00	14.50	16.00	40.00	80.00	235	875
1927	848,000	13.00	24.00	34.00	36.00	40.00	47.50	70.00	140	270	2,350
1927D	1,268,900	11.00	22.50	24.00	25.00	27.50	78.00	150	300	625	5,100
1927S	866,000	14.00	26.00	32.00	35.00	40.00	70.00	135	300	725	11,250
1928	360,649	250	365	415	425	440	470	510	750	1,150	4,500
1928S	1,632,000	13.00	30.00	32.50	35.00	38.50	60.00	140	575	1,300	19,000
1934	954,057	12.00	19.00	20.00	22.00	23.00	40.00	105	250	425	1,100
1934D	1,569,500	11.00	18.00	19.00	19.50	21.00	41.50	110	375	595	1,850
1934S	1,011,000	12.00	23.50	28.00	62.50	175	500	1,800	4,150	5,300	7,500
1935	1,576,000	11.00	16.00	20.00	21.50	23.00	30.00	62.50	100.00	165	670
1935S	1,964,000	11.00	16.00	17.00	20.00	27.00	96.00	250	365	525	1,250

Eisenhower Dollar.

KM# 203 **Designer:** Frank Gasparro. **Diameter:** 38.1 **Weight:** 22.6800 g. **Composition:** Copper-Nickel Clad Copper.

Date	Mintage	Proof	MS-63	Prf-65
1971	47,799,000	—	3.75	—
1971D	68,587,424	—	2.00	—
1972	75,890,000	—	2.75	—
1972D	92,548,511	—	2.25	—
1973	2,000,056	—	11.00	—
1973D	2,000,000	—	11.00	—
1973S	2,769,624	—	—	11.00
1974	27,366,000	—	3.00	—
1974D	35,466,000	—	2.75	—
1974S	—	(2,617,350)	—	6.50

Eisenhower Dollar.

KM# 203a **Designer:** Frank Gasparro. **Diameter:** 38.1 **Weight:** 24.5900 g. **Composition:** Silver.

Date	Mintage	Proof	MS-63	Prf-65
1971S	6,868,530	(4,265,234)	6.00	7.00
1972S	2,193,056	(1,811,631)	7.50	7.00
1973S	1,833,140	(1,005,617)	8.50	30.00
1974S	1,720,000	(1,306,579)	7.50	7.25

Eisenhower Dollar. Bicentennial design, moon behind Liberty Bell.

KM# 206 **Rev. Designer:** Dennis R. Williams. **Diameter:** 38.1 **Weight:** 22.6800 g. **Composition:** Copper-Nickel Clad Copper. **Notes:** In 1976 the lettering on the reverse was changed to thinner letters, resulting in Type I and Type II varieties for that year.

Type I

Type II

Date	Mintage	Proof	MS-63	Prf-65
1976 type I	117,337,000	—	4.00	—
1976 type II	Inc. above	—	2.00	—
1976D type I	103,228,274	—	3.25	—
1976D type II	Inc. above	—	2.00	—
1976S type I	—	(2,909,369)	—	5.75
1976S type II	—	(4,149,730)	—	5.75

Eisenhower Dollar. Bicentennial design, moon behind Liberty Bell.

KM# 206a **Rev. Designer:** Dennis R. Williams. **Weight:** 24.5900 g. **Composition:** 0.4000 Silver, 0.3162 oz. ASW.

Date	Mintage	Proof	MS-63	Prf-65
1976S	4,908,319	(3,998,621)	14.00	12.50

Eisenhower Dollar. Regular design resumed.

KM# A203 Diameter: 38.1 **Composition:** Copper-Nickel Clad Copper.

Date	Mintage	Proof	MS-63	Prf-65
1977	12,596,000	—	4.25	—
1977D	32,983,006	—	3.25	—
1977S	—	(3,251,152)	—	8.00
1978	25,702,000	—	2.75	—
1978D	33,012,890	—	3.00	—
1978S	—	(3,127,788)	—	10.00

Susan B. Anthony Dollar.

KM# 207 Designer: Frank Gasparro. **Diameter:** 26.5 **Weight:** 8.1000 g. **Composition:** Copper-Nickel Clad Copper, 0 oz. **Notes:** The 1979-S and 1981-S Type II coins have a clearer mint mark than the Type I varieties for those years.

Date	Mintage	MS-63	Prf-65
1979S Proof, Type I	(3,677,175)	—	8.00
1979S Proof, Type II	Inc. above	—	110
1980P	27,610,000	2.00	—
1980D	41,628,708	2.00	—
1980S	20,422,000	2.00	—
1980S Proof	3,547,030	—	8.00
1981P	3,000,000	5.75	—
1981D	3,250,000	5.75	—
1981S	3,492,000	6.00	—
1981S Proof, Type I	4,063,083	—	8.00
1981S Proof, Type II	Inc. above	—	230
1999P	29,592,000	1.50	—
1999D	11,776,000	1.75	—
1999P Proof; *maximum mintage	(750,000)	—	22.50

Date	Mintage	MS-63	Prf-65
1979P	360,222,000	2.00	—
1979P Near date	Inc. above	12.00	—
1979D	288,015,744	1.75	—
1979S	109,576,000	2.00	—

Sacagawea Dollar.

KM# 310 Diameter: 26.4 **Weight:** 8.0700 g. **Composition:** Copper-Zinc-Manganese-Nickel Clad Copper.

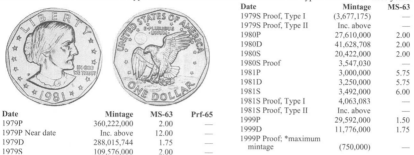

Date	Mintage	MS-63	Prf-65
2000D	518,916,000	2.00	—
2000S	(4,048,865)	—	10.00
2001P	62,468,000	4.00	—
2001D	70,909,500	4.00	—
2001S	(3,084,600)	—	37.50
2002P	3,865,610	2.00	—
2002D	3,732,000	2.00	—
2002S	(3,157,739)	—	26.00
2003P	3,090,000	2.50	—
2003D	3,090,000	2.50	—
2003S	(3,116,590)	—	10.00
2004S	—	—	—

Date	Mintage	MS-63	Prf-65
2000P	767,140,000	2.00	—

DOLLAR
GOLD

Liberty Head - Type 1.

KM# 73 Designer: James B. Longacre. **Diameter:** 13 **Weight:** 1.6720 g. **Composition:** 0.9000 Gold, 0.0484 oz. AGW. **Notes:** On the "closed wreath" varieties of 1849, the wreath on the reverse extends closer to the numeral 1.

Date	Mintage	F-12	VF-20	XF-40	AU-50	MS-60
1849 open wreath	688,567	100.00	140	190	225	450
1849 closed wreath	Inc. above	100.00	135	185	210	365
1849C closed wreath	11,634	800	950	1,250	1,900	8,000
1849C open wreath	Inc. above	—	—	—	—	—
1849D open wreath	21,588	950	1,150	1,600	1,950	5,000
1849O open wreath	215,000	120	150	230	310	700
1850	481,953	100.00	135	190	200	340
1850C	6,966	800	950	1,250	2,250	7,500
1850D	8,382	950	1,150	1,650	2,600	8,500
1850O	14,000	185	245	350	725	2,700
1851	3,317,671	100.00	135	190	200	250
1851C	41,267	800	950	1,250	1,600	4,900
1851D	9,882	950	1,150	1,600	2,000	5,400
1851O	290,000	135	160	200	230	725
1852	2,045,351	100.00	135	190	200	245
1852C	9,434	800	950	1,250	1,600	3,800
1852D	6,360	950	1,150	1,600	2,150	8,500

Date	Mintage	F-12	VF-20	XF-40	AU-50	MS-60
1852O	140,000	115	140	230	320	1,100
1853	4,076,051	100.00	135	190	200	245
1853C	11,515	800	950	1,250	1,750	5,000
1853D	6,583	950	1,150	1,600	2,400	8,500
1853O	290,000	130	160	210	225	600
1854	736,709	100.00	135	190	200	250
1854D	2,935	950	1,150	2,000	5,300	11,000
1854S	14,632	245	290	420	700	2,100

Indian Head - Type 2.

KM# 83 **Designer:** James B. Longacre. **Diameter:** 15
Weight: 1.6720 g. **Composition:** 0.9000 Gold,
0.0484 oz. AGW.

Date	Mintage	F-12	VF-20	XF-40	AU-50	MS-60
1854	902,736	210	280	415	550	3,300
1855	758,269	210	280	415	550	3,300
1855C	9,803	800	1,100	3,000	8,500	24,500
1855D	1,811	3,000	4,250	8,250	22,000	48,000
1855O	55,000	330	400	540	1,250	6,750
1856S	24,600	440	725	1,200	2,200	7,700

Indian Head - Type 3.

KM# 86 **Designer:** James B. Longacre. **Diameter:** 15
Weight: 1.6720 g. **Composition:** 0.9000 Gold,
0.0484 oz. AGW. **Notes:** The 1856 varieties are
distinguished by whether the 5 in the date is slanted or
upright. The 1873 varieties are distinguished by the
amount of space between the upper left and lower left
serifs in the 3.

Date	Mintage	F-12	VF-20	XF-40	AU-50	MS-60	Prf-65
1856 upright 5	1,762,936	125	145	195	225	465	—
1856 slanted 5	Inc. above	130	140	190	210	260	50,000
1856D	1,460	2,200	3,400	5,400	7,500	30,000	—
1857	774,789	110	135	190	210	260	31,000
1857C	13,280	800	950	1,400	2,750	10,500	—
1857D	3,533	950	1,150	1,750	3,650	10,000	—
1857S	10,000	250	500	600	1,100	5,600	—
1858	117,995	110	135	190	215	265	27,500
1858D	3,477	950	1,150	1,500	2,750	10,000	—
1858S	10,000	280	375	500	1,150	5,000	—
1859	168,244	110	135	190	205	260	16,000
1859C	5,235	800	950	1,500	3,100	9,000	—
1859D	4,952	950	1,150	1,500	2,850	10,000	—
1859S	15,000	185	225	480	1,000	5,000	—
1860	36,668	110	135	190	205	280	14,500
1860D	1,566	2,000	2,500	3,800	6,000	15,000	—
1860S	13,000	280	325	465	700	2,250	—
1861	527,499	110	135	190	205	265	13,500
1861D mintage unrecorded	—	4,600	6,400	9,000	16,500	28,000	—
1862	1,361,390	110	135	190	205	260	14,500
1863	6,250	370	425	825	1,600	3,650	16,500
1864	5,950	270	350	440	750	950	16,000
1865	3,725	270	350	550	700	1,450	16,000
1866	7,130	275	360	425	650	900	16,000
1867	5,250	300	400	485	600	1,100	16,000
1868	10,525	250	275	400	465	900	16,500
1869	5,925	315	335	520	800	1,000	15,000
1870	6,335	245	270	385	475	850	14,000
1870S	3,000	280	440	725	1,100	2,150	—
1871	3,930	245	270	365	450	700	16,500
1872	3,530	245	275	350	440	850	16,500
1873 closed 3	125,125	300	400	750	900	1,600	—
1873 open 3	Inc. above	110	135	190	200	260	—
1874	198,820	110	135	190	200	260	16,500
1875	420	1,600	1,850	3,650	4,700	5,900	32,500
1876	3,245	220	275	345	440	600	15,500
1877	3,920	140	175	330	440	900	16,500
1878	3,020	175	200	350	450	600	14,000
1879	3,030	160	180	270	315	500	12,500
1880	1,636	140	160	200	225	440	12,500
1881	7,707	140	160	200	225	425	10,500
1882	5,125	150	170	200	225	425	8,500
1883	11,007	140	160	200	225	425	8,500
1884	6,236	135	150	200	225	415	8,500
1885	12,261	140	160	200	225	400	8,500

Date	Mintage	F-12	VF-20	XF-40	AU-50	MS-60	Prf-65
1886	6,016	140	160	200	225	400	8,500
1887	8,543	140	160	200	225	400	8,500
1888	16,580	140	160	200	225	400	8,500
1889	30,729	140	160	200	225	400	8,500

$2.50 (QUARTER EAGLE)

GOLD

Liberty Cap.

KM# 27 Designer: Robert Scot. **Diameter:** 20
Weight: 4.3700 g. **Composition:** 0.9160 Gold,
0.1289 oz. AGW. **Notes:** The 1796 "no stars" variety
does not have stars on the obverse. The 1804 varieties
are distinguished by the number of stars on the obverse.

Date	Mintage	F-12	VF-20	XF-40	MS-60
1796 no stars	963	25,000	37,500	70,000	110,000
1796 stars	432	22,500	33,500	60,000	140,000
1797	427	14,000	16,500	21,500	100,000
1798	1,094	4,350	6,250	7,750	49,000
1802/1	3,035	4,350	6,250	7,500	20,000
1804 13-star reverse	3,327	23,500	31,250	70,000	200,000
1804 14-star reverse	Inc. above	4,350	6,250	7,250	20,000
1805	1,781	4,350	6,250	7,250	20,000
1806/4	1,616	4,500	6,350	7,500	21,000
1806/5	Inc. above	5,600	8,000	11,500	70,000
1807	6,812	4,350	6,250	7,250	18,500

Turban Head.

KM# 40 Designer: John Reich. **Diameter:** 20
Weight: 4.3700 g. **Composition:** 0.9160 Gold,
0.1289 oz. AGW.

Date	Mintage	F-12	VF-20	XF-40	MS-60
1808	2,710	22,500	28,000	34,000	80,000

Turban Head.

KM# 46 Designer: John Reich. **Diameter:** 18.5
Weight: 4.3700 g. **Composition:** 0.9160 Gold,
0.1289 oz. AGW.

Date	Mintage	F-12	VF-20	XF-40	MS-60
1821	6,448	5,000	6,250	7,500	20,000
1824/21	2,600	5,000	6,250	7,250	18,500
1825	4,434	5,000	6,250	7,250	15,500
1826/25	760	5,250	6,500	8,000	31,500
1827	2,800	5,350	7,000	8,500	19,000

Turban Head.

KM# 49 Designer: John Reich. **Diameter:** 18.2
Weight: 4.3700 g. **Composition:** 0.9160 Gold,
0.1289 oz. AGW.

Date	Mintage	F-12	VF-20	XF-40	MS-60
1829	3,403	4,600	5,500	6,500	12,500
1830	4,540	4,600	5,500	6,500	12,500
1831	4,520	4,600	5,500	6,500	12,500
1832	4,400	4,600	5,500	6,500	12,500
1833	4,160	4,600	5,500	6,600	12,750
1834	4,000	7,000	9,750	15,500	33,500

Classic Head.

KM# 56 **Designer:** William Kneass. **Diameter:** 18.2
Weight: 4.1800 g. **Composition:** 0.8990 Gold,
0.1209 oz. AGW.

Date	Mintage	VF-20	XF-40	AU-50	MS-60	MS-65
1834	112,234	325	465	700	2,000	24,000
1835	131,402	325	465	700	2,250	31,000
1836	547,986	325	465	700	2,000	27,500
1837	45,080	415	650	1,175	3,250	32,500
1838	47,030	325	465	800	2,000	27,000
1838C	7,880	1,200	2,000	6,100	23,500	50,000
1839	27,021	360	650	1,440	4,250	—
1839C	18,140	1,100	2,200	3,500	22,500	—
1839D	13,674	1,125	2,800	6,000	21,000	—
1839O	17,781	500	925	1,500	5,600	—

Coronet Head.

KM# 72 **Designer:** Christian Gobrecht. **Diameter:** 18
Weight: 4.1800 g. **Composition:** 0.9000 Gold, 0.121 oz.
AGW. **Notes:** Varieties for 1843 are distinguished by the
size of the numerals in the date. One 1848 variety has
"Cal." inscribed on the reverse, indicating it was made
from California gold. The 1873 "closed-3" and "open-3"
varieties are distinguished by the amount of space between
the upper left and lower left serifs in the 3 in the date.

1948 "Cal."

Date	Mintage	F-12	VF-20	XF-40	AU-50	MS-60	Prf-65
1840	18,859	150	180	850	2,950	6,000	—
1840C	12,822	650	1,100	1,600	4,700	13,000	—
1840D	3,532	800	2,400	8,000	15,500	35,000	—
1840O	33,580	225	270	800	1,700	10,000	—
1841	—	—	50,000	90,000	95,000	—	—
1841C	10,281	650	1,100	1,600	3,250	18,500	—
1841D	4,164	850	1,650	3,850	9,900	25,000	—
1842	2,823	500	900	2,900	6,500	20,000	140,000
1842C	6,729	700	1,300	2,800	7,500	27,000	—
1842D	4,643	900	1,650	3,350	11,750	36,500	—
1842O	19,800	220	350	1,100	2,400	11,000	—
1843	100,546	150	170	220	325	1,150	140,000
1843C small date	26,064	1,100	2,150	5,000	8,400	22,000	—
1843C large date	Inc. above	600	1,100	1,600	3,100	8,500	—
1843D small date	36,209	700	1,250	1,850	2,750	9,500	—
1843O small date	288,002	150	180	240	350	1,600	—
1843O large date	76,000	200	250	450	1,600	7,000	—
1844	6,784	225	400	850	1,900	7,250	140,000
1844C	11,622	600	1,100	1,850	6,250	19,000	—
1844D	17,332	650	1,250	1,850	2,650	7,800	—
1845	91,051	180	245	300	440	1,150	140,000
1845D	19,460	650	1,250	1,850	2,750	13,000	—
1845O	4,000	525	950	2,000	5,900	16,000	—
1846	21,598	200	275	500	850	5,500	140,000
1846C	4,808	650	1,250	3,500	8,500	18,750	—
1846D	19,303	650	1,250	1,850	2,500	10,500	—
1846O	66,000	170	280	400	1,050	6,100	—
1847	29,814	140	220	360	825	3,400	—
1847C	23,226	600	1,100	1,600	2,300	6,500	—
1847D	15,784	650	1,250	1,850	2,500	10,000	—
1847O	124,000	150	220	375	1,000	3,500	—
1848	7,497	315	500	850	1,700	6,000	125,000
1848 "Cal."	1,389	6,000	10,000	20,000	29,000	40,000	—
1848C	16,788	600	1,100	1,650	2,800	14,000	—
1848D	13,771	650	1,250	1,850	2,750	10,000	—
1849	23,294	200	275	475	900	2,500	—
1849C	10,220	600	1,100	1,750	5,000	23,500	—
1849D	10,945	650	1,250	1,850	3,500	16,000	—
1850	252,923	140	170	215	350	1,100	—
1850C	9,148	600	1,100	1,600	2,400	17,500	—
1850D	12,148	650	1,250	1,850	3,150	11,500	—
1850O	84,000	160	225	450	1,150	4,750	—
1851	1,372,748	135	170	200	225	325	—
1851C	14,923	600	1,100	1,600	4,400	12,000	—
1851D	11,264	650	1,250	1,850	3,800	12,000	—

Date	Mintage	F-12	VF-20	XF-40	AU-50	MS-60	Prf-65
1851O	148,000	140	185	215	900	4,650	—
1852	1,159,681	135	170	200	225	325	—
1852C	9,772	600	1,100	1,700	4,250	19,000	—
1852D	4,078	700	1,300	2,550	7,250	17,000	—
1852O	140,000	145	185	300	950	5,000	—
1853	1,404,668	135	170	200	225	350	—
1853D	3,178	950	1,700	3,250	4,900	18,500	—
1854	596,258	135	170	200	225	350	—
1854C	7,295	600	1,100	2,000	5,000	14,750	—
1854D	1,760	1,750	2,750	5,000	11,000	27,500	—
1854O	153,000	140	170	215	415	1,500	—
1854S	246	32,500	43,500	80,000	185,000	300,000	—
1855	235,480	135	170	200	225	350	—
1855C	3,677	700	1,350	3,000	6,000	25,000	—
1855D	1,123	1,750	3,250	7,500	18,500	48,500	—
1856	384,240	135	170	200	225	380	9,500
1856C	7,913	650	1,150	2,200	4,400	15,500	—
1856D	874	3,500	6,400	9,800	2,500	72,500	—
1856O	21,100	150	200	700	1,250	7,700	—
1856S	71,120	145	195	360	900	4,400	—
1857	214,130	135	170	200	225	380	78,000
1857D	2,364	650	1,250	2,500	3,750	13,000	—
1857O	34,000	145	195	350	1,000	4,400	—
1857S	69,200	145	195	330	850	5,500	—
1858	47,377	135	170	235	350	1,250	62,500
1858C	9,056	600	1,100	1,600	2,900	9,250	—
1859	39,444	135	170	250	400	1,250	62,500
1859D	2,244	900	1,650	2,900	4,750	20,000	—
1859S	15,200	180	425	900	2,500	6,500	—
1860	22,675	135	170	245	450	1,100	33,500
1860C	7,469	600	1,100	1,800	3,650	22,500	—
1860S	35,600	160	250	675	1,150	4,000	—
1861	1,283,878	135	170	200	230	325	33,000
1861S	24,000	175	350	900	2,900	7,250	—
1862	98,543	145	190	300	500	1,250	33,000
1862/1	Inc. above	450	900	1,750	3,300	8,000	—
1862S	8,000	400	850	2,100	4,250	17,000	—
1863	30	—	—	—	—	—	80,000
1863S	10,800	300	500	1,500	3,200	13,500	—
1864	2,874	2,500	5,500	11,000	22,000	37,500	27,000
1865	1,545	2,400	4,650	7,250	19,000	36,500	31,500
1865S	23,376	150	215	610	1,200	4,400	—
1866	3,110	650	1,200	3,500	6,000	11,500	25,000
1866S	38,960	170	300	650	1,500	6,250	—
1867	3,250	185	365	800	1,150	4,800	27,000
1867S	28,000	150	250	600	1,600	4,000	—
1868	3,625	170	220	400	650	1,600	27,000
1868S	34,000	135	190	290	1,000	4,000	—
1869	4,345	150	230	450	715	3,000	23,000
1869S	29,500	135	215	440	775	5,000	—
1870	4,555	150	220	400	725	3,650	23,500
1870S	16,000	135	200	400	750	4,750	—
1871	5,350	150	230	325	575	2,200	23,500
1871S	22,000	135	185	275	525	2,200	—
1872	3,030	200	400	750	1,000	4,650	22,000
1872S	18,000	135	190	400	900	4,300	—
1873 closed 3	178,025	135	170	200	250	515	22,500
1873 open 3	Inc. above	135	165	195	240	285	—
1873S	27,000	135	225	400	850	2,750	—
1874	3,940	150	240	365	700	2,100	33,000
1875	420	1,750	3,500	5,000	8,000	12,500	43,500
1875S	11,600	135	180	300	750	3,350	—
1876	4,221	160	275	6,400	900	3,300	21,000
1876S	5,000	145	225	500	950	3,300	—
1877	1,652	250	380	750	1,050	3,000	21,500
1877S	35,400	135	160	195	230	615	—
1878	286,260	135	160	195	225	275	34,000
1878S	178,000	135	160	195	225	340	—
1879	88,990	135	160	195	225	275	21,500
1879S	43,500	135	195	275	525	215	—
1880	2,996	160	200	335	600	1,300	21,000
1881	691	850	1,850	2,800	4,350	9,000	19,000
1882	4,067	150	210	290	400	675	15,000
1883	2,002	150	220	440	975	2,300	15,500
1884	2,023	150	210	400	590	1,500	16,000
1885	887	400	700	1,750	2,350	4,400	15,500
1886	4,088	150	190	260	425	1,100	16,500
1887	6,282	150	175	245	325	700	16,500
1888	16,098	140	165	225	270	325	15,000

Date	Mintage	F-12	VF-20	XF-40	AU-50	MS-60	Prf-65
1889	17,648	150	165	200	250	325	17,500
1890	8,813	150	180	225	280	500	14,000
1891	11,040	150	165	200	230	400	14,000
1892	2,545	155	175	235	325	725	15,000
1893	30,106	145	165	190	225	280	14,000
1894	4,122	155	170	225	325	750	13,500
1895	6,199	135	160	205	275	395	12,500
1896	19,202	135	160	195	225	285	12,500
1897	29,904	135	160	195	225	285	12,500
1898	24,165	135	160	195	225	285	12,500
1899	27,350	135	160	195	225	285	12,500
1900	67,205	135	160	250	340	425	12,500
1901	91,322	135	160	195	220	275	12,500
1902	133,733	135	160	195	220	275	12,500
1903	201,257	135	160	195	220	275	13,000
1904	160,960	135	160	195	225	275	12,500
1905	217,944	135	160	195	225	275	12,500
1906	176,490	135	160	195	225	275	12,500
1907	336,448	135	160	195	225	275	12,500

Indian Head.

KM# 128   Designer: Bela Lyon Pratt. **Diameter:** 18
Weight: 4.1800 g. **Composition:** 0.9000 Gold, 0.121 oz.
AGW.

Date	Mintage	VF-20	XF-40	AU-50	MS-60	MS-63	MS-65	Prf-65
1908	565,057	135	175	185	280	1,400	5,000	16,000
1909	441,899	135	175	185	275	2,200	7,500	30,000
1910	492,682	135	175	185	265	2,150	8,500	18,000
1911	704,191	135	175	185	250	1,400	8,500	16,000
1911D	55,680	700	1,000	1,450	3,100	22,500	80,000	16,000
1912	616,197	135	175	185	285	2,500	11,000	16,000
1913	722,165	135	175	185	270	1,350	9,500	16,500
1914	240,117	135	175	200	450	6,000	17,500	16,500
1914D	448,000	135	175	185	300	2,200	21,000	23,000
1915	606,100	135	175	185	240	1,400	8,500	15,250
1925D	578,000	135	175	185	230	1,150	4,200	—
1926	446,000	135	175	185	230	1,150	4,200	—
1927	388,000	135	175	185	230	1,150	4,200	—
1928	416,000	135	175	185	230	1,150	4,200	—
1929	532,000	135	175	185	230	1,150	6,000	—

$3

GOLD

KM# 84   Designer: James B. Longacre. **Diameter:**
20.5 **Weight:** 5.0150 g. **Composition:** 0.9000 Gold,
0.1452 oz. AGW. **Notes:** The 1873 "closed-3" and
"open-3" varieties are distinguished by the amount of
space between the upper left and lower left serifs of the 3
in the date.

Date	Mintage	VF-20	XF-40	AU-50	MS-60	MS-65	Prf-65
1854	138,618	675	1,000	1,350	2,450	15,500	125,000
1854D	1,120	8,000	14,000	25,500	65,000	—	—
1854O	24,000	950	1,750	3,000	16,500	55,000	—
1855	50,555	700	1,000	1,300	2,400	30,000	125,000
1855S	6,600	1,000	2,000	5,000	22,000	—	—
1856	26,010	700	1,000	1,400	2,400	27,000	85,000
1856S	34,500	750	1,150	2,000	9,000	50,000	—
1857	20,891	700	1,000	1,400	3,000	32,500	62,500
1857S	14,000	800	1,750	4,500	15,500	—	—
1858	2,133	800	1,450	2,600	7,000	35,000	62,500
1859	15,638	700	1,000	1,400	2,550	18,500	45,000
1860	7,155	750	1,000	1,400	3,150	21,000	46,000
1860S	7,000	850	1,550	6,100	14,000	—	—
1861	6,072	750	1,025	1,600	3,300	27,000	46,000
1862	5,785	750	1,000	1,600	3,300	28,000	46,500
1863	5,039	800	1,150	1,600	3,400	20,000	40,000
1864	2,680	800	1,050	1,600	3,300	29,000	40,000

Date	Mintage	VF-20	XF-40	AU-50	MS-60	MS-65	Prf-65
1865	1,165	1,150	2,200	4,500	7,500	40,000	40,000
1866	4,030	850	1,000	1,600	3,300	27,500	40,000
1867	2,650	850	1,000	1,800	3,350	28,000	40,000
1868	4,875	700	950	1,500	2,800	22,000	38,000
1869	2,525	825	1,000	1,700	3,650	34,500	40,000
1870	3,535	725	1,000	1,750	3,700	40,000	47,000
1870S unique	—	—	—	—	—	—	—
Note: Est. value, $1.25 million, AU50 cleaned, Bass Collection.							
1871	1,330	825	1,150	1,700	3,700	27,500	47,000
1872	2,030	750	1,000	1,500	3,250	35,000	33,000
1873 open 3, proof only	25	3,300	5,000	8,700	—	—	65,000
1873 closed 3, mintage unknown	—	4,000	6,000	10,000	—	—	40,000
1874	41,820	650	950	1,300	2,300	12,500	38,000
1875 proof only	20	20,000	28,000	47,500	—	—	175,000
1876	45	5,500	10,000	14,000	—	—	50,000
1877	1,488	1,200	2,700	5,000	11,500	67,000	42,000
1878	82,324	650	1,000	1,300	2,500	11,000	47,500
1879	3,030	700	1,000	1,500	2,400	12,000	32,000
1880	1,036	750	1,600	2,000	2,800	15,500	31,000
1881	554	1,200	2,250	4,000	5,250	22,500	25,000
1882	1,576	850	1,000	1,750	3,000	20,000	25,000
1883	989	800	1,300	20,000	3,200	18,000	24,000
1884	1,106	1,150	1,500	2,200	2,750	22,000	24,000
1885	910	1,150	1,500	2,250	3,300	22,500	25,000
1886	1,142	1,100	1,700	2,100	4,000	35,000	24,000
1887	6,160	700	1,000	1,600	2,800	14,000	24,000
1888	5,291	750	1,000	1,500	2,450	13,000	24,000
1889	2,429	725	1,000	1,400	2,500	13,500	24,000

$5 (HALF EAGLE)

GOLD

Liberty Cap.

KM# 19 **Designer:** Robert Scot. **Diameter:** 25 **Weight:** 8.7500 g. **Composition:** 0.9160 Gold, 0.258 oz. AGW.
Notes: From 1795 through 1798, varieties exist with either a "small eagle" or a "large (heraldic) eagle" on the reverse. After 1798, only the heraldic eagle was used. Two 1797 varieties are distinguished by the size of the 8 in the date. 1806 varieties are distinguished by whether the top of the 6 has a serif.

Small eagle

Large eagle

Date	Mintage	F-12	VF-20	XF-40	MS-60
1795 small eagle	8,707	11,500	17,000	20,000	40,000
1795 large eagle	Inc. above	8,800	13,500	20,000	89,000
1796/95 small eagle	6,196	12,000	17,500	22,500	67,500
1797/95 large eagle	3,609	8,600	12,500	21,000	165,000
1797 15 stars, small eagle	Inc. above	13,500	19,000	33,000	150,000
1797 16 stars, small eagle	Inc. above	12,000	17,500	27,500	137,500
1798 small eagle	—	96,000	165,000	300,000	—
1798 large eagle, small 8	24,867	2,800	3,600	4,900	22,000
1798 large eagle, large 8, 13-star reverse	Inc. above	2,750	3,500	4,500	17,500
1798 large eagle, large 8, 14-star reverse	Inc. above	2,900	3,850	7,000	25,000
1799	7,451	2,850	3,450	4,500	16,500
1800	37,628	2,750	3,300	3,700	8,700
1802/1	53,176	2,750	3,300	3,700	8,700
1803/2	33,506	2,750	3,300	3,700	8,700
1804 small 8	30,475	2,750	3,300	3,700	8,700
1804 large 8	Inc. above	2,750	3,300	3,700	9,600
1805	33,183	2,750	3,300	3,700	8,600
1806 pointed 6	64,093	2,800	3,350	3,750	9,000
1806 round 6	Inc. above	2,750	3,300	3,700	8,600
1807	32,488	2,750	3,300	3,700	8,700

Turban Head. Capped draped bust.

KM# 38   Designer: John Reich. **Diameter:** 25 **Weight:** 8.7500 g. **Composition:** 0.9160 Gold, 0.258 oz. AGW. **Notes:** The 1810 varieties are distinguished by the size of the numerals in the date and the size of the 5 in the "5D." on the reverse. The 1811 varieties are distinguished by the size of the 5 in the "5D." on the reverse.

Date	Mintage	F-12	VF-20	XF-40	MS-60
1807	51,605	2,000	2,400	3,150	6,800
1808	55,578	2,000	2,400	3,150	6,900
1808/7	Inc. above	3,100	3,300	3,750	12,000
1809/8	33,875	2,000	2,400	3,150	6,900
1810 small date, small 5	100,287	9,600	22,500	35,000	102,500
1810 small date, large 5	Inc. above	2,100	2,400	3,200	7,000
1810 large date, small 5	Inc. above	13,500	25,000	37,000	124,000
1810 large date, large 5	Inc. above	2,000	2,400	3,150	6,800
1811 small 5	99,581	2,000	2,400	3,150	6,800
1811 large 5	Inc. above	1,950	2,350	3,100	7,000
1812	58,087	2,000	2,400	3,150	6,800

Turban Head. Capped head.

KM# 43   Designer: John Reich. **Diameter:** 25 **Weight:** 8.7500 g. **Composition:** 0.9160 Gold, 0.258 oz. AGW. **Notes:** 1820 varieties are distinguished by whether the 2 in the date has a curved base or square base and by the size of the letters in the reverse inscriptions. 1832 varieties are distinguished by whether the 2 in the date has a curved base or square base and by the number of stars on the reverse. 1834 varieties are distinguished by whether the 4 has a serif at its far right.

Date	Mintage	F-12	VF-20	XF-40	MS-60
1813	95,428	2,400	2,750	3,400	7,800
1814/13	15,454	2,500	2,800	3,500	9,800
1815	635	—	—	—	—
Note: 1815, private sale, Jan. 1994, MS-61, $150,000					
1818	48,588	2,475	2,750	3,400	8,000
1819	51,723	9,600	16,500	275,000	62,000
1820 curved-base 2, small letters	263,806	2,450	2,800	3,600	10,500
1820 curved-base 2, large letters	Inc. above	2,500	3,000	3,750	20,000
1820 square-base 2	Inc. above	2,450	2,800	3,600	10,500
1821	34,641	5,800	13,500	20,000	72,000
1822 3 known	—	55,000	1,000,000	1,500,000	—
Note: 1822, private sale, 1993, VF-30, $1,000,000.					
1823	14,485	2,500	3,400	4,700	16,000
1824	17,340	5,000	10,000	16,000	38,000
1825/21	29,060	5,150	8,250	12,000	38,000
1825/24	Inc. above	—	—	250,000	350,000
Note: 1825/4, Bowers & Merena, March 1989, XF, $148,500.					
1826	18,069	3,600	7,500	9,300	25,000
1827	24,913	5,600	9,600	12,250	34,000
1828/7	28,029	15,000	27,500	41,000	125,000
Note: 1828/7, Bowers & Merena, June 1989, XF, $20,900.					
1828	Inc. above	5,500	12,500	19,000	65,000
1829 large planchet	57,442	15,000	27,500	50,000	110,000
Note: 1829 large planchet, Superior, July 1985, MS-65, $104,500.					
1829 small planchet	Inc. above	37,500	50,000	82,500	140,000
Note: 1829 small planchet, private sale, 1992 (XF-45), $89,000.					
1830 small "5D."	126,351	14,500	17,500	21,000	40,000
1830 large "5D."	Inc. above	14,500	17,500	21,000	40,000
1831	140,594	14,500	17,500	21,000	42,500
1832 curved-base 2, 12 stars	157,487	45,000	65,000	125,000	—
1832 square-base 2, 13 stars	Inc. above	14,500	17,500	21,000	40,000
1833	193,630	14,500	17,500	21,000	40,000
1834 plain 4	50,141	14,500	17,500	21,000	40,000
1834 crosslet 4	Inc. above	14,500	17,500	21,000	40,000

Classic Head.

KM# 57 Designer: William Kneass. **Diameter:** 22.5
Weight: 8.3600 g. **Composition:** 0.8990 Gold,
0.2418 oz. AGW. **Notes:** 1834 varieties are
distinguished by whether the 4 has a serif at its far right.

Date	Mintage	VF-20	XF-40	AU-50	MS-60	MS-65
1834 plain 4	658,028	390	550	890	2,850	48,000
1834 crosslet 4	Inc. above	1,650	2,750	5,500	20,000	—
1835	371,534	390	560	960	3,150	70,000
1836	553,147	390	550	890	2,900	70,000
1837	207,121	390	585	1,200	3,500	75,000
1838	286,588	390	5,500	890	3,700	58,000
1838C	17,179	1,900	3,850	12,500	38,500	—
1838D	20,583	1,500	3,400	8,250	23,000	—

Coronet Head. No motto above eagle.

KM# 69 Designer: Christian Gobrecht. **Diameter:**
21.6 **Weight:** 8.3590 g. **Composition:** 0.9000 Gold,
0.242 oz. AGW. **Notes:** Varieties for the 1842
Philadelphia strikes are distinguished by the size of the
letters in the reverse inscriptions. Varieties for the 1842-
C and -D strikes are distinguished by the size of the
numerals in the date. Varieties for the 1843-O strikes are
distinguished by the size of the letters in the reverse
inscriptions.

Date	Mintage	F-12	VF-20	XF-40	MS-60	Prf-65
1839	118,143	250	275	480	4,000	—
1839/8 curved date	Inc. above	275	325	700	2,250	—
1839C	17,205	700	1,450	2,700	24,000	—
1839D	18,939	700	1,450	2,200	22,000	—
1840	137,382	190	235	360	3,700	—
1840C	18,992	700	1,450	2,600	25,000	—
1840D	22,896	700	1,450	2,000	15,000	—
1840O	40,120	200	325	850	11,000	—
1841	15,833	210	375	1,750	10,500	—
1841C	21,467	650	1,400	1,925	18,500	—
1841D	30,495	700	1,450	1,925	14,500	—
1841O 2 known	50	—	—	—	—	—
1842 small letters	27,578	165	345	1,100	1,375	—
1842 large letters	Inc. above	300	750	2,000	11,000	—
1842C small date	28,184	4,500	9,000	23,000	125,000	—
1842C large date	Inc. above	650	1,400	2,000	18,000	—
1842D small date	59,608	700	1,450	1,925	15,000	—
1842D large date	Inc. above	1,000	2,200	5,800	48,000	—
1842O	16,400	450	1,000	3,000	22,000	—
1843	611,205	170	220	260	1,850	—
1843C	44,201	650	1,375	1,925	12,500	—
1843D	98,452	650	1,450	1,925	12,500	—
1843O small letters	19,075	250	500	1,400	20,000	—
1843O large letters	82,000	175	250	1,125	12,000	—
1844	340,330	150	220	240	2,000	—
1844C	23,631	650	1,375	3,000	22,000	—
1844D	88,982	700	1,450	1,925	11,000	—
1844O	364,600	175	250	375	4,000	—
1845	417,099	150	220	240	2,000	—
1845D	90,629	700	1,450	1,925	12,000	—
1845O	41,000	200	410	750	9,900	—
1846	395,942	150	220	240	2,400	—
1846C	12,995	700	1,450	2,900	22,500	—
1846D	80,294	700	1,450	1,925	12,000	—
1846O	58,000	200	375	960	11,500	—
1847	915,981	150	220	250	1,650	—
1847C	84,151	650	1,375	1,925	13,000	—
1847D	64,405	700	1,450	1,925	10,000	—
1847O	12,000	1,925	7,500	9,600	26,000	—
1848	260,775	150	225	275	1,500	—
1848C	64,472	650	1,375	1,925	19,250	—
1848D	47,465	700	1,450	1,925	14,500	—
1849	133,070	150	220	270	2,750	—
1849C	64,823	650	1,375	1,925	13,500	—
1849D	39,036	700	1,450	1,925	14,000	—
1850	64,491	185	275	600	3,700	—
1850C	63,591	650	1,375	1,925	12,000	—
1850D	43,984	700	1,450	1,925	27,500	—

Date	Mintage	F-12	VF-20	XF-40	MS-60	Prf-65
1851	377,505	150	220	240	2,800	—
1851C	49,176	650	1,375	1,925	16,500	—
1851D	62,710	700	1,450	1,925	15,000	—
1851O	41,000	275	565	1,500	12,000	—
1852	573,901	150	220	245	1,250	—
1852C	72,574	650	1,375	1,925	6,750	—
1852D	91,584	700	1,450	1,925	12,500	—
1853	305,770	150	220	240	1,500	—
1853C	65,571	650	1,375	1,925	8,500	—
1853D	89,678	700	1,450	1,925	10,000	—
1854	160,675	150	220	250	2,000	—
1854C	39,283	650	1,375	1,925	14,000	—
1854D	56,413	700	1,450	1,925	10,500	—
1854O	46,000	200	300	525	8,250	—
1854S	268	—	—	—	—	—
Note: 1854S, Bowers & Merena, Oct. 1982, AU-55, $170,000.						
1855	117,098	140	220	235	1,800	—
1855C	39,788	650	1,375	2,000	15,000	—
1855D	22,432	700	1,450	1,925	16,500	—
1855O	11,100	275	650	2,100	20,000	—
1855S	61,000	200	390	975	15,500	—
1856	197,990	150	220	240	2,300	—
1856C	28,457	650	1,375	1,925	20,000	—
1856D	19,786	700	1,450	1,925	11,000	—
1856O	10,000	330	650	1,250	12,500	—
1856S	105,100	175	300	625	6,900	—
1857	98,188	150	220	240	1,600	123,500
1857C	31,360	650	1,375	1,925	9,000	—
1857D	17,046	700	1,450	1,925	13,000	—
1857O	13,000	325	640	1,400	17,000	—
1857S	87,000	180	300	525	9,600	—
1858	15,136	150	240	550	3,850	190,000
1858C	38,856	650	1,375	1,925	10,000	—
1858D	15,362	700	1,450	1,925	12,500	—
1858S	18,600	300	700	2,350	30,000	—
1859	16,814	185	325	625	7,250	—
1859C	31,847	650	1,375	1,925	15,000	—
1859D	10,366	700	1,450	1,925	14,500	—
1859S	13,220	500	1,250	3,500	29,000	—
1860	19,825	175	275	575	2,700	100,000
1860C	14,813	650	1,375	2,200	15,000	—
1860D	14,635	700	1,450	2,000	17,000	—
1860S	21,200	400	1,100	2,100	25,000	—
1861	688,150	150	220	245	1,200	100,000
1861C	6,879	700	1,850	3,900	25,000	—
1861D	1,597	2,400	4,400	7,000	53,500	—
1861S	18,000	450	1,000	4,500	36,500	—
1862	4,465	300	700	1,850	20,000	96,000
1862S	9,500	1,600	3,000	6,300	62,000	—
1863	2,472	450	1,200	3,750	27,500	90,000
1863S	17,000	600	1,450	3,900	35,500	—
1864	4,220	350	630	1,850	14,500	72,000
1864S	3,888	2,300	5,000	16,000	55,000	—
1865	1,295	500	1,300	4,100	20,000	82,500
1865S	27,612	450	1,300	2,400	20,000	—
1866S	9,000	700	1,650	4,000	40,000	—

Coronet Head.
"In God We Trust" above eagle.

KM# 101 Designer: Christian Gobrecht. **Diameter:** 21.6 **Weight:** 8.3590 g. **Composition:** 0.9000 Gold, 0.242 oz. AGW. **Notes:** The 1873 "closed-3" and "open-3" varieties are known and are distinguished by the amount of space between the upper left and lower left serifs of the 3 in the date.

Date	Mintage	VF-20	XF-40	AU-50	MS-60	MS-63	MS-65	Prf-65
1866	6,730	800	1,650	3,500	16,500	—	—	70,000
1866S	34,920	900	2,600	8,000	25,000	—	—	—
1867	6,920	500	1,700	3,700	11,500	—	—	70,000
1867S	29,000	1,300	2,700	8,000	34,500	—	—	—
1868	5,725	650	1,000	3,500	11,000	—	—	70,000
1868S	52,000	400	1,550	4,000	20,000	—	—	—
1869	1,785	925	2,400	3,500	17,500	33,500	—	65,000
1869S	31,000	500	1,750	4,000	26,000	—	—	—
1870	4,035	800	2,000	2,850	18,000	—	—	75,000
1870CC	7,675	5,000	13,000	26,000	110,000	137,500	200,000	—
1870S	17,000	950	2,600	8,250	29,000	—	—	—
1871	3,230	950	1,850	3,300	12,500	—	—	70,000

Date	Mintage	VF-20	XF-40	AU-50	MS-60	MS-63	MS-65	Prf-65
1871CC	20,770	1,100	3,300	11,000	60,000	—	—	—
1871S	25,000	500	1,000	3,150	13,000	—	—	—
1872	1,690	850	1,925	3,000	15,000	20,000	—	60,000
1872CC	16,980	1,100	4,800	20,000	60,000	—	—	—
1872S	36,400	445	800	3,600	13,000	—	—	—
1873 closed 3	49,305	180	225	400	1,175	6,500	24,000	70,000
1873 open 3	63,200	180	215	350	850	3,800	—	—
1873CC	7,416	2,200	12,500	27,500	60,000	—	—	—
1873S	31,000	525	1,400	3,250	22,000	—	—	—
1874	3,508	660	1,675	2,500	12,500	26,000	—	66,000
1874CC	21,198	800	1,700	9,500	38,000	—	—	—
1874S	16,000	640	2,100	4,600	22,500	—	—	—
1875	220	34,000	45,000	60,000	200,000	—	—	185,000
1875CC	11,828	1,400	4,400	11,500	52,000	—	—	—
1875S	9,000	675	2,250	4,800	16,500	32,500	—	—
1876	1,477	1,100	2,500	4,125	11,000	14,500	55,000	60,000
1876CC	6,887	1,200	5,000	14,000	46,500	82,500	165,000	—
1876S	4,000	2,000	3,600	9,500	30,000	—	—	—
1877	1,152	900	2,750	4,000	13,750	29,000	—	75,000
1877CC	8,680	1,000	3,300	11,000	52,500	—	—	—
1877S	26,700	400	650	1,400	9,200	—	—	—
1878	131,740	160	190	240	425	2,000	—	50,000
1878CC	9,054	3,000	7,200	20,000	60,000	—	—	—
1878S	144,700	165	190	3,000	675	4,250	—	—
1879	301,950	165	180	225	400	2,000	12,000	55,000
1879CC	17,281	525	1,375	3,000	2,200	—	—	—
1879S	426,200	180	225	240	825	3,300	—	—
1880	3,166,436	160	175	180	220	840	7,500	54,000
1880CC	51,017	425	770	1,375	9,900	—	—	—
1880S	1,348,900	160	175	180	220	800	5,750	—
1881	5,708,802	160	175	180	220	775	4,800	54,000
1881/80	Inc. above	330	600	750	1,500	4,500	—	—
1881CC	13,886	515	1,400	6,750	22,500	60,000	—	—
1881S	969,000	160	175	180	220	775	7,150	—
1882	2,514,568	160	175	180	220	800	6,150	54,000
1882CC	82,817	390	550	800	7,500	40,000	—	—
1882S	969,000	160	175	180	220	800	4,500	—
1883	233,461	160	175	200	260	1,200	—	40,000
1883CC	12,958	450	1,000	3,200	18,000	—	—	—
1883S	83,200	200	240	300	1,000	2,950	—	—
1884	191,078	170	200	220	650	2,250	—	35,000
1884CC	16,402	550	975	3,000	17,000	—	—	—
1884S	177,000	170	200	215	360	2,000	—	—
1885	601,506	160	175	180	220	825	4,800	35,000
1885S	1,211,500	160	175	180	220	790	4,000	—
1886	388,432	160	175	180	230	1,100	5,600	44,000
1886S	3,268,000	160	175	180	220	790	4,500	—
1887	87	—	14,500	20,000	—	—	—	130,000
1887S	1,912,000	160	175	180	220	825	4,800	—
1888	18,296	175	230	300	550	1,550	—	28,000
1888S	293,900	175	200	320	1,200	4,000	—	—
1889	7,565	280	4,400	515	1,100	2,400	—	29,000
1890	4,328	400	475	550	2,200	6,500	—	27,000
1890CC	53,800	330	385	560	1,175	5,000	55,000	—
1891	61,413	170	200	225	450	1,900	5,400	28,000
1891CC	208,000	315	415	525	750	3,150	31,500	—
1892	753,572	160	175	180	220	880	7,000	30,000
1892CC	82,968	315	400	575	1,500	6,000	33,500	—
1892O	10,000	515	1,000	1,375	3,300	—	—	—
1892S	298,400	180	195	220	525	3,300	—	—
1893	1,528,197	160	175	180	220	790	3,900	34,000
1893CC	60,000	315	450	770	1,400	6,350	—	—
1893O	110,000	225	315	480	950	6,500	—	—
1893S	224,000	170	200	210	230	825	9,000	—
1894	957,955	160	175	180	220	790	2,000	35,000
1894O	16,600	200	360	570	1,300	5,500	—	—
1894S	55,900	240	375	575	2,900	10,000	—	—
1895	1,345,936	160	175	180	220	790	4,500	29,000
1895S	112,000	200	275	400	3,150	6,500	26,000	—
1896	59,063	160	175	175	235	9,750	4,500	30,000
1896S	155,400	200	240	300	1,150	6,000	24,500	—
1897	867,883	160	175	180	220	825	4,500	35,000
1897S	354,000	175	210	235	865	5,150	—	—
1898	633,495	160	175	180	225	885	6,000	30,000
1898S	1,397,400	175	200	210	230	950	—	—
1899	1,710,729	160	175	180	220	790	3,600	30,000
1899S	1,545,000	170	180	185	230	1,000	9,600	—
1900	1,405,730	160	175	180	220	790	3,600	30,000
1900S	329,000	170	190	200	230	900	14,000	—

Date	Mintage	VF-20	XF-40	AU-50	MS-60	MS-63	MS-65	Prf-65
1901	616,040	160	175	180	220	790	3,650	12,500
1901S	3,648,000	160	175	180	220	790	3,600	—
1902	172,562	160	175	180	220	790	4,400	22,000
1902S	939,000	160	175	180	220	790	3,600	—
1903	227,024	160	175	180	220	790	4,000	22,000
1903S	1,855,000	160	175	180	220	790	3,600	—
1904	392,136	160	175	180	220	790	3,600	25,000
1904S	97,000	175	215	285	900	3,850	9,600	—
1905	302,308	160	175	180	220	790	4,000	25,000
1905S	880,700	175	200	235	550	1,500	9,600	—
1906	348,820	160	175	180	220	790	3,600	22,000
1906D	320,000	160	175	180	220	790	400	—
1906S	598,000	165	185	200	230	1,000	4,500	—
1907	626,192	160	175	180	220	790	3,600	23,000
1907D	888,000	160	175	180	220	790	3,600	—
1908	421,874	160	175	180	220	790	3,600	—

Indian Head.

KM# 129   Designer: Bela Lyon Pratt. **Diameter:** 21.6 **Weight:** 8.3590 g. **Composition:** 0.9000 Gold, .2420 oz. AGW.

Date	Mintage	VF-20	XF-40	AU-50	MS-60	MS-63	MS-65	Prf-65
1908	578,012	180	200	235	320	1,800	12,500	25,500
1908D	148,000	180	200	235	320	1,800	22,500	—
1908S	82,000	195	435	470	1,250	2,600	15,000	—
1909	627,138	180	200	235	335	1,800	12,500	36,000
1909D	3,423,560	175	200	235	310	1,800	12,500	—
1909O	34,200	650	1,950	2,350	10,000	49,000	255,000	—
1909S	297,200	185	270	305	1,300	10,500	44,000	—
1910	604,250	175	200	235	325	1,800	18,500	37,000
1910D	193,600	175	215	260	370	1,950	41,500	—
1910S	770,200	175	280	305	990	5,400	42,500	—
1911	915,139	175	200	235	325	1,800	12,500	28,500
1911D	72,500	350	450	505	3,300	33,500	120,000	—
1911S	1,416,000	180	270	280	550	2,700	40,000	—
1912	790,144	180	200	235	325	1,800	12,500	28,500
1912S	392,000	195	320	350	1,650	13,000	90,000	—
1913	916,099	180	200	235	325	1,800	12,500	28,000
1913S	408,000	200	290	315	1,375	12,500	115,000	—
1914	247,125	180	200	235	340	1,800	12,500	28,500
1914D	247,000	185	230	235	335	2,700	25,500	—
1914S	263,000	260	300	335	1,220	12,000	100,000	—
1915	588,075	190	200	235	315	1,800	12,500	39,000
1915S	164,000	270	400	435	2,000	16,000	110,000	—
1916S	240,000	260	295	320	550	2,800	19,500	—
1929	662,000	2,400	5,400	5,900	6,500	8,800	40,000	—

$10 (EAGLE)

GOLD

Liberty Cap. Small eagle.

KM# 21   Designer: Robert Scot. **Diameter:** 33 **Weight:** 17.5000 g. **Composition:** 0.9160 Gold, 0.5159 oz. AGW.

Date	Mintage	F-12	VF-20	XF-40	MS-60
1795 13 leaves	5,583	17,000	22,000	31,500	60,000
1795 9 leaves	Inc. above	22,500	37,500	60,000	190,000

Date	Mintage	F-12	VF-20	XF-40	MS-60
1796	4,146	18,500	24,000	34,500	37,500
1797 small eagle	3,615	24,000	30,000	38,500	185,000

Liberty Cap. Heraldic eagle.

KM# 30 **Designer:** Robert Scot. **Diameter:** 33 **Weight:** 17.5000 g. **Composition:** 0.9160 Gold, 0.5159 oz. AGW.
Notes: The 1798/97 varieties are distinguished by the positioning of the stars on the obverse.

Date	Mintage	F-12	VF-20	XF-40	MS-60
1797 large eagle	10,940	8,250	10,000	12,500	3,150
1798/97 9 stars left, 4 right	900	9,600	14,500	26,500	90,000
1798/97 7 stars left, 6 right	842	17,500	27,500	60,000	—
1799	37,449	7,500	8,900	10,000	20,000
1800	5,999	7,500	8,900	10,000	26,000
1801	44,344	7,500	8,900	10,000	20,000
1803	15,017	7,500	9,000	10,000	21,000
1804	3,757	7,700	9,250	10,250	34,500

Coronet Head. Old-style head. No motto above eagle.

KM# 66.1 **Designer:** Christian Gobrecht. **Diameter:** 27 **Weight:** 16.7180 g. **Composition:** 0.9000 Gold, 0.4839 oz. AGW.

Date	Mintage	F-12	VF-20	XF-40	MS-60	Prf-65
1838	7,200	800	1,100	2,900	35,500	—
1839 large letters	38,248	800	1,000	1,950	30,000	—

Coronet Head. New-style head. No motto above eagle.

KM# 66.2 **Designer:** Christian Gobrecht. **Diameter:** 27 **Weight:** 16.7180 g. **Composition:** 0.9000 Gold, 0.4839 oz. AGW. **Notes:** The 1842 varieties are distinguished by the size of the numerals in the date.

Date	Mintage	F-12	VF-20	XF-40	MS-60	Prf-65
1839 small letters	Inc. above	800	1,500	3,500	30,000	—
1840	47,338	300	400	650	10,000	—
1841	63,131	300	385	500	9,500	—
1841O	2,500	1,100	2,200	5,000	30,000	—
1842 small date	81,507	275	375	650	16,500	—
1842 large date	Inc. above	250	325	475	9,200	—
1842O	27,400	250	370	500	22,500	—
1843	75,462	250	370	500	19,000	—
1843O	175,162	250	370	475	11,500	—
1844	6,361	800	1,350	2,700	16,750	—
1844O	118,700	245	325	475	15,000	—
1845	26,153	290	600	775	14,000	—
1845O	47,500	250	380	650	16,500	—
1846	20,095	410	625	900	20,000	—
1846O	81,780	250	425	770	14,750	—
1847	862,258	240	300	350	3,000	—
1847O	571,500	250	325	375	4,850	—
1848	145,484	260	340	375	4,300	—
1848O	38,850	325	525	1,050	14,000	—

Date	Mintage	F-12	VF-20	XF-40	MS-60	Prf-65
1849	653,618	240	300	350	3,400	—
1849O	23,900	375	710	2,100	21,000	—
1850	291,451	240	300	380	3,600	—
1850O	57,500	285	380	880	—	—
1851	176,328	275	325	475	5,150	—
1851O	263,000	250	315	440	5,750	—
1852	263,106	240	300	350	4,200	—
1852O	18,000	375	650	1,100	19,000	—
1853	201,253	240	300	350	3,500	—
1853O	51,000	285	325	485	12,500	—
1854	54,250	290	320	400	6,000	—
1854O small date	52,500	290	375	675	10,500	—
1854O large date	Inc. above	375	475	875	—	—
1854S	123,826	275	325	410	5,500	—
1855	121,701	250	300	350	4,150	—
1855O	18,000	400	625	1,250	20,000	—
1855S	9,000	700	1,250	2,100	29,500	—
1856	60,490	250	300	350	4,200	—
1856O	14,500	375	725	1,250	9,800	—
1856S	68,000	250	320	500	8,500	—
1857	16,606	325	490	850	12,000	—
1857O	5,500	600	975	1,850	18,000	—
1857S	26,000	300	375	950	9,500	—
1858	2,521	2,600	4,650	7,250	32,000	—
1858O	20,000	300	440	750	9,000	—
1858S	11,800	825	1,450	3,100	34,000	—
1859	16,093	325	390	750	10,500	—
1859O	2,300	1,850	3,800	8,200	47,500	—
1859S	7,000	1,000	1,800	4,500	40,000	—
1860	15,105	300	420	775	8,000	—
1860O	11,100	410	575	1,100	8,250	—
1860S	5,000	1,400	3,250	6,100	40,500	—
1861	113,233	250	300	350	3,600	—
1861S	15,500	690	1,600	2,950	32,500	—
1862	10,995	265	515	1,000	13,500	—
1862S	12,500	675	1,750	2,950	37,000	—
1863	1,248	2,400	3,650	10,000	42,500	—
1863S	10,000	625	1,600	3,350	24,000	—
1864	3,580	775	1,600	4,200	17,500	—
1864S	2,500	2,300	4,900	12,500	50,000	—
1865	4,005	875	1,950	3,500	31,500	—
1865S	16,700	1,700	5,350	10,500	45,000	—
1865S /inverted 186	—	1,250	2,850	6,100	47,000	—
1866S	8,500	950	2,400	3,300	44,000	—

Coronet Head. New-style head.
"In God We Trust" above eagle.

KM# 102 Designer: Christian Gobrecht. **Diameter:**
27 **Weight:** 16.7180 g. **Composition:** 0.9000 Gold,
0.4839 oz. AGW. **Notes:** The 1873 "closed-3" and
"open-3" varieties are distinguished by the amount of
space between the upper left and lower left serifs of the 3
in the date.

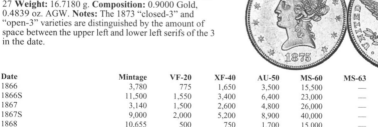

Date	Mintage	VF-20	XF-40	AU-50	MS-60	MS-63	MS-65	Prf-65
1866	3,780	775	1,650	3,500	15,500	—	—	75,000
1866S	11,500	1,550	3,400	6,400	23,000	—	—	—
1867	3,140	1,500	2,600	4,800	26,000	—	—	75,000
1867S	9,000	2,000	5,200	8,900	40,000	—	—	—
1868	10,655	500	750	1,700	15,000	—	—	60,000
1868S	13,500	1,250	2,100	3,800	24,000	—	—	—
1869	1,855	1,400	2,800	5,400	27,500	—	—	—
1869S	6,430	1,500	2,500	6,250	25,000	—	—	—
1870	4,025	800	1,175	2,350	17,000	—	—	60,000
1870CC	5,908	9,000	22,000	42,000	90,000	—	—	—
1870S	8,000	1,100	2,500	6,500	32,000	—	—	—
1871	1,820	1,450	2,400	4,000	19,500	—	—	75,000
1871CC	8,085	2,150	4,950	16,500	53,500	—	—	—
1871S	16,500	1,075	1,500	5,700	26,000	—	—	—
1872	1,650	2,200	3,600	9,500	16,500	32,000	—	60,000
1872CC	4,600	3,000	8,800	20,000	55,000	—	—	—
1872S	17,300	550	850	1,800	22,000	—	—	—
1873 closed 3	825	4,500	9,500	17,500	55,000	—	—	60,000
1873CC	4,543	5,000	12,000	26,000	57,500	—	—	—
1873S	12,000	950	1,950	4,750	24,500	—	—	—
1874	53,160	240	265	315	1,850	8,750	—	60,000

Date	Mintage	VF-20	XF-40	AU-50	MS-60	MS-63	MS-65	Prf-65
1874CC	16,767	850	2,500	8,000	40,000	—	—	—
1874S	10,000	1,150	3,250	6,800	39,500	—	—	—
1875	120	38,000	53,000	80,000	95,000	—	—	185,000
Note: 1875, Akers, Aug. 1990, Proof, $115,000.								
1875CC	7,715	3,700	8,800	25,000	65,000	—	—	—
1876	732	3,500	4,750	15,000	55,000	—	—	60,000
1876CC	4,696	3,200	6,500	20,500	50,000	—	—	—
1876S	5,000	1,250	2,000	5,500	38,000	—	—	—
1877	817	2,100	3,800	8,500	—	—	—	—
1877CC	3,332	2,300	4,750	14,000	47,000	—	—	—
1877S	17,000	500	700	2,200	22,500	—	—	—
1878	73,800	220	265	285	900	4,800	—	60,000
1878CC	3,244	3,600	7,500	14,000	47,000	—	—	—
1878S	26,100	450	550	1,650	15,000	—	—	—
1879	384,770	200	220	315	665	2,850	—	50,000
1879/78	Inc. above	300	400	700	800	900	—	—
1879CC	1,762	6,500	12,000	21,750	60,000	—	—	—
1879O	1,500	2,300	3,750	10,000	28,750	—	—	—
1879S	224,000	200	220	250	1,100	7,750	—	—
1880	1,644,876	210	225	250	280	2,250	—	45,000
1880CC	11,190	475	700	1,450	12,500	—	—	—
1880O	9,200	415	700	1,200	12,750	—	—	—
1880S	506,250	200	230	315	415	3,300	—	—
1881	3,877,260	200	225	240	275	800	—	45,000
1881CC	24,015	360	515	950	6,500	18,500	—	—
1881O	8,350	375	650	1,250	6,750	—	—	—
1881S	970,000	200	225	240	350	—	—	—
1882	2,324,480	200	225	240	270	800	—	41,500
1882CC	6,764	950	1,300	3,000	13,000	35,000	—	—
1882O	10,820	375	575	1,200	7,700	16,750	—	—
1882S	132,000	200	230	240	350	4,200	—	—
1883	208,740	200	225	240	300	1,300	—	41,500
1883CC	12,000	425	700	2,350	12,500	35,000	—	—
1883O	800	2,950	6,800	9,500	33,500	—	—	—
1883S	38,000	200	250	340	1,100	6,900	—	—
1884	76,905	190	225	250	750	2,600	—	46,000
1884CC	9,925	600	950	2,250	10,750	34,000	—	—
1884S	124,250	210	220	235	525	6,500	—	—
1885	253,527	210	220	230	375	2,750	—	43,000
1885S	228,000	210	225	250	375	3,600	6,500	—
1886	236,160	210	225	250	375	1,800	—	42,500
1886S	826,000	200	225	250	340	1,000	—	—
1887	53,680	200	225	295	800	3,800	—	37,000
1887S	817,000	200	225	240	315	1,950	—	—
1888	132,996	225	235	315	700	4,500	—	38,500
1888O	21,335	225	250	275	515	4,500	—	—
1888S	648,700	210	225	240	300	1,950	—	—
1889	4,485	575	700	1,100	2,700	6,800	—	43,000
1889S	425,400	210	220	240	350	1,400	4,200	—
1890	58,043	225	275	300	700	3,900	7,750	37,500
1890CC	17,500	385	450	650	2,000	13,500	—	—
1891	91,868	225	250	275	325	1,900	—	32,500
1891CC	103,732	350	400	515	750	4,200	—	—
1892	797,552	210	225	250	285	1,150	12,000	37,500
1892CC	40,000	350	450	625	3,100	8,000	—	—
1892O	28,688	250	275	300	400	2,500	—	—
1892S	115,500	210	220	250	360	2,950	—	—
1893	1,840,895	200	210	235	275	695	—	34,500
1893CC	14,000	425	625	1,450	6,200	14,500	—	—
1893O	17,000	260	315	350	625	5,100	—	—
1893S	141,350	220	230	250	440	2,750	—	—
1894	2,470,778	210	225	250	265	725	11,500	35,000
1894O	107,500	225	260	360	900	4,750	—	—
1894S	25,000	260	385	875	3,500	8,800	—	—
1895	567,826	200	210	240	280	775	8,800	33,000
1895O	98,000	220	230	280	480	3,500	—	—
1895S	49,000	225	300	600	2,250	9,000	—	—
1896	76,348	200	220	260	300	1,475	—	31,500
1896S	123,750	215	265	450	2,500	10,500	—	—
1897	1,000,159	200	215	250	285	685	6,500	35,000
1897O	42,500	225	265	335	700	2,000	—	—
1897S	234,750	200	250	335	870	3,300	—	—
1898	812,197	200	215	255	285	900	3,800	35,000
1898S	473,600	205	235	250	350	2,200	—	—
1899	1,262,305	200	220	245	285	650	2,800	31,000
1899O	37,047	230	275	325	550	2,700	—	—
1899S	841,000	200	235	265	320	1,300	—	—
1900	293,960	200	225	230	300	650	7,750	30,500
1900S	81,000	210	275	350	850	3,800	—	—

Date	Mintage	VF-20	XF-40	AU-50	MS-60	MS-63	MS-65	Prf-65
1901	1,718,825	200	215	240	285	615	2,800	30,500
1901O	72,041	225	250	285	400	1,850	—	—
1901S	2,812,750	200	215	240	285	615	2,500	—
1902	82,513	230	260	295	330	1,175	—	30,500
1902S	469,500	230	250	260	400	615	2,700	—
1903	125,926	215	260	290	315	850	—	30,000
1903O	112,771	225	250	295	375	1,875	—	—
1903S	538,000	200	225	250	290	640	2,650	—
1904	162,038	215	230	260	325	900	—	31,500
1904O	108,950	220	250	285	360	1,975	—	—
1905	201,078	200	220	250	285	850	4,800	30,000
1905S	369,250	210	230	300	1,100	4,500	—	—
1906	165,497	225	230	250	295	950	7,750	30,000
1906D	981,000	230	245	275	325	615	3,850	—
1906O	86,895	235	250	330	450	2,350	—	—
1906S	457,000	220	250	300	475	3,100	12,500	—
1907	1,203,973	195	210	220	275	615	—	30,000
1907D	1,030,000	230	240	250	310	850	—	—
1907S	210,500	240	260	280	600	2,400	—	—

Indian Head. No motto next to eagle.

KM# 125 Designer: Augustus Saint-Gaudens. **Diameter:** 27 **Weight:** 16.7180 g. **Composition:** 0.9000 Gold, 0.4839 oz. AGW. **Notes:** 1907 varieties are distinguished by whether the edge is rolled or wired, and whether the legend "E Pluribus Unum" has periods between each word.

Date	Mintage	VF-20	XF-40	AU-50	MS-60	MS-63	MS-65	Prf-65
1907 wire edge, periods before and after legend	500	7,500	12,000	13,000	17,500	23,500	47,000	—
1907 same, without stars on edge, unique	—	—	—	—	—	—	—	—
1907 rolled edge, periods	42	15,000	24,000	27,000	32,500	54,000	95,000	—
1907 without periods	239,406	350	375	400	550	2,500	7,200	—
1908 without motto	33,500	350	390	450	835	4,000	14,000	—
1908D without motto	210,000	335	375	400	700	6,400	40,000	—

Indian Head. "In God We Trust" left of eagle.

KM# 130 Designer: Augustus Saint-Gaudens. **Diameter:** 27 **Weight:** 16.7180 g. **Composition:** 0.9000 Gold, 0.4839 oz. AGW.

Date	Mintage	VF-20	XF-40	AU-50	MS-60	MS-63	MS-65	Prf-65
1908	341,486	315	360	400	475	1,700	5,700	37,000
1908D	836,500	320	360	400	725	6,300	20,000	—
1908S	59,850	360	390	400	1,675	5,800	20,000	—
1909	184,863	320	335	400	485	2,150	8,500	43,500
1909D	121,540	320	335	400	575	3,600	48,000	—
1909S	292,350	330	350	400	610	4,000	11,500	—
1910	318,704	335	375	400	480	1,125	5,700	43,500
1910D	2,356,640	330	365	400	465	1,100	5,700	—
1910S	811,000	330	370	400	600	6,000	45,000	—
1911	505,595	325	365	390	480	1,200	6,000	37,500
1911D	30,100	425	725	800	3,900	16,500	100,000	—
1911S	51,000	365	550	640	1,100	6,750	10,500	—
1912	405,083	330	335	400	450	1,200	7,500	37,500
1912S	300,000	330	350	400	715	5,150	48,500	—
1913	442,071	320	335	400	440	1,200	5,400	37,500
1913S	66,000	550	640	800	3,550	25,000	100,000	—
1914	151,050	325	340	390	520	1,700	7,000	37,500
1914D	343,500	320	340	390	545	1,700	10,500	—
1914S	208,000	320	340	390	675	5,400	38,000	—
1915	351,075	320	340	390	530	1,300	6,000	45,000
1915S	59,000	550	700	800	2,900	9,500	60,000	—
1916S	138,500	330	350	415	720	3,600	17,500	—
1920S	126,500	5,000	7,250	8,250	17,000	54,000	195,000	—
1926	1,014,000	290	325	380	415	1,000	4,300	—
1930S	96,000	4,000	6,000	8,000	9,500	17,500	28,000	—
1932	4,463,000	290	325	380	430	615	4,200	—
1933	312,500	10,000	30,000	42,500	60,000	110,000	400,000	—

$20 (DOUBLE EAGLE)

GOLD

Liberty. "Twenty D." below eagle. No motto above eagle.

KM# 74.1 **Designer:** James B. Longacre. **Diameter:** 34 **Weight:** 33.4360 g. **Composition:** 0.9000 Gold, 0.9677 oz. AGW.

Date	Mintage	VF-20	XF-40	AU-50	MS-60	MS-63	MS-65	Prf-65
1849 unique, in Smithsonian collection	1	—	—	—	—	—	—	—
1850	1,170,261	700	1,150	260	6,700	46,500	—	—
1850O	141,000	850	1,400	7,500	33,000	—	—	—
1851	2,087,155	650	700	925	3,200	20,000	—	—
1851O	315,000	750	925	1,650	17,000	—	—	—
1852	2,053,026	650	720	900	3,300	13,000	—	—
1852O	190,000	775	925	1,800	15,000	—	—	—
1853	1,261,326	650	720	925	4,400	21,000	—	—
1853O	71,000	750	1,200	2,500	25,000	—	—	—
1854	757,899	650	715	925	5,850	21,000	—	—
1854O	3,250	29,000	57,500	110,000	330,000	—	—	—
1854S	141,468	700	825	1,300	3,800	12,000	40,000	—
1855	364,666	650	725	1,150	8,250	—	—	—
1855O	8,000	2,350	5,750	17,500	75,000	—	—	—
1855S	879,675	650	675	1,100	7,200	15,000	—	—
1856	329,878	675	725	1,150	8,900	22,500	—	—
1856O	2,250	41,500	75,000	120,000	425,000	—	—	—
1856S	1,189,750	650	725	1,150	5,500	11,500	33,000	—
1857	439,375	650	675	900	3,400	26,000	—	—
1857O	30,000	1,050	1,750	4,250	27,500	115,000	—	—
1857S	970,500	650	700	950	4,800	7,150	—	—
1858	211,714	700	925	1,250	4,950	36,000	—	—
1858O	35,250	1,375	2,000	1,800	26,500	—	—	—
1858S	846,710	650	725	1,000	9,250	—	—	—
1859	43,597	960	2,100	4,000	31,500	—	—	—
1859O	9,100	3,400	6,750	17,000	82,500	—	—	—
1859S	636,445	650	675	1,000	4,950	—	—	—
1860	577,670	650	675	950	4,000	20,000	—	—
1860O	6,600	3,200	6,000	17,500	89,000	—	—	—
1860S	544,950	650	675	1,000	6,000	20,000	—	—
1861	2,976,453	650	675	950	2,500	9,500	36,000	—
1861O	17,741	2,400	4,000	13,750	90,000	—	—	—
1861S	768,000	650	720	1,600	8,500	30,000	—	—

Liberty. Paquet design.

KM# 93 **Weight:** 33.4360 g. **Composition:** 0.9000 Gold, 0.9677 oz. AGW. **Notes:** In 1861 the reverse was redesigned by Anthony C. Paquet, but it was withdrawn soon after its release. The letters in the inscriptions on the Paquet-reverse variety are taller than on the regular reverse.

Date	Mintage	VF-20	XF-40	AU-50	MS-60	MS-63	MS-65	Prf-65
1861 2 Known	—	—	—	—	—	—	—	—

Date	Mintage	VF-20	XF-40	AU-50	MS-60	MS-63	MS-65	Prf-65
Note: 1861 Paquet reverse, Bowers & Merena, Nov. 1988, MS-67, $660,000.								
1861S	—	11,000	22,500	34,000	170,000	—	—	—
Note: Included in mintage of 1861S, KM#74.1								

Liberty. Longacre design resumed.

KM# A74.1   **Weight:** 33.4360 g. **Composition:** 0.9000 Gold, 0.9677 oz. AGW.

Date	Mintage	VF-20	XF-40	AU-50	MS-60	MS-63	MS-65	Prf-65
1862	92,133	925	1,450	2,900	15,500	33,000	—	—
1862S	854,173	650	775	1,600	10,000	—	—	—
1863	142,790	720	880	1,850	17,000	35,000	—	—
1863S	966,570	650	800	1,400	7,500	30,000	—	—
1864	204,285	775	1,000	1,750	14,000	—	—	—
1864S	793,660	650	675	1,700	6,600	—	—	—
1865	351,200	650	700	1,000	6,000	25,000	—	—
1865S	1,042,500	650	715	1,000	4,000	6,600	17,500	—
1866S	Inc. below	1,650	2,850	11,000	60,000	—	—	—

Liberty. "Twenty D." below eagle. "In God We Trust" above eagle.

KM# 74.2   **Designer:** James B. Longacre. **Diameter:** 34 **Weight:** 33.4360 g. **Composition:** 0.9000 Gold, 0.9677 oz. AGW. **Notes:** The 1873 "closed-3" and "open-3" varieties are known and are distinguished by the amount of space between the upper left and lower left serif in the 3 in the date.

Date	Mintage	VF-20	XF-40	AU-50	MS-60	MS-63	MS-65	Prf-65
1866	698,775	675	825	1,300	4,800	28,500	—	—
1866S	842,250	625	700	1,250	15,500	—	—	—
1867	251,065	625	650	925	2,400	20,000	—	—
1867S	920,750	625	725	1,600	14,000	—	—	—
1868	98,600	925	1,150	2,000	10,000	40,000	—	—
1868S	837,500	625	750	1,200	8,500	—	—	—
1869	175,155	700	950	1,250	6,000	21,000	—	—
1869S	686,750	625	650	1,100	5,300	30,000	—	—
1870	155,185	750	1,000	1,650	9,000	—	—	—
1870CC	3,789	85,000	115,000	240,000	675,000	—	—	—
1870S	982,000	650	675	925	5,000	24,000	—	—
1871	80,150	825	960	1,500	4,000	26,000	—	—
1871CC	17,387	6,000	9,600	19,000	50,000	—	—	—
1871S	928,000	625	750	750	4,400	22,000	—	—
1872	251,880	650	740	740	2,700	25,000	—	—
1872CC	26,900	1,900	2,400	5,500	27,500	—	—	—
1872S	780,000	625	740	715	3,000	24,000	—	—
1873 closed 3	Est. 208,925	675	800	1,100	2,600	—	—	—
1873 open 3	Est. 1,500,900	625	650	660	990	11,000	—	—
1873CC	22,410	2,250	3,500	6,000	30,000	100,000	—	—
1873S	1,040,600	625	650	660	1,500	21,000	—	—
1874	366,800	625	650	660	1,150	20,000	—	—
1874CC	115,085	1,100	1,500	2,400	8,500	—	—	—
1874S	1,214,000	625	650	660	1,375	26,000	—	—
1875	295,740	625	650	660	1,000	11,000	—	—
1875CC	111,151	1,100	1,300	1,500	2,300	17,500	—	—
1875S	1,230,000	625	650	660	1,000	16,500	—	—
1876	583,905	625	650	660	990	11,500	—	—
1876CC	138,441	1,100	1,300	1,650	4,500	35,000	—	—
1876S	1,597,000	625	650	660	990	11,500	—	—

Liberty. "Twenty Dollars" below eagle.

KM# 74.3   **Weight:** 33.4360 g. **Composition:** 0.9000 Gold, 0.9677 oz. AGW.

Date	Mintage	VF-20	XF-40	AU-50	MS-60	MS-63	MS-65	Prf-65
1877	397,670	585	590	600	825	5,250	—	—
1877CC	42,565	1,250	1,550	2,300	16,500	—	—	—
1877S	1,735,000	585	590	600	750	12,500	—	—
1878	543,645	585	590	600	675	5,600	—	—
1878CC	13,180	2,000	2,800	4,600	26,000	—	—	—
1878S	1,739,000	585	590	600	750	22,000	—	—
1879	207,630	585	590	600	1,000	125,000	—	—
1879CC	10,708	2,000	3,000	5,750	30,000	—	—	—
1879O	2,325	4,500	6,750	15,000	75,000	120,000	—	—
1879S	1,223,800	585	590	600	1,375	—	—	—
1880	51,456	585	590	600	3,000	16,500	—	—
1880S	836,000	585	590	600	950	16,000	—	—
1881	2,260	4,500	6,750	13,750	44,000	—	—	105,000
1881S	727,000	585	590	600	850	17,500	—	—
1882	630	7,000	15,000	28,000	66,000	135,000	—	—
1882CC	39,140	1,150	1,375	1,900	6,500	—	—	—
1882S	1,125,000	585	590	600	750	16,000	—	—
1883 proof only	92	—	—	10,000	—	—	—	—
1883CC	59,962	1,100	1,250	1,650	4,000	20,000	—	—
1883S	1,189,000	585	590	600	675	8,500	—	—
1884 proof only	71	—	—	10,000	—	—	—	150,000
1884CC	81,139	1,100	1,300	1,600	2,750	—	—	—
1884S	916,000	585	590	600	675	7,000	—	—
1885	828	6,500	8,500	11,000	35,000	—	—	—
1885CC	9,450	2,100	3,000	5,500	11,000	—	—	—
1885S	683,500	585	590	600	675	7,000	—	—
1886	1,106	8,250	11,500	30,000	45,000	55,000	—	67,000
1887	121	—	—	8,000	—	—	—	85,000
1887S	283,000	585	590	600	675	14,000	—	—
1888	226,266	585	590	600	675	4,500	32,000	—
1888S	859,600	585	590	600	675	5,500	—	—
1889	44,111	625	650	700	750	11,000	—	57,500
1889CC	30,945	1,250	1,450	2,100	3,400	15,000	—	—
1889S	774,700	585	590	600	675	6,750	—	—
1890	75,995	585	590	600	675	5,500	—	27,000
1890CC	91,209	1,100	1,400	1,400	2,300	27,500	—	—
1890S	802,750	585	590	600	675	8,500	—	—
1891	1,442	3,300	5,000	8,500	40,000	—	—	62,500
1891CC	5,000	3,500	5,000	7,500	15,000	44,000	—	—
1891S	1,288,125	585	590	600	650	3,350	—	—
1892	4,523	1,150	1,650	2,600	5,500	18,500	—	55,000
1892CC	27,265	1,200	1,400	2,000	3,300	25,000	—	—
1892S	930,150	585	590	600	650	4,000	—	—
1893	344,339	585	590	600	650	2,400	—	60,000
1893CC	18,402	1,400	1,750	2,000	3,000	15,000	—	—
1893S	996,175	585	590	600	650	3,850	—	—
1894	1,368,990	585	590	600	650	1,500	—	55,000
1894S	1,048,550	585	590	600	650	2,400	—	—
1895	1,114,656	585	590	600	650	1,300	11,500	54,000
1895S	1,143,500	585	590	600	650	2,400	12,500	—
1896	792,663	585	590	600	650	2,000	11,500	49,000
1896S	1,403,925	585	590	600	650	2,150	—	—
1897	1,383,261	585	590	600	650	1,350	—	55,000
1897S	1,470,250	585	590	600	650	1,350	9,600	—
1898	170,470	585	590	625	675	4,800	—	49,000
1898S	2,575,175	585	590	600	650	1,300	12,000	—
1899	1,669,384	585	590	600	650	1,000	8,500	49,000
1899S	2,010,300	585	590	600	650	1,800	12,500	—
1900	1,874,584	585	590	600	650	900	6,000	49,000
1900S	2,459,500	585	590	600	650	2,300	—	—
1901	111,526	585	590	600	650	975	6,000	—

Date	Mintage	VF-20	XF-40	AU-50	MS-60	MS-63	MS-65	Prf-65
1901S	1,596,000	585	590	600	650	3,850	—	—
1902	31,254	585	590	600	900	10,000	—	—
1902S	1,753,625	585	590	600	650	4,000	—	—
1903	287,428	585	590	600	650	900	6,000	51,500
1903S	954,000	585	590	600	650	1,800	10,000	—
1904	6,256,797	585	590	600	650	900	5,500	50,000
1904S	5,134,175	585	590	600	650	950	6,600	
1905	59,011	585	590	600	1,000	14,000	—	—
1905S	1,813,000	585	590	600	650	3,850	16,500	—
1906	69,690	585	590	600	650	6,600	15,000	52,500
1906D	620,250	585	590	600	650	2,000	13,000	—
1906S	2,065,750	585	590	600	650	2,300	19,000	—
1907	1,451,864	585	590	600	650	960	7,500	—
1907D	842,250	585	590	600	650	2,000	7,000	—
1907S	2,165,800	585	590	600	650	2,400	13,500	—

Saint-Gaudens. Roman numerals in date. No motto below eagle.

KM# 126 **Designer:** Augustus Saint-Gaudens. **Diameter:** 34 **Weight:** 33.4360 g. **Composition:** 0.9000 Gold, 0.9677 oz. AGW.

Date	Mintage	VF-20	XF-40	AU-50	MS-60	MS-63	MS-65	Prf-65
MCMVII (1907) high relief, unique, AU-55, $150,000	—	—	—	—	—	—	—	—
MCMVII (1907) high relief, wire rim	11,250	6,100	6,700	7,900	10,000	17,000	32,500	—
MCMVII (1907) high relief, flat rim	Inc. above	6,250	6,900	8,250	10,500	17,750	35,000	—

Saint-Gaudens. Arabic numerals in date. No motto below eagle.

KM# 127 **Designer:** Augustus Saint-Gaudens. **Diameter:** 34 **Weight:** 33.4360 g. **Composition:** 0.9000 Gold, 0.9677 oz. AGW.

Date	Mintage	VF-20	XF-40	AU-50	MS-60	MS-63	MS-65	Prf-65
1907 large letters on edge, unique	—	—	—	—	—	—	—	—
1907 small letters on edge	361,667	465	475	485	565	950	2,500	—
1908	4,271,551	455	465	475	560	675	1,200	—
1908D	663,750	460	475	490	565	900	10,500	—

Saint-Gaudens. Roman numerals in date. No motto below eagle.

KM# Pn1874 **Designer:** Augustus Saint-Gaudens. **Diameter:** 34 **Weight:** 33.4360 g. **Composition:** 0.9000 Gold, 0.9677 oz. AGW. **Notes:** The "Roman numerals" varieties for 1907 use Roman numerals for the date instead of Arabic numerals. The lettered-edge varieties have "E Pluribus Unum" on the edge, with stars between the words.

Date	Mintage	VF-20	XF-40	AU-50	MS-60	MS-63	MS-65	Prf-65
1907 extremely high relief, unique	—	—	—	—	—	—	—	—
1907 extremely high relief, lettered edge	—	—	—	—	—	—	—	—

Note: 1907 extremely high relief, lettered edge, Prf-68, private sale, 1990, $1,500,000.

Saint-Gaudens. "In God We Trust" below eagle.

KM# 131 **Designer:** Augustus Saint-Gaudens. **Diameter:** 34 **Weight:** 33.4360 g. **Composition:** 0.9000 Gold, 0.9677 oz. AGW.

Date	Mintage	VF-20	XF-40	AU-50	MS-60	MS-63	MS-65	Prf-65
1908	156,359	465	510	585	595	1,350	20,000	49,500
1908D	349,500	460	470	495	560	990	5,300	—
1908S	22,000	750	1,400	1,750	4,400	11,000	37,500	—
1909/8	161,282	525	580	700	1,150	5,850	29,000	—
1909	Inc. above	470	560	625	775	3,350	37,500	49,000
1909D	52,500	500	690	775	1,200	6,750	35,000	—
1909S	2,774,925	470	485	525	700	1,550	5,750	—
1910	482,167	465	475	510	595	700	7,350	49,000
1910D	429,000	465	475	500	595	700	3,450	—
1910S	2,128,250	460	485	500	610	850	8,850	—
1911	197,350	455	465	495	580	1,850	14,000	39,500
1911D	846,500	455	465	485	565	680	1,600	—
1911S	775,750	460	470	500	600	750	6,200	—
1912	149,824	455	485	495	585	1,200	17,500	44,000
1913	168,838	455	465	495	585	2,750	31,000	44,000
1913D	393,500	465	475	495	575	900	6,200	—
1913S	34,000	550	800	840	1,350	3,650	38,500	—
1914	95,320	460	515	530	625	1,650	15,200	41,500
1914D	453,000	465	475	495	585	750	3,250	—
1914S	1,498,000	465	475	495	580	725	2,150	—
1915	152,050	465	485	520	665	2,100	24,500	47,500
1915S	567,500	465	475	485	585	725	2,150	—
1916S	796,000	465	475	495	675	900	2,500	—
1920	228,250	465	475	450	610	825	36,500	—
1920S	558,000	4,950	8,000	10,500	25,000	48,500	185,000	—
1921	528,500	8,000	14,400	20,000	36,000	125,000	285,000	—
1922	1,375,500	455	465	485	560	680	3,900	—
1922S	2,658,000	500	750	800	975	1,450	39,500	—
1923	566,000	455	465	495	545	650	6,250	—
1923D	1,702,250	165	475	495	560	775	1,650	—
1924	4,323,500	455	465	495	545	650	1,500	—
1924D	3,049,500	800	1,325	1,500	2,000	6,200	56,000	—
1924S	2,927,500	750	1,200	1,440	2,600	6,100	36,500	—
1925	2,831,750	455	465	485	545	650	1,550	—
1925D	2,938,500	1,000	1,750	2,300	4,400	8,250	55,000	—
1925S	3,776,500	900	1,350	1,550	5,800	18,500	86,500	—
1926	816,750	455	465	485	545	650	1,575	—
1926D	481,000	1,100	2,850	3,200	7,900	21,000	105,000	—
1926S	2,041,500	700	1,250	1,375	1,850	4,000	35,000	—
1927	2,946,750	455	465	485	545	650	1,550	—
1927D	180,000	—	195,000	245,000	300,000	485,000	785,000	—
1927S	3,107,000	2,500	4,400	4,550	12,500	50,000	105,000	—
1928	8,816,000	455	465	485	550	655	1,550	—
1929	1,779,750	4,750	7,000	8,000	13,000	20,000	35,000	—
1930S	74,000	6,000	8,500	9,300	25,000	44,500	115,000	—
1931	2,938,250	4,850	8,000	9,250	18,500	27,500	52,000	—
1931D	106,500	5,500	8,000	8,500	25,500	32,500	64,500	—
1932	1,101,750	7,000	10,000	11,500	19,000	26,000	44,500	—
1933 Sotheby/Stack Sale, July 2002	445,500	—	—	—	—	—	7,590,000	—

COMMEMORATIVE COINAGE
1892-1954

All commemorative half dollars of 1892-1954 have the following specifications: diameter -- 30.6 millimeters; weight -- 12.5000 grams; composition -- 0.9000 silver, 0.3617 ounces actual silver weight. Values for "PDS sets" contain one example each from the Philadelphia, Denver and San Francisco mints. "Type coin" prices are the most inexpensive single coin available from the date and mint-mark combinations listed.

QUARTER

Columbian Exposition. KM# 115 **Obverse:** Queen Isabella **Diameter:** 24.3 **Weight:** 6.2500 g. **Composition:** 0.9000 Silver, 0.1808 oz. ASW.

Date	Mintage	AU-50	MS-60	MS-63	MS-64	MS-65
1893	24,214	575	720	950	1,440	3,125

HALF DOLLAR

Columbian Exposition. KM# 117 **Obv. Designer:** Charles E. Barber **Rev. Designer:** George T. Morgan

Lincoln-Illinois. KM# 143 **Obv. Designer:** George T. Morgan **Rev. Designer:** John R. Sinnock

Date	Mintage	AU-50	MS-60	MS-63	MS-64	MS-65
1892	950,000	19.00	28.00	80.00	200	700
1893	1,550,405	16.00	27.50	80.00	200	950

Panama-Pacific Exposition. KM# 135 **Designer:** Charles E. Barber.

Date	Mintage	AU-50	MS-60	MS-63	MS-64	MS-65
1918	100,058	100.00	135	150	250	500

Maine Centennial. KM# 146 **Designer:** Anthony de Francisci.

Date	Mintage	AU-50	MS-60	MS-63	MS-64	MS-65
1920	50,028	115	140	160	325	600

Date	Mintage	AU-50	MS-60	MS-63	MS-64	MS-65
1915S	27,134	375	425	775	1,525	2,850

Pilgrim Tercentenary. **KM# 147.1 Designer:** Cyrus E. Dallin.

Date	Mintage	AU-50	MS-60	MS-63	MS-64	MS-65
1920	152,112	67.50	82.50	90.00	160	450

Alabama Centennial. **KM# 148.1 Designer:** Laura G. Fraser. **Obverse:** "2x2" at right above stars

 2X2

Date	Mintage	AU-50	MS-60	MS-63	MS-64	MS-65
1921	6,006	250	300	625	1,050	2,525

Alabama Centennial. **KM# 148.2 Obv. Designer:** Laura G. Fraser

Date	Mintage	AU-50	MS-60	MS-63	MS-64	MS-65
1921	59,038	160	225	535	825	2,525

Missouri Centennial. **KM# 149.1 Designer:** Robert Aitken.

Date	Mintage	AU-50	MS-60	MS-63	MS-64	MS-65
1921	15,428	225	410	775	1,400	5,000

Missouri Centennial. **KM# 149.2 Designer:** Robert Aitken. **Obverse:** 2 star 4 in field at left

 2★4

Date	Mintage	AU-50	MS-60	MS-63	MS-64	MS-65
1921	5,000	525	635	1,100	1,950	5,750

Pilgrim Tercentenary. **KM# 147.2 Designer:** Cyrus E. Dallin. **Obverse:** 1921 date next to Pilgrim

Date	Mintage	AU-50	MS-60	MS-63	MS-64	MS-65
1921	20,053	135	150	160	300	650

Grant Memorial. **KM# 151.1 Designer:** Laura G. Fraser.

Date	Mintage	AU-50	MS-60	MS-63	MS-64	MS-65
1922	67,405	96.00	105	170	325	925

Grant Memorial. **KM# 151.2 Designer:** Laura G. Fraser. **Obverse:** Star above the word "Grant"

Date	Mintage	AU-50	MS-60	MS-63	MS-64	MS-65
1922	4,256	790	1,300	1,850	2,700	8,000

Monroe Doctrine Centennial. KM# 153
Designer: Chester Beach.

Date	Mintage	AU-50	MS-60	MS-63	MS-64	MS-65
1923S	274,077	43.50	57.50	150	550	3,600

Huguenot-Walloon Tercentenary. KM# 154
Designer: George T. Morgan.

Date	Mintage	AU-50	MS-60	MS-63	MS-64	MS-65
1924	142,080	125	135	185	270	550

California Diamond Jubilee. KM# 155
Designer: Jo Mora.

Date	Mintage	AU-50	MS-60	MS-63	MS-64	MS-65
1925S	86,594	150	160	200	420	1,250

Fort Vancouver Centennial. KM# 158
Designer: Laura G. Fraser.

Date	Mintage	AU-50	MS-60	MS-63	MS-64	MS-65
1925	14,994	285	350	430	625	1,525

Lexington-Concord Sesquicentennial.
KM# 156 Designer: Chester Beach.

Date	Mintage	AU-50	MS-60	MS-63	MS-64	MS-65
1925	162,013	80.00	92.50	110	185	645

Stone Mountain Memorial. KM# 157.1
Designer: Gutzon Borglum.

Date	Mintage	AU-50	MS-60	MS-63	MS-64	MS-65
1925	1,314,709	52.50	62.50	75.00	90.00	265

Oregon Trail Memorial. KM# 159 Designer:
James E. and Laura G. Fraser.

Date	Mintage	AU-50	MS-60	MS-63	MS-64	MS-65
1926	47,955	120	150	160	165	340
1926S	83,055	120	150	160	165	340
Type coin	—	120	150	160	165	340
1928	6,028	180	200	210	215	385
1933D	5,008	290	300	325	335	575
1934D	7,006	165	180	200	205	335
1936	10,006	125	150	160	165	300
1936S	5,006	140	150	175	210	375
1937D	12,008	150	160	170	185	300
1938 PDS set	6,005	500	550	675	700	900
1939 PDS set	3,004	1,050	1,200	1,350	1,450	1,750

U.S. Sesquicentennial. KM# 160 Designer: John R. Sinnock.

Date	Mintage	AU-50	MS-60	MS-63	MS-64	MS-65
1926	141,120	70.00	90.00	160	625	5,500

Vermont Sesquicentennial. KM# 162
Obv. Designer: Charles Keck

Date	Mintage	AU-50	MS-60	MS-63	MS-64	MS-65
1927	28,142	200	220	230	350	950

Hawaiian Sesquicentennial. KM# 163 Designer: Juliette M. Fraser.

Date	Mintage	AU-50	MS-60	MS-63	MS-64	MS-65
1928	10,008	1,450	2,000	2,500	3,500	5,500

Daniel Boone Bicentennial. KM# 165.1
Designer: Augustus Lukeman.

Date	Mintage	AU-50	MS-60	MS-63	MS-64	MS-65
1934	10,007	100.00	110	125	128	215
1935 PDS set	2,003	675	750	850	1,150	2,100

Daniel Boone Bicentennial. KM# 165.2
Designer: Augustus Lukeman. **Reverse:** "1934" added above the word "Pioneer."

Date	Mintage	AU-50	MS-60	MS-63	MS-64	MS-65
1935 PDS set	5,005	300	350	375	385	675
Type coin	—	100.00	110	120	125	210
1936 PDS set	5,005	300	350	375	385	675

Date	Mintage	AU-50	MS-60	MS-63	MS-64	MS-65
1937 PDS set	2,506	635	715	750	850	1,300
1938 PDS set	2,100	850	950	1,100	1,300	1,825

Maryland Tercentenary. KM# 166 Designer: Hans Schuler.

Date	Mintage	AU-50	MS-60	MS-63	MS-64	MS-65
1934	25,015	140	150	175	200	350

Texas Centennial. KM# 167 Designer: Pompeo Coppini.

Date	Mintage	AU-50	MS-60	MS-63	MS-64	MS-65
1934	61,463	115	125	130	135	220
Type coin	—	115	125	130	135	220
1935 PDS set	9,994	350	390	400	415	650
1936 PDS set	8,911	350	415	420	430	650
1937 PDS set	6,571	350	390	400	415	650
1938 PDS set	3,775	575	650	800	925	1,500

Arkansas Centennial. KM# 168 Designer: Edward E. Burr.

Date	Mintage	AU-50	MS-60	MS-63	MS-64	MS-65
Type coin	—	82.50	85.00	90.00	100.00	220
1935 PDS set	5,505	250	265	280	350	825
1936 PDS set	9,600	250	265	280	310	850
1937 PDS set	5,505	250	265	315	340	1,025
1938 PDS set	3,155	325	400	450	525	2,000
1939 PDS set	—	650	750	900	1,150	3,500

Connecticut Tercentenary. KM# 169 Designer: Henry Kreiss.

Date	Mintage	AU-50	MS-60	MS-63	MS-64	MS-65
1935	25,018	220	250	275	385	635

Hudson, N.Y., Sesquicentennial. KM# 170 Designer: Chester Beach.

Date	Mintage	AU-50	MS-60	MS-63	MS-64	MS-65
1935	10,008	585	675	775	1,050	1,660

Old Spanish Trail. KM# 172 Designer: L.W. Hoffecker.

Date	Mintage	AU-50	MS-60	MS-63	MS-64	MS-65
1935	10,008	975	1,050	1,075	1,150	1,400

San Diego, California - Pacific Exposition. KM# 171 Designer: Robert Aitken.

Date	Mintage	AU-50	MS-60	MS-63	MS-64	MS-65
1935S	70,132	75.00	105	110	115	150
1936D	30,092	75.00	125	130	135	150

Albany, N.Y., Charter Anniversary. KM# 173 Designer: Gertrude K. Lathrop.

Date	Mintage	AU-50	MS-60	MS-63	MS-64	MS-65
1936	17,671	260	275	300	315	390

Arkansas Centennial. KM# 187 Obv. Designer: Henry Kreiss **Rev. Designer:** Edward E. Burr **Obverse:** Sen. Joseph T. Robinson

Date	Mintage	AU-50	MS-60	MS-63	MS-64	MS-65
1936	25,265	125	130	135	140	410

Battle of Gettysburg 75th Anniversary. KM# 181 Designer: Frank Vittor.

Date	Mintage	AU-50	MS-60	MS-63	MS-64	MS-65
1936	26,928	350	385	410	425	735

Bridgeport, Conn., Centennial. KM# 175 Designer: Henry Kreiss.

Date	Mintage	AU-50	MS-60	MS-63	MS-64	MS-65
1936	25,015	150	160	165	180	250

Cincinnati Music Center. KM# 176 Designer: Constance Ortmayer.

Date	Mintage	AU-50	MS-60	MS-63	MS-64	MS-65
Type coin	—	275	280	290	390	700
1936 PDS set	5,005	800	840	880	1,150	2,850

Cleveland-Great Lakes Exposition. KM# 177 Designer: Brenda Putnam.

Date	Mintage	AU-50	MS-60	MS-63	MS-64	MS-65
1936	50,030	62.00	68.00	75.00	95.00	220

Columbia, S.C., Sesquicentennial. KM# 178 Designer: A. Wolfe Davidson.

Date	Mintage	AU-50	MS-60	MS-63	MS-64	MS-65
1936 PDS set	9,007	675	690	715	730	900
Type coin	—	225	230	235	245	300

Delaware Tercentenary. KM# 179 Designer: Carl L. Schmitz.

Date	Mintage	AU-50	MS-60	MS-63	MS-64	MS-65
1936	20,993	275	300	315	330	435

Elgin, Ill., Centennial. KM# 180 Designer: Trygve Rovelstad.

Date	Mintage	AU-50	MS-60	MS-63	MS-64	MS-65
1936	20,015	200	225	235	250	265

Long Island Tercentenary. KM# 182 Designer: Howard K. Weinman.

Date	Mintage	AU-50	MS-60	MS-63	MS-64	MS-65
1936	81,826	75.00	85.00	90.00	125	425

Lynchburg, Va., Sesquicentennial. KM# 183 Designer: Charles Keck.

Date	Mintage	AU-50	MS-60	MS-63	MS-64	MS-65
1936	20,013	200	235	240	250	350

Norfolk, Va., Bicentennial. KM# 184 Designer: William M. and Marjorie E. Simpson.

Date	Mintage	AU-50	MS-60	MS-63	MS-64	MS-65
1936	16,936	440	465	470	480	485

Rhode Island Tercentenary. KM# 185
Designer: Arthur G. Carey and John H. Benson.

Date	Mintage	AU-50	MS-60	MS-63	MS-64	MS-65
1936 PDS set	15,010	250	270	290	345	775
Type coin	—	82.50	85.00	95.00	110	260

San Francisco-Oakland Bay Bridge. KM# 174
Designer: Jacques Schnier.

Date	Mintage	AU-50	MS-60	MS-63	MS-64	MS-65
1936	71,424	150	160	180	190	300

Wisconsin Territorial Centennial. KM# 188
Designer: David Parsons.

Date	Mintage	AU-50	MS-60	MS-63	MS-64	MS-65
1936	25,015	200	220	240	250	315

York County, Maine, Tercentenary. KM# 189
Designer: Walter H. Rich.

Date	Mintage	AU-50	MS-60	MS-63	MS-64	MS-65
1936	25,015	190	200	215	225	280

Battle of Antietam 75th Anniversary. KM# 190
Designer: William M. Simpson.

Date	Mintage	AU-50	MS-60	MS-63	MS-64	MS-65
1937	18,028	570	580	650	815	950

Roanoke Island, N.C.. KM# 186 **Designer:**
William M. Simpson.

Date	Mintage	AU-50	MS-60	MS-63	MS-64	MS-65
1937	29,030	210	240	250	265	325

New Rochelle, N.Y.. KM# 191 **Designer:**
Gertrude K. Lathrop.

Date	Mintage	AU-50	MS-60	MS-63	MS-64	MS-65
1938	15,266	340	360	385	400	480

Booker T. Washington. KM# 198 **Designer:**
Isaac S. Hathaway.

Date	Mintage	AU-50	MS-60	MS-63	MS-64	MS-65
1946 PDS set	200,113	44.00	48.00	70.00	75.00	160
Type coin	—	14.00	16.00	17.50	18.00	55.00
1947 PDS set	100,017	50.00	75.00	85.00	115	280
1948 PDS set	8,005	85.00	140	150	160	210
1949 PDS set	6,004	160	225	240	250	350
1950 PDS set	6,004	75.00	125	135	140	220
1951 PDS set	7,004	80.00	110	140	150	220

Iowa Statehood Centennial. KM# 197 Designer: Adam Pietz.

Date	Mintage	AU-50	MS-60	MS-63	MS-64	MS-65
1946	100,057	85.00	120	125	130	140

Booker T. Washington and George Washington Carver. KM# 200 Designer: Isaac S. Hathaway.

Date	Mintage	AU-50	MS-60	MS-63	MS-64	MS-65
1951 PDS set	10,004	65.00	85.00	95.00	120	550
Type coin	—	13.00	16.00	18.00	20.00	48.00
1952 PDS set	8,006	65.00	80.00	110	125	400
1953 PDS set	8,003	57.50	80.00	110	130	600
1954 PDS set	12,006	55.00	80.00	90.00	110	440

DOLLAR

Lafayette. KM# 118 Designer: Charles E. Barber. **Diameter:** 38.1 **Weight:** 26.7300 g. **Composition:** 0.9000 Silver, 0.7736 oz. ASW.

Date	Mintage	AU-50	MS-60	MS-63	MS-64	MS-65
1900	36,026	500	775	2,000	4,000	10,500

Louisiana Purchase Exposition. KM# 119 Designer: Charles E. Barber. **Obverse:** Jefferson **Diameter:** 15 **Weight:** 1.6720 g. **Composition:** 0.9000 Gold, 0.0484 oz. AGW.

Date	Mintage	AU-50	MS-60	MS-63	MS-64	MS-65
1903	17,500	650	700	940	2,000	3,150

Louisiana Purchase Exposition. KM# 120 **Obv. Designer:** Charles E. Barber **Obverse:** McKinley **Diameter:** 15 **Weight:** 1.6720 g. **Composition:** 0.9000 Gold, 0.0484 oz. AGW.

Date	Mintage	AU-50	MS-60	MS-63	MS-64	MS-65
1903	17,500	650	700	940	1,900	3,000

Lewis and Clark Exposition. KM# 121 **Obv. Designer:** Charles E. Barber **Diameter:** 15 **Weight:** 1.6720 g. **Composition:** 0.9000 Gold, 0.7736 oz. AGW.

Date	Mintage	AU-50	MS-60	MS-63	MS-64	MS-65
1904	10,025	975	1,000	2,250	4,850	10,500
1905	10,041	1,100	1,150	2,900	7,000	17,500

Panama-Pacific Exposition. KM# 136 **Obv.** Designer: Charles Keck **Diameter:** 15 **Weight:** 1.6720 g. **Composition:** 0.9000 Gold, 0.0484 oz. AGW.

Date	Mintage	AU-50	MS-60	MS-63	MS-64	MS-65
1915S	15,000	575	590	770	1,200	2,500

McKinley Memorial. KM# 144 **Obv. Designer:** Charles E. Barber **Rev. Designer:** George T. Morgan **Diameter:** 15 **Weight:** 1.6720 g. **Composition:** 0.9000 Gold, 0.0484 oz. AGW.

Date	Mintage	AU-50	MS-60	MS-63	MS-64	MS-65
1916	9,977	560	575	785	1,250	2,400
1917	10,000	690	715	1,250	2,000	3,200

Grant Memorial. KM# 152.1 **Obv. Designer:** Laura G. Fraser **Obverse:** Without a star above the word "Grant" **Diameter:** 15 **Weight:** 1.6720 g. **Composition:** 0.9000 Gold, 0.0484 oz. AGW. **Notes:** The Grant gold-dollar varieties are distinguished by whether a star appears on the obverse above the word 'Grant.'

Date	Mintage	AU-50	MS-60	MS-63	MS-64	MS-65
1922	5,016	1,500	1,550	2,000	3,200	4,000

Grant Memorial. KM# 152.3 **Obv. Designer:** Laura G. Fraser **Obverse:** With a star above the word "Grant" **Diameter:** 15 **Weight:** 1.6720 g. **Composition:** 0.9000 Gold, 0.0484 oz. AGW.

Star

Date	Mintage	AU-50	MS-60	MS-63	MS-64	MS-65
1922	5,000	1,500	1,550	2,250	3,200	3,800

$2.50 (QUARTER EAGLE)

Panama Pacific Exposition. KM# 137 **Obv. Designer:** Charles E. Barber **Rev. Designer:** George T. Morgan **Diameter:** 18 **Weight:** 4.1800 g. **Composition:** 0.9000 Gold, 0.121 oz. AGW.

Date	Mintage	AU-50	MS-60	MS-63	MS-64	MS-65
1915S	6,749	1,500	1,550	3,600	4,500	5,850

Philadelphia Sesquicentennial. KM# 161 **Obv. Designer:** John R. Sinnock **Diameter:** 18 **Weight:** 4.1800 g. **Composition:** 0.9000 Gold, 0.121 oz. AGW.

Date	Mintage	AU-50	MS-60	MS-63	MS-64	MS-65
1926	46,019	460	480	690	1,200	3,850

$50

Panama-Pacific Exposition. KM# 138 **Obv. Designer:** Robert Aitken **Diameter:** 44 **Weight:** 83.5900 g. **Composition:** 0.9000 Gold, 2.419 oz. AGW.

Date	Mintage	AU-50	MS-60	MS-63	MS-64	MS-65
1915S	483	31,500	40,000	59,000	75,000	135,000

Panama-Pacific Exposition. **KM# 139** **Obv. Designer:** Robert Aitken **Diameter:** 44 **Weight:** 83.5900 g. **Composition:** 0.9000 Gold, 2.419 oz. AGW.

Date	Mintage	AU-50	MS-60	MS-63	MS-64	MS-65
1915S	645	30,000	35,000	50,000	70,000	11,500

1982-PRESENT

All commemorative silver dollar coins of 1982-present have the following specifications: diameter -- 38.1 millimeters; weight -- 26.7300 grams; composition -- 0.9000 silver, 0.7736 ounces actual silver weight. All commemorative $5 coins of 1982-present have the following specificiations: diameter -- 21.6 millimeters; weight -- 8.3590 grams; composition: 0.9000 gold, 0.242 ounces actual gold weight.

Note: In 1982, after a hiatus of nearly 20 years, coinage of commemorative half dollars resumed. Those designated with a 'W' were struck at the West Point Mint. Some issues were struck in copper--nickel. Those struck in silver have the same size, weight and composition as the prior commemorative half--dollar series.

HALF DOLLAR

George Washinton, 250th Birth Anniversary. **KM# 208** **Obv. Designer:** Elizabeth Jones **Diameter:** 30.6 **Weight:** 12.5000 g. **Composition:** 0.9000 Silver, 0.3618 oz. ASW.

Date	Mintage	Proof	MS-65	Prf-65
1982D	2,210,458	—	5.50	—
1982S	—	(4,894,044)	—	5.75

Statue of Liberty Centennial. **KM# 212** **Obv. Designer:** Edgar Z. Steever **Rev. Designer:** Sherl Joseph Winter **Weight:** 11.3400 g. **Composition:** Copper-Nickel Clad Copper

Date	Mintage	Proof	MS-65	Prf-65
1986D	928,008	—	6.75	—
1986S	—	(6,925,627)	—	6.50

Bicentennial of the Congress. **KM# 224** **Obv. Designer:** Patricia L. Verani **Rev. Designer:** William Woodward and Edgar Z. Steever **Weight:** 11.3400 g. **Composition:** Copper-Nickel Clad Copper

Date	Mintage	Proof	MS-65	Prf-65
1989D	163,753	—	8.00	—
1989S	—	—	—	8.00

Mount Rushmore 50th Anniversary. **KM# 228** **Obv. Designer:** Marcel Jovine **Rev. Designer:** T. James Ferrell **Weight:** 11.3400 g. **Composition:** Copper-Nickel Clad Copper

Date	Mintage	Proof	MS-65	Prf-65
1991D	172,754	—	20.00	—
1991S	—	—	—	21.50

1992 Olympics. **KM# 233** **Obv. Designer:** William Cousins **Rev. Designer:** Steven M. Bieda **Weight:** 11.3400 g. **Composition:** Copper-Nickel Clad Copper

Date	Mintage	Proof	MS-65	Prf-65
1992P	161,607	—	8.25	—
1992S	—	(519,645)	—	8.00

500th Anniversary of Columbus Discovery. **KM# 237** **Designer:** T. James Ferrell. **Weight:** 11.3400 g. **Composition:** Copper-Nickel Clad Copper

Date	Mintage	Proof	MS-65	Prf-65
1992D	135,702	—	11.50	—
1992S	—	(390,154)	—	11.50

James Madison and Bill of Rights. **KM# 240** **Obv. Designer:** T. James Ferrell **Rev. Designer:** Dean McMullen **Weight:** 12.5000 g. **Composition:** 0.9000 Silver, 0.3618 oz. ASW.

Date	Mintage	Proof	MS-65	Prf-65
1993W	173,224	—	20.00	—
1993S	—	(559,758)	—	16.50

World War II 50th Anniversary. **KM# 243** **Obv. Designer:** George Klauba **Rev. Designer:** William J. Leftwich **Weight:** 11.3400 g. **Composition:** Copper-Nickel Clad Copper

Date	Mintage	Proof	MS-65	Prf-65
1993P	192,968	(290,343)	35.00	37.50

1994 World Cup Soccer. **KM# 246** **Obv. Designer:** Richard T. LaRoche **Rev. Designer:** Dean McMullen **Weight:** 11.3400 g. **Composition:** Copper-Nickel Clad Copper

Date	Mintage	Proof	MS-65	Prf-65
1994D	168,208	—	10.00	—
1994P	122,412	(609,354)	10.00	—

Atlanta Olympics. **KM# 257** **Obverse:** Basketball **Weight:** 11.3400 g. **Composition:** Copper-Nickel Clad Copper

Date	Mintage	Proof	MS-65	Prf-65
1995S	171,001	(169,655)	22.00	18.50

Atlanta Olympics. **KM# 262** **Obv. Designer:** Edgar Z. Steever **Obverse:** Baseball **Weight:** 11.3400 g. **Composition:** Copper-Nickel Clad Copper

Date	Mintage	Proof	MS-65	Prf-65
1995S	164,605	(118,087)	23.50	19.00

Civil War. **KM# 254** **Obv. Designer:** Don Troiani **Rev. Designer:** T. James Ferrell **Weight:** 11.3400 g. **Composition:** Copper-Nickel Clad Copper

Date	Mintage	Proof	MS-65	Prf-65
1995S	119,510	(330,099)	42.50	42.50

Atlanta Olympics. KM# 271 **Obverse:** Soccer **Weight:** 11.3400 g. **Composition:** Copper-Nickel Clad Copper

Date	Mintage	Proof	MS-65	Prf-65
1996S		52,836(122,412)	90.00	105

Atlanta Olympics. KM# 267 **Obverse:** Swimming **Weight:** 11.3400 g. **Composition:** Copper-Nickel Clad Copper

Date	Mintage	Proof	MS-65	Prf-65
1996S	49,533	(114,315)	155	33.50

U. S. Capitol Visitor Center. KM# 323 **Obv. Designer:** Dean McMullen **Rev. Designer:** Alex Shagin and Marcel Jovine **Weight:** 11.3400 g. **Composition:** Copper-Nickel Clad Copper

Date	Mintage	Proof	MS-65	Prf-65
2001		99,157 (77,962)	13.50	18.00

First Flight Centennial. KM# 348 **Obv. Designer:** John Mercanti **Rev. Designer:** Donna Weaver **Weight:** 11.3400 g. **Composition:** Copper-Nickel Clad Copper

Date	Mintage	Proof	MS-65	Prf-65
2003P	—	—	16.00	18.00

DOLLAR

Los Angeles XXIII Olympiad. KM# 209 **Obv. Designer:** Elizabeth Jones

Date	Mintage	Proof	MS-65	Prf-65
1983P	294,543	—	11.50	—
1983D	174,014	—	12.00	—
1983S	174,014	(1,577,025)	11.50	13.00

Los Angeles XXIII Olympiad. KM# 210 **Obv. Designer:** Robert Graham

Date	Mintage	Proof	MS-65	Prf-65
1984P	217,954	—	13.50	—
1984D	116,675	—	18.00	—
1984S	116,675	(1,801,210)	19.00	13.00

Statue of Liberty Centennial. KM# 214 Obv.
Designer: John Mercanti **Rev. Designer:** John Mercanti and Matthew Peloso

Olympics. KM# 222 Obv. Designer: Patricia L.
Verani **Rev. Designer:** Sherl Joseph Winter

Date	Mintage	Proof	MS-65	Prf-65
1988D	191,368	—	13.50	—
1988S	—	(1,359,366)	—	13.50

Bicentennial of the Congress. KM# 225
Designer: William Woodward and Chester Y. Martin.

Date	Mintage	Proof	MS-65	Prf-65
1986P	723,635	—	16.00	—
1986S	—	(6,414,638)	—	16.50

Constitution Bicentennial. KM# 220 Obv.
Designer: Patricia L. Verani

Date	Mintage	Proof	MS-65	Prf-65
1987P	451,629	—	13.00	—
1987S	—	(2,747,116)	—	12.50

Date	Mintage	Proof	MS-65	Prf-65
1989D	135,203	—	16.00	—
1989S	—	(762,198)	—	20.00

Eisenhower Centennial. KM# 227 Obv.
Designer: John Mercanti **Rev. Designer:** Marcel Jovine
and John Mercanti

Date	Mintage	Proof	MS-65	Prf-65
1990W	241,669	—	18.00	—
1990P	—	(638,333)	—	22.50

Korean War. KM# 231 Obv. **Designer:** John
Mercanti **Rev. Designer:** T. James Ferrell

Date	Mintage	Proof	MS-65	Prf-65
1991D	213,049	—	16.00	—
1991P	—	(618,488)	—	19.00

Mount Rushmore Golden Anniversary. KM#
229 Obv. **Designer:** Marika Somogyi **Rev. Designer:**
Frank Gasparro

Date	Mintage	Proof	MS-65	Prf-65
1991P	133,139	—	33.00	—
1991S	—	(738,419)	—	41.50

USO 50th Anniversary. KM# 232 Obv.
Designer: Robert Lamb **Rev. Designer:** John Mercanti

Date	Mintage	Proof	MS-65	Prf-65
1991D	124,958	—	16.00	—
1991S	—	(321,275)	—	22.50

Columbus Quincentenary. KM# 238 Obv.
Designer: John Mercanti **Rev. Designer:** Thomas D. Rogers, Sr.

Date	Mintage	Proof	MS-65	Prf-65
1992D	106,949	—	30.00	—
1992P	—	(385,241)	—	46.00

Olympics. KM# 234 Obv. **Designer:** John R. Deecken and Chester Y. Martin **Rev. Designer:** Marcel Jovine

Date	Mintage	Proof	MS-65	Prf-65
1992D	187,552	—	26.00	—
1992S	—	(504,505)	—	28.50

White House Bicentennial. KM# 236 Obv.
Designer: Edgar Z. Steever **Rev. Designer:** Chester Y. Martin

Date	Mintage	Proof	MS-65	Prf-65
1992D	123,803	—	38.50	—
1992W	—	(375,851)	—	46.00

James Madison and Bill of Rights. KM# 241
Obv. Designer: William Krawczewicz and Thomas D. Rogers, Sr. **Rev. Designer:** Dean McMullen and Thomas D. Rogers, Sr.

Date	Mintage	Proof	MS-65	Prf-65
1993D	98,383	—	20.00	—
1993S	—	(534,001)	—	21.50

Thomas Jefferson 250th Birth Anniversary.
KM# 249 Designer: T. James Ferrell.

Date	Mintage	Proof	MS-65	Prf-65
1993P	266,927	—	27.00	—
1993S	—	(332,891)	—	30.50

World War II 50th Anniversary. KM# 244
Designer: Thomas D. Rogers, Sr..

Date	Mintage	Proof	MS-65	Prf-65
1993D	94,708	—	35.00	—
1993W		—(322,422)	—	42.50

National Prisoner of War Museum. KM# 251
Obv. Designer: Thomas Nielson and Alfred Maletsky
Rev. Designer: Edgar Z. Steever

Date	Mintage	Proof	MS-65	Prf-65
1994W	54,790	—	85.00	—
1994P	—	(220,100)	—	63.50

U.S. Capitol Bicentennial. KM# 253

Date	Mintage	Proof	MS-65	Prf-65
1994D	68,352	—	22.50	—
1994S	—	(279,416)	—	25.50

Vietnam Veterans Memorial. KM# 250
Obv. Designer: John Mercanti **Rev. Designer:** Thomas D. Rogers, Sr.

Date	Mintage	Proof	MS-65	Prf-65
1994W	57,317	—	85.00	—
1994P	—	(226,262)	—	100.00

Women in Military Service Memorial.
KM# 252 **Obv. Designer:** T. James Ferrell **Rev. Designer:** Thomas D. Rogers, Sr.

Date	Mintage	Proof	MS-65	Prf-65
1994W	53,054	—	62.50	—
1994P	—	(213,201)	—	65.00

World Cup Soccer. KM# 247 Obv. Designer:
Dean McMullen and T. James Ferrell

Date	Mintage	Proof	MS-65	Prf-65
1994D	81,698	—	27.00	—
1994S	—	(576,978)	—	30.00

Atlanta Olympics. KM# 264 Obv. Designer:
John Mercanti **Obverse:** Track and field

Date	Mintage	Proof	MS-65	Prf-65
1995D	24,796	—	85.00	—
1995P	—	(136,935)	—	38.50

Atlanta Olympics. KM# 263 Obv. Designer: John Mercanti **Obverse:** Cycling

Date	Mintage	Proof	MS-65	Prf-65
1995D	19,662	—	135	—
1995P	—	(118,795)	—	45.00

Atlanta Olympics. KM# 260 **Obverse:** Gymnastics

Date	Mintage	Proof	MS-65	Prf-65
1995D	42,497	—	80.00	—
1995P	—	(182,676)	—	62.50

Atlanta Olympics, Paralympics. KM# 259 **Obverse:** Blind runner

Date	Mintage	Proof	MS-65	Prf-65
1995D	28,649	—	97.50	—
1995P	—	(138,337)	—	66.00

Civil War. KM# 255 Obv. Designer: Don Troiani and Edgar Z. Steever Rev. Designer: John Mercanti

Date	Mintage	Proof	MS-65	Prf-65
1995P	45,866	—	77.50	—
1995S	—	(437,114)	—	90.00

U.S. COMMEMORATIVES

Special Olympics World Games. KM# 266
Obv. Designer: Jamie Wyeth and T. James Ferrell
Rev. Designer: Thomas D. Rogers, Sr.

Date	Mintage	Proof	MS-65	Prf-65
1995W	89,301	—	25.00	—
1995P	—	(351,764)	—	27.50

Atlanta Olympics. KM# 269 **Rev. Designer:**
Thomas D. Rogers, Sr. **Obverse:** Tennis

Date	Mintage	Proof	MS-65	Prf-65
1996D	15,983	—	300	—
1996P	—	(92,016)	—	96.00

Atlanta Olympics. KM# 272A **Rev. Designer:**
Thomas D. Rogers, Sr. **Obverse:** High jumper

Date	Mintage	Proof	MS-65	Prf-65
1996D	15,697	—	375	—
1996P	—	(124,502)	—	62.50

Atlanta Olympics. KM# 272 **Rev. Designer:**
Thomas D. Rogers, Sr. **Obverse:** Rowing

Date	Mintage	Proof	MS-65	Prf-65
1996D	16,258	—	330	—
1996P	—	(151,890)	—	75.00

Atlanta Olympics, Paralympics. KM# 268
Rev. Designer: Thomas D. Rogers, Sr. **Obverse:**
Wheelchair racer

Date	Mintage	Proof	MS-65	Prf-65
1996D	14,497	—	375	—
1996P	—	(84,280)	—	90.00

National Community Service. KM# 275 **Obv.**
Designer: Thomas D. Rogers, Sr. **Rev. Designer:**
William C. Cousins

Date	Mintage	Proof	MS-65	Prf-65
1996S	23,500	—	285	—
1996S	—	(101,543)	—	96.00

Smithsonian 150th Anniversary. KM# 276
Obv. Designer: Thomas D. Rogers, Sr. **Rev. Designer:**
John Mercanti

Date	Mintage	Proof	MS-65	Prf-65
1996D	31,230	—	135	—
1996P	—	(129,152)	—	72.50

Jackie Robinson 50th Anniversary. KM# 279
Obv. Designer: Alfred Maletsky **Rev. Designer:** T.
James Ferrell

Date	Mintage	Proof	MS-65	Prf-65
1997S	30,007(110,495)		92.50	85.00

National Law Enforcement Officers Memorial. KM# 281 Designer: Alfred Maletsky.

Date	Mintage	Proof	MS-65	Prf-65
1997P	28,575	(110,428)	175	165

U.S. Botanic Gardens 175th Anniversary.
KM# 278 Designer: Edgar Z. Steever.

Date	Mintage	Proof	MS-65	Prf-65
1997P	57,272	(264,528)	47.50	46.00

Black Revolutionary War Patriots. KM# 288
Obv. Designer: John Mercanti Rev. Designer: Ed Dwight Obverse: Crispus Attucks

Date	Mintage	Proof	MS-65	Prf-65
1998S	37,210	(75,070)	175	123

Robert F. Kennedy. KM# 287 Obv. Designer:
Thomas D. Rogers, Sr. Rev. Designer: James M. Peed and Thomas D. Rogers, Sr.

Date	Mintage	Proof	MS-65	Prf-65
1998S	106,422	(99,020)	32.00	45.00

Dolley Madison. KM# 298 **Designer:** Tiffany & Co.. **Obv. Designer:** T. James Ferrell **Rev. Designer:** Thomas D. Rogers, Sr.

Date	Mintage	Proof	MS-65	Prf-65
1999P	22,948	(158,247)	60.00	57.50

Yellowstone. KM# 299 **Obv. Designer:** Edgar Z. Steever **Rev. Designer:** William C. Cousins

Date	Mintage	Proof	MS-65	Prf-65
1999P	23,614	(128,646)	57.50	60.00

Leif Ericson. KM# 313 **Obv. Designer:** John Mercanti **Rev. Designer:** T. James Ferrell

Date	Mintage	Proof	MS-65	Prf-65
2000P	28,150	(58,612)	92.50	72.50
2000 Iceland	—	(15,947)	—	72.50

Library of Congress Bicentennial. KM# 311 **Obv. Designer:** Thomas D. Rogers, Sr. **Rev. Designer:** John Mercanti

Date	Mintage	Proof	MS-65	Prf-65
2000P	52,771	(196,900)	45.00	45.00

American Buffalo. KM# 325 Designer: James E. Fraser.

Date	Mintage	Proof	MS-65	Prf-65
2001	197,131	(272,869)	130	135

Capitol Visitor Center. KM# 324 Obv. Designer: Marika Somogyi Rev. Designer: John Mercanti

Date	Mintage	Proof	MS-65	Prf-65
2001	66,636	(143,793)	41.50	46.00

West Point Military Academy Bicentennial. KM# 338 Obv. Designer: T. James Ferrell Rev. Designer: John Mercanti

Date	Mintage	Proof	MS-65	Prf-65
2002	103,201	(288,293)	32.50	36.00

Winter Olympics - Salt Lake City. KM# 336 Obv. Designer: John Mercanti Rev. Designer: Donna Weaver

Date	Mintage	Proof	MS-65	Prf-65
2002	35,388	(142,873)	39.00	42.00

First Flight Centennial. KM# 349 Obv. Designer: T. James Ferrell Rev. Designer: Norman E. Nemeth
Obverse: Orville and Wilbur Wright Reverse: Wright Brothers airplane

Date	Mintage		Proof	MS-65	Prf-65
2003P	—		—	38.50	42.50

125th Anniversary of Edison's Electric Light.
KM# 362 Obv. Designer: Donna Weaver Rev.
Designer: John Mercanti

Date	Mintage	Proof	MS-65	Prf-65
2004P	—	—	38.50	42.50

**Lewis and Clark Corps of Discovery
Bicentennial.** KM# 363

Date	Mintage	Proof	MS-65	Prf-65
2004P	—	—	38.50	42.50

$5 (HALF EAGLE)

Statue of Liberty Centennial. KM# 215
Designer: Elizabeth Jones.

Date	Mintage	Proof	MS-65	Prf-65
1986W	95,248	(404,013)	140	140

Constitution Bicentennial. KM# 221 Designer:
Marcel Jovine.

Date	Mintage	Proof	MS-65	Prf-65
1987W	214,225	(651,659)	140	140

Olympics. KM# 223 Obv. Designer: Elizabeth
Jones Rev. Designer: Marcel Jovine

Date	Mintage	Proof	MS-65	Prf-65
1988W	62,913	(281,456)	140	140

Bicentennial of the Congress. KM# 226 Obv.
Designer: John Mercanti

Date	Mintage	Proof	MS-65	Prf-65
1989W	46,899	(164,690)	140	140

Mount Rushmore Golden Anniversary. KM#
230 Obv. Designer: John Mercanti Rev. Designer:
Robert Lamb and William C. Cousins

Date	Mintage	Proof	MS-65	Prf-65
1991W	31,959	(111,991)	185	155

Columbus Quincentenary. KM# 239 Obv.
Designer: T. James Ferrell Rev. Designer: Thomas D.
Rogers, Sr.

Date	Mintage	Proof	MS-65	Prf-65
1992W	24,329	(79,730)	205	170

Olympics. **KM# 235** **Obv. Designer:** James C. Sharpe and T. James Ferrell **Rev. Designer:** James M. Peed

Date	Mintage	Proof	MS-65	Prf-65
1992W	27,732	(77,313)	175	150

James Madison and Bill of Rights. **KM# 242**
Obv. Designer: Scott R. Blazek **Rev. Designer:** Joseph D. Peña

Date	Mintage	Proof	MS-65	Prf-65
1993W	22,266	(78,651)	210	185

World War II 50th Anniversary. **KM# 245**
Obv. Designer: Charles J. Madsen **Rev. Designer:** Edward S. Fisher

Date	Mintage	Proof	MS-65	Prf-65
1993W	23,089	(65,461)	215	210

World Cup Soccer. **KM# 248** **Obv. Designer:** William J. Krawczewicz **Rev. Designer:** Dean McMullen

Date	Mintage	Proof	MS-65	Prf-65
1994W	22,464	(89,619)	200	165

Civil War. **KM# 256** **Obv. Designer:** Don Troiani
Rev. Designer: Alfred Maletsky

Date	Mintage	Proof	MS-65	Prf-65
1995W	12,735	(55,246)	585	385

Olympics. **KM# 261** **Obverse:** Torch runner

Date	Mintage	Proof	MS-65	Prf-65
1995W	14,675	(57,442)	350	250

Olympics. **KM# 265** **Obverse:** Stadium

Date	Mintage	Proof	MS-65	Prf-65
1995W	10,579	(43,124)	385	290

1996 Atlanta Olympics. **KM# 270** **Obverse:** Cauldron

Date	Mintage	Proof	MS-65	Prf-65
1996W	9,210	(38,555)	465	375

Olympics. **KM# 274** **Obverse:** Flag bearer

Date	Mintage	Proof	MS-65	Prf-65
1996W	9,174	(32,886)	485	375

Smithsonian Institution 150th Anniversary.
KM# 277 Obv. Designer: Alfred Maletsky **Rev. Designer:** T. James Ferrell

Date	Mintage	Proof	MS-65	Prf-65
1996W	9,068	(21,772)	850	385

Franklin Delano Roosevelt. KM# 282 Obv. Designer: T. James Ferrell **Rev. Designer:** James M. Peed and Thomas D. Rogers, Sr.

Date	Mintage	Proof	MS-65	Prf-65
1997W	11,894	(29,474)	350	375

**Jackie Robinson 50th Anniversary. KM# 280
Obv. Designer:** William C. Cousins **Rev. Designer:** James M. Peed

Date	Mintage	Proof	MS-65	Prf-65
1997W	5,202	(24,546)	2,900	570

George Washington Death Bicentennial. KM# 300 Designer: Laura G. Fraser.

Date	Mintage	Proof	MS-65	Prf-65
1999W	22,511	(41,693)	300	315

Capitol Visitor Center. KM# 326 Designer: Elizabeth Jones.

Date	Mintage	Proof	MS-65	Prf-65
2001	6,761	(27,652)	650	285

2002 Salt Lake City Winter Olympics. KM# 337 Designer: Donna Weaver.

Date	Mintage	Proof	MS-65	Prf-65
2002	10,585	(32,877)	330	300

$10 (EAGLE)

Los Angeles XXIII Olympiad. **KM# 211** **Obv. Designer:** James M. Peed and John Mercanti **Rev. Designer:** John Mercanti **Diameter:** 27 **Weight:** 16.7180 g. **Composition:** 0.9000 Gold, 0.4839 oz. AGW.

Date	Mintage	Proof	MS-65	Prf-65
1984W	75,886	(381,085)	275	275
1984P	33,309	—	—	275
1984D	34,533	—	—	290
1984S	48,551	—	—	275

Library of Congress. **KM# 312** **Obv. Designer:** John Mercanti **Rev. Designer:** Thomas D. Rogers, Sr. **Weight:** 16.2590 g. **Composition:** Platinum-Gold-Alloy **Notes:** Composition is 48 percent platinum, 48 percent gold, and 4 percent alloy.

Date	Mintage	Proof	MS-65	Prf-65
2000W	6,683	(27,167)	1,600	650

First Flight Centennial. **KM# 350** **Designer:** Donna Weaver. **Weight:** 16.7180 g. **Composition:** 0.9000 Gold, .4839 oz. AGW

Date	Mintage	Proof	MS-65	Prf-65
2003P	—	—	340	400

AMERICAN EAGLE BULLION COINS

GOLD $5

KM# 216   Obv. Designer: Augustus Saint-Gaudens.
Rev. Designer: Miley Busiek. Diameter: 16.5 Weight:
3.3930 g. Composition: 0.9167 GOLD, 0.1 oz.

Date	Mintage	Unc	Prf.
MCMLXXXVI (1986)	912,609	60.00	—
MCMLXXXVII (1987)	580,266	60.00	—
MCMLXXXVIII (1988)	159,500	192	—
MCMLXXXVIII (1988)P	(143,881)	—	80.00
MCMLXXXIX (1989)	264,790	96.00	—
MCMLXXXIX (1989)P	(82,924)	—	80.00
MCMXC (1990)	210,210	72.00	—
MCMXC (1990)P	(99,349)	—	80.00
MCMXCI (1991)	165,200	125	—
MCMXCI (1991)P	(70,344)	—	80.00
1992	209,300	60.00	—
1992P	(64,902)	—	80.00
1993	210,709	70.00	—

Date	Mintage	Unc	Prf.
1993P	(58,649)	—	80.00
1994	206,380	56.00	—
1994W	(62,100)	—	80.00
1995	223,025	56.00	—
1995W	(62,650)	—	80.00
1996	401,964	56.00	—
1996W	(58,440)	—	80.00
1997	528,515	56.00	—
1997W	(35,000)	—	91.00
1998	1,344,520	53.00	—
1998W	(39,653)	—	80.00
1999	2,750,338	53.00	—
1999W	(48,426)	—	80.00
2000	569,153	56.00	—
2000W	(50,000)	—	90.00
2001	269,147	56.00	—
2001W	(37,547)	—	80.00
2002	230,027	56.00	—
2002W	(40,864)	—	80.00
2003	245,029	56.00	—
2003W	—	—	85.00
2004	—	56.00	—
2004W	—	—	—

GOLD $10

KM# 217   Obv. Designer: Augustus Saint-Gaudens.
Rev. Designer: Miley Busiek. Diameter: 22 Weight:
8.4830 g. Composition: 0.9167 GOLD, 0.25 oz.

Date	Mintage	Unc	Prf.
MCMLXXXVI (1986)	726,031	160	—
MCMLXXXVII (1987)	269,255	160	—
MCMLXXXVIII (1988)	49,000	170	—
MCMLXXXVIII (1988)P	(98,028)	—	160
MCMLXXXIX (1989)	81,789	135	—
MCMLXXXIX (1989P)	(53,593)	—	160
MCMXC (1990)	41,000	160	—
MCMXC (1990)P	(62,674)	—	160
MCMXCI (1991)	36,100	290	—
MCMXCI (1991)P	(50,839)	—	160
1992	59,546	150	—
1992P	(46,290)	—	160

Date	Mintage	Unc	Prf.
1993	71,864	150	—
1993P	(46,271)	—	150
1994	72,650	145	—
1994W	(47,600)	—	160
1995	83,752	145	—
1995W	(47,545)	—	160
1996	60,318	145	—
1996W	(39,190)	—	160
1997	108,805	145	—
1997W	(29,800)	—	160
1998	309,829	135	—
1998W	(29,733)	—	160
1999	564,232	135	—
1999W	(34,416)	—	160
2000	128,964	135	—
2000W	(36,000)	—	160
2001	71,280	150	—
2001W	(25,630)	—	160
2002	62,027	135	—
2002W	(29,242)	—	160
2003	74,029	150	—
2003W	—	—	165
2004	—	135	—
2004W	—	—	—

GOLD $25

KM# 218   Obv. Designer: Augustus Saint-Gaudens.
Rev. Designer: Miley Busiek. Diameter: 27 Weight:
16.9660 g. Composition: 0.9167 GOLD, 0.5 oz.

Date	Mintage	Unc	Prf.
MCMLXXXVI (1986)	599,566	335	—
MCMLXXXVII (1987)	131,255	300	—
MCMLXXXVII (1987)P	(143,398)	—	320
MCMLXXXVIII (1988)	45,000	385	—
MCMLXXXVIII (1988)P	(76,528)	—	320
MCMLXXXIX (1989)	44,829	480	—
MCMLXXXIX (1989)P	(44,264)	—	320
MCMXC (1990)	31,000	500	—
MCMXC (1990)P	(51,636)	—	320
MCMXCI (1991)	24,100	800	—
MCMXCI (1991)P	(53,125)	—	320
1992	54,404	360	—
1992P	(40,982)	—	320
1993	73,324	280	—
1993P	(43,319)	—	320
1994	62,400	280	—

BULLION COINAGE

Date	Mintage	Unc	Prf.
1994W	(44,100)	—	320
1995	53,474	325	—
1995W	(45,511)	—	320
1996	39,287	325	—
1996W	(35,937)	—	320
1997	79,605	265	—
1997W	(26,350)	—	320
1998	169,029	260	—
1998W	(25,896)	—	320
1999	263,013	260	—
1999W	(30,452)	—	320

Date	Mintage	Unc	Prf.
2000	79,287	280	—
2000W	(32,000)	—	320
2001	48,047	325	—
2001W	(23,261)	—	320
2002	70,027	275	—
2002W	(26,646)	—	320
2003	79,029	265	—
2003W	—	—	320
2004	—	260	—
2004W	—	—	—

GOLD $50

Date	Mintage	Unc	Prf.
MCMXCI (1991)	243,100	252	—
MCMXCI (1991)W	(50,411)	—	620
1992	275,000	525	—
1992W	(44,835)	—	620
1993	480,192	525	—
1993W	(34,389)	—	620
1994	221,633	525	—
1994W	(36,300)	—	620
1995	200,636	525	—
1995W	(46,553)	—	620
1996	189,148	525	—
1996W	(37,302)	—	620
1997	664,508	525	—
1997W	(28,000)	—	620
1998	1,468,530	525	—
1998W	(26,060)	—	620
1999	1,505,026	525	—
1999W	(31,446)	—	620
2000	433,319	525	—
2000W	(33,000)	—	620
2001	143,605	525	—
2001W	(24,580)	—	—
2002	222,029	525	—
2002W	(24,242)	—	620
2003	416,032	525	—
2003W	—	—	620
2004	—	525	—
2004W	—	—	—

KM# 219 **Obv. Designer:** Augustus Saint-Gaudens. **Rev. Designer:** Miley Busiek. **Diameter:** 32.7 **Weight:** 33.9310 g. **Composition:** 0.9167 GOLD, 1 oz.

Date	Mintage	Unc	Prf.
MCMLXXXVI (1986)	1,362,650	525	—
MCMLXXXVI (1986)W	(446,290)	—	620
MCMLXXXVII (1987)	1,045,500	525	—
MCMLXXXVII (1987)W	(147,498)	—	620
MCMLXXXVIII (1988)	465,000	525	—
MCMLXXXVIII (1988)W	(87,133)	—	620
MCMLXXXIX (1989)	415,790	525	—
MCMLXXXIX (1989)W	(53,960)	—	620
MCMXC (1990)	373,210	525	—
MCMXC (1990)W	(62,401)	—	620

SILVER DOLLAR

Date	Mintage	Unc	Prf.
1988S	(557,370)	—	90.00
1989	5,203,327	11.00	—
1989S	(617,694)	—	47.50
1990	5,840,210	12.00	—
1990S	(695,510)	—	42.50
1991	7,191,066	10.50	—
1991S	(511,924)	—	60.00
1992	5,540,068	13.00	—
1992S	(498,552)	—	55.00
1993	6,763,762	10.50	—
1993P	(403,625)	—	210
1994	4,227,319	11.00	—
1994P	(372,168)	—	200
1995	4,672,051	11.00	—
1995P	(395,400)	—	200
1995W 10th Anniversary	(30,125)	—	3,000
1996	3,603,386	38.00	—
1996P	(473,021)	—	60.00
1997	4,295,004	11.00	—
1997P	(429,682)	—	90.00
1998	4,847,549	10.50	—
1998P	(452,319)	—	62.50
1999	7,408,640	10.50	—
1999P	(549,769)	—	82.50
2000P	(600,000)	—	41.00
2000	9,239,132	10.50	—
2001	9,001,711	10.50	—
2001W	(746,154)	—	35.00
2002	10,539,026	10.50	—
2002W	(647,342)	—	35.00
2003	8,495,008	10.50	—

KM# 273 **Obv. Designer:** Adolph A. Weinman. **Rev. Designer:** John Mercanti. **Diameter:** 40.6 **Weight:** 31.1010 g. **Composition:** 0.9993 SILVER, 1 oz.

Date	Mintage	Unc	Prf.
1986	5,393,005	17.50	—
1986S	(1,446,778)	—	35.00
1987	11,442,335	10.00	—
1987S	(904,732)	—	35.00
1988	5,004,646	11.00	—

Date	Mintage	Unc	Prf.	Date	Mintage	Unc	Prf.
2003W	—	—	38.50	2004W	—	—	—
2004	—	10.50	—				

PLATINUM $10

KM# 283 Obv. Designer: John Mercanti. **Rev. Designer:** Thomas D. Rogers Sr. **Weight:** 3.1100 g. **Composition:** 0.9995 PLATINUM, .1000 oz.

Date	Mintage	Unc	Prf.
1997	70,250	125	—
1997W	(36,996)	—	125
1998	39,525	138	—
1999	55,955	125	—
2000	34,027	125	—
2001	52,017	125	—
2002	23,005	150	—
2003	22,007	132	—
2004	—	125	—

KM# 289 Obv. Designer: John Mercanti. **Weight:** 3.1100 g. **Composition:** 0.9995 PLATINUM, .1000 oz.

Date	Mintage	Unc	Prf.
1998W	(19,832)	—	125

KM# 301 Obv. Designer: John Mercanti. **Weight:** 3.1100 g. **Composition:** 0.9995 PLATINUM, .1000 oz.

Date	Mintage	Unc	Prf.
1999W	(19,123)	—	125

KM# 314 Obv. Designer: John Mercanti. **Weight:** 3.1100 g. **Composition:** 0.9995 PLATINUM, .1000 oz.

Date	Mintage	Unc	Prf.
2000W	(15,651)	—	125

KM# 327 Obv. Designer: John Mercanti. **Weight:** 3.1100 g. **Composition:** 0.9995 PLATINUM, .1000 oz.

Date	Mintage	Unc	Prf.
2001W	(12,193)	—	125

KM# 339 Obv. Designer: John Mercanti. **Weight:** 3.1100 g. **Composition:** 0.9995 PLATINUM, .1000 oz.

Date	Mintage	Unc	Prf.
2002W	(12,365)	—	135

KM# 351 Obv. Designer: John Mercanti. **Rev. Designer:** Al Maletsky. **Weight:** 3.1100 g. **Composition:** 0.9995 PLATINUM, .1000 oz.

Date	Mintage	Unc	Prf.
2003W	—	—	135

KM# 364 Obv. Designer: John Mercanti. **Weight:** 3.1100 g. **Composition:** 0.9995 PLATINUM, .1000 oz.

Date	Mintage	Unc	Prf.
2004W	—	—	—

PLATINUM $25

KM# 284 Obv. Designer: John Mercanti. **Rev. Designer:** Thomas D. Rogers Sr. **Weight:** 7.7857 g. **Composition:** 0.9995 PLATINUM, 0.2500 oz.

Date	Mintage	Unc	Prf.
1997	27,100	300	—
1997W	(18,628)	—	300
1998	38,887	300	—
1999	39,734	300	—
2000	20,054	300	—
2001	21,815	325	—
2002	27,405	290	—
2003	25,207	325	—
2004	—	305	—

KM# 290 Obv. Designer: John Mercanti. **Weight:** 7.7857 g. **Composition:** 0.9995 PLATINUM, .2500 oz.

Date	Mintage	Unc	Prf.
1998W	(14,860)	—	300

KM# 302 Obv. Designer: John Mercanti. **Weight:** 7.7857 g. **Composition:** 0.9995 PLATINUM, .2500 oz.

Date	Mintage	Unc	Prf.
1999W	(13,514)	—	300

KM# 315 Obv. Designer: John Mercanti. **Weight:** 7.7857 g. **Composition:** 0.9995 PLATINUM, .2500 oz.

Date	Mintage	Unc	Prf.
2000W	(11,995)	—	300

KM# 328 Obv. Designer: John Mercanti. **Weight:** 7.7857 g. **Composition:** 0.9995 PLATINUM, .2500 oz.

Date	Mintage	Unc	Prf.
2001W	(8,858)	—	300

KM# 340 Obv. Designer: John Mercanti. **Weight:** 7.7857 g. **Composition:** 0.9995 PLATINUM, .2500 oz.

Date	Mintage	Unc	Prf.
2002W	(9,282)	—	385

KM# 352 Obv. Designer: John Mercanti. **Rev. Designer:** Al Maletsky. **Weight:** 7.7857 g. **Composition:** 0.9995 PLATINUM, .2500 oz.

Date	Mintage	Unc	Prf.
2003W	—	—	385

KM# 365 Obv. Designer: John Mercanti. **Weight:** 7.7857 g. **Composition:** 0.9995 PLATINUM, .2500 oz.

Date	Mintage	Unc	Prf.
2004W	—	—	—

BULLION COINAGE

PLATINUM $50

KM# 285 Obv. Designer: John Mercanti. **Rev. Designer:** Thomas D. Rogers Sr. **Weight:** 15.5520 g. **Composition:** 0.9995 PLATINUM, 0.5000 oz.

Date	Mintage	Unc	Prf.
1997	20,500	575	—
1997W	(15,432)	—	575
1998	32,415	575	—
1999	32,309	575	—
2000	18,892	575	—
2001	12,815	600	—
2002	24,005	565	—
2003	17,409	575	—
2004	—	575	—

KM# 291 Obv. Designer: John Mercanti. **Weight:** 15.5520 g. **Composition:** 0.9995 PLATINUM, .5000 oz.

Date	Mintage	Unc	Prf.
1998W	(13,821)	—	575

KM# 303 Obv. Designer: John Mercanti. **Weight:** 15.5520 g. **Composition:** 0.9995 PLATINUM, .5000 oz.

Date	Mintage	Unc	Prf.
1999W	(11,098)	—	575

KM# 316 Obv. Designer: John Mercanti. **Weight:** 15.5520 g. **Composition:** 0.9995 PLATINUM, .5000 oz.

Date	Mintage	Unc	Prf.
2000W	(11,049)	—	575

KM# 329 Obv. Designer: John Mercanti. **Weight:** 15.5520 g. **Composition:** 0.9995 PLATINUM, .5000 oz.

Date	Mintage	Unc	Prf.
2001W	(8,268)	—	575

KM# 341 Obv. Designer: John Mercanti. **Weight:** 15.5520 g. **Composition:** 0.9995 PLATINUM, .5000 oz.

Date	Mintage	Unc	Prf.
2002W	(8,772)	—	630

KM# 353 Obv. Designer: John Mercanti. **Rev. Designer:** Al Maletsky. **Weight:** 15.5520 g. **Composition:** 0.9995 PLATINUM, .5000 oz.

Date	Mintage	Unc	Prf.
2003W	—	—	630

KM# 366 Obv. Designer: John Mercanti. **Weight:** 15.5520 g. **Composition:** 0.9995 PLATINUM, .5000 oz.

Date	Mintage	Unc	Prf.
2004W	—	—	—

PLATINUM $100

KM# 286 Obv. Designer: John Mercanti. **Rev. Designer:** Thomas D. Rogers Sr. **Weight:** 31.1050 g. **Composition:** 0.9995 PLATINUM, 1.000 oz.

Date	Mintage	Unc	Prf.	Date	Mintage	Unc	Prf.
1997	56,000	1,115	—	2001	14,070	1,115	—
1997W	(15,885)	—	1,115	2002	11,502	1,115	—
1998	133,002	1,115	—	2003	8,007	1,115	—
1999	56,707	1,115	—	2004	—	1,115	—
2000	18,892	1,115	—				

KM# 292 Obv. Designer: John Mercanti. **Weight:** 31.1050 g. **Composition:** 0.9995 PLATINUM, 1.000 oz.

Date	Mintage	Unc	Prf.
1998W	(14,203)	—	1,115

KM# 304   **Obv. Designer:** John Mercanti. **Weight:** 31.1050 g. **Composition:** 0.9995 PLATINUM, 1.000 oz.

Date	Mintage	Unc	Prf.
1999W	—	—	1,115

KM# 317   **Obv. Designer:** John Mercanti. **Weight:** 31.1050 g. **Composition:** 0.9995 PLATINUM, 1.000 oz.

Date	Mintage	Unc	Prf.
2000W	—	—	1,115

KM# 330   **Obv. Designer:** John Mercanti. **Weight:** 31.1050 g. **Composition:** 0.9995 PLATINUM, 1.000 oz.

Date	Mintage	Unc	Prf.
2001W	(8,990)	—	1,115

KM# 342   **Obv. Designer:** John Mercanti. **Weight:** 31.1050 g. **Composition:** 0.9995 PLATINUM, 1.000 oz.

Date	Mintage	Unc	Prf.
2002W	(9,834)	—	1,115

KM# 354   **Obv. Designer:** John Mercanti. **Rev. Designer:** Al Maletsky. **Weight:** 31.1050 g. **Composition:** 0.9995 PLATINUM, 1.000 oz.

Date	Mintage	Unc	Prf.
2003W	—	—	1,215

KM# 367   **Obv. Designer:** John Mercanti. **Rev. Designer:** Donna Weaver. **Weight:** 31.1050 g. **Composition:** 0.9995 PLATINUM, 1.000 oz.

Date	Mintage	Unc	Prf.
2004W	—	—	1,215

BULLION COINAGE

MINT SETS

Mint, or uncirculated, sets contain one uncirculated coin of each denomination from each mint produced for circulation that year. Values listed here are only for those sets sold by the U.S. Mint. Sets were not offered in years not listed. In years when the Mint did not offer the sets, some private companies compiled and marketed uncirculated sets. Mint sets from 1947 through 1958 contained two examples of each coin mounted in cardboard holders, which caused the coins to tarnish. Beginning in 1959, the sets have been packaged in sealed Pliofilm packets and include only one specimen of each coin struck for that year. Listings for 1965, 1966 and 1967 are for "special mint sets," which were of higher quality than regular mint sets and were prooflike. They were packaged in plastic cases. The 1970 large-date and small-date varieties are distinguished by the size of the date on the coin. The 1976 three-piece set contains the quarter, half dollar and dollar with the Bicentennial design. The 1971 and 1972 sets do not include a dollar coin; the 1979 set does not include an S-mint-marked dollar.

Date	Sets Sold	Issue Price	Value	Date	Sets Sold	Issue Price	Value
1947 Est. 5,000	—	4.87	1,300	1976 3 coins	4,908,319	9.00	17.50
1948 Est. 6,000	—	4.92	600	1976	1,892,513	6.00	10.00
1949 Est. 5,200	—	5.45	900	1977	2,006,869	7.00	7.50
1950 None issued	—	—	—	1978	2,162,609	7.00	9.00
1951	8,654	6.75	850	1979	2,526,000	8.00	5.50
1952	11,499	6.14	750	1980	2,815,066	9.00	6.25
1953	15,538	6.14	575	1981	2,908,145	11.00	14.00
1954	25,599	6.19	290	1982 & 1983 None issued	—	—	—
1955	49,656	3.57	170	1984	1,832,857	7.00	5.50
1956	45,475	3.34	165	1985	1,710,571	7.00	7.00
1957	32,324	4.40	260	1986	1,153,536	7.00	20.00
1958	50,314	4.43	160	1987	2,890,758	7.00	6.50
1959	187,000	2.40	50.00	1988	1,646,204	7.00	6.50
1960	260,485	2.40	27.50	1989	1,987,915	7.00	5.50
1961	223,704	2.40	45.00	1990	1,809,184	7.00	6.50
1962	385,285	2.40	19.00	1991	1,352,101	7.00	8.50
1963	606,612	2.40	14.00	1992	1,500,143	7.00	6.50
1964	1,008,108	2.40	11.50	1993	1,297,094	8.00	10.25
1965 Special Mint Set	2,360,000	4.00	12.50	1994	1,234,813	8.00	9.00
1966 Special Mint Set	2,261,583	4.00	14.00	1995	1,038,787	8.00	27.50
1967 Special Mint Set	1,863,344	4.00	21.50	1996	1,457,949	8.00	28.50
1968	2,105,128	2.50	5.00	1997	950,473	8.00	40.00
1969	1,817,392	2.50	6.50	1998	1,187,325	8.00	14.00
1970 large date	2,038,134	2.50	24.00	1999	1,421,625	14.95	37.00
1970 small date	Inc. above	2.50	56.00	2000	1,490,160	14.95	15.50
1971	2,193,396	3.50	5.50	2001	1,066,900	14.95	20.00
1972	2,750,000	3.50	5.50	2002	1,139,388	14.95	16.50
1973	1,767,691	6.00	26.50	2003	1,002,555	14.95	25.00
1974	1,975,981	6.00	7.00	2004	—	14.95	62.50
1975	1,921,488	6.00	11.00				

MODERN
COMMEMORATIVE COIN SETS

Olympic, 1983-1984

Date	Price
1983 & 1984 proof dollars	21.50
1983 & 1984S gold and silver proof set: One 1983 and one 1984 proof dollar and one 1984 proof gold $10; KM209, 210, 211.	280
1983 & 1984 6 coin set: One 1983 and one 1984 uncirculated and proof dollar, one uncirculated and one proof gold $10; KM209, 210, 211.	575
1983 collectors set: 1983 PDS uncirculated dollars; KM209.	34.00
1983 & 1984 gold and silver uncirculated set: One 1983 and one 1984 uncirculated dollar and one 1984P uncirculated gold $10; KM209, 210, 211.	280
1984 collectors set: 1984 PDS uncirculated dollars; KM210.	42.50

Statue of Liberty

Date	Price
1986 3 coin set: proof silver dollar, clad half dollar and gold $5; KM212, 214, 215.	160
1986 2 coin set: uncirculated silver dollar and clad half dollar; KM212, 214.	21.00
1986 2 coin set: proof silver dollar and clad half dollar; KM212, 214.	21.00
1986 3 coin set: uncirculated silver dollar, clad half dollar and gold $5; KM212, 214, 215.	160
1986 6 coin set: 1 each of the proof and uncirculated issues; KM212, 214, 215.	275

Constitution

Date	Price
1987 2 coin set: uncirculated silver dollar and gold $5; KM220, 221.	145
1987 2 coin set: proof silver dollar and gold $5; KM220, 221.	145
1987 4 coin set: 1 each of the proof and uncirculated issues; KM220, 221.	285

Olympic, 1988

Date	Price
1988 2 coin set: uncirculated silver dollar and gold $5; KM222, 223.	150
1988 2 coin set: Proof silver dollar and gold $5; KM222, 223.	150
1988 4 coin set: 1 each of proof and uncirculated issues; KM222, 223.	300

Congress

Date	Price
1989 2 coin set: uncirculated silver dollar and clad half dollar; KM224, 225.	22.00
1989 2 coin set: proof silver dollar and clad half dollar; KM224, 225.	23.00
1989 3 coin set: uncirculated silver dollar, clad half and gold $5; KM224, 225, 226.	170
1989 3 coin set: proof silver dollar, clad half and gold $5; KM224, 225, 226.	170
1989 6 coin set: 1 each of the proof and uncirculated issues; KM224, 225, 226.	325

Mt. Rushmore

Date	Price
1991 2 coin set: uncirculated half dollar and silver dollar; KM228, 229.	47.50
1991 2 coin set: proof half dollar and silver dollar; KM228, 229.	56.00
1991 3 coin set: uncirculated half dollar, silver dollar and gold $5; KM228, 229, 230.	220
1991 3 coin set: proof half dollar, silver dollar and gold $5; KM228, 229, 230.	200
1991 6 coin set: 1 each of proof and uncirculated issues; KM228, 229, 230.	440

Olympic, 1992

Date	Price
1992 2 coin set: uncirculated half dollar and silver dollar; KM233, 234.	30.00
1992 2 coin set: proof half dollar and silver dollar; KM233, 234.	32.00
1992 3 coin set: uncirculated half dollar, silver dollar and gold $5; KM233, 234, 235.	200
1992 3 coin set: proof half dollar, silver dollar and gold $5; KM233, 234, 235.	190
1992 6 coin set: 1 each of proof and uncirculated issues; KM233, 234, 235.	360

Columbus Quincentenary

Date	Price
1992 2 coin set: uncirculated half dollar and silver dollar; KM237, 238.	35.00
1992 2 coin set: proof half dollar and silver dollar; KM237, 238.	47.50
1992 3 coin set: uncirculated half dollar, silver dollar and gold $5; KM237, 238, 239.	240
1992 3 coin set: proof half dollar, silver dollar and gold $5; KM237, 238, 239.	210
1992 6 coin set: 1 each of proof and uncirculated issues; KM237, 238, 239.	440

Jefferson

Date	Price
1993 Jefferson: dollar, nickel and $2 note; KM249, 192.	95.00

Madison / Bill of Rights

Date	Price
1993 2 coin set: uncirculated half dollar and silver dollar; KM240, 241.	30.00
1993 2 coin set: proof half dollar and silver dollar; KM240, 241.	33.50
1993 3 coin set: uncirculated half dollar, silver dollar and gold $5; KM240, 241, 242.	240
1993 3 coin set: proof half dollar, silver dollar and gold $5; KM240, 241, 242.	215
1993 6 coin set: 1 each of proof and uncirculated issues; KM240, 241, 242.	440

World War II

Date	Price
1993 6 coin set: 1 each of proof and uncirculated issues; KM243, 244, 245.	500
1993 2 coin set: uncirculated half dollar and silver dollar; KM243, 244.	55.00
1993 2 coin set: proof half dollar and silver dollar; KM243, 244.	62.50
1993 3 coin set: uncirculated half dollar, silver dollar and gold $5; KM243, 244, 245.	265
1993 3 coin set: proof half dollar, silver dollar and gold $5; KM243, 244, 245.	245

World Cup

Date	Price
1994 2 coin set: uncirculated half dollar and silver dollar; KM246, 247.	35.00
1994 2 coin set: proof half dollar and silver dollar; KM246, 247.	37.00
1994 3 coin set: uncirculated half dollar, silver dollar and gold $5; KM246, 247, 248.	220
1994 3 coin set: proof half dollar, silver dollar and gold $5; KM246, 247, 248.	195
1994 6 coin set: 1 each of proof and uncirculated issues; KM246, 247, 248.	395

U.S. Veterans

Date	Price
1994 3 coin set: uncirculated POW, Vietnam, Women dollars; KM250, 251, 252.	245
1994 3 coin set: proof POW, Vietnam, Women dollars; KM250, 251, 252.	200

Olympic, 1995-96

Date	Price
1995 4 coin set: uncirculated basketball half, $1 gymnast & blind runner, $5 torch runner; KM257, 259, 260, 261.	465
1995 4 coin set: proof basketball half, $1 gymnast & blind runner, $5 torch runner; KM257, 259, 260, 261.	270
1995-96 4 coin set: proof halves, basketball, baseball, swimming, soccer; KM257, 262, 267, 271.	135
1996P 2 coin set: proof $1 gymnast & blind runner; KM259, 260.	72.50
1996P 2 coin set: proof $1 track & field, cycling; KM263, 264.	80.00
1996P 2 coin set: proof $1 wheelchair & tennis; KM268, 269.	120
1996P 2 coin set: proof $1 rowing & high jump; KM272, 272A.	110

Civil War

Date	Price
1995 2 coin set: uncirculated half and dollar; KM254, 255.	100.00
1995 2 coin set: proof half and dollar; KM254, 255.	120
1995 3 coin set: uncirculated half, dollar and gold $5; KM254, 255, 256.	590
1995 3 coin set: proof half, dollar and gold $5; KM254, 255, 256.	465
1995 6 coin set: 1 each of proof and uncirculated issues; KM254, 255, 256.	1,000

Smithsonian

Date	Price
1996 2 coin set: proof dollar and $5 gold; KM276, 277.	380
1996 4 coin set: proof and B.U. ; KM276, 277.	1,150

Botanic Garden

Date	Price
1997 2 coin set: dollar, Jefferson nickel and $1 note; KM278, 192.	225

Jackie Robinson

Date	Price
1997 2 coin set: proof dollar & $5 gold; KM279, 280.	510
1997 4 coin set: proof & BU; KM279, 280.	3,500
1997 legacy set.	510

Franklin Delano Roosevelt

Date	Price
1997W 2 coin set: uncirculated and proof; KM282.	575

Kennedy

Date	Price
1998 2 coin set: proof; KM287.	75.00
1998 2 coin collectors set: Robert Kennedy dollar and John Kennedy half dollar; KM287, 202b. Matte finished.	325

Black Patriots

Date	Price
1998S 2 coin set: uncirculated and proof; KM288.	205

Dolley Madison

Date	Price
1999 2 coin set: proof and uncirculated silver dollars; KM298.	82.50

George Washington

Date	Price
1999 2 coin set: proof and uncirculated gold $5; KM300.	580

Yellowstone National Park

Date	Price
1999 2 coin set: proof and uncirculated silver dollars; KM299.	96.00

Leif Ericson

Date	Price
2000 2 coin set: proof and uncirculated silver dollars; KM313.	95.00

Millennium Coin & Currency

Date	Price
2000 2 coin set: uncirculated Sacagewea $1, silver Eagle & $1 note	70.00

American Buffalo

Date	Price
2001 2 coin set: 90% Silver unc. & proof $1.; KM325.	260
2001 coin & currency set 90% unc. dollar & replicas of 1899 $5 silver cert.; KM325.	140

Capitol Visitor Center

Date	Price
2001 3 coin set: proof half, silver dollar, gold $5; KM323, 324, 326.	340

Winter Olympics - Salt Lake City

Date	Price
2002 2 coin set: Proof 90% silver dollar; KM336 & $5.00 Gold; KM337	310
2002 4 coin set: 90% Silver unc. & proof $1, KM336 & unc. & proof gold $5, KM337.	740

SETS & ROLLS

PROOF SETS

Proof coins are produced through a special process involving specially selected, highly polished planchets and dies. They usually receive two strikings from the coin press at increased pressure. The result is a coin with mirrorlike surfaces and, in recent years, a cameo effect on its raised design surfaces. Proof sets have been sold off and on by the U.S. Mint since 1858. Listings here are for sets from what is commonly called the modern era, since 1936. Values for earlier proofs are included in regular date listings. Sets were not offered in years not listed. Since 1968, proof coins have been produced at the San Francisco Mint; before that they were produced at the Philadelphia Mint. In 1942 the five-cent coin was struck in two compositions. Some proof sets for that year contain only one type (five-coin set); others contain both types. Two types of packaging were used in 1955 -- a box and a flat, plastic holder. The 1960 large-date and small-date sets are distinguished by the size of the date on the cent. Some 1968 sets are missing the mint mark on the dime, the result of an error in the preparation of an obverse die. The 1970 large-date and small-date sets are distinguished by the size of the date on the cent. Some 1970 sets are missing the mint mark on the dime, the result of an error in the preparation of an obverse die. Some 1971 sets are missing the mint mark on the five-cent piece, the result of an error in the preparation of an obverse die. The 1976 three-piece set contains the quarter, half dollar and dollar with the Bicentennial designs. The 1979 and 1981 Type II sets have clearer mint marks than the Type I sets for those years. Some 1983 sets are missing the mint mark on the dime, the result of an error in the preparation of an obverse die. Prestige sets contain the five regular-issue coins plus a commemorative silver dollar from that year.

Date	Sets Sold	Issue Price	Value
1936	3,837	1.89	8,000
1937	5,542	1.89	4,400
1938	8,045	1.89	2,000
1939	8,795	1.89	1,850
1940	11,246	1.89	1,550
1941	15,287	1.89	1,550
1942 6 coins	21,120	1.89	1,550
1942 5 coins	Inc. above	1.89	1,400
1950	51,386	2.10	765
1951	57,500	2.10	675
1952	81,980	2.10	380
1953	128,800	2.10	335
1954	233,300	2.10	195
1955 box	378,200	2.10	150
1955 flat pack	Inc. above	2.10	195
1956	669,384	2.10	70.00
1957	1,247,952	2.10	33.50
1958	875,652	2.10	80.00
1959	1,149,291	2.10	27.00
1960 large date	1,691,602	2.10	21.00
1960 small date	Inc. above	2.10	48.00
1961	3,028,244	2.10	10.50
1962	3,218,019	2.10	11.25
1963	3,075,645	2.10	14.00
1964	3,950,762	2.10	11.00
1968S	3,041,509	5.00	7.50
1968S no mint mark dime	Inc. above	5.00	11,000
1969S	2,934,631	5.00	7.50
1970S large date	2,632,810	5.00	16.00
1970S small date	Inc. above	5.00	105
1970S no mint mark dime	Inc. above	5.00	1,750
1971S	3,224,138	5.00	6.00
1971S no mint mark nickel Est. 1,655	1,655	5.00	1,350
1972S	3,267,667	5.50	4.75
1973S	2,769,624	7.00	12.50
1974S	2,617,350	7.00	8.00
1975S	2,909,369	7.00	14.50
1975S no mint mark dime	Inc. above	7.00	50,000
1976S 3 coins	3,998,621	12.00	17.50
1976S	4,149,730	7.00	8.50
1977S	3,251,152	9.00	7.50
1978S	3,127,788	9.00	9.00
1979S Type I	3,677,175	9.00	8.00
1979S Type II	Inc. above	9.00	115
1980S	3,547,030	10.00	6.25
1981S Type I	4,063,083	11.00	9.50
1981S Type II	Inc. above	11.00	410
1982S	3,857,479	11.00	4.00
1983S	3,138,765	11.00	5.50
1983S Prestige Set	140,361	59.00	115
1983S no mint mark dime	Inc. above	11.00	1,350
1984S	2,748,430	11.00	8.50
1984S Prestige Set	316,680	59.00	24.00
1985S	3,362,821	11.00	4.50
1986S	2,411,180	11.00	22.50
1986S Prestige Set	599,317	48.50	36.00
1987S	3,972,233	11.00	4.00

Date	Sets Sold	Issue Price	Value
1987S Prestige Set	435,495	45.00	24.00
1988S	3,031,287	11.00	8.50
1988S Prestige Set	231,661	45.00	30.00
1989S	3,009,107	11.00	7.50
1989S Prestige Set	211,087	45.00	39.50
1990S	2,793,433	11.00	8.00
1990S no S 1¢	3,555	11.00	8,000
1990S Prestige Set	506,126	45.00	28.00
1990S Prestige Set, no S 1¢	Inc. above	45.00	8,000
1991S	2,610,833	11.00	15.00
1991S Prestige Set	256,954	59.00	67.50
1992S	2,675,618	12.00	6.25
1992S Prestige Set	183,285	59.00	135
1992S Silver	1,009,585	21.00	17.50
1992S Silver premier	308,055	37.00	17.50
1993S	2,337,819	12.50	14.00
1993S Prestige Set	224,045	57.00	49.00
1993S Silver	570,213	21.00	42.50
1993S Silver premier	191,140	37.00	42.50
1994S	2,308,701	13.00	22.00
1994S Prestige Set	175,893	57.00	65.00
1994S Silver	636,009	21.00	52.50
1994S Silver premier	149,320	37.50	52.50
1995S	2,010,384	12.50	97.50
1995S Prestige Set	17,112	57.00	275
1995S Silver	549,878	21.00	130
1995S Silver premier	130,107	37.50	130
1996S	2,085,191	16.00	17.00
1996S Prestige Set	55,000	57.00	575
1996S Silver	623,655	21.00	62.50
1996S Silver premier	151,366	37.50	62.50
1997S	1,975,000	12.50	60.00
1997S Prestige Set	80,000	57.00	260
1997S Silver	605,473	21.00	110
1997S Silver premier	136,205	37.50	110
1998S	2,078,494	12.50	34.00
1998S Silver	638,134	21.00	55.00
1998S Silver premier	240,658	37.50	55.00
1999S	2,557,899	19.95	85.00
1999S 5 quarter set	1,169,958	13.95	77.50
1999S Silver	804,565	31.95	315
2000S	3,097,442	19.95	23.00
2000S 5 quarter set	995,803	13.95	14.00
2000S Silver	965,421	31.95	35.00
2001S	2,249,498	19.95	135
2001S 5 quarter set	774,800	13.95	55.00
2001S Silver	849,600	31.95	175
2002S	2,319,766	19.95	50.00
2002S 5 quarter set	764,419	13.95	27.00
2002S Silver	892,229	31.95	80.00
2003S	—	19.95	45.00
2003S 5 quarter set	—	13.95	23.50
2003S Silver	—	31.95	62.50
2004S 11 pieces	—	22.95	58.50
2004S 5 quarter set	—	15.95	16.00
2004S 5 silver quarter set	600,000	23.95	42.50
2004S Silver 11 pieces	—	37.95	83.50

UNCIRCULATED ROLLS

Date	Cents	Nickels	Dimes	Quarters	Halves	Date	Cents	Nickels	Dimes	Quarters	Halves
1938	235	250	1,000	3,250	1,900	1953D	15.00	16.50	130	230	190
1938D	340	210	900	—	—	1953S	24.00	38.00	56.00	340	575
1938S	215	280	1,250	3,400	—	1954	15.00	44.00	55.00	365	240
1939	88.00	80.00	600	1,125	1,200	1954D	15.00	30.00	48.50	360	225
1939D	190	3,400	540	1,800	2,000	1954S	17.50	78.00	37.50	215	225
1939S	135	1,150	1,350	3,250	2,400	1955	15.00	24.00	40.00	150	440
1940	110	60.00	470	1,675	1,000	1955D	12.50	7.50	40.00	120	—
1940D	125	94.00	630	4,400	—	1955S	20.00	—	35.00	—	—
1940S	120	145	600	1,300	1,200	1956	11.00	7.50	35.00	225	230
1941	88.00	68.00	385	750	725	1956D	11.00	7.00	35.00	165	—
1941D	165	170	635	2,900	1,200	1957	10.00	13.00	35.00	145	150
1941S	200	165	400	2,200	3,200	1957D	10.00	7.00	40.00	80.00	170
1942	50.00	245	385	420	700	1958	10.00	7.00	35.00	60.00	110
1942P	—	400				1958D	10.00	4.25	35.00	60.00	150
1942D	30.00	1,700	580	1,000	1,300	1959	1.50	4.25	35.00	60.00	125
1942S	485	400	850	4,700	1,400	1959D	1.50	5.40	35.00	60.00	140
1943	70.00	220	390	415	700	1960 large date	1.50	4.25	35.00	60.00	125
1943D	115	260	475	2,000	1,800	1960 small date	225	—	—	—	—
1943S	350	175	575	2,000	1,400	1960D large date	1.50	4.25	35.00	60.00	125
1944	22.00	530	400	415	700	1960D small date	2.00	—	35.00	—	—
1944D	19.50	400	470	800	1,200	1961	1.50	4.25	35.00	60.00	130
1944S	22.00	240	415	850	1,250	1961D	1.50	5.00	35.00	60.00	105
1945	32.00	270	380	380	700	1962	1.50	6.50	35.00	60.00	100.00
1945D	40.00	210	380	1,100	1,000	1962D	1.50	7.00	35.00	60.00	95.00
1945S	22.00	210	380	650	950	1963	1.50	5.00	35.00	60.00	95.00
1946	15.00	80.00	155	420	1,000	1963D	1.50	5.40	35.00	60.00	95.00
1946D	18.00	80.00	160	415	850	1964	1.50	4.25	35.00	60.00	70.00
1946S	22.00	38.00	190	400	880	1964D	1.50	4.25	35.00	60.00	70.00
1947	85.00	46.00	250	825	1,000	1965	2.70	4.60	9.50	26.00	30.00
1947D	16.00	52.00	335	740	950	1966	4.50	4.25	11.00	27.00	30.00
1947S	30.00	52.00	180	670	—	1967	10.00	8.00	11.00	27.00	30.00
1948	30.00	52.00	185	280	475	1968	4.00	—	8.50	40.00	—
1948D	36.50	110	175	675	340	1968D	2.50	5.40	10.00	34.00	30.00
1948S	95.00	80.00	165	460	—	1968S	1.75	4.25			
1949	72.50	160	1,300	2,200	1,700	1969	8.00	—	42.00	95.00	—
1949D	44.00	96.00	550	1,500	1,425	1969D	1.50	4.80	12.50	60.00	30.00
1949S	110	90.00	2,000	—	2,350	1969S	3.25	4.70	—	—	—
1950	32.00	110	440	360	880	1970	4.50	—	8.00	25.00	—
1950D	29.00	540	210	300	920	1970D	3.25	4.25	9.00	16.00	375
1950S	39.00	—	1,800	520	—	1970S	3.25	4.25	—	—	—
1951	36.50	140	130	450	420	1970S small date	1,350	—	—	—	—
1951D	13.50	270	100.00	430	780	1971	7.00	30.00	13.00	40.00	27.50
1951S	41.50	125	550	1,200	650	1971D	7.00	6.00	9.50	21.00	17.50
1952	95.00	52.00	80.00	430	380	1971S	5.00	—	—	—	—
1952D	13.50	190	115	370	250						
1952S	135	35.00	250	1,100	1,100						
1953	18.00	13.50	130	465	390						

Date	Cents	Nickels	Dimes	Quarters	Halves	Date	Cents	Nickels	Dimes	Quarters	Halves
1972	2.75	6.00	9.50	23.00	30.00	1987D	3.50	4.25	7.50	16.00	80.00
1972D	2.75	4.25	11.00	21.00	30.00	1988	7.00	5.40	10.25	40.00	90.00
1972S	2.75	—	—	—	—	1988D	7.00	8.00	9.50	23.50	57.50
1973	1.50	4.25	9.50	21.00	32.00	1989	2.40	5.40	11.50	20.00	57.50
1973D	1.40	6.00	8.50	23.50	23.00	1989D	2.40	8.00	11.00	21.00	42.00
1973S	2.75	—	—	—	—	1990	2.40	10.00	13.00	26.00	50.00
1974	1.20	4.25	8.00	21.50	21.50	1990D	2.40	11.00	12.50	30.00	70.00
1974D	1.20	6.00	7.50	18.00	23.00	1991	2.40	12.00	10.50	35.00	70.00
1974S	3.00	—	—	—	—	1991D	2.40	12.00	13.50	35.00	110
1975	2.00	11.00	10.00	—	—	1992	2.60	48.00	8.00	26.00	30.00
1975D	2.00	4.25	12.50	—	—	1992D	2.60	8.00	10.00	34.00	55.00
1976	1.80	15.00	20.00	22.00	21.00	1993	2.60	11.50	9.50	42.00	42.00
1976D	4.25	12.50	16.00	22.00	21.00	1993D	2.60	12.50	12.50	37.50	65.00
1977	2.00	4.25	12.50	17.00	28.50	1994	2.25	7.00	8.50	42.00	15.00
1977D	2.00	6.00	8.50	17.50	35.00	1994D	2.25	6.00	8.50	42.00	23.00
1978	2.00	4.25	7.50	16.00	44.00	1995	2.25	7.50	12.50	42.00	16.00
1978D	2.00	5.00	8.00	17.00	78.00	1995D	2.25	20.00	17.50	42.00	13.00
1979	1.75	5.00	8.50	17.00	27.50	1996	2.00	5.40	11.00	22.00	15.00
1979D	1.75	5.40	8.00	18.50	28.50	1996D	2.00	7.50	11.50	28.00	13.00
1980	1.75	4.25	8.50	17.00	20.00	1997	2.00	12.50	27.50	23.50	15.00
1980D	1.75	4.25	8.00	18.50	22.50	1997D	2.00	28.00	8.50	34.00	16.00
1981	1.75	4.25	8.00	16.00	30.00	1998	2.00	12.50	10.50	30.00	15.00
1981D	1.50	4.25	8.50	16.00	26.00	1998D	2.00	13.50	9.50	25.00	15.00
1982	1.75	160	275	210	62.50	1999P	1.75	4.25	13.50	—	18.50
1982D	1.75	48.00	58.00	90.00	60.00	1999D	1.75	5.40	9.50	—	17.50
1983	2.25	80.00	185	1,150	80.00	2000P	1.75	5.40	9.00	—	14.00
1983D	10.50	36.00	30.00	500	58.00	2000D	1.75	3.40	7.00	—	15.00
1984	3.50	25.00	9.50	17.50	37.50	2001P	1.75	4.25	9.00	—	18.00
1984D	15.00	5.00	21.50	30.00	47.50	2001D	1.75	4.25	7.00	—	15.00
1985	7.00	10.00	9.50	37.50	75.00	2002P	1.50	3.40	7.50	—	42.00
1985D	3.50	8.00	9.50	13.50	70.00	2002D	1.50	3.40	7.50	—	42.00
1986	35.00	8.00	27.50	125	130	2003	1.50	3.50	8.00	—	27.50
1986D	33.00	28.00	26.00	285	115	2003D	1.50	3.50	8.00	—	27.50
1987	4.00	6.00	7.50	16.00	92.50						

COLONIAL COINAGE

MARYLAND
LORD BALTIMORE

PENNY (DENARIUM)

KM#1 **Composition:** COPPER.

Date	AG	Good	VG	Fine	VF	XF	Unc
(1659) 4 known	—	—	—	—	—	—	—

4 PENCE (GROAT)

KM#2 **Composition:** SILVER. **Obverse:** Large bust.
Reverse: Large shield.

Date	AG	Good	VG	Fine	VF	XF	Unc
(1659)	750	1,250	2,500	4,500	8,500	15,000	—

KM#3 **Composition:** SILVER. **Obverse:** Small bust.
Reverse: Small shield.

Date	AG	Good	VG	Fine	VF	XF	Unc
(1659) unique	—	—	—	—	—	—	—

Note: Norweb $26,400

6 PENCE

KM#4 **Composition:** SILVER. **Obverse:** Small bust.
Note: Known in two other rare small-bust varieties and
two rare large-bust varieties.

Date	AG	Good	VG	Fine	VF	XF	Unc
(1659)	450	950	1,750	3,500	6,750	12,500	—

SHILLING

KM#6 **Composition:** SILVER. **Note:** Varieties exist;
one is very rare.

Date	AG	Good	VG	Fine	VF	XF	Unc
(1659)	500	1,000	2,000	4,000	8,000	14,500	—

MASSACHUSETTS
NEW ENGLAND

3 PENCE

KM#1 **Composition:** SILVER. **Obverse:** NE.
Reverse: III.

Date	AG	Good	VG	Fine	VF	XF	Unc
(1652) 2 known	—	—	—	—	—	—	—

6 PENCE

KM#2 **Composition:** SILVER. **Obverse:** NE.
Reverse: VI.

Date	AG	Good	VG	Fine	VF	XF	Unc
(1652) 8 known	—	—	—	—	—	—	—

Note: Garrett $75,000

SHILLING

KM#3 **Composition:** SILVER. **Obverse:** NE.
Reverse: XII.

Date	AG	Good	VG	Fine	VF	XF	Unc
(1652)	2,000	4,500	7,500	15,000	35,000	—	—

OAK TREE

2 PENCE

KM#7 **Composition:** SILVER.

Date	AG	Good	VG	Fine	VF	XF	Unc
1662	150	300	550	850	2,150	—	—

3 PENCE

KM#8 **Composition:** SILVER. **Note:** Two types of legends.

Date	AG	Good	VG	Fine	VF	XF	Unc
1652	200	400	650	1,000	2,600	—	—

6 PENCE

KM#9 **Composition:** SILVER. **Note:** Three types of legends.

Date	AG	Good	VG	Fine	VF	XF	Unc
1652	250	450	750	1,250	3,000	—	—

SHILLING

KM#10 **Composition:** SILVER. **Note:** Two types of legends.

Date	AG	Good	VG	Fine	VF	XF	Unc
1652	175	300	650	1,150	2,850	—	—

PINE TREE

3 PENCE

KM#11 **Composition:** SILVER. **Obverse:** Tree without berries.

Date	AG	Good	VG	Fine	VF	XF	Unc
1652	150	300	450	750	1,600	—	—

KM#12 **Composition:** SILVER. **Obverse:** Tree with berries.

Date	AG	Good	VG	Fine	VF	XF	Unc
1652	165	325	500	850	1,850	—	—

6 PENCE

KM#13 **Composition:** SILVER. **Obverse:** Tree without berries; "spiney tree".

Date	AG	Good	VG	Fine	VF	XF	Unc
1652	525	950	1,650	2,000	3,000	—	—

KM#14 **Composition:** SILVER. **Obverse:** Tree with berries.

Date	AG	Good	VG	Fine	VF	XF	Unc
1652	150	300	575	1,150	2,100	—	—

SHILLING

KM#15 **Composition:** SILVER. **Note:** Large planchet. Many varieties exist; some are very rare.

Date	AG	Good	VG	Fine	VF	XF	Unc
1652	200	425	775	1,350	2,650	—	—

KM#16 **Composition:** SILVER. **Note:** Small planchet; large dies. All examples are thought to be contemporary fabrications.

Date	AG	Good	VG	Fine	VF	XF	Unc
1652	—	—	—	—	—	—	—

KM#17 **Composition:** SILVER. **Note:** Small planchet; small dies. Many varieties exist; some are very rare.

Date	AG	Good	VG	Fine	VF	XF	Unc
1652	150	300	575	1,250	2,300	—	—

WILLOW TREE

3 PENCE

KM#4 **Composition:** SILVER.

Date	AG	Good	VG	Fine	VF	XF	Unc
1652 3 known	—	—	—	—	—	—	—

6 PENCE

KM#5   Composition: SILVER.

Date	AG	Good	VG	Fine	VF	XF	Unc
1652	3,500	7,500	10,000	18,000	35,000	—	—

SHILLING

KM#6   Composition: SILVER.

Date	AG	Good	VG	Fine	VF	XF	Unc
1652	4,000	10,000	12,500	20,000	36,500	—	—

NEW JERSEY

ST. PATRICK OR MARK NEWBY

FARTHING

KM#1   Composition: COPPER.

Date	AG	Good	VG	Fine	VF	XF	Unc
(1682)	20.00	40.00	80.00	200	425	—	—

KM#1a   Composition: SILVER.

Date	AG	Good	VG	Fine	VF	XF	Unc
(1682)	350	550	1,150	1,650	2,750	—	—

HALFPENNY

KM#2   Composition: COPPER.

Date	AG	Good	VG	Fine	VF	XF	Unc
(1682)	50.00	100.00	200	400	900	—	—

EARLY AMERICAN TOKENS

AMERICAN PLANTATIONS

1/24 REAL

KM#Tn5.1 **Composition:** TIN. **Obverse Legend:** ET HIB REX.

Date	AG	Good	VG	Fine	VF	XF	Unc
(1688)	65.00	125	165	210	285	450	—

KM#Tn5.3 **Composition:** TIN. **Reverse:** Horizontal 4.

Date	AG	Good	VG	Fine	VF	XF	Unc
(1688)	175	300	400	500	650	1,350	—

KM#Tn5.4 **Composition:** TIN. **Obverse Legend:** ET HIB REX.

Date	AG	Good	VG	Fine	VF	XF	Unc
(1688)	—	—	—	—	—	—	6,000

KM#Tn6 **Composition:** TIN. **Reverse:** Arms of Scotland left, Ireland right.

Date	AG	Good	VG	Fine	VF	XF	Unc
(1688)	450	750	1,250	2,000	2,500	—	—

KM#Tn5.2 **Composition:** TIN. **Obverse:** Rider's head left of "B" in legend. **Note:** Restrikes made in 1828 from two obverse dies.

Date	AG	Good	VG	Fine	VF	XF	Unc
(1828)	35.00	65.00	100.00	150	225	325	—

ELEPHANT

KM#Tn1.1 **Composition:** COPPER. **Note:** Thick planchet.

Date	AG	Good	VG	Fine	VF	XF	Unc
(1664)	60.00	100.00	150	250	450	850	—

KM#Tn1.2 **Composition:** COPPER. **Note:** Thin planchet.

Date	AG	Good	VG	Fine	VF	XF	Unc
(1664)	80.00	150	200	350	600	1,250	—

KM#Tn2 **Composition:** COPPER. **Reverse:** Diagonals tie shield.

Date	AG	Good	VG	Fine	VF	XF	Unc
(1664)	120	185	225	400	700	1,450	—

KM#Tn3 **Composition:** COPPER. **Reverse:** Sword right side of shield..

Date	AG	Good	VG	Fine	VF	XF	Unc
(1664) 3 known	—	—	—	—	—	—	—

Note: Norweb $1,320

KM#Tn4 **Composition:** COPPER. **Reverse Legend:** LON DON..

Date	AG	Good	VG	Fine	VF	XF	Unc
(1684)	175	300	500	1,000	1,850	3,750	—

KM#Tn7 **Composition:** COPPER. **Reverse Legend:** NEW ENGLAND..

Date	AG	Good	VG	Fine	VF	XF	Unc
(1694) 2 known	—	—	—	—	—	—	—

Note: Norweb $25,300

KM#Tn8.1 **Composition:** COPPER. **Reverse Legend:** CAROLINA (PROPRIETORS)..

Date	AG	Good	VG	Fine	VF	XF	Unc
(1694) 5 known	—	—	—	—	—	—	—

Note: Norweb $35,200

KM#Tn8.2 **Composition:** COPPER. **Reverse Legend:** CAROLINA (PROPRIETORS, O over E)..

Date	AG	Good	VG	Fine	VF	XF	Unc
1694	700	1,100	1,700	2,750	5,750	11,000	—

Note: Norweb $17,600

GLOUCESTER

KM#Tn15   Composition: COPPER.

Date	AG	Good	VG	Fine	VF	XF	Unc
(1714) 2 known	—	—	—	—	—	—	—

Note: Garrett $36,000

HIBERNIA-VOCE POPULI

FARTHING

KM#Tn21.1   Composition: COPPER. **Note:** Large letters

Date	AG	Good	VG	Fine	VF	XF	Unc
1760	90.00	150	275	450	750	1,550	—

KM#Tn21.2   Composition: COPPER. **Note:** Small letters

Date	AG	Good	VG	Fine	VF	XF	Unc
1760 extremely rare	—	—	—	—	—	—	—

Note: Norweb $5,940.

HALFPENNY

KM#Tn22   Composition: COPPER.

Date	AG	Good	VG	Fine	VF	XF	Unc
1700 date is error, extremely rare	—	—	—	—	—	—	—

Note: ex-Roper $575. Norweb $577.50. Stack's Americana, VF, $2,900

Date	AG	Good	VG	Fine	VF	XF	Unc
1760 varieties		10.00	30.00	50.00	100.00	185	350	—
1760 legend VOOE POPULI	20.00	35.00	60.00	110	200	400	—

HIGLEY OR GRANBY

KM#Tn16   Composition: COPPER. **Obverse Legend:** CONNECTICVT.. **Note:** THE VALVE OF THREE PENCE.

Date	AG	Good	VG	Fine	VF	XF	Unc
1737	—	—	—	—	—	—	—

Note: Garrett $16,000

KM#Tn17   Composition: COPPER. **Obverse Legend:** THE VALVE OF THREE PENCE.. **Reverse Legend:** I AM GOOD COPPER..

Date	AG	Good	VG	Fine	VF	XF	Unc
1737 2 known	—	—	—	—	—	—	—

Note: ex-Norweb $6,875

KM#Tn18.1   Composition: COPPER. **Obverse Legend:** VALUE ME AS YOU PLEASE.. **Reverse Legend:** I AM GOOD COPPER..

Date	AG	Good	VG	Fine	VF	XF	Unc
1737	6,500	8,500	10,500	14,500	25,000	—	—

KM#Tn18.2   Composition: COPPER. **Obverse Legend:** VALVE ME AS YOU PLEASE.. **Reverse Legend:** I AM GOOD COPPER..

Date	AG	Good	VG	Fine	VF	XF	Unc
1737 2 known	—	—	—	—	—	—	—

KM#Tn19   Composition: COPPER. **Reverse:** Broad axe..

Date	AG	Good	VG	Fine	VF	XF	Unc
(1737)	—	—	—	—	—	—	—

Note: Garrett $45,000

Date	AG	Good	VG	Fine	VF	XF	Unc
1739 5 known	—	—	—	—	—	—	—

Note: Eliasberg $12,650. Oechsner $9,900. Steinberg (holed) $4,400.

Date	AG	Good	VG	Fine	VF	XF	Unc
1739 5 known	—	—	—	—	—	—	—

Note: Eliasberg $12,650. Oechsner $9,900. Steinberg (holed) $4,400.

KM#Tn20   Composition: COPPER. **Obverse Legend:** THE WHEELE GOES ROUND.. **Reverse:** J CUT MY WAY THROUGH..

Date	AG	Good	VG	Fine	VF	XF	Unc
(1737) unique	—	—	—	—	—	—	—

Note: Roper $60,500

NEW YORKE

KM#Tn9 **Composition:** BRASS. **Note:** The 1700 date is circa.

Date	AG	Good	VG	Fine	VF	XF	Unc
1700	650	1,250	2,850	4,500	7,500	—	—

KM#Tn9a **Composition:** WHITE METAL.

Date	AG	Good	VG	Fine	VF	XF	Unc
1700 4 known	—	—	—	—	—	—	—

PITT

FARTHING

KM#Tn23 **Composition:** COPPER.

Date	AG	Good	VG	Fine	VF	XF	Unc
1766	—	—	—	1,350	2,850	6,000	—

HALFPENNY

KM#Tn24 **Composition:** COPPER.

Date	AG	Good	VG	Fine	VF	XF	Unc
1766	45.00	85.00	175	350	700	1,500	—

COLONIAL COINAGE

ROYAL PATENT COINAGE

HIBERNIA

FARTHING

KM#20 **Composition:** COPPER. **Note:** Pattern.

Date	AG	Good	VG	Fine	VF	XF	Unc
1722	25.00	50.00	125	220	325	700	—

KM#24 **Composition:** COPPER. **Obverse:** 1722 obverse. **Obverse Legend:** …D:G:REX..

Date	AG	Good	VG	Fine	VF	XF	Unc
1723	20.00	40.00	60.00	90.00	150	350	—

KM#25 **Composition:** COPPER. **Obverse Legend:** DEI • GRATIA • REX •.

Date	AG	Good	VG	Fine	VF	XF	Unc
1723	10.00	20.00	40.00	65.00	90.00	200	—

KM#25a **Composition:** SILVER.

Date	Good	VG	Fine	VF	XF	Unc	Proof
1723	—	—	—	800	1,600	—	2,700
1724	45.00	75.00	125	250	485		

HALFPENNY

KM#21 **Composition:** COPPER. **Reverse:** Harp left, head right.

Date	AG	Good	VG	Fine	VF	XF	Unc
1722	—	15.00	35.00	65.00	135	350	—

KM#22 **Composition:** COPPER. **Obverse:** Harp left, head right. **Note:** Pattern.

Date	AG	Good	VG	Fine	VF	XF	Unc
1722	7.00	—	—	1,150	1,750	3,000	—

KM#23.1 **Composition:** COPPER. **Reverse:** Harp right.

Date	AG	Good	VG	Fine	VF	XF	Unc
1722	2.00	15.00	35.00	60.00	125	250	—
1723	7.00	15.00	25.00	40.00	80.00	175	—
1723/22	10.00	20.00	45.00	90.00	185	375	—
1724	7.00	15.00	35.00	60.00	125	265	—

KM#23.2 **Composition:** COPPER. **Obverse:** DEII error in legend.

Date	AG	Good	VG	Fine	VF	XF	Unc
1722	40.00	90.00	180	300	500	750	—

KM#26 **Composition:** COPPER. **Reverse:** Large head. **Note:** Rare. Generally mint state only. Probably a pattern.

Date	AG	Good	VG	Fine	VF	XF	Unc
1723	—	—	—	—	—	—	—

KM#27 **Composition:** COPPER. **Reverse:** Continuous legend over head.

Date	AG	Good	VG	Fine	VF	XF	Unc
1724	30.00	65.00	150	300	475	750	—

ROSA AMERICANA

HALFPENNY

KM#1 **Composition:** COPPER. **Obverse Legend:** D • G • REX •.

Date	AG	Good	VG	Fine	VF	XF	Unc
1722	20.00	40.00	60.00	100.00	220	475	—

KM#2 **Composition:** COPPER. **Obverse:** Uncrowned rose. **Obverse Legend:** DEI GRATIA REX.. **Note:** Several varieties exist.

Date	AG	Good	VG	Fine	VF	XF	Unc
1722	18.00	35.00	55.00	100.00	200	475	—
1723	285	525	750	1,350	2,250	—	—

KM#3 **Composition:** COPPER. **Reverse Legend:** VTILE DVLCI.

Date	AG	Good	VG	Fine	VF	XF	Unc
1722	250	450	650	1,100	—	—	—

KM#9 **Composition:** COPPER. **Reverse:** Crowned
rose.

Date	AG	Good	VG	Fine	VF	XF	Unc
1723	18.00	35.00	55.00	100.00	200	450	—

PENNY

KM#4 **Composition:** COPPER. **Reverse Legend:**
UTILE DULCI. **Note:** Several varieties exist.

Date	AG	Good	VG	Fine	VF	XF	Unc
1722	18.00	35.00	55.00	100.00	175	385	—

KM#5 **Composition:** COPPER. **Note:** Several
varieties exist. Also known in two rare pattern types with
long hair ribbons, one with V's for U's on the obverse.

Date	AG	Good	VG	Fine	VF	XF	Unc
1722	18.00	35.00	55.00	100.00	220	475	—

KM#10 **Composition:** COPPER. **Note:** Several
varieties exist.

Date	AG	Good	VG	Fine	VF	XF	Unc
1723	18.00	35.00	55.00	100.00	200	420	—

KM#12 **Composition:** COPPER. **Note:** Pattern.

Date	AG	Good	VG	Fine	VF	XF	Unc
1724 2 known	—	—	—	—	—	—	—

KM#13 **Composition:** COPPER.

Date	AG	Good	VG	Fine	VF	XF	Unc
(1724) 5 known	—	—	—	—	—	—	—

Note: Norweb $2,035

KM#14 **Composition:** COPPER. **Obverse:** George
II. **Note:** Pattern.

Date	AG	Good	VG	Fine	VF	XF	Unc
1727 2 known	—	—	—	—	—	—	—

2 PENCE

KM#6 **Composition:** COPPER. **Reverse:** Motto with
scroll.

Date	AG	Good	VG	Fine	VF	XF	Unc
(1722)	35.00	60.00	110	200	350	700	—

KM#7 **Composition:** COPPER. **Reverse:** Motto
without scroll.

Date	AG	Good	VG	Fine	VF	XF	Unc
(1722) 3 known	—	—	—	—	—	—	—

COLONIAL COINAGE

KM#8.1   Composition: COPPER. **Obverse:** Period after REX. **Reverse:** Dated.

Date	AG	Good	VG	Fine	VF	XF	Unc
1722	25.00	40.00	70.00	125	265	500	—

KM#8.2   Composition: COPPER. **Obverse:** Without period after REX.

Date	AG	Good	VG	Fine	VF	XF	Unc
1722	22.00	40.00	70.00	125	275	525	—

KM#11   Composition: COPPER. **Note:** Several varieties exist.

Date	AG	Good	VG	Fine	VF	XF	Unc
1723	25.00	45.00	75.00	140	285	550	—

KM#15   Composition: COPPER. **Note:** Pattern. Two varieties exist; both extremely rare.

Date	AG	Good	VG	Fine	VF	XF	Unc
1724	—	—	—	—	—	—	—

Note: ex-Garrett $5,775. Stack's Americana, XF, $10,925

KM#16   Composition: COPPER. **Note:** Pattern.

Date	AG	Good	VG	Fine	VF	XF	Unc
1733 4 known	—	—	—	—	—	—	—

Note: Norweb $19,800

VIRGINIA HALFPENNY

KM#Tn25.1   Composition: COPPER. **Reverse:** Small 7s in date.. **Note:** Struck on Irish halfpenny planchets.

Date	Good	VG	Fine	VF	XF	Unc	Proof
1773	—	—	—	—	—	—	3,500

KM#Tn25.2   Composition: COPPER. **Obverse:** Period after GEORGIVS.. **Reverse:** Varieties with 7 or 8 strings in harp..

Date	AG	Good	VG	Fine	VF	XF	Unc
1773	6.00	12.00	25.00	50.00	100.00	250	465

KM#Tn25.3   Composition: COPPER. **Obverse:** Without period after GEORGIVS.. **Reverse:** Varieties with 6, 7 or 8 strings in harp..

Date	AG	Good	VG	Fine	VF	XF	Unc
1773	7.00	15.00	30.00	60.00	135	275	525

KM#Tn25.4   Composition: COPPER. **Obverse:** Without period after GEORGIVS.. **Reverse:** 8 harp strings, dot on cross..

Date	AG	Good	VG	Fine	VF	XF	Unc
1773	—	—	—	—	—	—	—

Note: ex-Steinberg $2,600

KM#Tn26   Composition: SILVER. **Note:** So-called "shilling" silver proofs.

Date	AG	Good	VG	Fine	VF	XF	Unc
1774 6 known	—	—	—	—	—	—	—

Note: Garrett $23,000

REVOLUTIONARY COINAGE
CONTINENTAL "DOLLAR".

KM#EA1   **Composition:** PEWTER   **Obverse Legend:** CURRENCY.

Date	AG	Good	VG	Fine	VF	XF	Unc
1776	—	—	1,850	3,000	4,750	8,750	18,500

KM#EA2   **Composition:** PEWTER   **Obverse Legend:** CURRENCY, EG FECIT.

Date	AG	Good	VG	Fine	VF	XF	Unc
1776	—	—	1,750	2,850	4,250	7,750	16,000

KM#EA2a   **Composition:** SILVER   **Obverse Legend:** CURRENCY, EG FECIT.

Date	AG	Good	VG	Fine	VF	XF	Unc
1776 2 known	—	—	—	—	—	—	—

KM#EA3   **Composition:** PEWTER   **Obverse Legend:** CURRENCY.

Date	AG	Good	VG	Fine	VF	XF	Unc
1776 extremely rare	—	—	—	—	—	—	—

KM#EA4   **Composition:** PEWTER   **Obverse Legend:** CURRENCY. **Reverse:** Floral cross.

Date	AG	Good	VG	Fine	VF	XF	Unc
1776 3 recorded	—	—	—	—	—	—	—

Note: Norweb $50,600. Johnson $25,300

KM#EA5   **Composition:** PEWTER   **Obverse Legend:** CURENCY.

Date	AG	Good	VG	Fine	VF	XF	Unc
1776	—	—	1,650	2,750	4,000	8,000	16,000

KM#EA5a   **Composition:** BRASS   **Obverse Legend:** CURENCY. **Note:** Two varieties exist.

Date	AG	Good	VG	Fine	VF	XF	Unc
1776	—	—	—	—	13,500	17,500	—

KM#EA5b   **Composition:** SILVER   **Obverse Legend:** CURENCY.

Date	AG	Good	VG	Fine	VF	XF	Unc
1776 unique	—	—	—	—	—	—	—

Note: Romano $99,000

COLONIAL COINAGE

STATE COINAGE
CONNECTICUT

KM#1   **Composition:** COPPER **Obverse:** Bust facing right.

Date	AG	Good	VG	Fine	VF	XF	Unc
1785	20.00	30.00	50.00	85.00	190	450	—

KM#2   **Composition:** COPPER **Obverse:** "African head."

Date	AG	Good	VG	Fine	VF	XF	Unc
1785	25.00	45.00	85.00	200	450	1,500	—

KM#3.1   **Composition:** COPPER **Obverse:** Bust facing left.

Date	AG	Good	VG	Fine	VF	XF	Unc
1785	60.00	100.00	150	275	400	750	—
1786	20.00	30.00	50.00	90.00	185	465	—
1787	22.00	35.00	60.00	110	125	350	—
1788	20.00	30.00	50.00	100.00	220	500	—

KM#4   **Composition:** COPPER **Obverse:** Small mailed bust facing left. **Reverse Legend:** ETLIB INDE.

Date	AG	Good	VG	Fine	VF	XF	Unc
1786	22.00	35.00	55.00	85.00	165	400	—

KM#5   **Composition:** COPPER **Obverse:** Small mailed bust facing right. **Reverse Legend:** INDE ET LIB.

Date	AG	Good	VG	Fine	VF	XF	Unc
1786	30.00	55.00	75.00	115	225	475	—

KM#6   **Composition:** COPPER **Obverse:** Large mailed bust facing right.

Date	AG	Good	VG	Fine	VF	XF	Unc
1786	30.00	50.00	90.00	165	350	850	—

COLONIAL COINAGE

KM#7 **Composition:** COPPER **Obverse:** "Hercules head."

Date	AG	Good	VG	Fine	VF	XF	Unc
1786	25.00	40.00	75.00	135	300	700	—

KM#8.1 **Composition:** COPPER **Obverse:** Draped bust.

Date	AG	Good	VG	Fine	VF	XF	Unc
1786	22.00	35.00	65.00	120	275	600	—

KM#9 **Composition:** COPPER **Obverse:** Small head. **Reverse Legend:** ETLIB INDE.

Date	AG	Good	VG	Fine	VF	XF	Unc
1787	25.00	40.00	90.00	150	350	800	—

KM#10 **Composition:** COPPER **Obverse:** Small head. **Reverse Legend:** INDE ET LIB.

Date	AG	Good	VG	Fine	VF	XF	Unc
1787	75.00	135	175	275	450	950	—

KM#11 **Composition:** COPPER **Obverse:** Medium bust. **Note:** Two reverse legend types exist.

Date	AG	Good	VG	Fine	VF	XF	Unc
1787	50.00	80.00	140	200	325	625	—

KM#12 **Composition:** COPPER **Obverse:** "Muttonhead" variety. **Note:** Extremely rare with legend INDE ET LIB.

Date	AG	Good	VG	Fine	VF	XF	Unc
1787	30.00	50.00	120	250	650	1,500	—

KM#3.3 **Composition:** COPPER **Obverse:** Perfect date. **Reverse Legend:** IN DE ET.

Date	AG	Good	VG	Fine	VF	XF	Unc
1787	35.00	65.00	85.00	135	250	600	—

KM#13   **Composition:** COPPER   **Obverse:** "Laughing head."

Date	AG	Good	VG	Fine	VF	XF	Unc
1787	22.00	35.00	60.00	110	250	700	—

KM#14   **Composition:** COPPER   **Obverse:** "Horned head."

Date	AG	Good	VG	Fine	VF	XF	Unc
1787	15.00	25.00	40.00	70.00	175	475	—

KM#15   **Composition:** COPPER **Reverse Legend:** IND ET LIB.

Date	AG	Good	VG	Fine	VF	XF	Unc
1787/8	25.00	40.00	75.00	130	250	650	—
1787/1887	20.00	30.00	50.00	90.00	200	520	—

KM#16   **Composition:** COPPER   **Obverse Legend:** CONNECT. **Reverse Legend:** INDE ET LIB. **Note:** Two additional scarce reverse legend types exist.

Date	AG	Good	VG	Fine	VF	XF	Unc
1787	22.00	37.50	60.00	115	220	550	—

KM#8.2   **Composition:** COPPER   **Obverse:** Draped bust. **Note:** Many varieties.

Date	AG	Good	VG	Fine	VF	XF	Unc
1787	12.00	20.00	40.00	80.00	135	275	—

KM#8.3   **Composition:** COPPER   **Obverse Legend:** AUCIORI.

Date	AG	Good	VG	Fine	VF	XF	Unc
1787	15.00	25.00	50.00	110	250	600	—

KM#8.4   **Composition:** COPPER   **Obverse Legend:** AUCTOPI.

Date	AG	Good	VG	Fine	VF	XF	Unc
1787	20.00	30.00	60.00	125	265	650	—

KM#8.5   **Composition:** COPPER   **Obverse Legend:** AUCTOBI.

Date	AG	Good	VG	Fine	VF	XF	Unc
1787	15.00	25.00	50.00	110	225	550	—

KM#8.6   **Composition:** COPPER   **Obverse Legend:** CONNFC.

Date	AG	Good	VG	Fine	VF	XF	Unc
1787	12.00	20.00	40.00	85.00	200	525	—

KM#8.7   **Composition:** COPPER   **Obverse Legend:** CONNLC.

Date	AG	Good	VG	Fine	VF	XF	Unc
1787	—	30.00	60.00	125	265	650	—

KM#8.8   **Composition:** COPPER **Reverse Legend:** FNDE.

Date	AG	Good	VG	Fine	VF	XF	Unc
1787	15.00	25.00	45.00	90.00	210	535	—

KM#8.9   **Composition:** COPPER **Reverse Legend:** ETLIR.

Date	AG	Good	VG	Fine	VF	XF	Unc
1787	15.00	25.00	45.00	90.00	210	535	—

KM#8.10   **Composition:** COPPER **Reverse Legend:** ETIIB.

Date	AG	Good	VG	Fine	VF	XF	Unc
1787	20.00	30.00	50.00	100.00	225	550	—

KM#20   **Composition:** COPPER   **Obverse:** Mailed bust facing right.

Date	AG	Good	VG	Fine	VF	XF	Unc
1788	15.00	25.00	45.00	90.00	200	425	—

KM#21   **Composition:** COPPER   **Obverse:** Small mailed bust facing right.

Date	AG	Good	VG	Fine	VF	XF	Unc
1788	75.00	150	285	550	1,100	2,500	—

KM#3.4   **Composition:** COPPER   **Obverse Legend:** CONNLC.

Date	AG	Good	VG	Fine	VF	XF	Unc
1788	15.00	25.00	40.00	80.00	175	400	—

KM#22.1   **Composition:** COPPER   **Obverse:** Draped bust facing left. **Reverse Legend:** INDE ET LIB.

Date	AG	Good	VG	Fine	VF	XF	Unc
1788	12.00	20.00	35.00	55.00	135	375	—

KM#22.2   **Composition:** COPPER **Reverse Legend:** INDLET LIB.

Date	AG	Good	VG	Fine	VF	XF	Unc
1788	20.00	30.00	55.00	90.00	185	400	—

KM#22.3   **Composition:** COPPER   **Obverse Legend:** CONNLC. **Reverse Legend:** INDE ET LIB.

Date	AG	Good	VG	Fine	VF	XF	Unc
1788	22.00	35.00	60.00	100.00	200	425	—

KM#22.4   **Composition:** COPPER   **Obverse Legend:** CONNLC. **Reverse Legend:** INDL ET LIB.

Date	AG	Good	VG	Fine	VF	XF	Unc
1788	22.00	35.00	60.00	100.00	200	425	—

MASSACHUSETTS

HALFPENNY

KM#17   Composition: COPPER

Date	AG	Good	VG	Fine	VF	XF	Unc
1776 unique	—	—	—	—	—	—	—

Note: Garrett $40,000

PENNY

KM#18   Composition: COPPER

Date	AG	Good	VG	Fine	VF	XF	Unc
1776 unique	—	—	—	—	—	—	—

HALF CENT

KM#19   Composition: COPPER **Note:** Varieties exist; some are rare.

Date	AG	Good	VG	Fine	VF	XF	Unc
1787	30.00	50.00	90.00	175	350	800	—
1788	35.00	55.00	100.00	185	375	850	—

CENT

KM#20.1   Composition: COPPER **Reverse:** Arrows in right talon

Date	AG	Good	VG	Fine	VF	XF	Unc
1787 7 known	—	—	—	—	—	—	—

Note: Ex-Bushnell-Brand $8,800. Garrett $5,500

KM#20.2 **Composition:** COPPER **Reverse:** Arrows in left talon

Date	AG	Good	VG	Fine	VF	XF	Unc
1787	25.00	40.00	65.00	120	285	785	—

KM#20.3 **Composition:** COPPER **Reverse:** "Horned eagle" die break

Date	AG	Good	VG	Fine	VF	XF	Unc
1787	28.00	45.00	70.00	130	300	785	—

KM#20.4 **Composition:** COPPER **Reverse:** Without period after Massachusetts

Date	AG	Good	VG	Fine	VF	XF	Unc
1788	28.00	45.00	70.00	135	320	850	—

KM#20.5 **Composition:** COPPER **Reverse:** Period after Massachusetts, normal S's

Date	AG	Good	VG	Fine	VF	XF	Unc
1788	28.00	45.00	70.00	120	275	775	—

KM#20.6 **Composition:** COPPER **Reverse:** Period after Massachusetts, S's like 8's

Date	AG	Good	VG	Fine	VF	XF	Unc
1788	22.00	35.00	60.00	120	275	775	—

COLONIAL COINAGE

NEW HAMPSHIRE

KM#1 **Composition:** COPPER

Date	AG	Good	VG	Fine	VF	XF	Unc
1776 extremely rare	—	—	—	—	—	—	—

Note: Garrett $13,000

NEW JERSEY

KM#8 **Composition:** COPPER **Obverse:** Date below draw bar.

Date	AG	Good	VG	Fine	VF	XF	Unc
1786 extremely rare	—	—	—	—	—	—	—

Note: Garrett $52,000

KM#9 **Composition:** COPPER **Obverse:** Large horse head, date below plow, no coulter on plow.

Date	AG	Good	VG	Fine	VF	XF	Unc
1786	75.00	150	285	550	1,450	5,500	—

KM#10 **Composition:** COPPER **Reverse:** Narrow shield, straight beam.

Date	AG	Good	VG	Fine	VF	XF	Unc
1786	25.00	40.00	65.00	150	350	975	—

KM#11.1 **Composition:** COPPER **Reverse:** Wide shield, curved beam. **Note:** Varieties exist.

Date	AG	Good	VG	Fine	VF	XF	Unc
1786	28.00	45.00	85.00	180	425	1,000	—

KM#11.2 **Composition:** COPPER **Obverse:** Bridle variety (die break). **Note:** Reverse varieties exist.

Date	AG	Good	VG	Fine	VF	XF	Unc
1786	30.00	50.00	90.00	185	425	1,000	—

KM#12.1 **Composition:** COPPER **Reverse:** Plain shield. **Note:** Small planchet. Varieties exist.

Date	AG	Good	VG	Fine	VF	XF	Unc
1787	20.00	30.00	60.00	100.00	200	675	—

KM#12.2 **Composition:** COPPER **Reverse:** Shield heavily outlined. **Note:** Small planchet.

Date	AG	Good	VG	Fine	VF	XF	Unc
1787	22.00	35.00	75.00	125	285	800	—

KM#13 **Composition:** COPPER **Obverse:** "Serpent head."

Date	AG	Good	VG	Fine	VF	XF	Unc
1787	40.00	60.00	120	285	700	1,275	—

KM#14 **Composition:** COPPER **Reverse:** Plain shield. **Note:** Large planchet. Varieties exist.

Date	AG	Good	VG	Fine	VF	XF	Unc
1787	22.00	35.00	75.00	135	300	850	—

KM#15 **Composition:** COPPER **Reverse Legend:** PLURIBS.

Date	AG	Good	VG	Fine	VF	XF	Unc
1787	30.00	50.00	100.00	225	600	1,100	—

KM#16 **Composition:** COPPER **Obverse:** Horse's head facing right. **Note:** Varieties exist.

Date	AG	Good	VG	Fine	VF	XF	Unc
1788	20.00	30.00	65.00	125	375	750	—

KM#17 **Composition:** COPPER **Reverse:** Fox before legend. **Note:** Varieties exist.

Date	AG	Good	VG	Fine	VF	XF	Unc
1788	—	55.00	110	275	725	1,550	—

KM#18 **Composition:** COPPER **Obverse:** Horse's head facing left. **Note:** Varieties exist.

Date	AG	Good	VG	Fine	VF	XF	Unc
1788	65.00	125	285	575	1,150	3,000	—

NEW YORK

NOVA EBORACS

KM#1 **Composition:** COPPER **Obverse Legend:** NON VI VIRTUTE VICI.

Date	AG	Good	VG	Fine	VF	XF	Unc
1786	1,200	2,200	3,750	6,000	11,500	—	—

KM#2 **Composition:** COPPER **Obverse:** Eagle on globe facing right.

Date	AG	Good	VG	Fine	VF	XF	Unc
1787	175	750	1,250	3,500	6,500	12,750	—

KM#3   Composition: COPPER **Obverse:** Eagle on globe facing left.

Date	AG	Good	VG	Fine	VF	XF	Unc
1787	350	700	1,200	3,250	6,000	12,000	—

KM#4   Composition: COPPER **Reverse:** Large eagle, arrows in right talon.

Date	AG	Good	VG	Fine	VF	XF	Unc
1787 2 known	—	—	—	—	—	—	—

Note: Norweb $18,700

KM#5   Composition: COPPER **Obverse:** George Clinton.

Date	AG	Good	VG	Fine	VF	XF	Unc
1787	2,250	4,000	5,500	9,500	20,000	—	—

KM#6   Composition: COPPER **Obverse:** Indian. **Reverse:** New York arms.

Date	AG	Good	VG	Fine	VF	XF	Unc
1787	1,000	2,000	4,000	6,500	10,500	25,000	—

KM#7   Composition: COPPER **Obverse:** Indian. **Reverse:** Eagle on globe.

Date	AG	Good	VG	Fine	VF	XF	Unc
1787	1,650	3,000	6,500	11,500	23,500	35,000	—

KM#8   Composition: COPPER **Obverse:** Indian. **Reverse:** George III.

Date	AG	Good	VG	Fine	VF	XF	Unc
1787	125	200	350	650	1,350	4,200	—

COLONIAL COINAGE

KM#9 **Composition:** COPPER **Obverse Legend:** NOVA EBORAC. **Reverse:** Figure seated right.

Date	AG	Good	VG	Fine	VF	XF	Unc
1787	40.00	75.00	125	260	525	1,100	—

KM#10 **Composition:** COPPER **Reverse:** Figure seated left.

Date	AG	Good	VG	Fine	VF	XF	Unc
1787	35.00	55.00	110	225	500	1,000	—

KM#11 **Composition:** COPPER **Obverse:** Small head, star above. **Obverse Legend:** NOVA EBORAC.

Date	AG	Good	VG	Fine	VF	XF	Unc
1787	300	600	1,750	3,000	4,500	6,500	—

KM#12 **Composition:** COPPER **Obverse:** Large head, two quatrefoils left. **Obverse Legend:** NOVA EBORAC.

Date	AG	Good	VG	Fine	VF	XF	Unc
1787	200	300	400	650	1,150	2,500	—

MACHIN MILL

KM#13 Composition: COPPER **Note:** Crude, lightweight imitations of the British Halfpenny were struck at Machin's Mill in large quantities bearing the Obverse legends: GEORGIVS II REX, GEORGIVS III REX, and GEORGIUS III REX, with the BRITANNIA reverse, and dates of: 1747, 1771, 1772, 1774, 1775, 1776, 1777, 1778, 1784, 1785, 1786, 1787 and 1788. Other dates may exist. There are many different mulings. These pieces, which have plain crosses in the shield of Britannia, are not to be confused with the very common British made imitations, which usually have outlined crosses in the shield. Some varieties are very rare.

Date	AG	Good	VG	Fine	VF	XF	Unc
	—	—	—	—	—	—	—

VERMONT

KM#1 Composition: COPPER **Reverse Legend:** IMMUNE COLUMBIA.

Date	AG	Good	VG	Fine	VF	XF	Unc
(1785)	1,250	2,000	3,000	5,000	9,000	—	—

KM#2 Composition: COPPER **Obverse Legend:** VERMONTIS.

Date	AG	Good	VG	Fine	VF	XF	Unc
1785	120	200	300	600	1,150	—	—

KM#3 Composition: COPPER **Obverse Legend:** VERMONTS.

Date	AG	Good	VG	Fine	VF	XF	Unc
1785	85.00	150	225	450	900	3,200	—

KM#4 **Composition:** COPPER **Obverse Legend:** VERMONTENSIUM.

Date	AG	Good	VG	Fine	VF	XF	Unc
1786	75.00	125	200	450	950	3,250	—

KM#5 **Composition:** COPPER **Obverse:** "Baby head." **Reverse:** AUCTORI: VERMONS.

Date	AG	Good	VG	Fine	VF	XF	Unc
1786	120	200	300	550	1,150	4,500	—

KM#6 **Composition:** COPPER **Obverse:** Bust facing left. **Obverse Legend:** VERMON: AUCTORI:.

Date	AG	Good	VG	Fine	VF	XF	Unc
1786	60.00	100.00	185	300	750	2,250	—
1787 extremely rare	—	—	—	—	—	—	—

KM#7 **Composition:** COPPER **Obverse:** Bust facing right. **Note:** Varieties exist.

Date	AG	Good	VG	Fine	VF	XF	Unc
1787	—	—	—	—	—	—	—

KM#8   Composition: COPPER Note: Britannia mule.

Date	AG	Good	VG	Fine	VF	XF	Unc
1787	25.00	40.00	65.00	140	285	950	—

KM#9.2   Composition: COPPER Obverse: "C" backward in AUCTORI.

Date	AG	Good	VG	Fine	VF	XF	Unc
1788 extremely rare	—	—	—	—	—	—	—

Note: Stack's Americana, Fine, $9,775

KM#10   Composition: COPPER Reverse Legend: ET LIB INDE.

Date	AG	Good	VG	Fine	VF	XF	Unc
1788	75.00	125	300	600	1,100	—	—

KM#11   Composition: COPPER Note: George III Rex mule.

Date	AG	Good	VG	Fine	VF	XF	Unc
1788	85.00	145	325	650	1,250	2,750	—

KM#9.1   Composition: COPPER Reverse Legend: INDE ET LIB. Note: Varieties exist.

Date	AG	Good	VG	Fine	VF	XF	Unc
1788	40.00	65.00	120	220	550	1,850	—

EARLY AMERICAN TOKENS

ALBANY CHURCH "PENNY"

KM#Tn54.1 **Composition:** COPPER **Obverse:** Without "D" above church. **Note:** Uniface.

Date	AG	Good	VG	Fine	VF	XF	Unc
5 known	—	—	3,500	7,000	14,000	—	—

KM#Tn54.2 **Composition:** COPPER **Obverse:** With "D" above church. **Note:** Uniface.

Date	AG	Good	VG	Fine	VF	XF	Unc
rare	—	—	3,000	5,000	10,000	—	—

AUCTORI PLEBIS

KM#Tn50 **Composition:** COPPER

Date	AG	Good	VG	Fine	VF	XF	Unc
1787	20.00	45.00	90.00	150	300	600	—

BAR "CENT"

KM#Tn49 **Composition:** COPPER

Date	AG	Good	VG	Fine	VF	XF	Unc
	85.00	150	275	675	1,200	2,500	—

CASTORLAND "HALF DOLLAR"

KM#Tn87.1 Composition: SILVER Edge: Reeded.

Date	AG	Good	VG	Fine	VF	XF	Unc
1796	—	—	—	—	—	3,550	—

KM#Tn87.1a Composition: COPPER Edge: Reeded.

Date	AG	Good	VG	Fine	VF	XF	Unc
1796 3 known	—	—	—	—	—	1,650	—

KM#Tn87.1b Composition: BRASS Edge: Reeded.

Date	AG	Good	VG	Fine	VF	XF	Unc
1796 unique	—	—	—	—	—	—	—

KM#Tn87.2 Composition: COPPER Edge: Plain. Note: Thin planchet.

Date	AG	Good	VG	Fine	VF	XF	Unc
1796 unique	—	—	—	—	—	—	—

KM#Tn87.3 Composition: SILVER Edge: Reeded. Note: Thin planchet. Restrike.

Date	Good	VG	Fine	VF	XF	Unc	Proof
1796	—	—	—	—	—	325	—

KM#Tn87.4 Composition: SILVER Edge: Lettered. Edge Lettering: ARGENT. Note: Thin planchet. Restrike.

Date	Good	VG	Fine	VF	XF	Unc	Proof
1796	—	—	—	—	—	60.00	—

KM#Tn87.3a Composition: COPPER Edge: Reeded. Note: Thin planchet. Restrike.

Date	Good	VG	Fine	VF	XF	Unc	Proof
1796	—	—	—	—	—	285	—

KM#Tn87.5 Composition: COPPER Edge: Lettered. Edge Lettering: CUIVRE. Note: Thin planchet. Restrike.

Date	Good	VG	Fine	VF	XF	Unc	Proof
1796	—	—	—	—	—	40.00	—

CHALMERS

3 PENCE

KM#Tn45 Composition: SILVER

Date	AG	Good	VG	Fine	VF	XF	Unc
1783	250	500	1,000	1,500	2,650	5,500	—

6 PENCE

KM#Tn46.1 Composition: SILVER Reverse: Small date

Date	AG	Good	VG	Fine	VF	XF	Unc
1783	350	700	1,500	2,250	5,500	12,000	—

KM#Tn46.2 Composition: SILVER Reverse: Large date

Date	AG	Good	VG	Fine	VF	XF	Unc
1783	300	600	1,300	2,000	4,000	10,000	—

SHILLING

KM#Tn47.1 **Composition:** SILVER **Reverse:** Birds with long worm

Date	AG	Good	VG	Fine	VF	XF	Unc
1783	180	300	500	1,000	2,000	4,500	—

KM#Tn47.2 **Composition:** SILVER **Reverse:** Birds with short worm

Date	AG	Good	VG	Fine	VF	XF	Unc
1783	150	250	475	900	1,850	4,500	—

KM#Tn48 **Composition:** SILVER **Reverse:** Rings and stars

Date	AG	Good	VG	Fine	VF	XF	Unc
1783 4 known	—	—	—	—	—	—	—

Note: Garrett $75,000

COPPER COMPANY OF UPPER CANADA

HALFPENNY

KM#Tn86 **Composition:** COPPER

Date	Good	VG	Fine	VF	XF	Unc	Proof
1796	—	—	—	—	—	—	3,750

FRANKLIN PRESS

KM#Tn73 **Composition:** COPPER **Edge:** Plain.

Date	AG	Good	VG	Fine	VF	XF	Unc
1794	18.00	35.00	55.00	85.00	175	300	600

KENTUCKY TOKEN

KM#Tn70.1 **Composition:** COPPER **Edge:** Plain. **Note:** 1793 date is circa.

Date	AG	Good	VG	Fine	VF	XF	Unc
1793	12.00	25.00	40.00	60.00	100.00	265	575

KM#Tn70.2 **Composition:** COPPER **Edge:** Engrailed.

Date	AG	Good	VG	Fine	VF	XF	Unc
	35.00	75.00	125	200	350	950	1,850

KM#Tn70.3 **Composition:** COPPER **Edge:** Lettered. **Edge Lettering:** PAYABLE AT BEDWORTH.

Date	AG	Good	VG	Fine	VF	XF	Unc
unique	—	—	—	—	—	1,980	—

KM#Tn70.4 **Composition:** COPPER **Edge:** Lettered. **Edge Lettering:** PAYABLE AT LANCASTER.

Date	AG	Good	VG	Fine	VF	XF	Unc
	14.00	28.00	45.00	65.00	110	285	725

KM#Tn70.5 **Composition:** COPPER **Edge:** Lettered. **Edge Lettering:** PAYABLE AT I.FIELDING.

Date	AG	Good	VG	Fine	VF	XF	Unc
unique	—	—	—	—	—	—	—

KM#Tn70.6 **Composition:** COPPER **Edge:** Lettered. **Edge Lettering:** PAYABLE AT W. PARKERS.

Date	AG	Good	VG	Fine	VF	XF	Unc
unique	—	—	—	—	1,800	—	—

KM#Tn70.7 **Composition:** COPPER **Edge:** Ornamented branch with two leaves.

Date	AG	Good	VG	Fine	VF	XF	Unc
unique	—	—	—	—	—	—	—

MOTT TOKEN

KM#Tn52.1 **Composition:** COPPER **Note:** Thin planchet.

Date	AG	Good	VG	Fine	VF	XF	Unc
1789	30.00	60.00	120	220	350	850	—

KM#Tn52.2 **Composition:** COPPER **Note:** Thick planchet. Weight generally about 170 grams.

Date	AG	Good	VG	Fine	VF	XF	Unc
1789	25.00	50.00	100.00	175	300	700	—

KM#Tn52.3 **Composition:** COPPER **Edge:** Fully engrailed. **Note:** Specimens struck with perfect dies are scarcer and generally command higher prices.

Date	AG	Good	VG	Fine	VF	XF	Unc
1789	40.00	85.00	175	350	600	1,250	—

MYDDELTON TOKEN

KM#Tn85 **Composition:** COPPER

Date	Good	VG	Fine	VF	XF	Unc	Proof
1796	—	—	—	—	—	—	6,500

KM#Tn85a **Composition:** SILVER

Date	Good	VG	Fine	VF	XF	Unc	Proof
1796	—	—	—	—	—	—	5,500

NEW YORK THEATRE

KM#Tn90 **Composition:** COPPER **Note:** 1796 date is circa.

Date	AG	Good	VG	Fine	VF	XF	Unc
1796	—	—	300	900	2,000	3,250	8,000

NORTH AMERICAN

HALFPENNY

KM#Tn30 **Composition:** COPPER

Date	AG	Good	VG	Fine	VF	XF	Unc
1781	6.50	12.50	25.00	75.00	135	365	750

RHODE ISLAND SHIP

KM#Tn27a **Composition:** BRASS **Obverse:** Without wreath below ship.

Date	AG	Good	VG	Fine	VF	XF	Unc
1779	50.00	100.00	175	275	500	1,000	2,000

KM#Tn27b **Composition:** PEWTER **Obverse:** Without wreath below ship.

Date	AG	Good	VG	Fine	VF	XF	Unc
1779	—	—	—	—	1,250	2,500	5,500

KM#Tn28a **Composition:** BRASS **Obverse:** Wreath below ship.

Date	AG	Good	VG	Fine	VF	XF	Unc
1779	60.00	120	200	325	600	1,150	2,200

KM#Tn28b **Composition:** PEWTER **Obverse:** Wreath below ship.

Date	AG	Good	VG	Fine	VF	XF	Unc
1779	—	—	—	—	1,500	3,000	6,500

KM#Tn29 **Composition:** BRASS **Obverse:** VLUGTENDE below ship

Date	AG	Good	VG	Fine	VF	XF	Unc
1779 unique	—	—	—	—	—	—	—

Note: Garrett $16,000

STANDISH BARRY

3 PENCE

KM#Tn55 **Composition:** SILVER

Date	AG	Good	VG	Fine	VF	XF	Unc
1790	850	1,350	2,000	3,000	6,500	12,000	—

TALBOT, ALLUM & LEE

CENT

KM#Tn71.1 **Composition:** COPPER **Reverse:** NEW YORK above ship **Edge:** Lettered. **Edge Lettering:** PAYABLE AT THE STORE OF

Date	AG	Good	VG	Fine	VF	XF	Unc
1794	12.00	25.00	45.00	90.00	175	300	925

KM#Tn71.2 **Composition:** COPPER **Reverse:** NEW YORK above ship **Edge:** Plain. **Note:** Size of ampersand varies on Obverse and reverse dies.

Date	AG	Good	VG	Fine	VF	XF	Unc
1794 4 known	—	—	—	—	2,350	3,000	—

KM#Tn72.1 **Composition:** COPPER **Reverse:** Without NEW YORK above ship **Edge:** Lettered. **Edge Lettering:** PAYABLE AT THE STORE OF

Date	AG	Good	VG	Fine	VF	XF	Unc
1794	100.00	200	350	650	1,000	2,250	4,550

KM#Tn72.2 **Composition:** COPPER **Edge:** Lettered. **Edge Lettering:** WE PROMISE TO PAY THE BEARER ONE CENT.

Date	AG	Good	VG	Fine	VF	XF	Unc
1795	10.00	20.00	40.00	75.00	160	300	725

KM#Tn72.3 **Composition:** COPPER **Edge:** Lettered. **Edge Lettering:** CURRENT EVERYWHERE.

Date	AG	Good	VG	Fine	VF	XF	Unc
1795 unique	—	—	—	—	—	—	—

KM#Tn72.4 **Composition:** COPPER **Edge:** Olive leaf.

Date	AG	Good	VG	Fine	VF	XF	Unc
1795 unique	—	—	—	—	—	—	—

Note: Norweb $4,400

KM#Tn72.5 **Composition:** COPPER **Edge:** Plain.

Date	AG	Good	VG	Fine	VF	XF	Unc
1795 plain edge, 2 known	—	—	—	—	—	—	—
1795 edge: Cambridge Bedford Huntington.X.X., unique	—	—	—	—	—	—	—

Note: Norweb, $3,960

WASHINGTON PIECES

KM#Tn35 **Composition:** COPPER **Obverse Legend:** GEORGIVS TRIUMPHO.

Date	AG	Good	VG	Fine	VF	XF	Unc
1783	25.00	40.00	65.00	150	325	750	—

KM#Tn36 **Composition:** COPPER **Obverse:** Large military bust. **Note:** Varieties exist.

Date	AG	Good	VG	Fine	VF	XF	Unc
1783	8.00	15.00	25.00	50.00	110	280	—

KM#Tn37.1 **Composition:** COPPER **Obverse:** Small military bust. **Edge:** Plain.

Date	AG	Good	VG	Fine	VF	XF	Unc
1783	10.00	20.00	35.00	65.00	125	300	—

Note: One proof example is known. Value: $12,500

KM#Tn37.2 **Composition:** COPPER **Obverse:** Small military bust. **Edge:** Engrailed.

Date	AG	Good	VG	Fine	VF	XF	Unc
1783	18.00	35.00	50.00	80.00	175	345	—

KM#Tn38.1   **Composition:** COPPER **Obverse:** Draped bust, no button on drapery, small letter.

Date	AG	Good	VG	Fine	VF	XF	Unc
1783	10.00	20.00	35.00	65.00	125	285	—

KM#Tn38.2   **Composition:** COPPER **Obverse:** Draped bust, button on drapery, large letter.

Date	AG	Good	VG	Fine	VF	XF	Unc
1783	25.00	40.00	60.00	100.00	200	350	—

KM#Tn38.4   **Composition:** COPPER **Edge:** Engrailed. **Note:** Restrike.

Date	Good	VG	Fine	VF	XF	Unc	Proof
1783	—	—	—	—	—	—	400

KM#Tn38.4a   **Composition:** COPPER **Note:** Bronzed. Restrike.

Date	Good	VG	Fine	VF	XF	Unc	Proof
1783	—	—	—	—	—	—	—

KM#Tn83.3   **Composition:** COPPER **Obverse:** Large modern lettering. **Edge:** Plain. **Note:** Restrike.

Date	Good	VG	Fine	VF	XF	Unc	Proof
1783	—	—	—	—	—	—	500

KM#Tn83.4b   **Composition:** SILVER **Note:** Restrike.

Date	Good	VG	Fine	VF	XF	Unc	Proof
1783	—	—	—	—	—	—	1,000

KM#Tn83.4c   **Composition:** GOLD **Note:** Restrike.

Date	AG	Good	VG	Fine	VF	XF	Unc
1783 2 known	—	—	—	—	—	—	—

KM#Tn60.1   **Composition:** COPPER **Obverse Legend:** WASHINGTON PRESIDENT. **Edge:** Plain.

Date	AG	Good	VG	Fine	VF	XF	Unc
1792	850	1,450	3,250	5,000	7,500	—	—

Note: Steinberg $12,650. Garrett $15,500

KM#Tn60.2   **Composition:** COPPER **Obverse Legend:** WASHINGTON PRESIDENT. **Edge:** Lettered. **Edge Lettering:** UNITED STATES OF AMERICA.

Date	AG	Good	VG	Fine	VF	XF	Unc
1792	1,350	2,250	4,500	7,500	12,500	—	—

KM#Tn61.1   **Composition:** COPPER **Obverse Legend:** BORN VIRGINIA. **Note:** Varieties exist.

Date	AG	Good	VG	Fine	VF	XF	Unc
	250	500	1,000	2,200	3,750	7,500	—

KM#Tn61.2   **Composition:** SILVER **Edge:** Lettered. **Edge Lettering:** UNITED STATES OF AMERICA.

Date	AG	Good	VG	Fine	VF	XF	Unc
2 known	—	—	—	—	—	—	—

KM#Tn61.1a   **Composition:** SILVER **Edge:** Plain.

Date	AG	Good	VG	Fine	VF	XF	Unc
4 known	—	—	—	—	—	—	—

Note: Roper $16,500

KM#Tn62   **Composition:** SILVER **Reverse:** Heraldic eagle. 1792 half dollar. **Note:** Mule.

Date	AG	Good	VG	Fine	VF	XF	Unc
3 known	—	—	—	—	—	—	—

KM#Tn77.1 **Composition:** COPPER **Obverse Legend:** LIBERTY AND SECURITY. **Edge:** Lettered. **Note:** "Penny."

Date	AG	Good	VG	Fine	VF	XF	Unc
	25.00	40.00	75.00	135	275	625	2,000

KM#Tn77.2 **Composition:** COPPER **Edge:** Plain. **Note:** "Penny."

Date	AG	Good	VG	Fine	VF	XF	Unc
extremely rare	—	—	—	—	—	—	—

KM#Tn77.3 **Composition:** COPPER **Note:** "Penny." Engine-turned borders.

Date	AG	Good	VG	Fine	VF	XF	Unc
12 known	—	—	—	—	—	—	3,750

KM#Tn78 **Composition:** COPPER **Note:** Similar to "Halfpenny" with date on reverse.

Date	AG	Good	VG	Fine	VF	XF	Unc
1795 very rare	—	—	—	—	—	—	—

Note: Roper $6,600

KM#Tn81.2 **Composition:** COPPER **Obverse Legend:** NORTH WALES. **Edge:** Lettered.

Date	AG	Good	VG	Fine	VF	XF	Unc
	120	250	400	600	950	2,000	4,500

CENT

KM#Tn39 **Composition:** COPPER **Obverse Legend:** UNITY STATES

Date	AG	Good	VG	Fine	VF	XF	Unc
1783	12.00	22.00	40.00	70.00	160	325	—

KM#Tn40 **Composition:** COPPER **Note:** Double head.

Date	AG	Good	VG	Fine	VF	XF	Unc
(1783)	10.00	20.00	35.00	65.00	135	300	—

KM#Tn41 **Composition:** COPPER **Obverse:** "Ugly head." **Note:** 3 known in copper, 1 in white metal.

Date	AG	Good	VG	Fine	VF	XF	Unc
1784	—	—	—	—	—	—	—

Note: Roper $14,850

KM#Tn57 **Composition:** COPPER **Reverse:** Small eagle

Date	AG	Good	VG	Fine	VF	XF	Unc
1791	30.00	60.00	125	250	335	675	—

KM#Tn58 **Composition:** COPPER **Reverse:** Large eagle

Date	AG	Good	VG	Fine	VF	XF	Unc
1791	35.00	65.00	145	275	375	725	—

KM#Tn65 **Composition:** COPPER **Obverse:** "Roman" head

Date	Good	VG	Fine	VF	XF	Unc	Proof
1792	—	—	—	—	—	—	17,600

HALF DOLLAR

KM#Tn59.1 **Composition:** COPPER **Edge:** Lettered. **Edge Lettering:** UNITED STATES OF AMERICA

Date	AG	Good	VG	Fine	VF	XF	Unc
1792 2 known	—	—	—	—	—	—	—

Note: Roper $2,860. Benson, EF, $48,300

KM#Tn59.2 **Composition:** COPPER **Edge:** Plain.

Date	AG	Good	VG	Fine	VF	XF	Unc
1792 3 known	—	—	—	—	—	—	—

KM#Tn59.1a **Composition:** SILVER **Edge:** Lettered. **Edge Lettering:** UNITED STATES OF AMERICA

Date	AG	Good	VG	Fine	VF	XF	Unc
1792 rare	—	—	—	—	—	—	—

Note: Roper $35,200

KM#Tn59.2a **Composition:** SILVER **Edge:** Plain.

Date	AG	Good	VG	Fine	VF	XF	Unc
1792 rare	—	—	—	—	—	—	—

KM#Tn59.1b **Composition:** GOLD **Edge:** Lettered. **Edge Lettering:** UNITED STATES OF AMERICA

Date	AG	Good	VG	Fine	VF	XF	Unc
1792 unique	—	—	—	—	—	—	—

COLONIAL COINAGE

KM#Tn63.1   **Composition:** SILVER **Reverse:** Small eagle **Edge:** Plain.

Date	AG	Good	VG	Fine	VF	XF	Unc
1792	4,500	7,000	9,000	12,500	20,000	37,500	—

KM#Tn63.2   **Composition:** SILVER **Edge:** Ornamented, circles and squares.

Date	AG	Good	VG	Fine	VF	XF	Unc
1792 5 known	—	—	—	—	—	—	—

KM#Tn63.1a   **Composition:** COPPER **Edge:** Plain.

Date	AG	Good	VG	Fine	VF	XF	Unc
1792	750	1,500	3,500	5,750	8,500	—	—

Note: Garrett $32,000

KM#Tn63.3   **Composition:** SILVER **Edge:** Two olive leaves.

Date	AG	Good	VG	Fine	VF	XF	Unc
1792 unique	—	—	—	—	—	—	—

KM#Tn64   **Composition:** SILVER **Reverse:** Large heraldic eagle

Date	AG	Good	VG	Fine	VF	XF	Unc
1792 unique	—	—	—	—	—	—	—

Note: Garrett $16,500

HALF PENNY

KM#Tn56   **Composition:** COPPER **Obverse Legend:** LIVERPOOL HALFPENNY

Date	AG	Good	VG	Fine	VF	XF	Unc
1791	300	450	550	850	1,650	2,350	—

COLONIAL COINAGE

KM#Tn66.1   **Composition:** COPPER **Reverse:** Ship **Edge:** Lettered.

Date	AG	Good	VG	Fine	VF	XF	Unc
1793	20.00	30.00	60.00	110	235	500	—

KM#Tn66.2   **Composition:** COPPER **Reverse:** Ship **Edge:** Plain.

Date	AG	Good	VG	Fine	VF	XF	Unc
1793 5 known	—	—	—	—	2,000	—	—

KM#Tn75.1   **Composition:** COPPER **Obverse:** Large coat buttons **Reverse:** Grate **Edge:** Reeded.

Date	AG	Good	VG	Fine	VF	XF	Unc
1795	12.00	20.00	30.00	60 00	120	265	575

KM#Tn75.2   **Composition:** COPPER **Reverse:** Grate **Edge:** Lettered.

Date	AG	Good	VG	Fine	VF	XF	Unc
1795	45.00	85.00	165	225	300	625	1,200

KM#Tn75.3   **Composition:** COPPER **Obverse:** Small coat buttons **Reverse:** Grate **Edge:** Reeded.

Date	AG	Good	VG	Fine	VF	XF	Unc
1795	10.00	35.00	60.00	100.00	175	375	850

KM#Tn76.1   **Composition:** COPPER **Obverse Legend:** LIBERTY AND SECURITY. **Edge:** Plain.

Date	AG	Good	VG	Fine	VF	XF	Unc
1795	18.00	35.00	60.00	100.00	175	435	975

KM#Tn76.2   **Composition:** COPPER **Edge:** Lettered. **Edge Lettering:** PAYABLE AT LONDON ...

Date	AG	Good	VG	Fine	VF	XF	Unc
1795	12.00	20.00	30.00	60.00	125	375	800

KM#Tn76.3   **Composition:** COPPER **Edge:** Lettered. **Edge Lettering:** BIRMINGHAM ...

Date	AG	Good	VG	Fine	VF	XF	Unc
1795	14.00	22.00	35.00	70.00	150	425	950

KM#Tn76.4   **Composition:** COPPER **Edge:** Lettered. **Edge Lettering:** AN ASYLUM ...

Date	AG	Good	VG	Fine	VF	XF	Unc
1795	18.00	35.00	60.00	100.00	225	450	1,000

KM#Tn76.5   **Composition:** COPPER **Edge:** Lettered. **Edge Lettering:** PAYABLE AT LIVERPOOL ...

Date	AG	Good	VG	Fine	VF	XF	Unc
1795 unique	—	—	—	—	—	—	—

KM#Tn76.6   **Composition:** COPPER **Edge:** Lettered. **Edge Lettering:** PAYABLE AT LONDON-LIVERPOOL.

Date	AG	Good	VG	Fine	VF	XF	Unc
1795 unique	—	—	—	—	—	—	—

COLONIAL COINAGE

KM#Tn81.1 **Composition:** COPPER **Obverse Legend:** NORTH WALES. **Edge:** Plain.

Date	AG	Good	VG	Fine	VF	XF	Unc
(1795)	25.00	45.00	85.00	145	250	550	1,450

KM#Tn82 **Composition:** COPPER **Obverse Legend:** NORTH WALES. **Reverse:** Four stars at bottom

Date	AG	Good	VG	Fine	VF	XF	Unc
(1795)	200	400	700	1,500	2,850	5,500	—

EARLY AMERICAN PATTERNS
CONFEDERATIO

KM#EA22 **Composition:** COPPER **Reverse:** Small circle of stars.

Date	AG	Good	VG	Fine	VF	XF	Unc
1785	—	—	—	—	8,800	16,500	—

KM#EA23 **Composition:** COPPER **Reverse:** Large circle of stars. **Note:** The Confederatio dies were struck in combination with 13 other dies of the period. All surviving examples of these combinations are extremely rare.

Date	AG	Good	VG	Fine	VF	XF	Unc
extremely rare	—	—	—	—	—	—	—

IMMUNE COLUMBIA

KM#EA17 **Composition:** COPPER **Reverse Legend:** CONSTELLATIO.

Date	AG	Good	VG	Fine	VF	XF	Unc
1785	—	—	—	—	—	14,375	—

KM#EA17a   **Composition:** SILVER **Reverse Legend:** CONSTELLATIO.

Date	AG	Good	VG	Fine	VF	XF	Unc
	—	—	—	—	—	20,700	—

KM#EA18   **Composition:** COPPER **Obverse Legend:** Extra star in border. **Reverse Legend:** CONSTELLATIO.

Date	AG	Good	VG	Fine	VF	XF	Unc
1785	—	—	—	—	—	—	—

Note: Caldwell $4,675

KM#EA19   **Composition:** COPPER **Reverse:** Blunt rays.

Date	AG	Good	VG	Fine	VF	XF	Unc
1785 2 known	—	—	—	—	—	—	—

Note: Norweb $22,000

KM#EA19a   **Composition:** GOLD **Reverse Legend:** CONSTELATIO.

Date	AG	Good	VG	Fine	VF	XF	Unc
1785 unique	—	—	—	—	—	—	—

KM#EA20   **Composition:** COPPER **Obverse:** George III.

Date	AG	Good	VG	Fine	VF	XF	Unc
1785	750	1,250	1,850	2,250	5,000	9,000	—

KM#EA21   **Composition:** COPPER **Obverse:** Vermon.

Date	AG	Good	VG	Fine	VF	XF	Unc
1785	600	1,000	1,650	2,000	4,750	8,500	—

KM#EA24   **Composition:** COPPER **Obverse:** Washington.

Date	AG	Good	VG	Fine	VF	XF	Unc
1786 3 known	—	—	—	—	—	—	—

Note: Garrett $50,000. Steinberg $12,650

KM#EA25   **Composition:** COPPER **Obverse:** Eagle.

Date	AG	Good	VG	Fine	VF	XF	Unc
1786 unique	—	—	—	—	—	—	—

Note: Garrett $37,500

KM#EA26   **Composition:** COPPER **Obverse:** Washington. **Reverse:** Eagle.

Date	AG	Good	VG	Fine	VF	XF	Unc
1786 2 known	—	—	—	—	—	—	—

KM#EA27 **Composition:** COPPER **Obverse Legend:** IMMUNIS COLUMBIA.

Date	AG	Good	VG	Fine	VF	XF	Unc
1786 extremely rare	—	—	—	—	—	—	—

Note: Rescigno, AU, $33,000. Steinberg, VF, $11,000

KM#EA28 **Composition:** COPPER **Obverse Legend:** IMMUNIS COLUMBIA. **Reverse:** Eagle.

Date	AG	Good	VG	Fine	VF	XF	Unc
1786 3 known	—	—	—	—	—	—	—

NOVA CONSTELLATIO

KM#EA6.1 **Composition:** COPPER **Obverse:** Pointed rays. **Obverse Legend:** CONSTELLATIO. **Reverse:** Small "US".

Date	AG	Good	VG	Fine	VF	XF	Unc
1783	20.00	35.00	65.00	125	255	585	—

KM#EA6.2 **Composition:** COPPER **Obverse:** Pointed rays. **Obverse Legend:** CONSTALLATIO. **Reverse:** Large "US".

Date	AG	Good	VG	Fine	VF	XF	Unc
1783	20.00	35.00	70.00	140	285	650	—

KM#EA7 **Composition:** COPPER **Obverse:** Blunt rays. **Obverse Legend:** CONSTELATIO.

Date	AG	Good	VG	Fine	VF	XF	Unc
1783	22.00	40.00	80.00	150	350	750	—

KM#EA8 **Composition:** COPPER **Obverse:** Blunt rays. **Obverse Legend:** CONSTELATIO.

Date	AG	Good	VG	Fine	VF	XF	Unc
1785	22.00	40.00	80.00	160	375	775	—

KM#EA9 **Composition:** COPPER **Obverse:** Pointed rays. **Obverse Legend:** CONSTELLATIO.

Date	AG	Good	VG	Fine	VF	XF	Unc
1785	20.00	35.00	70.00	140	285	650	—

KM#EA10 **Composition:** COPPER **Note:** Contemporary circulating counterfeit. Similar to previously listed coin.

Date	AG	Good	VG	Fine	VF	XF	Unc
1786 extremely rare	—	—	—	—	—	—	—

5

KM#EA12 **Composition:** COPPER

Date	AG	Good	VG	Fine	VF	XF	Unc
1783 unique	—	—	—	—	—	—	—

100 (BIT)

KM#EA13.1 **Composition:** SILVER **Edge:** Leaf.

Date	AG	Good	VG	Fine	VF	XF	Unc
1783 2 known	—	—	—	—	—	—	—

Note: Garrett $97,500. Stack's auction, May 1991, $72,500

KM#EA13.2 **Composition:** SILVER **Edge:** Plain.

Date	AG	Good	VG	Fine	VF	XF	Unc
1783 unique	—	—	—	—	—	—	—

COLONIAL COINAGE

5OO (QUINT)

KM#EA14   **Composition:** SILVER   **Obverse Legend:** NOVA CONSTELLATIO

Date	AG	Good	VG	Fine	VF	XF	Unc
1783 unique	—	—	—	—	—	—	—

Note: Garrett $165,000

KM#EA15   **Composition:** SILVER   **Obverse:** Without legend

Date	AG	Good	VG	Fine	VF	XF	Unc
1783 unique	—	—	—	—	—	—	—

Note: Garrett $55,000

1000 (MARK)

KM#EA16   **Composition:** SILVER

Date	AG	Good	VG	Fine	VF	XF	Unc
1783 unique	—	—	—	—	—	—	—

Note: Garrett $190,000

EARLY FEDERAL COINAGE

BRASHER

KM#Tn51.1   **Composition:** GOLD **Reverse:** EB on wing.

Date	AG	Good	VG	Fine	VF	XF	Unc
1787 6 known	—	—	—	—	—	—	—

Note: Heritage FUN Sale, January 2005, AU-55, $2.415 million.

KM#Tn51.2   **Composition:** GOLD **Reverse:** EG on breast.

Date	AG	Good	VG	Fine	VF	XF	Unc
1787 unique	—	—	—	—	—	—	—

Note: Heritage FUN Sale, January 2005, XF-45, $2.99 million.

FUGIO "CENT"

KM#EA30.1   **Composition:** COPPER **Obverse:** Club rays, round ends.

Date	AG	Good	VG	Fine	VF	XF	Unc
1787	40.00	75.00	150	375	850	1,600	—

KM#EA30.2   **Composition:** COPPER **Obverse:** Club rays, concave ends.

Date	AG	Good	VG	Fine	VF	XF	Unc
1787	250	700	1,800	2,750	5,000	—	—

KM#EA30.3   **Composition:** COPPER **Obverse Legend:** FUCIO.

Date	AG	Good	VG	Fine	VF	XF	Unc
1787	—	750	1,850	2,850	55,000	—	—

KM#EA31.1   **Composition:** COPPER **Obverse:** Pointed rays. **Reverse:** UNITED above, STATES below.

Date	AG	Good	VG	Fine	VF	XF	Unc
1787	100.00	250	550	1,000	1,500	3,500	—

KM#EA31.2   **Composition:** COPPER **Reverse:** UNITED STATES at sides of ring.

Date	AG	Good	VG	Fine	VF	XF	Unc
1787	20.00	45.00	90.00	175	300	650	—

KM#EA31.3   **Composition:** COPPER **Reverse:** STATES UNITED at sides of ring.

Date	AG	Good	VG	Fine	VF	XF	Unc
1787	25.00	55.00	110	220	350	700	—

KM#EA31.4   **Composition:** COPPER **Reverse:** Eight-pointed stars on ring.

Date	AG	Good	VG	Fine	VF	XF	Unc
1787	30.00	65.00	120	250	400	800	—

KM#EA31.5   **Composition:** COPPER **Reverse:** Raised rims on ring, large lettering in center.

Date	AG	Good	VG	Fine	VF	XF	Unc
1787	35.00	75.00	135	275	450	950	—

KM#EA32.1   **Composition:** COPPER **Obverse:** No cinquefoils, cross after date. **Obverse Legend:** UNITED STATES.

Date	AG	Good	VG	Fine	VF	XF	Unc
1787	50.00	110	250	425	650	1,250	—

KM#EA32.2   **Composition:** COPPER **Obverse:** No cinquefoils, cross after date. **Obverse Legend:** STATES UNITED.

Date	AG	Good	VG	Fine	VF	XF	Unc
1787	60.00	110	250	425	650	1,250	—

KM#EA32.3   **Composition:** COPPER **Obverse:** No cinquefoils, cross after date. **Reverse:** Raised rims on ring.

Date	AG	Good	VG	Fine	VF	XF	Unc
1787	—	—	—	—	2,600	—	—

KM#EA33   **Composition:** COPPER **Obverse:** No cinquefoils, cross after date. **Reverse:** With rays. **Reverse Legend:** AMERICAN CONGRESS.

Date	AG	Good	VG	Fine	VF	XF	Unc
1787 extremely rare	—	—	—	—	—	—	—

Note: Norweb $63,800

KM#EA34   **Composition:** BRASS **Note:** New Haven restrike.

Date	AG	Good	VG	Fine	VF	XF	Unc
	—	—	—	—	—	—	500

KM#EA34a   **Composition:** COPPER **Note:** New Haven restrike.

Date	AG	Good	VG	Fine	VF	XF	Unc
	—	—	—	—	—	500	—

KM#EA34b	**Composition:** SILVER **Note:** New Haven restrike.						
Date	**AG**	**Good**	**VG**	**Fine**	**VF**	**XF**	**Unc**
	—	—	—	—	—	—	1,850

KM#EA34c	**Composition:** GOLD **Note:** New Haven restrike.						
Date	**AG**	**Good**	**VG**	**Fine**	**VF**	**XF**	**Unc**
2 known	—	—	—	—	—	—	—

Note: Norweb (holed) $1,430

ISSUES OF 1792

CENT

KM#PnE1	**Composition:** Copper around Silver **Note:** Silver plug in center.						
Date	**AG**	**Good**	**VG**	**Fine**	**VF**	**XF**	**Unc**
1792 12 known	—	—	—	—	—	—	—

Note: Norweb, MS-60, $143,000

KM#PnF1	**Composition:** COPPER **Note:** No silver center.						
Date	**AG**	**Good**	**VG**	**Fine**	**VF**	**XF**	**Unc**
1792 8 known	—	—	—	—	—	—	—

Note: Norweb, EF-40, $35,200; Benson, VG-10, $57,500

KM#PnG1	**Composition:** COPPER **Edge:** Plain **Note:** Commonly called "Birch cent."						
Date	**AG**	**Good**	**VG**	**Fine**	**VF**	**XF**	**Unc**
1792 unique	—	—	—	—	—	—	—

KM#PnH1	**Composition:** COPPER **Obverse:** One star in edge legend **Note:** Commonly called "Birch cent."						
Date	**AG**	**Good**	**VG**	**Fine**	**VF**	**XF**	**Unc**
1792 2 known	—	—	—	—	—	—	—

Note: Norweb, EF-40, $59,400

KM#PnI1	**Composition:** COPPER **Obverse:** Two stars in edge legend **Note:** Commonly called "Birch cent."						
Date	**AG**	**Good**	**VG**	**Fine**	**VF**	**XF**	**Unc**
1792 6 known	—	—	—	—	—	—	—

Note: Hawn, strong VF, $57,750

KM#PnJ1	**Composition:** WHITE METAL **Reverse:** "G.W.Pt." below wreath tie **Note:** Commonly called "Birch cent."						
Date	**AG**	**Good**	**VG**	**Fine**	**VF**	**XF**	**Unc**
1792 unique	—	—	—	—	—	—	—

COLONIAL COINAGE

Date	AG	Good	VG	Fine	VF	XF	Unc

Note: Garrett, $90,000

HALF DISME

KM#5   **Composition:** SILVER

Date	AG	Good	VG	Fine	VF	XF	Unc
1792	1,250	—	3,500	6,500	8,500	16,500	—

KM#PnA1   **Composition:** COPPER

Date	AG	Good	VG	Fine	VF	XF	Unc
1792 unique	—	—	—	—	—	—	—

DISME

KM#PnB1   **Composition:** SILVER

Date	AG	Good	VG	Fine	VF	XF	Unc
1792 3 known	—	—	—	—	—	—	—

Note: Norweb, EF-40, $28,600

KM#PnC1   **Composition:** COPPER **Edge:** Reeded

Date	AG	Good	VG	Fine	VF	XF	Unc
1792 14 known	—	—	—	—	—	—	—

Note: Hawn, VF, $30,800; Benson, EF-45, $109,250

KM#PnD1   **Composition:** COPPER **Edge:** Plain

Date	AG	Good	VG	Fine	VF	XF	Unc
1792 2 known	—	—	—	—	—	—	—

Note: Garrett, $45,000

QUARTER

KM#PnK1   **Composition:** COPPER **Edge:** Reeded **Note:** Commonly called "Wright quarter."

Date	AG	Good	VG	Fine	VF	XF	Unc
1792 2 known	—	—	—	—	—	—	—

KM#PnL1   **Composition:** WHITE METAL **Edge:** Plain **Note:** Commonly called "Wright quarter."

Date	AG	Good	VG	Fine	VF	XF	Unc
1792 2 known	—	—	—	—	—	—	—

Note: Norweb, VF-30 to EF-40, $28,600

KM#PnM1   **Composition:** WHITE METAL **Note:** Commonly called "Wright quarter."

Date	AG	Good	VG	Fine	VF	XF	Unc
1792 die trial	—	—	—	—	—	—	—

Note: Garrett, $12,000

US TERRITORIAL GOLD

Territorial gold pieces (also referred to as "Private" and "Pioneer" gold) are those struck outside the U.S. Mint and not recognized as official issues by the federal government. The pieces so identified are of various shapes, denominations, and degrees of intrinsic value, and were locally required because of the remoteness of the early gold fields from a federal mint and/or an insufficient quantity of official coinage in frontier areas.

The legality of these privately issued pieces derives from the fact that federal law prior to 1864 prohibited a state from coining money, but did not specifically deny that right to an individual, providing that the privately issued coins did not closely resemble those of the United States.

In addition to coin-like gold pieces, the private minters of the gold rush days also issued gold in ingot and bar form. Ingots were intended for circulation and were cast in regular values and generally in large denominations. Bars represent a miner's deposit after it had been assayed, refined, cast into convenient form (generally rectangular), and stamped with the appropriate weight, fineness, and value. Although occasionally cast in even values for the convenience of banks, bars were more often of odd denomination, and when circulated were rounded off to the nearest figure. Ingots and bars are omitted from this listing.

CALIFORNIA
Fractional and Small Size Gold Coinage

During the California gold rush a wide variety of U.S. and foreign coins were used for small change, but only limited quantities of these coins were available. Gold dust was in common use, although this offered the miner a relatively low value for his gold.

By 1852 California jewelers had begun to manufacture 25¢, 50¢ and $1 gold pieces in round and octagonal shapes. Makers included M. Deriberpe, Antoine Louis Nouizillet, Isadore Routhier, Robert B. Gray, Pierre Frontier, Eugene Deviercy, Herman J. Brand, and Herman and Jacob Levison. Reuben N. Hershfield and Noah Mitchell made their coins in Leavenworth, Kansas and most of their production was seized in August 1871. Herman Kroll made California gold coins in New York City in the 1890s. Only two or three of these companies were in production at any one time. Many varieties bear the makers initials. Frontier and his partners made most of the large Liberty Head, Eagle reverse, and Washington Head design types. Most of the small Liberty Head types were made first by Nouizillet and later by Gray and then the Levison brothers and lastly by the California Jewelry Co. Coins initialed "G.G." are apparently patterns made by Frontier and Deviercy for the New York based firm of Gaime, Guillemot & Co.

Most of the earlier coins were struck from gold alloys and had an intrinsic value of about 50-60 percent of face value. They were generally struck from partially hubbed dies and with reeded collars. A few issues were struck with a plain collar or a collar with reeding on only 7 of the 8 sides. Many issues are too poorly struck or too thin to have a clear and complete image of the collar. The later coins and some of the earlier coins were struck from laminated or plated gold planchets, or from gold plated silver planchets. Most of the last dates of issue are extremely thin and contain only token amounts of gold.

Circumstantial evidence exists that the coins issued through 1856 circulated as small change. The San Francisco mint was established in 1854, and by 1856 it had ramped up its production enough to satisfy the local need for small change. However, some evidence exists that these small gold coins may have continued to circulate on occasion through to 1871. After 1871, the gold content of the coins dramatically decreases and it is very unlikely that any of these last issues circulated.

Although the Private Coinages Act of 1864 outlawed all private coinage, this law was not enforced in California and production of small denominated gold continued through 1882. In the spring of 1883, Col. Henry Finnegass of the U.S. Secret Service halted production of the denominated private gold pieces. Non-denominated tokens (lacking DOLLARS, CENTS or the equivalent) were also made during this latter period, sometimes by the same manufacturing jeweler using the same obverse die and the same planchets as the small denomination gold coins. Production of these tokens continues to this day, with most issues made after the 1906 earthquake and fire being backdated to 1847-1865 and struck from brass or gold plated brass planchets.

Approximately 25,000 pieces of California small denomination gold coins are estimated to exist, in a total of over 500 varieties. A few varieties are undated, mostly gold rush era pieces; and a few of the issues are backdated, mostly those from the 1880's. This listing groups varieties together in easily identified categories. The prices quoted are for the most common variety in each group. UNC prices reflect the median auction prices realized of MS60 to MS62 graded coins. BU prices reflect the median auction prices realized of MS63 to MS64 graded coins. Pre-1871 true MS-65 coins are rare and sell for substantial premiums over the prices on this list. Post-1871 coins are rarely found with wear and often have a cameo proof appearance. Auction prices realized are highly volatile and it is not uncommon to find recent records of sales at twice or half of the values shown here. Many of the rarity estimates published in the 1980s and earlier have proven to be too high, so caution is advised when paying a premium for a rare variety. In addition, many varieties that have a refined appearance command higher prices than equivalent grade but scarcer varieties that have a more crude appearance.

Several counterfeits of California Fractional Gold coins exist. Beware of 1854 and 1858 dated round 1/2 dollars, and 1871 dated round dollars that have designs that do not match any of the published varieties. Beware of reeded edge Kroll coins being sold as originals (see the listings below).

For further information consult "California Pioneer Fractional Gold" by W. Breen and R.J. Gillio and "The Brasher Bulletin" the official newsletter of The Society of Private and Pioneer Numismatists.

1/4 DOLLAR (OCTAGONAL)

KM# 1.1   Obverse: Large Liberty head **Reverse:** Value and date within beaded circle

Date	XF	AU	Unc	BU
1853	100	150	200	300
1854	100	150	250	350
1855	100	150	250	350
1856	100	150	260	375

KM# 1.2   Reverse: Value and date within wreath

Date	XF	AU	Unc	BU
1859	65.00	110	200	450
1864	75.00	125	250	400
1866	75.00	125	250	400
1867	65.00	110	250	400
1868	70.00	125	200	350
1869	70.00	125	200	350
1870	65.00	110	200	350
1871	65.00	110	200	350

KM# 1.3   Obverse: Large Liberty head above date **Reverse:** Value and CAL within wreath

Date	XF	AU	Unc	BU
1872	65.00	110	250	400
1873	50.00	85.00	175	300

KM# 1.4   Obverse: Small Liberty head **Reverse:** Value and date within beaded circle

Date	XF	AU	Unc	BU
1853	125	250	325	425

KM# 1.5   Obverse: Small Liberty head above date **Reverse:** Value within wreath

Date	XF	AU	Unc	BU
1854	125	250	300	350

KM# 1.6   Obverse: Small Liberty head **Reverse:** Value and date within wreath

Date	XF	AU	Unc	BU
1855	—	—	—	—
1856	—	—	—	—
1857 Plain edge	—	—	—	—
Note: Kroll type date				
1857 Reeded edge	—	—	—	—
Note: Kroll type date				
1860	—	—	—	—
1870	—	—	—	—

KM# 1.7   Reverse: Value in shield and date within wreath

Date	XF	AU	Unc	BU
1863	150	350	500	—
1864	65.00	110	240	—
1865	85.00	145	250	550
1866	85.00	145	250	400
1867	75.00	125	200	400
1868	75.00	125	200	—
1869	75.00	125	190	300
1870	75.00	125	200	350

KM# 1.8   Obverse: Small Liberty head above date **Reverse:** Value and CAL within wreath

Date	XF	AU	Unc	BU
1870	65.00	110	200	300
1871	65.00	110	175	250
1871	65.00	110	175	250
1873	175	250	400	—
1874	65.00	110	175	275
1875/3	350	700	1,000	—
1876	65.00	110	200	300

KM# 1.9   Obverse: Goofy Liberty head **Reverse:** Value and date within wreath

Date	XF	AU	Unc	BU
1870	85.00	145	200	300

KM# 1.10   Obverse: Oriental Liberty head above date **Reverse:** 1/4 CALDOLL within wreath

Date	XF	AU	Unc	BU
1881	—	—	1,000	3,000

KM# 1.11   Obverse: Large Liberty head above 1872 **Reverse:** Value and 1871 within wreath

Date	XF	AU	Unc	BU
1872-71	—	—	1,000	3,000

KM# 2.1   Obverse: Large Indian head above date **Reverse:** Value within wreath

Date	XF	AU	Unc	BU
1852	100	175	240	450
Note: Back dated issue				
1868	100	175	240	450
Note: Back dated issue				
1874	85.00	160	220	400
Note: Back dated issue				
1876	85.00	160	220	400
1880	75.00	150	200	350
1881	85.00	160	220	400

KM# 2.2   Reverse: Value and CAL within wreath

Date	XF	AU	Unc	BU
1872	65.00	110	210	300
1873/2	200	350	550	800
1873	90.00	160	250	350
1874	65.00	110	210	300
1875	90.00	160	250	350
1876	90.00	160	250	350

KM# 2.3 Obverse: Small indian head above date

Date	XF	AU	Unc	BU
1875	90.00	160	250	350
1876	90.00	160	250	500
1881	—	—	500	1,100

KM# 2.4 Obverse: Aztec indian head above date

Date	XF	AU	Unc	BU
1880	65.00	110	210	300

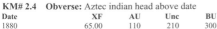

KM# 2.6 Obverse: Dumb indian head above date
Reverse: Value and CAL within wreath

Date	XF	AU	Unc	BU
1881	—	—	650	—

KM# 2.7 Obverse: Young indian head above date
Reverse: Value within wreath

Date	XF	AU	Unc	BU
1881	—	—	450	—

KM# 2.8 Reverse: Value and CAL within wreath

Date	XF	AU	Unc	BU
1882	—	—	500	750

KM# 3 Obverse: Washington head above date

Date	XF	AU	Unc	BU
1872	—	—	400	950

1/4 DOLLAR (ROUND)

KM# 4 Obverse: Defiant eagle above date **Reverse:** 25¢ within wreath

Date	XF	AU	Unc	BU
1854	11,000	22,000	33,000	44,000

KM# 5.1 Obverse: Large Liberty head **Reverse:** Value and date within wreath

Date	XF	AU	Unc	BU
1853	400	700	1,000	1,500
1854	150	250	400	600
1859	70.00	120	225	275
1865	90.00	160	250	350
1866	—	—	200	300
1867	—	—	200	300
1868	—	—	200	300
1870	—	—	200	300

Date	XF	AU	Unc	BU
1871	—	—	200	300

KM# 5.2 Obverse: Large Liberty head above date
Reverse: Value and CAL within wreath

Date	XF	AU	Unc	BU
1871	—	—	200	275
1872	—	—	200	275
1873	—	—	180	260

KM# 5.3 Obverse: Small Liberty head **Reverse:** 25¢ in wreath

Date	XF	AU	Unc	BU
ND	1,000	1,650	2,450	3,500

KM# 5.4 Reverse: 1/4 DOLL. or DOLLAR and date in wreath

Date	XF	AU	Unc	BU
ND	90.00	150	200	350
Note: Rare counterfeit exists				
1853	500	800	1,200	2,500
1853 10 stars	120	200	275	365
Note: Kroll type				
1855 11 stars	—	–	50.00	100
Note: Kroll type				
1856	100	175	250	350
1860	65.00	110	175	275
1864	75.00	125	200	300
1865	90.00	135	225	350
1866	125	210	600	350
1867	65.00	110	175	350
1869	65.00	100	175	300
1870	125	210	250	450

KM# 5.5 Reverse: Value in shield and date within wreath

Date	XF	AU	Unc	BU
1863	80.00	160	200	—

KM# 5.6 Obverse: Small Liberty head above date
Reverse: Value and CAL within wreath

Date	XF	AU	Unc	BU
	100	175	500	—
1870	80.00	160	200	250
1871	80.00	160	200	250
1871	—	—	210	350
1873	—	—	300	500
1874	—	—	300	500
1875	—	—	250	475
1876	—	—	225	450

KM# 5.7 Obverse: Goofy Liberty head **Reverse:** Value and date within wreath

Date	XF	AU	Unc	BU
1870	110	160	220	250

KM# 5.8 Obverse: Liberty head with H and date below **Reverse:** Value and CAL in wreath

Date	XF	AU	Unc	BU
1871	80.00	125	160	250

KM# 6.1 Obverse: Large indian head above date **Reverse:** Value within wreath

Date	XF	AU	Unc	BU
1852	—	—	200	300
Note: Back dated issue				
1868	—	—	250	375
Note: Back dated issue				
1874	—	—	190	275
Note: Back dated issue				
1876	—	—	200	325
1878/6	—	—	200	300
1880	—	—	200	325
1881	—	—	200	325

KM# 6.2 Reverse: Value and CAL within wreath

Date	XF	AU	Unc	BU
1872/1	—	—	200	300
1873	—	—	180	275
1874	—	—	180	275
1875	—	—	200	300
1876	—	—	200	300

KM# 6.3 Obverse: Small indian head above date

Date	XF	AU	Unc	BU
1875	75.00	125	250	400
1876	65.00	110	200	350
1881 Rare	—	—	—	—

KM# 6.4 Obverse: Young indian head above date

Date	XF	AU	Unc	BU
1882	400	725	1,225	1,750

KM# 7 Obverse: Washington head above date

Date	XF	AU	Unc	BU
1872	—	—	600	900

1/2 DOLLAR (OCTAGONAL)

KM# 8.1 Obverse: Liberty head above date **Reverse:** 1/2 DOLLAR in beaded circle, CALIFORNIA GOLD around circle

Date	XF	AU	Unc	BU
1853	165	280	350	450
1854	110	225	285	350
Note: Rare counterfeit exists				
1854	165	280	350	450

Date	XF	AU	Unc	BU
1856	165	285	365	450

KM# 8.2 Reverse: Small eagle with rays ("peacock")

Date	XF	AU	Unc	BU
1853	400	600	1,000	1,500

KM# 8.3 Obverse: Large Liberty head **Reverse:** Large eagle with date

Date	XF	AU	Unc	BU
1853	750	1,350	2,250	—

KM# 8.4 Reverse: Value and date within wreath

Date	XF	AU	Unc	BU
1859	—	130	200	275
1866	—	200	300	400
1867	—	130	225	300
1868	—	130	225	300
1869	—	130	250	350
1870	—	130	250	350
1871	—	130	225	300

KM# 8.5 Obverse: Large Liberty head above date **Reverse:** Value and CAL within wreath

Date	XF	AU	Unc	BU
1872	—	130	250	350
1873	—	130	225	300

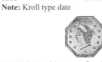

KM# 8.6 Obverse: Liberty head **Reverse:** Date in wreath, HALF DOL. CALIFORNIA GOLD around wreath

Date	XF	AU	Unc	BU
1854	100	250	350	500
1855	90.00	200	300	400
1856	90.00	200	265	325
1856	165	350	1,100	—
Note: Back date issue struck in 1864				
1868	60.00	110	185	275
Note: Kroll type date				

KM# 8.7 Obverse: Small Liberty head **Reverse:** HALF DOLLAR and date in wreath

Date	XF	AU	Unc	BU
1864	—	175	275	350
1870	—	175	275	—

KM# 8.8 Reverse: CAL. GOLD HALF DOL and date in wreath

Date	XF	AU	Unc	BU
1869	—	175	200	350
1870	—	175	200	350

KM# 8.9 **Obverse:** Small Liberty head above date
Reverse: Value and CAL in wreath

Date	XF	AU	Unc	BU
1870	55.00	110	200	300
1871	55.00	110	200	250
1871	55.00	100	165	250
1873	85.00	200	300	600
1874	85.00	200	300	600
1875	250	475	1,000	—
1876	55.00	110	200	250

KM# 8.10 **Obverse:** Goofy Liberty head **Reverse:** Value and date within wreath

Date	XF	AU	Unc	BU
1870	55.00	110	200	300

KM# 8.11 **Obverse:** Oriental Liberty head above date **Reverse:** 1/2 CALDOLL within wreath

Date	XF	AU	Unc	BU
1881	250	450	750	1,150

KM# 9.1 **Obverse:** Large indian head above date **Reverse:** Value within wreath

Date	XF	AU	Unc	BU
1852	—	—	500	900
Note: Back dated issue				
1868	—	—	650	1,000
Note: Back dated issue				
1874	—	175	500	900
Note: Back dated issue				
1876	—	—	300	400
1880	—	—	300	400
1881	—	—	300	400

KM# 9.2 **Reverse:** Value and CAL within wreath

Date	XF	AU	Unc	BU
1852	—	—	450	700
Note: Back dated issue				
1868	—	—	260	550
Note: Back dated issue				
1872	—	—	200	300
1873/2	—	—	200	400
1873	—	—	200	300
1874/3	—	—	250	350
1874	—	—	200	300
1875	—	—	250	425
1876	—	—	250	400
1878/6	—	—	250	400
1880	—	—	500	1,000
1881	—	—	250	400

KM# 9.3 **Obverse:** Small indian head above date

Date	XF	AU	Unc	BU
1875	—	175	225	350
1876	—	175	225	350

KM# 9.4 **Obverse:** Young indian head above date

Date	XF	AU	Unc	BU
1881	—	—	550	850
1882 Rare	—	—	—	—

1/2 DOLLAR (ROUND)

KM# 10 **Obverse:** Arms of California and date **Reverse:** Eagle and legends

Date	XF	AU	Unc	BU
1853	1,250	3,500	4,500	5,500

KM# 11.1 **Obverse:** Liberty head **Reverse:** Large eagle and legends

Date	XF	AU	Unc	BU
1854	1,000	2,700	6,000	—

KM# 11.2 **Obverse:** Liberty head and date **Reverse:** HALF DOL. CALIFORNIA GOLD around wreath

Date	XF	AU	Unc	BU
1854	175	210	300	450

KM# 11.3 **Obverse:** Liberty head **Reverse:** Date in wreath, value and CALIFORNIA GOLD around wreath

Date	XF	AU	Unc	BU
1852	145	180	275	400
1852	145	180	275	400
1853	145	180	275	400
1853	165	200	300	425
1853	165	200	300	425
1853 Date on reverse	125	160	225	300
Note: Kroll type				
1854 Large head	300	600	1,000	1,600
1854 Small head	—	—	100	200
Note: Common counterfeits exist				
1855 Date on reverse	175	210	325	550
Note: Kroll type				
1856	100	135	225	325
1860/56	125	185	250	400

KM# 11.4 **Reverse:** Small eagle and legends

Date	XF	AU	Unc	BU
1853 Rare	—	—	—	—
1853	5,000	8,000	10,000	15,000

TERRITORIAL GOLD

KM# 11.5 **Reverse:** Value in wreath; CALIFORNIA GOLD and date around wreath

Date	XF	AU	Unc	BU
1853	150	250	750	1,500

KM# 11.6 **Reverse:** Value and date within wreath

Date	XF	AU	Unc	BU
Rare	—	—	—	—
1854	850	2,000	—	—

Note: Common counterfeit without FD beneath truncation

Date	XF	AU	Unc	BU
1855	155	300	450	600
1859	140	250	350	500
1859	—	150	175	250
1865	—	150	225	350
1866	—	165	250	400
1867	—	150	225	350
1868	—	165	250	400
1869	—	165	250	400
1870	—	132	225	350
1871	—	125	200	300
1873	—	170	250	450

KM# 11.7 **Obverse:** Liberty head above date **Reverse:** Value and CAL within wreath

Date	XF	AU	Unc	BU
1870	—	125	250	400
1871	—	125	250	400
1871	—	200	400	—
1872	—	—	250	400
1873	—	200	400	1,000
1874	—	125	250	750
1875	—	125	300	800
1876	—	100	250	—

KM# 11.8 **Obverse:** Liberty head **Reverse:** Value and date within wreath, CALIFORNIA GOLD outside

Date	XF	AU	Unc	BU
1863	265	425	675	950

Note: This issue is a rare Kroll type. All 1858 dates of this type are counterfeits

KM# 11.9 **Obverse:** Liberty head **Reverse:** HALF DOLLAR and date in wreath

Date	XF	AU	Unc	BU
1864	100	165	250	350
1866	200	330	500	700
1867	100	165	250	350
1868	100	165	250	350
1869	125	200	300	—
1870	—	200	350	—

KM# 11.11 **Obverse:** Goofy Liberty head **Reverse:** Value and date within wreath

Date	XF	AU	Unc	BU
1870	125	225	400	700

KM# 11.12 **Obverse:** Liberty head with H and date below **Reverse:** Value and CAL within wreath

Date	XF	AU	Unc	BU
1871	90.00	175	200	275

KM# 12.1 **Obverse:** Large indian head above date **Reverse:** Value within wreath

Date	XF	AU	Unc	BU
1852	—	—	350	675
1868	—	—	300	600
1874	—	—	300	600
1876	—	—	200	250
1878/6	—	—	300	450
1880	—	—	250	400
1881	—	—	250	400

KM# 12.2 **Reverse:** Value and CAL within wreath

Date	XF	AU	Unc	BU
1872	—	—	200	300
1873/2	—	—	350	650
1873	—	—	200	300
1874/3	—	—	300	450
1874	—	—	200	300
1875/3	—	—	200	300
1875	—	—	300	500
1876/5	—	—	200	300
1876	—	—	340	600

KM# 12.3 **Obverse:** Small indian head above date

Date	XF	AU	Unc	BU
1875	100	165	250	450
1876	75.00	100	200	300

KM# 12.4 **Obverse:** Young indian head above date

Date	XF	AU	Unc	BU
1882	—	350	850	—

DOLLAR (OCTAGONAL)

KM# 13.1 **Obverse:** Liberty head **Reverse:** Large eagle and legends

Date	XF	AU	Unc	BU
	1,000	1,500	2,000	4,000
1853	3,000	3,500	5,500	—
1854	1,000	1,500	2,000	4,000

KM# 13.2 **Reverse:** Value and date in beaded circle; CALIFORNIA GOLD, initials around circle

Date	XF	AU	Unc	BU
1853	275	500	750	1,100
1853	450	800	1,100	—
1853	300	450	900	—

Date	XF	AU	Unc	BU
1853	275	450	750	1,200
1854	450	800	1,100	—
1854	300	500	900	1,600
1855	350	600	900	—
1856	2,100	3,300	5,000	—
1863 Reeded edge	150	225	325	500
1863 Plain edge	—	—	40.00	80.00

Note: Reeded edge 1863 dates are Kroll types, while plain edge examples are Kroll restrikes

KM# 13.3   Reverse: Value and date inside wreath; legends outside wreath

Date	XF	AU	Unc	BU
1854 Rare	—	—	—	—

Note: Bowers and Marena sale 5-99, XF $9,775

1854	275	500	750	1,100
1855	275	500	750	1,100
1858	150	250	350	600

Note: 1858 dates are Kroll types

1859	1,900	—	—	—
1860	—	450	750	100
1868	—	450	750	1,100
1869	—	350	6,600	900
1870	—	350	600	900
1871	—	300	400	850

KM# 13.4   Obverse: Goofy Liberty head **Reverse:** Value and date inside wreath

Date	XF	AU	Unc	BU
1870	—	250	1,000	1,500

KM# 13.5   Obverse: Liberty head above date **Reverse:** Value and date within wreath; CALIFORNIA GOLD around wreath

Date	XF	AU	Unc	BU
1871	—	350	600	900
1874	—	3,000	—	—
1875	—	3,000	—	—
1876	—	2,000	—	—

KM# 14.1   Obverse: Large indian head above date **Reverse:** 1 DOLLAR inside wreath; CALIFORNIA GOLD around wreath

Date	XF	AU	Unc	BU
1872	—	350	600	900
1873/2	—	400	700	1,100
1873	—	600	750	—
1874	—	525	850	1,300
1875	—	475	600	1,000
1876/5	—	700	1,000	1,300

KM# 14.2   Obverse: Small indian head above date **Reverse:** 1 DOLLAR CAL inside wreath

Date	XF	AU	Unc	BU
1875	700	900	1,200	—
1876	—	1,000	1,400	—

KM# 14.3   Reverse: 1 DOLLAR inside wreath; CALIFORNIA GOLD around wreath

Date	XF	AU	Unc	BU
1876	—	500	750	—

DOLLAR (ROUND)

KM# 15.1   Obverse: Liberty head **Reverse:** Large eagle and legends

Date	XF	AU	Unc	BU
1853 Rare	—	—	—	—

Note: Superior sale Sept. 1987 MS-63 $35,200

KM# 15.2   Reverse: Value and date inside wreath; CALIFORNIA GOLD around wreath

Date	XF	AU	Unc	BU
1854	3,000	5,500	—	—
1854	5,000	7,500	—	—
1854 Rare	—	—	—	—

Note: Superior sale Sept. 1988 Fine $13,200

1857 2 known	—	—	—	—
1870	500	1,250	2,000	—
1871	850	1,450	2,500	—

Note: Coutnerfeits reported

KM# 15.3   Obverse: Liberty head above date **Reverse:** Value inside wreath; CALIFORNIA GOLD around wreath

Date	XF	AU	Unc	BU
1870	500	1,000	1,400	2,000
1871	500	1,000	1,400	2,000

KM# 15.4   Obverse: Goofy Liberty head **Reverse:** Value and date inside wreath; CALIFORNIA GOLD around wreath

Date	XF	AU	Unc	BU
1870	400	1,000	1,500	—

KM# 16   Obverse: Large indian head above date **Reverse:** Value inside wreath; CALIFORNIA GOLD outside wreath

Date	XF	AU	Unc	BU
1872	650	1,100	1,800	2,400

CALIFORNIA
Regular Issues

Norris, Grieg & Norris produced the first territorial gold coin struck in California, a $5 piece struck in 1849 at Benicia City, though it bears the imprint of San Francisco. The coining facility was owned by Thomas H. Norris, Charles Greig, and Hiram A. Norris, members of a New York engineering firm. A unique 1850 variety of this coin has the name STOCKTON beneath the date, instead of SAN FRANCISCO.

Early in 1849, John Little Moffat, a New York assayer, established an assay office at San Francisco in association with Joseph R. Curtis, Philo H. Perry, and Samuel Ward. The first issues of the **Moffat & Co.** assay office consisted of rectangular $16 ingots and assay bars of various and irregular denominations. In early August, the firm began striking $5 and $10 gold coins which resemble those of the U.S. Mint in design, but carry the legend S.M.V. (Standard Mint Value) CALIFORNIA GOLD on the reverse. Five-dollar pieces of the same design were also issued in 1850.

On Sept. 30, 1850, Congress directed the Secretary of the Treasury to establish an official Assay Office in California. Moffat & Co. obtained a contract to perform the duties of the U.S. Assay Office. **Augustus Humbert**, a New York watchcase maker, was appointed U.S. Assayer of Gold in California. Humbert stamped the first octagonal coin-ingots of the Provisional Government Mint on Jan. 31, 1851. The $50 pieces were accepted at par with standard U.S. gold coins, but were not officially recognized as coins. Officially, they were designated as "ingots." Colloquially, they were known as slugs, quintuple eagles, or 5-eagle pieces.

The $50 ingots failed to alleviate the need of California for gold coins. The banks regarded them as disadvantageous to their interests and utilized them only when compelled to do so by public need or convenience. Being of sound value, the ingots drove the overvalued $5, $10, and $20 territorial gold coins from circulation, bringing about a return to the use of gold dust for everyday transactions. Eventually, the slugs became so great a nuisance that they were discounted 3 percent when accepted. This unexpected turn of events forced Moffat & Co. to resume the issuing of $10 and $20 gold coins in 1852. The $10 piece was first issued with the Moffat & Co. imprint on Liberty's coronet, and later with the official imprint of Augustus Humbert on reverse. The $20 piece was issued with the Humbert imprint.

On Feb. 14, 1852, John L. Moffat withdrew from Moffat & Co. to enter the diving bell business, and Moffat & Co. was reorganized as the **United States Assay Office of Gold**, composed of Joseph R. Curtis, Philo H. Perry, and Samuel Ward. The U.S. Assay Office of Gold issued gold coins in denominations of $50 and $10 in 1852, and $20 and $10 in 1853. With the exception of the $50 slugs, they carry the imprint of the Assay Office on reverse. The .900 fine issues of this facility reflect an attempt to bring the issues of the U.S. Assay Office into conformity with the U.S. Mint standard.

The last territorial gold coins to bear the imprint of Moffat & Co. are $20 pieces issued in 1853, after the retirement of John L. Moffat. These coins do not carry a mark of fineness, and generally assay below the U.S. Mint standard.

Templeton Reid, previously mentioned in connection with the private gold issues of Georgia, moved his coining equipment to California when gold was discovered there, and in 1849 issued $10 and $25 gold pieces. No specimens are available to present-day collectors. The only known $10 piece is in the Smithsonian Collection. The only known specimen of the $25 piece was stolen from the U.S. Mint Cabinet Collection in 1858 and was never recovered.

Little is known of the origin and location of the **Cincinnati Mining & Trading Co.** It is believed that the firm was organized in the East and was forced to abandon most of its equipment while enroute to California. A few $5 and $10 gold coins were struck in 1849. Base metal counterfeits exist.

The **Massachusetts & California Co.** was organized in Northampton, Mass., in May 1849 by Josiah Hayden, S. S. Wells, Miles G. Moies, and others. Coining equipment was taken to San Francisco where $5 gold pieces were struck in 1849. The few pieces extant are heavily alloyed with copper.

Wright & Co., a brokerage firm located in Portsmouth Square, San Francisco, issued an undated $10 gold piece in the autumn of 1849 under the name of **Miners' Bank**. Unlike most territorial gold pieces, the Miners' Bank eagle was alloyed with copper. The coinage proved to be unpopular because of its copper-induced color and low intrinsic value. The firm was dissolved on Jan. 14, 1850.

In 1849, Dr. **J. S. Ormsby** and Major William M. Ormsby struck gold coins of $5 and $10 denominations at Sacramento under the name of Ormsby & Co. The coinage, which is identified by the initials J. S. O., is undated. Ormsby & Co. coinage was greatly over-valued, the eagle assaying at as little as $9.37.

The **Pacific Co.** of San Francisco issued $5 and $10 gold coins in 1849. The clouded story of this coinage is based on conjecture. It is believed that the well-struck pattern coins of this type were struck in the East by the Pacific Co. that organized in Boston and set sail for California on Feb. 20, 1849, and that the crudely hand-struck pieces were made by the jewelry firm of Broderick and Kohler after the dies passed into their possession. In any event, the intrinsic value of the initial coinage exceeded face value, but by the end of 1849, when they passed out of favor, the coins had been debased so flagrantly that the eagles assayed for as little as $7.86.

Dubosq & Co., a Philadelphia jewelry firm owned by Theodore Dubosq Sr. and Jr. and Henry Dubosq, took melting and coining equipment to San Francisco in 1849, and in 1850 issued $5 and $10 gold coins struck with dies allegedly made by U.S. Mint Engraver James B. Longacre. Dubosq & Co. coinage was immensely popular with the forty-niners because its intrinsic worth was in excess of face value.

The minting equipment of David C. Broderick and Frederick D. Kohler (see Pacific Co.) was acquired in May 1850 by San Francisco jewelers George C. Baldwin and Thomas S. Holman, who organized a private minting venture under the name of **Baldwin & Co**. The firm produced a $5 piece of Liberty Head design and a $10 piece with Horseman device in 1850. Liberty Head $10 and $20 pieces were coined in 1851. Baldwin & Co. produced the first $20 piece issued in California.

Schultz & Co. of San Francisco, a brass foundry located in the rear of the Baldwin & Co. establishment, and operated by Judge G. W. Schultz and William T. Garratt, issued $5 gold coins from early 1851 until April of that year. The inscription "SHULTS & CO." is a misspelling of SCHULTZ & CO.

Dunbar & Co. of San Francisco issued a $5 gold piece in 1851, after Edward E. Dunbar, owner of the California Bank in San Francisco, purchased the coining equipment of the defunct Baldwin & Co.

The San Francisco-based firm of **Wass, Molitor & Co.** was owned by 2 Hungarian exiles, Count S. C. Wass and A. P. Molitor, who initially founded the firm as a gold smelting and assaying plant. In response to a plea from the commercial community for small gold coins, Wass, Molitor & Co. issued $5 and $10 gold coins in 1852. The $5 piece was coined with small head and large head varieties, and the $10 piece with small head, large head, and small close-date varieties. The firm produced a second issue of gold coins in 1855, in denominations of $10, $20, and $50.

The U.S. Assay Office in California closed its doors on Dec. 14, 1853, to make way for the newly established San Francisco Branch Mint. The Mint, however, was unable to start immediate quantity production due to the lack of refining acids. During the interim, John G. Kellogg, a former employee of Moffat & Co., and John Glover Richter, a former assayer in the U.S. Assay Office, formed **Kellogg & Co.** for the purpose of supplying businessmen with urgently needed coinage. The firm produced $20 coins dated 1854 and 1855, after which Augustus Humbert replaced Richter and the enterprise reorganized as Kellogg & Humbert Melters, Assayers & Coiners. Kellogg & Humbert endured until 1860, but issued coins, $20 pieces, only in 1855.

BALDWIN & COMPANY

5 DOLLARS

20 DOLLARS

KM# 17

Date	XF	AU	Unc	BU
1850	10,000	—	25,000	—

10 DOLLARS

KM# 20

Date	Fine	VF	XF	Unc
1851	—	—	—	—

Note: Stack's Superior Sale Dec. 1988, XF-40 $52,800; Beware of copies cast in base metals

BLAKE & COMPANY

KM# 18

Date	XF	AU	Unc	BU
1850	48,500	—	85,000	—

Note: Bass Sale May 2000, MS-64 $149,500

20 DOLLARS

KM# 19

Date	Fine	VF	XF	Unc
1851	9,000	14,500	28,500	50,000

KM# 21

Date	Fine	VF	XF	Unc
1855 Rare	—	—	—	—

Note: Many modern copies exist

J. H. BOWIE

5 DOLLARS

KM# 22

Date	Fine	VF	XF	Unc
1849 Rare	—	—	—	—

Note: Americana Sale Jan. 2001, AU-58 $253,000

CINCINNATI MINING AND TRADING COMPANY

5 DOLLARS

KM# 23

Date	Fine	VF	XF	Unc
1849 Rare	—	—	—	—

10 DOLLARS

KM# 24

Date	Fine	VF	XF	Unc
1849 Rare	—	—	—	—

Note: Brand Sale 1984, XF $104,500

DUBOSQ & COMPANY

5 DOLLARS

KM# 26

Date	Fine	VF	XF	Unc
1850	25,000	42,500	—	—

10 DOLLARS

KM# 27

Date	Fine	VF	XF	Unc
1850	25,000	45,000	65,000	—

DUNBAR & COMPANY

5 DOLLARS

KM# 28

Date	Fine	VF	XF	Unc
1851	22,500	32,500	55,000	—

Note: Spink & Son Sale 1988, AU $62,000

AUGUSTUS HUMBERT / UNITED STATES ASSAYER

10 DOLLARS

KM# 29.1 **Note:** AUGUSTUS HUMBERT imprint.

Date	Fine	VF	XF	Unc
1852/1	2,000	3,500	5,500	15,000
1852	1,500	2,500	4,750	11,500

KM# 29.2 **Note:** Error: IINITED.

Date	Fine	VF	XF	Unc
1852/1 Rare	—	—	—	—
1852 Rare	—	—	—	—

20 DOLLARS

KM# 30

Date	Fine	VF	XF	Unc
1852/1	4,500	6,000	9,500	—

Note: Mory Sale June 2000, AU-53 $13,800; Garrett Sale Mar. 1980, Humberts Proof $325,000; Private Sale May 1989, Humberts Proof (PCGS Pr-65) $1,350,000; California Sale Oct. 2000, Humberts Proof (PCGS Pr-65) $552,000

50 DOLLARS

KM# 31.1   Obverse: 50 D C 880 THOUS, eagle **Reverse:** 50 in center

Date	Fine	VF	XF	Unc
1851	9,500	12,000	22,000	—

KM# 31.1a   Obverse: 887 THOUS

Date	Fine	VF	XF	Unc
1851	6,000	9,000	17,500	37,500

KM# 31.2   Obverse: 880 THOUS **Reverse:** Without 50

Date	Fine	VF	XF	Unc
1851	5,000	8,000	16,500	35,500

KM# 31.2a   Obverse: 887 THOUS

Date	Fine	VF	XF	Unc
1851	—	14,500	25,000	—

KM# 31.3   Note: ASSAYER inverted.

Date	Fine	VF	XF	Unc
1851 Unique	—	—	—	—

KM# 31.4   Obverse: 880 THOUS **Reverse:** Rays from central star

Date	Fine	VF	XF	Unc
1851 Unique	—	—	—	—

TERRITORIAL GOLD

KELLOGG & COMPANY

20 DOLLARS

KM# 32.1 **Obverse:** 880 THOUS **Reverse:** "Target"

Date	Fine	VF	XF	Unc
1851	5,000	8,000	16,000	35,000

KM# 32.1a **Obverse:** 887 THOUS

Date	Fine	VF	XF	Unc
1851	5,000	8,000	16,000	35,000

Note: Garrett Sale March 1980, Humberts Proof $500,000

KM# 32.2 **Reverse:** Small design

Date	Fine	VF	XF	Unc
1851	5,000	8,000	16,000	—
1852	4,500	7,500	18,500	40,000

Note: Bloomfield Sale December 1996, BU $159,500

KM# 33.1 **Obverse:** Thick date **Reverse:** Short arrows

Date	Fine	VF	XF	Unc
1854	1,200	2,000	4,000	17,500

KM# 33.2 **Obverse:** Medium date

Date	Fine	VF	XF	Unc
1854	1,200	2,000	4,000	17,500

KM# 33.3 **Obverse:** Thin date

Date	Fine	VF	XF	Unc
1854	1,200	2,000	4,000	17,500

KM# 33.4 **Reverse:** Long arrows

Date	Fine	VF	XF	Unc
1854	1,200	2,000	4,000	17,500
1855	1,200	2,250	4,250	18,500

Note: Garrett Sale March 1980 Proof $230,000

KM# 33.5 **Reverse:** Medium arrows

Date	Fine	VF	XF	Unc
1855	1,200	2,250	4,250	18,500

KM# 33.6 **Reverse:** Short arrows

Date	Fine	VF	XF	Unc
1855	1,200	2,250	4,250	18,500

50 DOLLARS

KM# 34

Date	Fine	VF	XF	Unc
1855	—	—	—	—

Note: Heritage ANA Sale August 1977, Proof $156,500

MASSACHUSETTES AND CALIFORNIA COMPANY

5 DOLLARS

KM# 35

Date	Fine	VF	XF	Unc
1849 Rare Proof	40,000	65,000	—	—

MINERS BANK

10 DOLLARS

Date	Fine	VF	XF	Unc
(1849)	—	8,500	17,500	45,000

Note: Garrett Sale March 1980, MS-65 $135,000

Date	Fine	VF	XF	Unc
(1849)	—	—	—	—

Note: Rare, as most specimens have heavy copper alloy

MOFFAT & COMPANY

5 DOLLARS

KM# 37.1

Date	Fine	VF	XF	Unc
1849	1,000	1,500	3,500	12,000

KM# 37.2 **Reverse:** Die break at DOL

Date	Fine	VF	XF	Unc
1849	1,000	1,500	3,500	12,000

KM# 37.3 **Reverse:** Die break on shield

Date	Fine	VF	XF	Unc
1849	1,000	1,500	3,500	12,000

KM# 37.4 **Reverse:** Small letters

Date	Fine	VF	XF	Unc
1850	1,100	1,650	4,200	14,000

KM# 37.5 **Reverse:** Large letters

Date	Fine	VF	XF	Unc
1850	1,100	1,650	4,200	14,000

Note: Garrett Sale March 1980, MS-60 $21,000

10 DOLLARS

KM# 38.1 **Reverse:** Value: TEN DOL., arrow below period

Date	Fine	VF	XF	Unc
1849	1,650	3,500	6,000	15,000

KM# 38.2 **Reverse:** Arrow above period

Date	Fine	VF	XF	Unc
1849	1,650	3,500	6,000	15,000

KM# 38.3 **Reverse:** Value: TEN D., large letters

Date	Fine	VF	XF	Unc
1849	2,250	5,000	7,500	16,500

KM# 38.4 **Reverse:** Small letters

Date	Fine	VF	XF	Unc
1849	—	5,000	7,500	16,500

KM# 39.1 **Note:** MOFFAT & CO. imprint, wide date

Date	Fine	VF	XF	Unc
1852	2,500	5,500	10,000	20,000

KM# 39.2 **Note:** Close date. Struck by Augustus Humbert.

Date	Fine	VF	XF	Unc
1852	2,000	4,250	9,000	18,500

20 DOLLARS

KM# 40 **Note:** Struck by Curtis, Perry, & Ward.

Date	Fine	VF	XF	Unc
1853	2,150	3,750	6,000	16,500

NORRIS, GREIG, & NORRIS

HALF EAGLE

KM# 41.1 **Reverse:** Period after ALLOY

Date	Fine	VF	XF	Unc
1849	2,250	3,750	7,250	20,000

KM# 41.2 **Reverse:** Without period after ALLOY

Date	Fine	VF	XF	Unc
1849	2,250	3,750	7,250	20,000

KM# 41.3 **Reverse:** Period after ALLOY

Date	Fine	VF	XF	Unc
1849	1,750	3,000	6,750	20,000

KM# 41.4 **Reverse:** Without period after ALLOY

Date	Fine	VF	XF	Unc
1849	1,750	3,000	6,750	20,000

KM# 42 **Obverse:** STOCKTON beneath date

Date	Fine	VF	XF	Unc
1850 Unique	—	—	—	—

TERRITORIAL GOLD

J. S. ORMSBY

5 DOLLARS

KM# 43.1

Date	Fine	VF	XF	Unc
(1849) Unique	—	—	—	—

KM# 43.2

Date	Fine	VF	XF	Unc
(1849) Unique	—	—	—	—

Note: Superior Auction 1989, VF $137,500

10 DOLLARS

KM# 44

Date	Fine	VF	XF	Unc
(1849) Rare	—	—	—	—

Note: Garrett Sale March 1980, F-12 $100,000; Ariagno Sale June 1999, AU-50 $145,000

PACIFIC COMPANY

5 DOLLARS

KM# 45

Date	Fine	VF	XF	Unc
1849 Rare	—	—	—	—

Note: Garrett Sale March 1980, VF-30 $180,000

10 DOLLARS

KM# 46.1

Date	Fine	VF	XF	Unc
1849 Rare	—	—	—	—

Note: Waldorf Sale 1964, $24,000

KM# 46.2

Date	Fine	VF	XF	Unc
1849 Rare	—	—	—	—

1 DOLLAR

KM# A45

Date	Fine	VF	XF	Unc
(1849) Unique	—	—	—	—

Note: Mory Sale June 2000, EF-40 $57,500

TEMPLETON REID

10 DOLLARS

KM# 47

Date	Fine	VF	XF	Unc
1849 Unique	—	—	—	—

20 DOLLARS

KM# 48

Date	Fine	VF	XF	Unc
1849 Unknown	—	—	—	—

Note: Only known specimen of above stolen from U.S. Mint in 1858 and never recovered; also see listings under Georgia

SCHULTZ & COMPANY

5 DOLLARS

KM# 49

Date	Fine	VF	XF	Unc
1851	—	36,800	50,000	—

UNITED STATES ASSAY OFFICE OF GOLD

10 DOLLARS

KM# 50.1   Obverse: TEN DOLS 884 THOUS
Reverse: O of OFFICE below I of UNITED

Date	Fine	VF	XF	Unc
1852	—	—	—	—

Note: Garrett Sale March 1980, MS-60 $18,000

KM# 51.2	**Reverse:** O below N, strong beads			
Date	Fine	VF	XF	Unc
1852	1,750	2,500	3,850	9,500
KM# 51.3	**Reverse:** Weak beads			
Date	Fine	VF	XF	Unc
1852	1,750	2,500	3,850	9,500

KM# 52   Obverse: TEN D, 884 THOUS

Date	Fine	VF	XF	Unc
1853	5,000	7,750	14,500	—

KM# 52a   Obverse: 900 THOUS

Date	Fine	VF	XF	Unc
1853	2,700	4,200	6,500	—

Note: Garrett Sale March 1980, MS-60 $35,000

20 DOLLARS

KM# 53   Obverse: 884/880 THOUS

Date	Fine	VF	XF	Unc
1853	8,500	12,500	17,500	23,500

KM# 53a   Obverse: 900/880 THOUS

Date	Fine	VF	XF	Unc
1853	1,550	2,750	4,250	10,000

Note: 1853 Liberty Head listed under Moffat & Company

50 DOLLARS

KM# 54   Obverse: 887 THOUS

Date	Fine	VF	XF	Unc
1852	4,000	6,500	13,500	26,500

KM# 54a   Obverse: 900 THOUS

Date	Fine	VF	XF	Unc
1852	5,000	7,000	14,500	28,500

WASS, MOLITOR & COMPANY

5 DOLLARS

KM# 55.1   Obverse: Small head, rounded bust

Date	Fine	VF	XF	Unc
1852	2,000	4,000	6,750	16,500

KM# 55.2   Note: Thick planchet.

Date	Fine	VF	XF	Unc
1852 Unique	—	—	—	—

KM# 56   Obverse: Large head, pointed bust

Date	Fine	VF	XF	Unc
1852	2,000	4,500	8,500	17,500

10 DOLLARS

KM# 57   Obverse: Long neck, large date

Date	Fine	VF	XF	Unc
1852	2,750	5,000	8,500	15,500

KM# 58   Obverse: Short neck, wide date

Date	Fine	VF	XF	Unc
1852	1,500	2,650	5,500	13,500

KM# 59.1   Obverse: Short neck, small date

Date	Fine	VF	XF	Unc
1852 Rare	—	—	—	—

Note: Eliasberg Sale May 1996, EF-45 $36,300; S.S. Central America Sale December 2000, VF-30 realized $12,650

TERRITORIAL GOLD

KM# 59.2 **Obverse:** Plugged date

Date	Fine	VF	XF	Unc
1855	6,000	8,000	12,500	28,500

20 DOLLARS

50 DOLLARS

KM# 62

Date	Fine	VF	XF	Unc
1855	—	—	—	—

Note: Bloomfield Sale December 1996, BU $170,500

KM# 60 **Obverse:** Large head

Date	Fine	VF	XF	Unc
1855 Rare	—	—	—	—

KM# 61 **Obverse:** Small head

Date	Fine	VF	XF	Unc
1855	7,000	11,000	20,000	—

TERRITORIAL GOLD

COLORADO

The discovery of gold in Colorado Territory was accompanied by the inevitable need for coined money. Austin M. Clark, Milton E. Clark, and Emanuel H. Gruber, bankers of Leavenworth, Kansas, moved to Denver where they established a bank and issued $2.50, $5, $10, and $20 gold coins in 1860 and 1861. To protect the holder from loss by abrasion, **Clark, Gruber & Co.** made their coins slightly heavier than full value required. The 1860 issues carry the inscription PIKE'S PEAK GOLD on reverse. CLARK, GRUBER & CO. appears on the reverse of the 1861 issues, and PIKE'S PEAK on the coronet of Liberty. The government purchased the plant of Clark, Gruber & Co. in 1863 and operated it as a federal Assay Office until 1906.

In the summer of 1861, **John Parsons**, an assayer whose place of business was located in South Park at the Tarryall Mines, Colorado, issued undated gold coins in the denominations of $2.50 and $5. They, too, carry the inscription PIKE'S PEAK GOLD on reverse.

J. J. Conway & Co., bankers of Georgia Gulch, Colorado operated the Conway Mint for a short period in 1861. Undated gold coins in the denominations of $2.50, $5, and $10 were issued. A variety of the $5 coin does not carry the numeral 5 on reverse. The issues of the Conway Mint were highly regarded for their scrupulously maintained value.

CLARK, GRUBER & COMPANY

2-1/2 DOLLARS

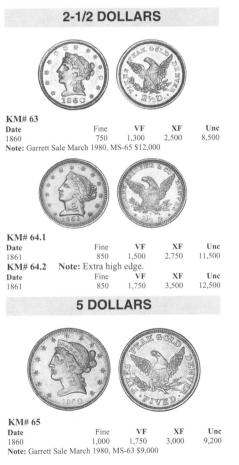

KM# 63

Date	Fine	VF	XF	Unc
1860	750	1,300	2,500	8,500

Note: Garrett Sale March 1980, MS-65 $12,000

KM# 64.1

Date	Fine	VF	XF	Unc
1861	850	1,500	2,750	11,500

KM# 64.2   **Note:** Extra high edge.

Date	Fine	VF	XF	Unc
1861	850	1,750	3,500	12,500

5 DOLLARS

KM# 65

Date	Fine	VF	XF	Unc
1860	1,000	1,750	3,000	9,200

Note: Garrett Sale March 1980, MS-63 $9,000

KM# 66

Date	Fine	VF	XF	Unc
1861	1,500	2,500	4,500	13,500

10 DOLLARS

KM# 67

Date	Fine	VF	XF	Unc
1860	2,750	3,750	8,000	21,500

KM# 68

Date	Fine	VF	XF	Unc
1861	1,500	2,500	4,500	15,500

TERRITORIAL GOLD

20 DOLLARS

KM# 69

Date	Fine	VF	XF	Unc
1860	25,000	55,000	75,000	100,000

Note: Eliasberg Sale May 1996, AU $90,200; Schoonmaker Sale June a997, VCF $62,700

KM# 70

Date	Fine	VF	XF	Unc
1861	7,000	10,000	21,500	—

J. J. CONWAY

2-1/2 DOLLARS

KM# 71

Date	Fine	VF	XF	Unc
(1861)	—	45,000	70,000	—

5 DOLLARS

KM# 72.1

Date	Fine	VF	XF	Unc
(1861) Rare	—	—	—	—

Note: Brand Sale June 1984, XF-40 $44,000

KM# 72.2   Reverse: Numeral 5 omitted

Date	Fine	VF	XF	Unc
(1861) Unique	—	—	—	—

10 DOLLARS

KM# 73

Date	Fine	VF	XF	Unc
(1861) Rare	—	60,000	—	—

JOHN PARSONS

2-1/2 DOLLARS

KM# 74

Date	Fine	VF	XF	Unc
(1861) Rare	—	—	—	—

Note: Garrett Sale March 1980, VF-20 $85,000

5 DOLLARS

KM# 75

Date	Fine	VF	XF	Unc
(1861) Rare	—	—	—	—

Note: Garrett Sale March 1980, VF-20 $100,000

GEORGIA

The first territorial gold pieces were struck in 1830 by **Templeton Reid**, a goldsmith and assayer who established a private mint at Gainesville, Georgia, at the time gold was being mined on a relatively large scale in Georgia and North Carolina. Reid's pieces were issued in denominations of $2.50, $5, and $10. Except for an undated variety of the $10 piece, all are dated 1830.

CHRISTOPHER BECHTLER

2-1/2 DOLLARS

KM# 76.1 Reverse: GEORGIA, 64 G, 22 CARATS

Date	Fine	VF	XF	Unc
ND	1,650	2,650	5,000	10,000

KM# 76.2 Reverse: GEORGIA, 64 G, 22 CARATS, even 22

Date	Fine	VF	XF	Unc
ND	1,850	2,850	5,500	11,500

5 DOLLARS

KM# 77 Obverse: RUTHERF Reverse: 128 G, 22 CARATS

Date	Fine	VF	XF	Unc
ND	2,000	3,500	5,500	11,500

KM# 78.1 Obverse: RUTHERFORD

Date	Fine	VF	XF	Unc
ND	2,000	3,750	6,000	12,500

KM# 78.2 Reverse: Colon after 128 G:

Date	Fine	VF	XF	Unc
ND	—	20,000	30,000	—

Note: Akers Pittman Sale October 1997, VF-XF $26,400

TEMPLETON REID

2-1/2 DOLLARS

KM# 79

Date	Fine	VF	XF	Unc
1830	12,500	32,500	55,000	—

5 DOLLARS

KM# 80

Date	Fine	VF	XF	Unc
1830 Rare	—	—	—	—

Note: Garrett Sale November 1979, XF-40 $200,000

10 DOLLARS

KM# 81 Obverse: With date

Date	Fine	VF	XF	Unc
1830 Rare	—	—	—	—

KM# 82 Obverse: Undated

Date	Fine	VF	XF	Unc
(1830) Rare	—	—	—	—

Note: Also see listings under California

NORTH CAROLINA

The southern Appalachians were also the scene of a private gold minting operation conducted by Christopher Bechtler Sr., his son August, and nephew Christopher Jr. The Bechtlers, a family of German metallurgists, established a mint at Rutherfordton, North Carolina, which produced territorial gold coins for a longer period than any other private mint in American history. Christopher Bechtler Sr. ran the Bechtler mint from July 1831 until his death in 1842, after which the mint was taken over by his son August who ran it until 1852.

The Bechtler coinage includes but 3 denominations -- $1, $2.50, and $5 - but they were issued in a wide variety of weights and sizes. The coinage is undated, except for 3 varieties of the $5 piece which carry the inscription "Aug. 1, 1834" to indicate that they conform to the new weight standard adopted by the U.S. Treasury for official gold coins. **Christopher Bechtler Sr.** produced $2.50 and $5 gold coins for Georgia, and $1, $2.50, and $5 coins for North Carolina. The dollar coins have the distinction of being the first gold coins of that denomination to be produced in the United States. While under the supervision of **August Bechtler**, the Bechtler mint issued $1 and $5 coins for North Carolina.

AUGUST BECHTLER

DOLLAR

KM# 83.1 **Reverse:** CAROLINA, 27 G. 21C.

Date	Fine	VF	XF	Unc
ND	450	650	1,150	2,950

KM# 83.2

Date	Fine	VF	XF	Unc
ND	450	650	1,150	2,950

KM# 84 **Reverse:** CAROLINA, 134 G. 21 CARATS

Date	Fine	VF	XF	Unc
ND	1,750	3,500	6,000	12,500

KM# 85 **Reverse:** CAROLINA, 128 G. 22 CARATS

Date	Fine	VF	XF	Unc
ND	3,000	5,500	8,000	15,000

KM# 86 **Reverse:** CAROLINA, 141 G: 20 CARATS

Date	Fine	VF	XF	Unc
ND	2,750	4,850	7,500	14,500

Note: Proof restrikes exist from original dies; in the Akers Pittman Sale October 1997, an example sold for $14,300.

CHRISTOPHER BECHTLER

DOLLAR

KM# 87 **Obverse:** 28 G. **Reverse:** CAROLINA, N reversed

Date	Fine	VF	XF	Unc
ND	900	1,200	1,700	3,750

KM# 88.1 **Obverse:** 28. G. centered without star **Reverse:** N. CAROLINA

Date	Fine	VF	XF	Unc
ND	1,500	2,200	3,500	8,000

KM# 88.2 **Obverse:** N. CAROLINA **Reverse:** 28 G high without star

Date	Fine	VF	XF	Unc
ND	2,500	4,500	6,500	12,000

KM# 89 **Obverse:** 30 G. **Reverse:** N. CAROLINA

Date	Fine	VF	XF	Unc
ND	850	1,200	2,750	5,500

2-1/2 DOLLARS

KM# 90.1 **Reverse:** CAROLINA, 67 G. 21 CARATS

Date	Fine	VF	XF	Unc
ND	1,250	2,250	5,500	11,500

KM# 90.2 **Reverse:** 64 G 22 CARATS, uneven 22

Date	Fine	VF	XF	Unc
ND	1,450	2,850	6,000	12,000

KM# 90.3 **Reverse:** Even 22

Date	Fine	VF	XF	Unc
ND	1,650	3,000	6,500	12,500

KM# 91 **Reverse:** CAROLINA, 70 G. 20 CARATS

Date	Fine	VF	XF	Unc
ND	1,650	3,000	6,750	18,500

Note: Bowers and Merena Long Sale May 1995, MS-63 $31,900

KM# 92.1 **Obverse:** RUTHERFORD in a circle, border of large beads **Reverse:** NORTH CAROLINA, 20 C. 75 G.

Date	Fine	VF	XF	Unc
ND	—	7,500	11,500	25,000

KM# 92.2 **Reverse:** NORTH CAROLINA, without 75 G, wide 20 C.

Date	Fine	VF	XF	Unc
ND	2,800	5,000	7,000	14,500

KM# 92.3 **Obverse:** Narrow 20 C

Date	Fine	VF	XF	Unc
ND	2,800	5,000	7,000	14,500

KM# 93.1 **Reverse:** NORTH CAROLINA without 75 G, CAROLINA above 250 instead of GOLD

Date	Fine	VF	XF	Unc
ND Unique	—	—	—	—

KM# 93.2 **Obverse:** NORTH CAROLINA, 20 C **Reverse:** 75 G, border finely serrated

Date	Fine	VF	XF	Unc
ND	4,500	7,500	10,500	—

5 DOLLARS

KM# 94 **Reverse:** CAROLINA, 134 G. star 21 CARATS

Date	Fine	VF	XF	Unc
ND	1,650	3,250	6,000	11,000

KM# 95 **Reverse:** 21 above CARATS, without star

Date	Fine	VF	XF	Unc
ND Unique	—	—	—	—

KM# 96.1 **Obverse:** RUTHERFORD **Reverse:** CAROLINA, 140 G. 20 CARATS

Date	Fine	VF	XF	Unc
1834	1,750	3,750	6,500	11,500

KM# 96.2

Date	Fine	VF	XF	Unc
1834	2,000	4,000	7,000	12,500

KM# 97.1 **Obverse:** RUTHERF **Reverse:** CARO-LINA. 140 G. 20 CARATS; 20 close to CARATS

Date	Fine	VF	XF	Unc
1834	1,800	3,850	6,750	12,000

KM# 97.2 **Reverse:** 20 away from CARATS

Date	Fine	VF	XF	Unc
1834	2,500	6,500	11,500	—

KM# 98 Obverse: RUTHERF **Reverse:** CAROLINA, 141 G, 20 CARATS

Date	Fine	VF	XF	Unc
Proof restrike	—	—	—	15,500

KM# 99.1 Reverse: NORTH CAROLINA, 150 G, below 20 CARATS

Date	Fine	VF	XF	Unc
ND	2,800	4,500	8,500	18,500

KM# 99.2 Reverse: Without 150 G

Date	Fine	VF	XF	Unc
ND	3,200	6,000	10,000	20,000

OREGON

The Oregon Exchange Co., a private mint located at Oregon City, Oregon Territory, issued $5 and $10 pieces of local gold in 1849. The initials K., M., T., A., W. R. C. (G on the $5 piece), and S. on the obverse represent the eight founders of the **Oregon Exchange Co.**: William Kilborne, Theophilus Magruder, James Taylor, George Abernathy, William Willson, William Rector, John Campbell, and Noyes Smith. Campbell is erroneously represented by a G on the $5 coin. For unknown reasons, the initials A and W are omitted from the $10 piece. O.T. (Oregon Territory) is erroneously presented as T.O. on the $5 coin.

OREGON EXCHANGE COMPANY

5 DOLLARS

KM# 100

Date	Fine	VF	XF	Unc
1849	10,000	18,500	33,350	—

10 DOLLARS

KM# 101

Date	Fine	VF	XF	Unc
1849	20,000	40,000	65,000	—

UTAH

In 1849, the **Mormons** settled in the Great Salt Lake Valley of Utah and established the Deseret Mint in a small adobe building in Salt Lake City. Operating under the direct supervision of Brigham Young, the Deseret Mint issued $2.50, $5, $10, and $20 gold coins in 1849. Additional $5 pieces were struck in 1850 and 1860, the latter in a temporary mint set up in Barlow's jewelry shop. The Mormon $20 piece was the first of that denomination to be struck in the United States. The initials G.S.L.C.P.G. on Mormon coins denotes "Great Salt Lake City Pure Gold." It was later determined that the coinage was grossly deficient in value, mainly because no attempt was made to assay or refine the gold.

MORMON ISSUES

2-1/2 DOLLARS

KM# 102

Date	Fine	VF	XF	Unc
1849	4,000	7,000	13,500	24,500

5 DOLLARS

KM# 103

Date	Fine	VF	XF	Unc
1849	4,000	7,000	12,000	23,500

KM# 104

Date	Fine	VF	XF	Unc
1850	4,500	7,500	15,000	25,500

KM# 105

Date	Fine	VF	XF	Unc
1860	6,500	12,000	25,000	37,500

10 DOLLARS

KM# 106

Date	Fine	VF	XF	Unc
1849 Rare	—	—	—	—

Note: Heritage ANA Sale July 1988, AU $93,000

20 DOLLARS

KM# 107

Date	Fine	VF	XF	Unc
1849	22,500	47,500	85,000	—

TERRITORIAL GOLD

HAWAII

KM# 1a CENT
Copper

Date	Mintage	VG	F	VF	XF	Unc
1847 Plain 4, 13 berries (6 left, 7 right)	100,000	175	250	325	550	1,000

KM# 1b CENT
Copper

Date	Mintage	VG	F	VF	XF	Unc
1847 Plain 4, 15 berries (8 left, 7 right)	Inc. above	175	250	325	550	1,000

KM# 1f CENT
Copper

Date	Mintage	VG	F	VF	XF	Unc
1847 Plain 4, 15 berries (7 left, 8 right)	Inc. above	550	800	1,500	2,000	—

KM# 1c CENT
Copper

Date	Mintage	VG	F	VF	XF	Unc
1847 Plain 4, 17 berries (8 left, 9 right)	Inc. above	175	250	325	550	1,200

KM# 1d CENT
Copper

Date	Mintage	VG	F	VF	XF	Unc
1847 Crosslet 4, 15 berries (7 left, 8 right)	Inc. above	150	225	325	500	1,000

KM# 1e CENT
Copper

Date	Mintage	VG	F	VF	XF	Unc
1847 Crosslet 4, 18 berries (9 left, 9 right)	Inc. above	250	400	550	750	6,000

KM# 2 5 CENTS (Pattern)
Nickel

Date	Mintage	VG	F	VF	XF	Unc
1881	200	2,500	3,500	5,500	7,500	12,500

Note: All original specimens of this pattern were struck on thin nickel planchets, presumably in Paris and have "MAILLECHORT" stamped on the edge. In the early 1900's, deceptive replicas of the issue were produced in Canada, on thick and thin nickel and aluminum, and thin copper planchets (thick about 2.7 to 3.1mm; thin about 1.4 to 1.7mm). The original patterns can be easily distiguished from the replicas, because on the former, a small cross surmounts the crown on the reverse; on the replicas the

KM# 3 10 CENTS (Umi Keneta)
2.5000 g., 0.9000 Silver .0724 oz. ASW

Date	Mintage	VG	F	VF	XF	Unc
1883	250,000	40.00	55.00	85.00	250	900
1883 Proof	26	Value: 7,500				

KM# 4a 1/8 DOLLAR (Hapawalu)
Copper **Note:** Pattern issue.

Date	Mintage	VG	F	VF	XF	Unc
1883 Proof	18	Value: 9,000				

KM# 4 1/8 DOLLAR (Hapawalu)
0.9000 Silver **Note:** Pattern issue.

Date	Mintage	VG	F	VF	XF	Unc
1883 Proof	20	Value: 25,000				

KM# 5 1/4 DOLLAR (Hapaha)
6.2200 g., 0.9000 Silver .1800 oz. ASW

Date	Mintage	VG	F	VF	XF	Unc
1883	500,000	35.00	45.00	60.00	90.00	200
1883/1883	Inc. above	40.00	50.00	80.00	125	275
1883 Proof	26	Value: 7,500				

KM# 5a 1/4 DOLLAR (Hapaha)
Copper **Note:** Pattern issue.

Date	Mintage	VG	F	VF	XF	Unc
1883 Proof	18	Value: 5,000				

KM# 6 1/2 DOLLAR (Hapalua)
12.5000 g., 0.9000 Silver .3618 oz. ASW

Date	Mintage	VG	F	VF	XF	Unc
1883	700,000	70.00	95.00	135	250	975
1883 Proof	26	Value: 8,000				

KM# 6a 1/2 DOLLAR (Hapalua)
Copper **Note:** Pattern issue.

Date	Mintage	VG	F	VF	XF	Unc
1883 Proof	18	Value: 6,000				

KM# 7 DOLLAR (Akahi Dala)
26.7300 g., 0.9000 Silver .7736 oz. ASW

Date	Mintage	VG	F	VF	XF	Unc
1883	500,000	225	255	400	750	4,000
1883 Proof	26	Value: 9,000				

KM# 7a DOLLAR (Akahi Dala)
Copper **Note:** Pattern issue.

Date	Mintage	VG	F	VF	XF	Unc
1883 Proof	18	Value: 9,000				

Note: Official records indicate the following quantities of the above issues were redeemed and melted: KM#1 - 88,305; KM#3 - 79; KM#5 - 257,400; KM#6 - 612,245; KM#7 - 453,652. That leaves approximate net mintages of: KM#1 - 11,600; KM#3 - 250,000; KM#5 (regular date) - 202,600, (overdate) 40,000; KM#6 - 87,700; KM#7 - 46,300.

PHILIPPINES
UNITED STATES ADMINISTRATION
100 Centavos = 1 Peso
DECIMAL COINAGE

KM# 162 1/2 CENTAVO
Bronze **Obv:** Man seated beside hammer and anvil; Mt. Mayon at right

Date	Mintage	F	VF	XF	Unc	BU
1903	12,084,000	0.50	1.00	2.00	15.00	18.00
1903 Proof	2,558	Value: 55.00				
1904	5,654,000	0.50	1.25	2.50	20.00	25.00
1904 Proof	1,355	Value: 60.00				
1905 Proof	471	Value: 130				
1906 Proof	500	Value: 110				
1908 Proof	500	Value: 110				

KM# 163 CENTAVO
Bronze **Obv:** Man seated beside hammer and anvil; Mt. Mayon at right

Date	Mintage	F	VF	XF	Unc	BU
1903	10,790,000	0.50	1.00	2.50	20.00	30.00
1903 Proof	2,558	Value: 50.00				
1904	17,040,000	0.50	1.00	2.50	20.00	35.00
1904 Proof	1,355	Value: 50.00				
1905	10,000,000	0.50	1.00	2.50	25.00	40.00
1905 Proof	471	Value: 150				
1906 Proof	500	Value: 125				
1908 Proof	500	Value: 125				
1908S	2,187,000	2.50	5.50	12.50	50.00	75.00
1909S	1,738,000	7.50	15.00	26.00	75.00	120
1910S	2,700,000	2.00	5.00	9.00	40.00	60.00
1911S	4,803,000	1.00	3.00	5.00	40.00	50.00
1912S	3,000,000	2.50	5.50	10.00	60.00	85.00
1913S	5,000,000	1.00	2.50	5.00	40.00	55.00
1914S	5,000,000	1.00	2.50	5.00	30.00	50.00
1914S Large S	Inc. above	—	—	—	—	—

Note: This variety has been questioned by leading authorities

Date	Mintage	F	VF	XF	Unc	BU
1915S	2,500,000	15.00	40.00	90.00	475	750
1916S	4,330,000	4.00	8.00	12.50	100	150
1917/6S	7,070,000	20.00	30.00	75.00	300	425
1917S	Inc. above	2.50	5.00	10.00	35.00	60.00
1918S	11,660,000	2.00	3.00	7.50	45.00	80.00
1918S Large S	Inc. above	80.00	150	250	1,200	1,800
1919S	4,540,000	0.75	2.00	6.00	35.00	65.00
1920S	2,500,000	4.00	8.00	15.00	125	265
1920	3,552,000	1.00	2.00	8.50	35.00	50.00
1921	7,283,000	0.75	1.50	5.00	40.00	70.00
1922	3,519,000	0.50	1.50	5.00	45.00	70.00
1925M	9,332,000	0.50	1.50	6.00	30.00	45.00
1926M	9,000,000	0.50	1.50	5.00	35.00	50.00
1927M	9,270,000	0.35	1.00	5.00	35.00	50.00
1928M	9,150,000	0.35	1.00	5.00	25.00	45.00
1929M	5,657,000	1.00	3.00	8.00	40.00	60.00
1930M	5,577,000	0.50	1.50	4.00	25.00	35.00
1931M	5,659,000	0.50	1.50	5.00	30.00	40.00
1932M	4,000,000	0.75	2.50	8.00	40.00	60.00
1933M	8,393,000	0.25	1.50	4.00	20.00	35.00
1934M	3,179,000	0.75	2.00	4.00	25.00	45.00
1936M	17,455,000	0.25	1.00	4.00	30.00	40.00

KM# 164 5 CENTAVOS
Copper-Nickel **Obv:** Man seated beside hammer and anvil; Mt. Mayon at right

Date	Mintage	F	VF	XF	Unc	BU
1903	8,910,000	0.50	1.00	2.50	22.00	30.00
1903 Proof	2,558	Value: 60.00				
1904	1,075,000	0.75	1.50	3.00	27.00	35.00
1904 Proof	1,355	Value: 65.00				
1905 Proof	471	Value: 150				
1906 Proof	500	Value: 100				
1908 Proof	500	Value: 110				
1916S	300,000	35.00	65.00	90.00	500	750
1917S	2,300,000	2.00	4.50	12.00	100	125
1918S	2,780,000	1.50	3.50	10.00	75.00	100
1919S	1,220,000	2.50	6.00	12.00	110	150
1920	1,421,000	3.00	8.00	17.50	125	150
1921	2,132,000	1.50	5.00	10.00	90.00	125
1925M	1,000,000	5.00	17.50	40.00	140	190
1926M	1,200,000	3.00	8.00	17.50	70.00	95.00
1927M	1,000,000	2.00	5.00	12.00	60.00	75.00
1928M	1,000,000	3.00	6.00	12.50	50.00	75.00

KM# 173 5 CENTAVOS
Copper-Nickel **Obv:** KM#164 **Rev:** 20 Centavos, KM#170 **Note:** Mule.

Date	Mintage	F	VF	XF	Unc	BU
1918S	—	150	400	1,200	2,500	3,000

KM# 175 5 CENTAVOS
Copper-Nickel **Obv:** Man seated beside hammer and anvil; Mt. Mayon at right

Date	Mintage	F	VF	XF	Unc	BU
1930M	2,905,000	1.00	2.00	5.00	50.00	65.00
1931M	3,477,000	1.00	2.50	6.00	55.00	70.00
1932M	3,956,000	1.00	2.00	5.00	50.00	65.00
1934M	2,154,000	1.00	3.00	10.00	80.00	100
1935M	2,754,000	1.00	1.50	10.00	85.00	125

KM# 165 10 CENTAVOS
2.6924 g., 0.9000 Silver .0779 oz. ASW **Obv:** Female standing beside hammer and anvil; Mt. Mayon at right

Date	Mintage	F	VF	XF	Unc	BU
1903	5,103,000	1.00	1.50	4.00	25.00	35.00
1903 Proof	2,558	Value: 75.00				
1903S	1,200,000	7.50	17.50	35.00	350	500
1904	11,000	10.00	18.00	35.00	100	160
1904 Proof	1,355	Value: 95.00				

Date	Mintage	F	VF	XF	Unc	BU
1904S	5,040,000	1.50	2.50	5.00	35.00	55.00
1905 Proof	471	Value: 160				
1906 Proof	500	Value: 125				

KM# 169   10 CENTAVOS
2.0000 g., 0.7500 Silver .0482 oz. ASW **Obv:** Female standing beside hammer and anvil; Mt. Mayon at right

Date	Mintage	F	VF	XF	Unc	BU
1907	1,501,000	1.50	3.00	5.00	40.00	60.00
1907S	4,930,000	1.00	2.00	3.50	40.00	50.00
1908 Proof	500	Value: 120				
1908S	3,364,000	1.00	2.00	5.00	50.00	75.00
1909S	312,000	12.50	35.00	60.00	350	450
1910S	—	—	—	—	—	—

Note: Unknown in any collection. Counterfeits of the 1910S are commonly encountered.

Date	Mintage	F	VF	XF	Unc	BU
1911S	1,101,000	1.50	3.00	10.00	60.00	85.00
1912S	1,010,000	2.00	4.00	12.00	70.00	90.00
1913S	1,361,000	1.50	3.00	9.00	50.00	75.00
1914S	1,180,000	3.00	5.00	10.00	150	225
1915S	450,000	7.50	17.50	35.00	250	350
1917S	5,991,000	1.00	2.00	3.50	35.00	50.00
1918S	8,420,000	0.50	1.50	2.00	27.50	35.00
1919S	1,630,000	1.00	2.50	5.00	45.00	60.00
1920	520,000	3.50	5.00	10.00	65.00	80.00
1921	3,863,000	0.50	1.00	2.00	30.00	40.00
1929M	1,000,000	0.50	1.00	2.00	15.00	20.00
1935M	1,280,000	0.50	1.00	2.00	20.00	25.00

KM# 166   20 CENTAVOS
5.3849 g., 0.9000 Silver .1558 oz. ASW **Obv:** Female standing beside hammer and anvil; Mt. Mayon at right

Date	Mintage	F	VF	XF	Unc	BU
1903	5,353,000	2.00	3.00	4.50	35.00	70.00
1903 Proof	2,558	Value: 85.00				
1903S	150,000	8.00	15.00	45.00	325	500
1904	11,000	15.00	25.00	35.00	90.00	120
1904 Proof	1,355	Value: 100				
1904S	2,060,000	2.00	3.50	7.50	35.00	75.00
1905 Proof	471	Value: 225				
1905S	420,000	7.50	10.00	17.50	140	175
1906 Proof	500	Value: 200				

KM# 170   20 CENTAVOS
4.0000 g., 0.7500 Silver .0965 oz. ASW **Obv:** Female standing beside hammer and anvil; Mt. Mayon at right

Date	Mintage	F	VF	XF	Unc	BU
1907	1,251,000	2.00	3.00	10.00	50.00	75.00
1907S	3,165,000	2.00	2.50	7.50	40.00	60.00
1908 Proof	500	Value: 185				
1908S	1,535,000	2.00	3.00	10.00	45.00	65.00
1909S	450,000	6.00	20.00	45.00	300	400
1910S	500,000	6.00	20.00	45.00	325	500
1911S	505,000	6.00	15.00	35.00	175	225

Date	Mintage	F	VF	XF	Unc	BU
1912S	750,000	5.00	10.00	20.00	150	170
1913S/S	949,000	8.00	20.00	35.00	175	250
1913S	Inc. above	3.00	5.00	15.00	120	150
1914S	795,000	2.50	4.00	22.00	140	175
1915S	655,000	4.50	12.00	28.00	250	350
1916S	1,435,000	3.00	8.00	15.00	85.00	125
1917S	3,151,000	1.50	3.00	5.00	50.00	70.00
1918S	5,560,000	1.00	2.00	4.00	40.00	50.00
1919S	850,000	1.50	4.00	8.00	55.00	70.00
1920	1,046,000	1.50	5.00	10.00	90.00	110
1921	1,843,000	1.00	2.50	4.00	40.00	50.00
1929M	1,970,000	1.50	2.50	4.00	35.00	50.00

KM# 174   20 CENTAVOS
4.0000 g., 0.7500 Silver .0965 oz. ASW **Obv:** KM#170 **Rev:** 5 Centavos, KM#164 **Note:** Mule.

Date	Mintage	F	VF	XF	Unc	BU
1928M	100,000	3.00	8.00	30.00	450	700

KM# 167   50 CENTAVOS
13.4784 g., 0.9000 Silver .3900 oz. ASW **Obv:** Female standing beside hammer and anvil; Mt. Mayon at right

Date	Mintage	F	VF	XF	Unc	BU
1903	3,102,000	5.00	7.50	10.00	75.00	90.00
1903 Proof	2,558	Value: 125				
1903S	—	—	—	22,000	—	—
1904	11,000	25.00	32.00	45.00	100	170
1904 Proof	1,355	Value: 125				
1904S	2,160,000	5.00	10.00	12.50	75.00	110
1905 Proof	471	Value: 350				
1905S	852,000	8.00	15.00	35.00	600	1,200
1906 Proof	500	Value: 275				

KM# 171   50 CENTAVOS
10.0000 g., 0.7500 Silver .2411 oz. ASW **Obv:** Female standing beside hammer and anvil; Mt. Mayon at right

Date	Mintage	F	VF	XF	Unc	BU
1907	1,201,000	5.00	9.00	17.50	140	200
1907S	2,112,000	2.50	7.50	12.50	100	125
1908 Proof	500	Value: 285				
1908S	1,601,000	2.50	9.00	20.00	150	250
1909S	528,000	5.00	12.50	30.00	275	350
1917S	674,000	5.00	10.00	22.00	125	150
1918S	2,202,000	3.00	6.00	9.00	70.00	90.00
1919S	1,200,000	3.50	5.50	10.00	100	130
1920	420,000	2.50	3.25	5.00	30.00	60.00
1921	2,317,000	2.50	3.00	4.00	20.00	50.00

UNITED STATES ADMINISTRATION
Commonwealth

DECIMAL COINAGE

KM# 179   CENTAVO
Bronze **Obv:** Male seated beside hammer and anvil; Mt. Mayon at right

Date	Mintage	F	VF	XF	Unc	BU
1937M	15,790,000	0.25	1.00	4.00	12.00	20.00
1938M	10,000,000	0.25	0.75	3.00	10.00	25.00
1939M	6,500,000	0.25	1.00	4.00	15.00	20.00
1940M	4,000,000	0.25	0.75	2.00	10.00	20.00
1941M	5,000,000	0.25	2.00	5.00	15.00	25.00
1944S	58,000,000	—	0.15	0.20	1.00	2.50

KM# 168   PESO
26.9568 g., 0.9000 Silver .7800 oz. ASW **Obv:** Female standing beside hammer and anvil; Mt. Mayon at right

Date	Mintage	F	VF	XF	Unc	BU
1903	2,791,000	12.00	18.00	30.00	150	200
1903 Proof	2,558	Value: 200				
1903S	11,361,000	9.00	15.00	20.00	100	150
1904	11,000	60.00	75.00	100	175	275
1904 Proof	1,355	Value: 300				
1904S	6,600,000	10.00	16.00	25.00	100	150
1905 Proof	471	Value: 700				
1905S straight serif on 1	—	20.00	35.00	50.00	225	325
1905S curved serif on 1	6,056,000	12.00	25.00	35.00	175	250
1906 Proof	500	Value: 575				
1906S	201,000	625	1,200	2,500	10,000	12,000

Note: Counterfeits of the 1906S exist

KM# 180   5 CENTAVOS
Copper-Nickel **Obv:** Male seated beside hammer and anvil; Mt. Mayon at right

Date	Mintage	F	VF	XF	Unc	BU
1937M	2,494,000	1.00	2.50	5.50	40.00	65.00
1938M	4,000,000	0.50	1.00	2.50	17.50	27.50
1941M	2,750,000	1.00	2.50	8.00	40.00	65.00

KM# 180a   5 CENTAVOS
Copper-Nickel-Zinc **Obv:** Male seated beside hammer and anvil; Mt. Mayon at right

Date	Mintage	F	VF	XF	Unc	BU
1944	21,198,000	—	0.15	0.50	1.25	2.00
1944S	14,040,000	—	0.15	0.25	0.75	1.75
1945S	72,796,000	—	0.15	0.20	0.65	1.50

KM# 181   10 CENTAVOS
2.0000 g., 0.7500 Silver .0482 oz. ASW **Obv:** Female standing beside hammer and anvil; Mt. Mayon at right

Date	Mintage	F	VF	XF	Unc	BU
1937M	3,500,000	0.75	2.00	3.00	15.00	20.00
1938M	3,750,000	0.50	0.75	2.00	10.00	15.00
1941M	2,500,000	0.65	1.00	2.00	12.50	18.00
1944D	31,592,000	—	BV	0.35	1.00	2.25
1945D	137,208,000	—	BV	0.35	1.00	2.00

Note: 1937, 1938, and 1941 dated strikes have inverted W's for M's

KM# 172   PESO
20.0000 g., 0.8000 Silver .5144 oz. ASW **Obv:** Female standing beside hammer and anvil; Mt. Mayon at right

Date	Mintage	F	VF	XF	Unc	BU
1907 Proof, 2 known	—	—	—	—	—	—
1907S	10,276,000	3.50	5.50	10.00	55.00	75.00
1908 Proof	500	Value: 575				
1908S	20,955,000	3.50	5.50	10.00	50.00	70.00
1909S	7,578,000	3.50	5.50	12.00	60.00	75.00
1910S	3,154,000	4.50	8.00	20.00	150	200
1911S	463,000	11.00	20.00	35.00	550	1,000
1912S	680,000	11.00	20.00	45.00	650	1,200

KM# 182   20 CENTAVOS
4.0000 g., 0.7500 Silver .0965 oz. ASW **Obv:** Female standing beside hammer and anvil; Mt. Mayon at right

Date	Mintage	F	VF	XF	Unc	BU
1937M	2,665,000	0.85	1.50	3.50	15.00	25.00
1938M	3,000,000	0.75	1.00	2.50	8.00	13.00
1941M	1,500,000	1.00	2.00	3.00	10.00	18.00
1944D	28,596,000	—	BV	0.75	1.25	3.00
1944D/S	—	12.00	16.50	20.00	45.00	55.00
1945D	82,804,000	—	BV	0.50	1.00	2.50

KM# 176   50 CENTAVOS
10.0000 g., 0.7500 Silver .2411 oz. ASW **Subject:**
Establishment of the Commonwealth

Date	Mintage	F	VF	XF	Unc	BU
1936	20,000	—	25.00	45.00	65.00	90.00

KM# 183   50 CENTAVOS
10.0000 g., 0.7500 Silver .2411 oz. ASW **Obv:** Female standing
beside hammer and anvil; Mt. Mayon at right

Date	Mintage	F	VF	XF	Unc	BU
1944S	19,187,000	—	BV	1.75	4.00	5.50
1945S	18,120,000	—	BV	1.75	4.00	5.50

KM# 177   PESO
20.0000 g., 0.9000 Silver .5787 oz. ASW **Subject:**
Establishment of the Commonwealth **Obv:** Conjoined busts of
Presidents Roosevelt and Quezon facing left

Date	Mintage	F	VF	XF	Unc	BU
1936	10,000	—	50.00	65.00	150	185

KM# 178   PESO
20.0000 g., 0.9000 Silver .5787 oz. ASW **Subject:**
Establishment of the Commonwealth **Obv:** Conjoined busts of
Governor General Murphy and President Quezon facing left
Rev: Similar to KM#177

Date	Mintage	F	VF	XF	Unc	BU
1936	10,000	—	50.00	65.00	150	185

HAWAII, PHILLIPINES, PUERTO RICO

PUERTO RICO
DECIMAL COINAGE

KM# 20   5 CENTAVOS
1.2500 g., 0.9000 Silver .0361 oz. ASW **Ruler:** Alfonso XIII
Obv: Denomination **Rev:** Crowned arms between columns

Date	Mintage	F	VF	XF	Unc	BU
1896 PGV	600,000	30.00	45.00	85.00	200	—

KM# 21   10 CENTAVOS
2.5000 g., 0.9000 Silver .0723 oz. ASW **Ruler:** Alfonso XIII
Obv: Bust of young Alfonso XIII left **Rev:** Crowned arms between
columns

Date	Mintage	F	VF	XF	Unc	BU
1896 PGV	700,000	35.00	60.00	110	275	—

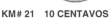

KM# 22   20 CENTAVOS
5.0000 g., 0.9000 Silver .1446 oz. ASW **Ruler:** Alfonso XIII
Obv: Bust of young Alfonso XIII left **Rev:** Crowned arms between
columns

Date	Mintage	F	VF	XF	Unc	BU
1895 PGV	3,350,000	45.00	70.00	135	325	—

KM# 23   40 CENTAVOS
10.0000 g., 0.9000 Silver .2893 oz. ASW **Ruler:** Alfonso XIII
Obv: Bust of young Alfonso XIII left **Rev:** Crowned arms between
columns

Date	Mintage	F	VF	XF	Unc	BU
1896 PGV	725,000	250	325	750	2,850	—

KM# 24   PESO
25.0000 g., 0.9000 Silver .7234 oz. ASW **Ruler:** Alfonso XIII
Obv: Bust of young Alfonso XIII left **Rev:** Crowned arms between
columns

Date	Mintage	F	VF	XF	Unc	BU
1895 PGV	8,500,000	275	350	800	1,650	—

Index

M

N

O

P

Q

R

S

262